KW-481-253

Integrating
Windows and
NetWare

J. Ranade Workstation Series

LOCKHART • *OSF DCE: Guide to Developing Distributed Applications,*
0-07-911481-4

WIGGINS • *The Internet for Everyone: A Guide for Users and Providers,*
0-07-067019-8

CHAKRAVARTY • *Power RISC System / 6000: Concepts, Facilities, and
Architecture,* 0-07-011047-6

SANCHEZ, CANTON • *High Resolution Video Graphics,* 0-07-911646-9

DEROEST • *AIX for RS / 6000: System and Administration Guide,* 0-07-036439-7

LAMB • *MicroFocus Workbench and Toolset Developer's Guide,* 0-07-036123-3

JOHNSTON • *OS / 2 Connectivity & Networking: A Guide to Communication
Managers / 2,* 0-07-032696-7

SANCHEZ, CANTON • *PC Programmer's Handbook, Second Edition,* 0-07-054948-6

WALKER, SCHWALLER • *CPI-C Programming in C: An Application Developer's
Guide to APPC,* 0-07-911733-3

SANCHEZ, CANTON • *Graphics Programming Solutions,* 0-07-911464-4

CHAKRAVARTY, CANNON • *PowerPC: Concepts, Architecture, and Design,*
0-07-011192-8

LEININGER • *UNIX Developer's Tool Kit,* 0-07-911646-9

HENRY, GRAHAM • *Solaris 2.X System Administrator's Guide,* 0-07-029368-6

RANADE, ZAMIR • *C + + Primer for C Programmers, Second Edition,*
0-07-051487-9

PETERSON • *DCE: A Guide to Developing Portable Applications,* 0-07-911801-1

LEININGER • *Solaris Developer's Tool Kit,* 0-07-911851-8

JOHNSTON • *OS / 2 Productivity Tool Kit,* 0-07-912029-6

LEININGER • *AIX / 6000 Developer's Tool Kit,* 0-07-911992-1

GRAHAM • *Solaris 2.X: Internals and Architecture,* 0-07-911876-3

BAMBARA, ALLEN • *PowerBuilder: A Guide for Developing Client / Server
Applications,* 0-07-005413-4

SANCHEZ, CANTON • *Solutions Handbook for PC Programmers,* Second Edition,
0-07-912249-3

LEININGER • *HP-UX Developer's Tool Kit,* 0-07-912174-8

ROBERTSON, KOOP • *Integrating Windows and Netware,* 0-07-912126-8

CERVONE • *AIX / 6000 System Guide,* 0-07-024129-5

CHAPMAN • *OS / 2 Power User's Reference: From OS / 2 2.0 through Warp,*
0-07-912218-3

KELLY • *AIX / 6000 Internals and Architecture,* 0-07-034061-7

MULLER • *The Webmaster's Guide to HTML,* 0-07-912273-6

LEININGER • *HP-UX Developer's Tool Kit,* 0-07-912175-6

GOPAUL • *OS / 2 Programmer's Desk Reference,* 0-07-023748-4

Integrating Windows and NetWare

A Professional's Guide

Wayne Robertson

Edward Koop

McGraw-Hill

New York   San Francisco   Washington, D.C.   Auckland   Bogotá
Caracas   Lisbon   London   Madrid   Mexico City   Milan
Montreal   New Delhi   San Juan   Singapore
Sydney   Tokyo   Toronto

Library of Congress Cataloging-in-Publication Data

Robertson, Wayne D.
    Integrating Windows and NetWare : a professional's guide / Wayne
Robertson, Edward Koop.
        p.   cm.—(J. Ranade workstation series)
    Includes index.
    ISBN 0-07-912126-8 (hardcover)
    1. Windows (Computer file)   2. NetWare (Computer file)
3. Operating systems (Computers) I. Koop, Edward. II. Title.
III. Series.
QA76.76.W56R6344   1996
005.7′1369—dc20   95-51365
                                              CIP

McGraw-Hill

A Division of The McGraw-Hill Companies

1 2 3 4 5 6 7 8 9 0 DOC/DOC 9 0 1 0 9 8 7 6

P/N 053216-8
PART OF
ISBN 0-07-912126-8

*The sponsoring editor for this book was Jerry Papke, the editing supervisor was
David E. Fogarty, and the production supervisor was Donald Schmidt. It was
set in Century Schoolbook by Victoria Khavkina of McGraw-Hill's Professional
Book Group composition unit.*

Printed and bound by R. R. Donnelley & Sons Company.

This book is printed on acid-free paper.

*My thanks to the greatest family a man could have.
To Donna who has been a great help and the greatest
wife who is always there during good times and
bad, and to Michael and Matthew who, despite their
young years, realized that Dad needed to give up
some fun times for this project.*

W. R.

*Many thanks to Mom and Dad for all the support, emotion-
ally and otherwise, over the past few years. To my lovely
wife Dawn, for daring to say "I do…," and to Bandit,
the wonder dog.*

E. K.

Contents

ABOUT THE AUTHORS

WAYNE ROBERTSON is owner of the Robertson Group, a Fresno, California consulting company specializing in network design and graphical systems, and project management services for clients nationwide. He is a Certified NetWare Engineer (CNE). He is also an internationally recognized instructor, speaker, and freelance writer in the areas of LAN planning, design, installation, maintenance, and training.

EDWARD KOOP is Senior Network Administrator for St. Agnes Medical Center in Fresno, California. He is an Enterprise Certified NetWare Engineer (ECNE) with extensive enterprise-wide experience in UNIX and Novell NetWare networking environments. He has written for *PC Week* and has been a featured speaker at Networld + Interop. In addition to his current position, he also acts as technical consultant for several companies.

ABOUT THE SERIES

The J. Ranade Workstations Series is McGraw-Hill's primary vehicle for providing workstation professionals with timely concepts, solutions, and applications. Jay Ranade is also Series Editor in Chief of more than 150 books in the J. Ranade IBM and DEC Series and Series Advisor to the McGraw-Hill Series on Computer Communications.

Jay Ranade, Series Editor in Chief and best-selling computer author, is a Technology Strategist and Systems Architect for a major financial services company in New York City.

Preface

Today's network administrators are faced with the never-ending challenge of integration and technology. The desire for Windows frequently comes from users who want to have that graphical system on their computers. Combine that desire with a network system, and and you have a complete data infrastructure that is efficient in delivering information to employees and managers.

Because Microsoft Windows and Novell NetWare are the most popular products in their fields, it is only natural that we look to combine these. The information in this book comes from our personal experience of designing and installing large network systems and integrating Windows across these systems. We wish there had been a book like this when we started doing large-scale network projects in the early 1990s.

With the knowledge that will come from reading this book, you will be able to make those tough decisions with confidence. You'll have a better understanding of how to integrate Windows with NetWare and have a more complete and thorough knowledge of how to approach a large-scale project.

This book is broken down logically into the following chapters:

Chapter 1 We first review the different Microsoft Windows versions and some of the features that are available in the current versions.

Chapter 2 After examining Windows, we take a look at Novell NetWare and the features that make it so popular. We take a look at the two major versions available (3.x and 4.x) and their major features.

Chapter 3 Using Windows and Windows applications on a network file server will increase the level of activity on the file server. To make sure Windows won't impair the operation of the file server, you may need to adjust a number of parameters. The file-server parameters and their effects on Windows systems and users are listed in Chap. 3.

Chapter 4 Before installing Windows on a workstation, it is important to look at the computers in your organization and make sure that their configurations and memory capacities are adequate for Windows to run efficiently.

Chapter 5   After modifying the configuration of the workstation, we take a look at workstation network communications and how to improve the network shell configuration.

Chapter 6   This chapter reviews the different locations and methods for installing and configuring Windows. You will be able to decide where to install Windows on the basis of your system and user needs.

Chapter 7   After Windows is installed, it is necessary to review the configuration files and make changes for network communications. The different .INI files and any required changes are described.

Chapter 8   It is almost impossible to run only Windows applications as there are a number of DOS applications still being used that we need to integrate with Windows. This chapter reviews the setup for DOS applications.

Chapter 9   When printing out of Windows and DOS applications, what happens with Windows and NetWare? We examine how Windows prints locally and on the network and give some ideas on how to increase the printing speed.

Chapter 10   NetWare 4 is the first version of Novell's operating system that is closely integrated with Windows. The Windows utilities provided for managing the network make network control much easier, and since many have not had experience with this version, we take an in-depth look at the features of NetWare 4.

Chapter 11   Everyone is talking about Windows 95 even though its release on the market was delayed greatly. How will it work with NetWare? Will it be difficult to set up and integrate? Chapter 11 looks at Windows 95 and reviews the important features you may want to investigate.

Appendixes.   The appendixes provide a checklist of items you need to be aware of for the Windows and NetWare project, different methods of cantacting Novell and Microsoft for technical support, a glossary of important terms specific for these two technologies, and a description of the installation utility and shareware programs included with this book.

Also included in this book is a Windows installation utility that automates the process of installing Windows or Windows for Workgroups on a local PC from the network. As an additional bonus, we have included a number of the latest shareware programs that we feel help enhance productivity and facilitate management of the network.

While it is impossible to give a complete review and in-depth guide to Windows and NetWare in one book, we have concentrated on those areas that affect or are affected by the use of those two systems.

We have concentrated on Windows for Workgroups v3.11 because it is the latest and most stable of the Windows systems. Many organizations are just converting to Windows now and will be waiting a year or two until installing Windows 95. However, even if you decide to install Windows 95 rather than Windows for Worgroups, much of the network and Windows information also applies to Windows 95.

We had several types of people in mind when writing this book. If you are technically oriented, this book will give you in-depth information on a variety of different items. While some of the information may not be new to you, we believe there are a number of items that can save you a lot of work. Network administrators, system technicians, and other management information system staff will benefit from this book.

This book is also useful to end users who don't work in a formal computer support capacity because the more they know about this technology, the better they will be able to handle problems and changes.

If you are a college student about to graduate or a recent graduate, and you want to work in the computer systems field, this book is invaluable because it gives inside information about these technologies that almost every organization is using. Take this book, study it as though you were preparing for a test, and you will become invaluable to your employer.

Sit down, get comfortable, and happy reading....

Acknowledgments

We would like to express our appreciate to the many people who assisted in this book. While there are too many to list here, a few people deserve special recognition.

Our thanks to Jay Ranade for his work on the topics and for finding out what readers wanted to see. Jerry Papke was a great help in working out the details of the project and with wise words of wisdom. We can't forget Donna Namorato whose patience and cheerfulness in coordinating the manuscript activities was extraordinary. David Fogarty had the unenviable task of bringing everything together, and Don Schmidt was responsible for supervising the typesetting and printing.

As anyone who has engaged in a project like this knows, creating the words is just the start of the process and an equal effort goes into the production of the book. We are grateful to all those who worked so hard on this project.

Wayne Robertson
Edward Koop

Microsoft Windows

Outside MS-DOS, Microsoft Windows (Fig. 1.1) is the most widely used operating system in the world today. It is rare to find a corporation or organization that doesn't have at least one copy of Windows running. However, it is common to find a whole company or division that has implemented Windows as a standard desktop system.

Figure 1.1 Windows logo screen.

In the 1980s, it was hard to believe that we would see this great acceptance of Windows. The early versions were not technically exciting in part because of the low performance of computer systems. Now that high-powered computers and new versions of Windows are available, it makes sense why so many are turning to this technology.

Windows by itself is helpful, but since a large percentage of microcomputers are networked together, there is a need to enable Windows to operate in a networked environment. Novell NetWare is the dominant leader in network operating systems, so it would seem logical to think about how to combine it with Windows.

Windows and NetWare Project

Unless your network is very small, you will need to take some time to review the project ahead of you and be aware of issues you will need to address. Although it is not possible to think of everything involved in the project, here are a number of items you should think about when planning to integrate Windows and NetWare systems.

Planning the project

Examine why you want to install Windows on desktops and connect to a NetWare server. Windows has been the hottest topic for the workstation desktop in the last couple of years, so much so that it is difficult to buy DOS-based applications anymore. You need to decide whether Windows will be installed on all or only some desktops. Will users be using Windows all of the time or will they be using it part time for some applications only?

Time frame

Now that you have decided to install Windows, how soon will it be accomplished? Picking a pace that is reasonable will go a long way toward a successful project. Depending on resources, it could take as long as a year to install Windows on a couple hundred workstations. Don't be in a rush.

User knowledge level

Another issue you will have to deal with is the level of user knowledge. If they have a high level of computer knowledge, you will need to give them flexibility in the configuration and implementation of Windows; if they have little knowledge of computer systems, then you will have to build a complete Windows system with fewer choices to cause problems.

Configuration changes

Once you have installed Windows on the desktop, should the users be able to make any changes? You will probably want to give users the maximum amount of freedom possible, but we have found that the more freedom users are given, the more problems that will arise, which means more support calls for you.

You need to decide whether the users will be able to change the Windows setup or hardware settings, be able to modify the type of Windows installation on their computers, and be allowed to drop down to the DOS command line and run their own utilities. Maybe some of the users will want to have a Windows version different from that which you have decided on for your organization.

User flexibility

Other issues that you may need to address include the level of uptime required for your system. We will address the issue of uptime later in the book with respect to NetWare fault-tolerance systems. The issue of where to install Windows is discussed in Chap. 6. If the users need to move from computer to computer, you will want to install Windows on the file server to give them this flexibility. However, if the users never use anyone else's computer, a local installation of Windows may be desired.

Remote access

Once users have Windows on their desktop computers, it may not be long before they wish to have remote capabilities. Accessing the network through Windows brings a whole new level of problems. Windows over a phone line even at 28.8 kbits/s (kilobits per second) is still a slow system. While users say that speed is not important, they probably don't realize how slow it will actually be. Not only will they want access to the network file servers; they may want access to their own workstations.

Host systems access

If you have minicomputers or mainframes in your organization, there may be a need to connect to those systems from Windows. In addition, if you are using a Windows NT Server, you may need to install NetBEUI or TCP/IP (Transmission Control Protocol/Internet Protocol) protocols along with IPX/SPX for NetWare.

Staff resources

Planning for a Windows installation requires taking staff resources into account. Even with the install utility included with this book (described in Chap. 6), it will still take some time to install all the copies of Windows on the server(s) and workstations. We have found it takes approximately one hour per workstation even with the install utility we have provided for you. If you are installing from "floppies" (floppy disks) or are not using the automated installation utility, each workstation install could take up to 2 h.

User education

Despite what Microsoft, Apple, and IBM say about their graphical products, training is required to run them properly. Why should users know that it takes two fast clicks of the mouse on an icon to start an application? Why should users automatically know that the Exit command is usually found in the File menu? Do they know about copying and pasting? What is the difference between Paste and Paste Special? If you don't educate the users about these issues, the acceptance of Windows will be lessened, even though you may have done an excellent job, technically, with the Windows installation.

"Training" does not mean a 1-h course on a Thursday afternoon, but maybe 1 or 2 h each week for several weeks with a refresher course session within 90 days. This will ensure that users can handle Windows with the greatest efficiency. We have found the method of in-depth training of a key user in each department useful. All support issues should be sent to this key user first and then to the MIS department if it cannot be answered.

Budgeting

Even though this is not the most exciting part of the Windows and NetWare implementation, the budget is nonetheless a critical element of the project. You need to include items such as conversion costs from previous versions, implementation of Windows including installation on workstations and servers, maintenance of the system once it is installed, technical support, training, and new applications required to replace the old DOS programs.

Taking stock

With the rapid increase of microcomputer installations, you might not have taken a recent inventory of the number of computers installed in your organization. Before starting the Windows and NetWare project, there is a need to do a thorough inventory of the system currently installed and determine whether there is a need to upgrade the hardware before installing Windows. The checklist at the end of this chapter can be used to determine the current system. Items to check include total number of users, number of users with computers, and number of users without computers, local area network (LAN) setup—configuration information, current protocols, and network segmentation.

Network communications

Windows places more strain on the network than do most other systems. Passing larger programs and data elements across the network has caused many networks to slow down considerably, requiring a fast upgrade to the communications system.

You will need to see if the speed [measured in megabits per second (Mbits/s)] is high enough, decide what protocol is installed (type and speed); and determine the current level of bandwidth utilization.

Network systems

In addition to checking the workstations and communications, you need to check out the servers and related equipment.

Workstation configuration

You will need to plan for the Windows and NetWare project by deciding on the amount of random-access memory (RAM) you wish to install for each workstation. You will need to become familiar with memory issues such as memory sizes, memory terminology, accessing the high-memory area, CONFIG.SYS, file handles, Windows use of extended memory, virtual memory, and Windows system resources.

Workstation communication

After becoming familiar with the memory issues of Windows, you will need to make some decisions about network drivers including monolithic drivers, ODI, NDIS, NETX, virtual loadable modules (VLMs), link driver statements, Packet Burst, and Large Internetworking Packets.

Windows Versions

Before starting our Windows integration project, we need to examine the Windows and NetWare versions to select the best combination. While Microsoft periodically releases new versions, many people have not upgraded to the latest version, and some are not using Windows at all. That brings up the question of which version of Windows is the best for a network installation.

Windows version 3.0, released in 1990, marked the first serious version that could be used consistently in an organization. Unknown to many, there were previous versions of Windows (1.01, 2.0, 2.1) which were used mainly to run specialized applications (e.g., Aldus PageMaker).

Version 3.0 changed the desktop layout by including a proportional font, three-dimensional shading, different color schemes, and a new icon-based system on the desktop. One of the most important enhancements was support for networking and the ability to connect to file servers and print queues. Prior versions recognized only the local hard disk and system.

Windows 3.0 was designed to work with as many different Intel-based systems as possible. Through real, standard, and enhanced modes, this version could be run on 8088, 8086, 286, 386, and 486 computers. While these modes enabled various systems to run Windows, only 386 and 486 computers can run Windows efficiently. To enable the older central processing units (CPUs) to run Windows, various features were removed in the real and standard modes. For example, only in enhanced mode could you run more than one DOS application in Windows.

It is our opinion that Windows 3.0, although still used in many sites, is not the best choice for network connectivity since subsequent versions handle network communication better. Version 3.0 suffered from instability as it was not unusual to have the system crash several times a day, especially when running DOS applications inside Windows.

Windows 3.1, released to address the problem of instability, also added new features. One of the biggest problems faced by Microsoft was running DOS and Windows applications together. At seemingly random times the whole system would lock up, usually resulting in a loss of data. Many users who refused to use version 3.0, because it would not run consistently, eagerly adopted version 3.1.

Several enhancements were added to version 3.1 that provided procedures and more information about why the problem occurred. Rather than just indicating a general protection error, this version gave more detailed information about the source of the problem. Users were able to reboot a DOS window or Windows application with the <Ctrl-Alt-Del> keys without affecting other applications. This saved other applications because the whole Windows system was not rebooted. Parameter validation was also added, and additional testing tools were made available to help software vendors create stable Windows applications.

We view Windows for Workgroups 3.11 as the evolution of Windows v3.1. Even though it has a different name, it takes Windows 3.1 and adds a number of enhancements. Since Windows for Workgroups v3.11 is the focus of this book, we will be explaining many features in the next few chapters.

Windows 95 is the next generation of Windows bringing true 32-bit operation and overcoming the problems that DOS-based Windows for Workgroups still struggles with. We will discuss Windows 95 in Chap. 11.

Windows Modes

Windows for Workgroups 3.11 does not support real or standard modes because these modes are so limited in their operation. In previous versions of Windows, one of the jobs of WIN.COM was to determine which was the best mode to run. It attempted to run enhanced mode first; if that wasn't possible, then it tried to start in standard mode. If that didn't work, then you saw an error message and an explanation of why WFW didn't start.

There were two basic reasons for using standard mode. Some older Windows applications wouldn't run in the enhanced mode, there wasn't enough memory, or the computer CPU was less than that of an 80386. The standard mode had minimal function.

Enhanced mode

Enhanced mode is the only method available in Windows for Workgroups v3.11 because it gives the greatest amount of flexibility. This mode is possible because of the 386 and higher CPU chip which provides access to the virtual-memory features of those chips. This enables you to load a number of applications that together take more memory than is available in RAM—because of the virtual memory. This enhanced mode enables multitasking of DOS applications and provides greater control over running applications.

The enhanced mode requires a 80386 or higher, at least 256 kbytes of conventional memory, 1 Mbyte of extended memory, and HIMEM.SYS loaded in CONFIG.SYS. The enhanced mode uses up about 600 kbytes of memory, which can be either conventional or extended memory.

Despite what many think, applications in the enhanced mode do not run faster because there is system overhead involved with this mode. However, with the 32-bit access, virtual memory, and other improvements, the overall speed of Windows in enhanced mode is faster than it would have been in standard mode.

Parameter Checking

Parameter validation was one of the best enhancements for stability in Windows 3.1. Because it is impossible for Microsoft to control how third-party applications behave inside Windows, an application might make a request to the Windows operating system that was invalid (e.g., call to wrong address in memory). In Windows 3.0, virtually any system request was executed without checking its validity. This might access an invalid hardware address or modify data currently in memory. As a result, it would cause Windows 3.0 to lock up and crash and users would lose the data they were working on.

Each time an application makes a call to any system resources, Windows 3.1 checks for validity. If the request is determined to be invalid, with a potential to cause a system crash, it is returned to the application as a failed request and the application must reissue the call. Under the worst of circumstances, the application making the invalid system request would lock up, requiring termination by the user. Other applications would not be affected.

Some of the instability of Windows 3.0 was due to the inability to handle

```
You can use CTRL+ALT+DEL to close the application that has stopped
responding to the system.  When possible, you should close the
application in the manner recommended in the documentation
provided by the application

* Press ESC to cancel and return the non-Windows application
* Press ENTER to close this application
  You will lose any unsaved information in this application.
* Press CTRL+ALT+DEL to restart your computer.  You will lose any
unsaved information in this application.
```

Figure 1.2 Rebooting an application in Windows 3.1.

serious errors. This was reported to the user as an unrecoverable application error (UAE). The only alternative was to restart Windows because the system had become unstable. Microsoft added code to Windows 3.1 that would identify the source of the error, allow the user to close application or save the data files before closing, and keep the emainder of Windows operational, if possible.

If an application freezes, it may be necessary to restart the application to continue operation. Unfortunately, it is usually necessary to close the current instance of the application before starting it again. To make that possible, Windows 3.1 allows the user to close the application with the three-finger salute: (<Ctrl-Alt-Delete>). When that key combination is pressed, a text screen appears that gives the user several options shown in Fig. 1.2. If the user attempts to close the application with this method, while the application is still operational, the user is advised, through a message on the screen, to press Escape and return to the application. This will prevent data loss. In the case of an application that has frozen, the user is advised by message on the screen to press Enter to close the application.

System Resources

Microsoft also considered other problems in Windows and built safeguards to prevent them. A common problem in Windows 3.0 was a tendency to run low on system resources. This would freeze current applications or make it impossible to load additional applications. Windows 3.1 allocates those system resources differently, so more applications can be loaded before running out of space.

System resources are 64-kbyte memory locations known as heaps to store system information. The User heap tracks objects such as windows and menus. The GDI heap tracks graphical activities such as device contexts, brushes, pens, regions, and bitmaps. The Memory heap controls memory available to Windows programs (including physical and swap file memory).

System resources can be seen in the Help About window (Fig. 1.3) of the program manager. The number shown there is the lowest of all three heaps.

Figure 1.4 shows a utility available from Microsoft that displays the three memory heaps.

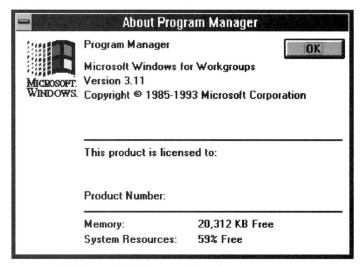

Figure 1.3   Windows for Workgroups About box.

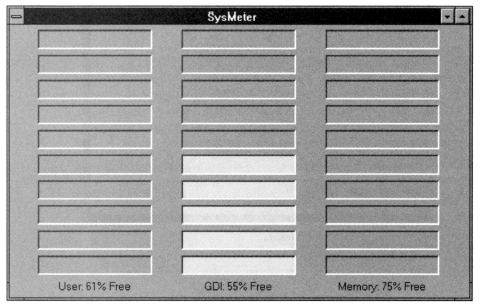

Figure 1.4   SysMeter utility showing system resources.

Windows 3.1 checks for terminate-and-stay-resident (TSR) utilities (listed in Fig. 1.5) known to cause problems with Windows during installation. If an incompatible TSR is found, the user is warned to remove it and restart the installation.

Norton Desktop/Windows Erase Protect TSR	Vaccine Antivirus Program
QMAPS Memory Manager	Newspace Disk Compression Utility
386 Max Disk Cache Utility	Newspace Disk Compression Utility
Disk Cache Utility	Trantor T100 SCSI driver
Flash Disk Cache Utility	Lasertools Printer Control Panel
Hyper Disk Cache Utility	HP Expanded Memory Manager
Hyper Disk Cache Utility	Ramtype Utility
Hyper Disk Cache Utility	Memory Manager
Hyper Disk Cache Utility	Intel Expanded Memory Emulator
Hyper Disk Cache Utility	Command Line Editor
Norton Disk Cache Utility	HP Memory Manager
Norton Utilities NCache	PCED Command Line Editor
Norton Speed Drive	CED Command Line Editor
PC-Kwik Disk Cache Utility	UMB Pro Memory Manager
PC Tools Disk Cache Utility	NetRoom Memory Manager
Super PC-Kwik Disk Cache Utility	IBM PC Support
IBM RAM Disk Utility	Command Line Editor
All Charge 386	DOSCUE Command Line Editor
Anarkey	PC Tools Datamon
Central Point Anti-Virus	MS-DOS SUBST Utility
Central Point Anti-Virus TSR	MS-DOS JOIN Utility
PC Tools VDefend	Data Physician Plus TSR
PC Tools VDefend	MS-DOS GRAPHICS Utility
KBFlow TSR by Artisoft	Le Menu Menuing Package
SoftIce	MS-DOS ASSIGN Utility
PC Tools Desktop TSR	MS-DOS APPEND Utility
Sidekick Version 2.0	Norton Disk Monitoring TSR
Sidekick Version 1.0	Double Disk Data Compression
Sidekick Plus	Printer Assist
MS-DOS PRINT Utility	Speedfxr
Pyro! Screen Saver	pcsxmaem Utility
8514 emulation driver	xmaem Utility
ASP Integrity Toolkit	Cubit
Lansight Network Utilities TSR	
Lansight Network Utilities TSR	

Figure 1.5 DOS TSRs that can cause problems for Windows.

Protection was provided in Windows for Workgroups 3.11 for applications written for pre-3.x versions. Microsoft has built as much compatibility as possible, and programs that aren't compatible will not run under Windows for Workgroups 3.11. These old applications can cause severe problems in the newer Windows versions.

Developer Assistance

To assist developers, Microsoft created a variety of tools for software developers to thoroughly test and debug their products, including emulating low-memory situations. Microsoft also provided a detailed list of new features in version 3.1 to ensure application integrity with Windows. In addition, many hardware systems were tested with Windows to ensure compatibility.

Additional Enhancements

Great emphasis was placed on application communication and integration with object linking and embedding (OLE). This utility provides a method of copying data from one application to another and preserves data links. Standard libraries, interfaces, and protocols were developed for Windows 3.1 to support OLE.

A significant new feature in Windows 3.1 was TrueType scalable-font technology. This provides outline fonts that can adapt to any monitor or printer supported by Windows. The fonts don't require a large amount of disk space as do bitmapped fonts. They provide an instant built-in system that allows easy interchange of documents using fonts; they also work with third-party font sets, and are scalable so that they can be created at almost any size and style. These fonts can be embedded in applications which enable data files created on one system to display fonts on another system without the fonts being present in the second copy of Windows.

Additional functionality was created for DOS applications in Windows 3.1. DOS versions 5 and 6 make a significantly larger amount of memory available and more room to run DOS. All DOS sessions in Windows inherit the free memory available when Windows started, so it is important to make the DOS base memory as large as possible before starting Windows. The new DOS function in Windows is a significant stabilizing factor for DOS applications in Windows.

DOS applications running VGA graphics are supported in Windows 3.1 in a DOS window or in the background. In addition, mouse support was provided for DOS applications in both full-screen and window modes. The 32-bit disk access provided in Windows 3.1 allows more DOS applications to run concurrently than under version 3.0.

Disk Access Enhancement

Disk access is a very important component of the operation of Windows. Because so many operations involve access to the computer's hard disk, an increase in the speed of disk access has a great impact on operation.

Microsoft developed the 32-bit disk access system that is operational in the enhanced mode of Windows 3.1. It intelligently manages communications between BIOS (basic input/output system) and the hard-disk controller. Microsoft had to struggle with system BIOSs from different IBM PCs and compatibles. These different BIOS systems handle hard-disk accesses in different methods. Some are quite old, and some are new with advanced technology to maximize the speed of access.

Microsoft had to not only improve access but also correct problems and inefficiencies in some BIOS systems. The method they developed uses protected-mode block devices that filter Interrupt 13H calls to the hard disk and reroute the calls through the 32-bit interface with the hard-disk controller or through BIOS, whichever is more efficient. The 32-bit disk access communicates with the hard-disk controller and will work with any controller compatible with the Western Digital 1003 controller interface. Most hard drives installed in Intel-based machines are compatible with this standard. This communication is provided through the WDCTRL driver.

Unfortunately, SCSI (small computer system interface) and ESDI (enhanced system device interface) drives do not support these same standards. Some drive manufacturers provide their own virtual device drivers to enable 32-bit functionality with SCSI and ESDI drives. So far, there are no drivers available on the market that provide 32-bit support for removable hard disks and floppy disks. Manufacturers can create these drivers for their systems because Microsoft has made their 32-bit technology available to ensure the largest number of drives that can take advantage of this technology. Because the 32-bit technology is an open standard, other utilities like SMARTDrive, Stacker, PC Tools, and Norton Utilities are compatible with 32-bit systems.

In version 3.0 of Windows, disk access was a long, complicated process and slowed the access of disk files. Windows, if run on top of DOS, has a schizophrenic operational mode. To run multiple applications in the same CPU, the system must run in protected mode to maintain division between the applications. However, calls made to hardware through DOS or BIOS need to be switched into virtual 8086 mode. Once the call is completed, the system must switch back to protected mode to resume Windows operation.

A DOS application running in Windows in virtual mode issues a call to the disk through Interrupt 21H. Windows intercepts the call and evaluates it in protected mode for any virtual drivers. If a driver does not interrupt the call, the call is sent to DOS by Windows switching to virtual mode, where DOS takes over and reads or writes data from or to a disk location.

Windows 3.1 handles disk calls more efficiently than does DOS by removing BIOS from the disk call procedure and handles disk access almost entirely in protected mode. This prevents switching back and forth when disk access is required.

DOS Application Problems

DOS applications are difficult for Windows to handle because they essentially mix two types of systems (DOS and Windows), which creates problems. DOS applications have no concept of multiple applications running on the same system and are designed to run without regard to any other system.

For Windows 3.x, memory problems can occur with DOS applications because of their architecture. Windows applications are designed to share the RAM and CPU with other applications so that portions can be swapped out to virtual memory on disk. Only small fragments of code need to be in RAM. It is possible to have more Windows than DOS applications running in Windows simultaneously.

To run multiple DOS applications, Windows has to create a virtual DOS machine for each application which requires 640 kybtes or more of contiguous memory. However, it is not possible to split DOS applications between RAM and virtual memory. The memory must be a single block regardless of whether the DOS application is in the foreground or background. If you need to run several DOS applications simultaneously, it is important to ensure that you have an adequate amount of RAM (12 Mbytes or higher) to avoid receiving out-of-memory errors.

A strange problem can occur when the amount of RAM available shown in the Help About box is large but you cannot load a DOS application. The amount of RAM shown in the box is both physical RAM and the size of the swap file on disk. There may be 5 Mbytes or more RAM listed as installed but only be a fraction of RAM available to the DOS application. The remainder of the RAM may be virtual memory which cannot be used by DOS.

Using 32-bit disk access can help load DOS applications because of the multiple requests Windows can handle. All DOS system calls are sequential and designed to complete before attempting the next instruction. If DOS is handling a disk access call, sending a second call will result in failure because DOS cannot handle it until the next call is completed. This results in a need to have all the code of a DOS application in RAM. The program would not continue because it would need more application code brought in from the virtual-memory swap file before processing the data from the disk. However, the data retrieval from disk must be completed before paging the code from the swap file resulting in a deadly embrace.

By using 32-bit disk access, this problem is avoided because DOS and BIOS are not used in disk access. This allows reentrant disk calls to be made from Windows protected mode. With 32-bit access, the amount of memory shown in the Help About box of program manager is available for Windows and DOS applications. 32-bit disk access also permits multiple requests to be sent to the disk controller simultaneously. They can execute as quickly as possible and provide a much faster method of accessing programs and data on the hard disk. Microsoft claims that 32-bit access will result in at least a 15 percent increase in disk access.

To enable 32-bit disk access (see Figs. 1.6 to 1.9), which is off by default, choose 386 enhanced mode in the control panel and click on the virtual-memory button. Click on the check box to select 32-bit access.

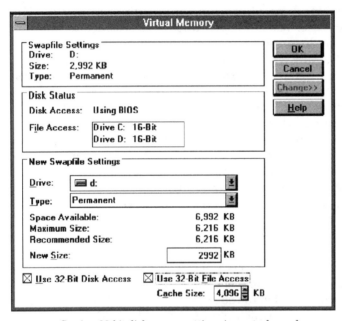

Figure 1.6   Setting 32-bit disk access settings in control panel.

WARNING: Make sure you always have a current backup before enabling 32-bit access. Microsoft has carefully tested the WDCTRL driver, but there have been a few cases where the disk controller is not totally compatible with 32-bit access. Disk files may be corrupted or destroyed as a result.

Figure 1.7   32-bit access problems.

NOTE
You must run a permanent swap file when using 32-bit access to gain maximum performance.

Figure 1.8   Permanent swap file setup requirement.

WARNING: Some laptop computers have controllers that are compatible with the WD 1003 instruction set but shut down the hard disk to save battery power. Disk calls made through the BIOS have no problems because they are delayed until the hard disk spins up and starts running. Since 32-bit access bypasses BIOS, there is no way to notify Windows that the drive is not active and data loss can result.

Figure 1.9 32-bit setup problem.

```
device=*Int13
device=*wdctrl
device=*BLOCKDEV
device=*PAGEFILE
```

Figure 1.10 Virtual disk drivers in SYSTEM.INI.

There are several virtual disk system drivers set up in the SYSTEM.INI file (Fig. 1.10) under the [386Enh] section during Windows loading. These lines are added automatically. The Int13 driver intercepts all calls to the hardware made through Interrupt 13H and passes the calls to the BLOCK-DEV driver. The PAGEFILE driver performs a function similar to that of the Int13 driver except it handles calls made to the virtual-memory swap file, then passes the information to BLOCKDEV. BLOCKDEV manages the read and write calls for the 32-bit disk access system. It creates and controls the list of calls to the hard-disk controller. It also handles all calls passed to it by the drivers by diverting read, write, and cancel calls to the controller directly. All other calls are routed to BIOS for processing.

The WDCTRL driver is the specific instruction set for Western Digital 1003 and compatible controllers. This driver will be installed only if the setup program finds a compatible controller during installation. If a disk manufacturer has developed its own driver for 32-bit access, it would load the driver and insert the appropriate line in the SYSTEM.INI file. That could be accomplished during the Windows installation or through a special installation routine later.

Entries in the SYSTEM.INI with an asterisk (*) in front of the driver name indicate an internal command. In the case of these drivers, they are appended to the WIN386.EXE file and available in memory as part of the Windows system.

SMARTDrive

Another utility upgraded by Microsoft for Windows 3.1 is the caching utility SMARTDrive. SMARTDrive provides greater performance when accessing the disk drive. DOS is slow in part because of its direct access to the disk drive. When data or programs are read from the drive, the calls are made as needed and the drive channel processes the request and then waits for another. This results in slow performance for users because they must wait until a disk access is performed before continuing their work.

The SMARTDrive utility was developed to speed up these accesses. It anticipates what data needs to be read from the drive, and then preloads it into memory. SMARTDrive also can perform lazy writes (write-behind cache) so that files can be written out when convenient and not when the user is waiting to continue. This utility greatly improves Windows performance.

Any calls made to a block device system (usually disks) are analyzed to determine whether they need disk system access. Once programs or data are cached in RAM, SMARTDrive will scan the cache area first to locate the request data. It then accesses the hard disk if it cannot be found in RAM. When data is loaded from the disk, SMARTDrive loads the request and additional programs or data into cache in anticipation of subsequent need.

SMARTDrive can use up to 16 Mbytes of memory for caching but will default somewhere around 0.2 to 5 Mbytes depending on available memory. SMARTDrive caching ability is not mandatory for Windows.

Previous versions of SMARTDrive tracked Interrupt 13H to detect calls to a disk system. The problem was that a growing number of disk systems (SCSI, optical, etc.) did not use the Interrupt 13H interface in BIOS. This meant that older versions of SMARTDrive didn't provide caching for these disk systems.

SMARTDrive 4.0 and higher was modified to be more flexible with different types of disk systems. It installs at the device driver level and can provide caching to any block device on the computer. The only drives missed by this new method are network drives. They cannot be called directly by DOS like CD-ROM drives because they are not addressed directly by DOS.

Some hard-disk manufacturers, in an effort to circumvent BIOS limitations and other problems, have created controllers or software disk managers that change the physical layout of the disk to enable DOS to see a logical disk system which then is interpreted to the physical layout. The SMARTDrive caching system depended on Interrupt 13H, and this caused problems. SMARTDrive 3.x was between the Interrupt 13H calls from the hard-disk drive and ROM (read-only memory) BIOS. Version 4.0 and higher moved up a layer. It now sits between the hard-disk driver and the Interrupt 13H calls. This new location eliminates many problems with physical and logical layout and solves the problem of those devices not using Interrupt 13H for their disk calls.

Busmastering

Busmastering is another device designed to speed up disk access on a hard disk. Since the internal communications of most computers cause the bottleneck, a busmastering controller takes over the bus and reads or writes to or from RAM without going through the CPU. There are two advantages to this configuration: bypassing the CPU eliminates one step the data has to go through before moving to RAM or the disk, and the CPU is now free to process requests from other devices or perform other duties. Busmastering is a good system for increasing performance.

It should be noted that a Busmastering controller interacting with a caching program can cause system lockup or data problems because of utilities that use virtual addressing. Any device driver that can load into upper memory may store data in a physical location in upper memory. It needs a conventional virtual-memory address for DOS to access; however, the translation between virtual memory and physical addresses is done by the CPU.

Because Busmastering bypasses the CPU, this translation doesn't occur, and wrong data can be written to the disk with disastrous consequences. SMARTDrive handles this problem by intercepting the call, writing the data to a conventional memory buffer, and then passing the information to the hard-disk drive controller. This procedure, called *double buffering,* ensures uniformity of the virtual and physical addresses. Few drives need double buffering; it's difficult for Windows 3.1 to determine whether it's needed. For reasons of safety, the Windows SETUP program will install double buffering regardless of whether it is a 386 CPU and if it is unable to determine whether 32-bit disk access is possible. SMARTDrive will report its status (Fig. 1.11) and whether it is using double buffering with the use of the /S switch.

SMARTDrive will also check to see if double buffering is necessary and will remove that feature, if it is determined to be unnecessary. In the example shown in Fig. 1.11 double buffering is not required for the disks and will not be used. You can force double buffering if you aren't comfortable with auto-

```
Microsoft SMARTDrive Disk Cache version 5.0
Copyright 1991,1993 Microsoft Corp.

Room for    256 elements of   8,192 bytes each
There have been    29 cache hits
    and    11 cache misses

Cache size: 2,097,152 bytes
Cache size while running Windows:  2,097,152 bytes

          Disk Caching Status
drive    read cache    write cache    buffering
---------------------------------------------
  A:       yes           no            no
  B:       yes           no            no
  C:       yes           yes           no

Write behind data will be committed before command prompt returns.
```

Figure 1.11 SMARTDrive caching status information.

matic detection. While SMARTDrive is loaded in the AUTOEXEC.BAT file, double buffering must be specified in the CONFIG.SYS file:

```
DEVICE=C:\WINDOWS\SMARTDRV.EXE /DOUBLE_BUFFER+
```

If you omit the plus (+) sign from the end of the line, the double-buffer detection feature will be loaded and SMARTDrive will not be forced to install double buffering. Double buffering takes additional resources to implement, so bypass this feature if possible.

There are some general rules to follow when installing SMARTDrive on your computer. Since it is a block-device-dependent utility, it is imperative to install it after block device drivers have been installed in CONFIG.SYS or AUTOEXEC.BAT. Any disk partitioning, compression, special disk drivers, or other similar utilities need to be installed first so that SMARTDrive can position itself properly.

The command-line options for SMARTDrive are listed in Fig. 1.12. You do not need to worry about these parameters; load SMARTDrive by itself. Invoking read-only caching is helpful, but it doesn't give you maximum performance. Saving data to the disk is time-consuming and can be a great

```
SMARTDRV [[/E:ELEMENTSIZE] [/B:BUFFERSIZE] [DRIVE [+]|[-]] [SIZE]
[WINSIZE]]...

drive letter            Specifies the letter of the disk drive to
                        cache.
                                (drive letter alone specifies read
                                caching only)
+                               Enables write-behind caching for the
                                specified drive.
-                               Disables all caching for the specified
drive.
size                    Specifies the amount of XMS memory (KB)
used by the cache.
winsize                 Specifies the amount of XMS memory (KB)
used in Windows.
/E:element size         Specifies the size of the cache elements (in
bytes).
/B:buffer size          Specifies the size of the read buffer.
/C                              Writes all write-behind information to
                                the hard disk.
/R                              Clears the contents of existing cache and
                                restarts SMARTDrive.
/L                              Loads SMARTDrive into low memory.
/Q                              Prevents the display of SMARTDrive
                                information on your screen.
/S                              Displays additional information about the
                                status of SMARTDrive.
```

Figure 1.12 SMARTDrive options.

source of delay when working with databases or other applications that need to write to the disk frequently.

The write-behind cache, also known as "lazy" writes, intercepts the write call to the hard disk and keeps it in RAM for a specific period. This type of delayed writing provides great efficiency for disk activities but also is in tension with data safety. The longer the data stays in RAM before being written out to disk, the more efficiently reads and writes can be grouped together. Disk access can be less frequent. A power failure or some other problem with the computer can wipe that data out and potentially cause data corruption.

SMARTDrive will never leave a write cache block in memory longer than 5 s, regardless of other activities. It will queue up the write request, and the data will be written out on the first available opportunity.

Occasionally the data will be written out to disk before it ages to 5 s. If there is a lot of disk activity taking place, the oldest data in cache will be written out to disk to make room for the new data. If the computer is idle, SMARTDrive will take the opportunity to write out the data to disk. While SMARTDrive cannot save data during power or other catastrophic failure of the computer, it intercepts a warm boot and writes out the data to the disk before passing on the reboot command to the system.

If you are running an older version of SMARTDrive, it is a good idea to upgrade to the latest version because of additional features but also to prevent a problem. This cannot be classified as a bug but it is a problem that needs to be dealt with. If you look back at Fig. 1.11 you will see near the bottom this line: Write-behind data will be committed before command prompt returns.

The /C switch has a curious history and points out how users regard computers. Older versions of SMARTDrive did not write out data to the disk until the parameters listed above were fulfilled. Some people assumed that when the DOS prompt appeared on the command line, it was safe to turn the computer off—and they did. They next time they accessed their data, information was missing or data corruption occurred. On those older versions of SMARTDrive, the reappearance of the DOS prompt did not necessarily mean that the data had been written out to disk.

If you are still running a 3.x or earlier version of SMARTDrive, you may want to start Windows from a batch file with the commands shown in Fig. 1.13.

```
c:
cd\windows
win.com
smartdrv.exe /c
```

Figure 1.13 Windows batch file with SMARTDrive command.

Running SMARTDrive with the /C parameter forces SMARTDrive to write the data in cache out to disk. Running from the batch file, this will be done before the DOS prompt appears.

Windows for Workgroups 3.11

Windows for Workgroups (WFW) has been a curious product. It was introduced after Windows 3.0 was shipped and was designed for peer-to-peer networking, but it did not have the power of Windows NT. Microsoft hoped to fill the gap between standard Windows and NT with WFW.

It wasn't long before it became known as Windows for Warehouses because it languished on shelves for months with low sales. Those who needed to network usually opted for a centralized file-server concept. Those who wanted peer-to-peer capabilities went with more established networks such as Lantastic or Novell Lite.

This all changed when WFW version 3.11 was released. Although Microsoft did not make an official announcement, it became clear that WFW 3.11 was the next generation of Windows beyond Windows 3.1. Whether you are running your Windows on a network or stand-alone, there are many benefits from upgrading to WFW 3.11.

NetWare Support

Windows for Workgroups 3.11 can now connect to a Novell NetWare server with the client computer running either Open Data-Link Interface (ODI) or

NETWARE.DRV -	This driver provides connectivity to NetWare file and servers, drive mapping capabilities, sends print jobs to file server print queues, and NetWare utilities.
VNETWARE.386 -	This provides the same functionality as the NETX.EXE shell except that it virtualizes the communication for the different windows and/or virtual machines. It is the same one shipped with Windows 3.1.
VIPX.386 -	Provides a similar function to VNETWARE.386 except it virtualizes the IPX protocol (IPXODI.COM) for multiple applications and virtual machines. This is also the same one that shipped with Windows 3.1.
NWPOPUP.COM -	This utility is unchanged from Windows 3.1 and presents SEND messages that would normally appear on a line at the top or bottom of the screen is now presented in a dialog box in Windows. If this utility is not loaded automatically in WIN.COM, the user will not see the message until they exit Windows or start a DOS virtual machine.

Figure 1.14 NetWare drivers for Windows for Workgroups.

the older monolithic drivers. Not only can WFW 3.11 attach to a NetWare server, it can also communicate peer-to-peer over IPX rather than the default NetBEUI protocol.

WFW 3.11 will connect to NetWare versions 2.0 through 4.1 inclusive. There are a variety of drivers and changes to .INI files required for stable NetWare connectivity. Figure 1.14 shows how these drivers work together.

A couple of new utilities have been added for WFW 3.11:

MSIPX.COM An implementation of the IPX protocol developed by Microsoft and Novell that is NDIS-compliant.

MSIPX.SYS A small utility that binds the MSIPX driver (above) to the NDIS driver for multiprotocol operation.

NDIS Specifications

The *Open-Systems Interconnect* (OSI) specification is a standard for transmitting data across a network. It provides a standard for manufacturers of hardware and software and makes it possible to interchange hardware and software on the same network.

The second layer of the OSI model is the data-link layer, which provides communication to network adapters and makes data available to other layers in the model so that it can be passed on to the CPU. Inside this level are utili-

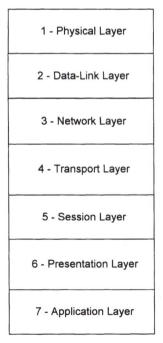

Figure 1.15 OSI model.

ties to handle data transmission and adapter management. The network card drivers operate at this level.

To further help interoperability, Microsoft and 3Com created a set of standards for communication at this level for communication between the MAC sublayer (in the data-link level), and the transport protocol that are located on layers 3 and 4 of the OSI model (Fig. 1.15).

The standard they developed became known as the *network device interface specification* (NDIS). NDIS is used to provide interoperability between network card manufacturers by allowing any protocol driver to communicate with any protocol as long as they conform to the NDIS specifications. Through this specification, different protocols can reside in the same computer and the system can communicate with IPX/SPX-, TCP/IP-, as well as NetBEUI-based systems. Under NDIS, each network card can handle four protocols, with a maximum of eight on a given computer (there can be as many as four network cards in a computer). As part of this specification, a packet of data being received by the workstation will be sent to the appropriate drive before being passed up the layers of the OSI models.

Microsoft Windows Design

Understanding the general design of Microsoft Windows can be a tremendous help in understanding how Windows works and for troubleshooting once you have installed the system. Confusing problems may arise at times, and this understanding may help solve a problem quickly.

Hardware independence

One of the best features of Microsoft Windows for Workgroups is the independence from hardware it provides for developers. One weakness of DOS was that all application developers had to create their own screens and communication to serial and parallel ports, printing devices, and other hardware systems.

Now, all screens can have a similar look, and developers don't have to completely create their own systems from the ground up. All the developer needs to know are the specific calls for an action, and Windows handles the rest.

Base systems

The basic Windows system is contained through a core set of files. These files handle the basic activities of Windows. The KRNL286.EXE and KRNL386.EXE files handle system input/output, manage memory, and schedule tasking so that the different applications running in separate windows will cooperate with each other. The KRNL286.EXE is used for running Windows in the standard mode, while the KRNL386.EXE is used for running Windows in enhanced mode.

The USER.EXE file takes care of the keyboard, mouse, communication through parallel and serial ports, and coordinates user elements such as windows currently open, icons on the screen, menus, and dialog boxes.

The third critical file in Windows is the GDI.EXE, which is the graphics interface. It handles the creation of graphic elements on the screen and handles any work with drivers. These drivers include printers and monitors that translate calls from the application to the hardware system.

Various other files provide services to Windows. The COMMDLG.DLL provides the look for dialog boxes when displaying messages or file lists. Multimedia devices are supported by the MMSYSTEM.DLL file, and data exchange between applications is provided by the DDEML.DLL file.

Device drivers

There are a number of device drivers in Windows to provide communication between the system and hardware items. Windows has routines for video monitors, printers, keyboards, and mice. These systems bring a standardization to Windows as you have to load only one driver for the particular hardware item and any application can communicate through standard Windows calls.

Dynamic link library (DLL) files

These files are a method of saving some disk space and bringing commonality to the system. Most DLL files contain code that can be accessed by almost any application. If you think about certain activities such as opening a file, it is the same process no matter what application does it. Rather than build these routines in each application, why not have common code files that can share these utilities? Some vendors who develop more than one application will build their own set of common DLLs to be shared among those applications.

Most DLL files have the extension .DLL following the file name, but some could have an .EXE extension to it. For example, KERNEL.EXE, USER.EXE, and GDI.EXE are technically .DLL files even though most people don't think of them as such.

The best definition of a DLL file is code, data, or routines available in Windows to any application that wishes to call it. A common method of including code into a program is to specify the file containing the code in the program code when the application is written. When the application is being compiled, the code in this external file is built into the program code and the application executable files contain all the code required to run the program.

DLL files don't use this method. They provide the same activity as building the code in the application, except it is done at the time the application is run. This keeps the executable files smaller. Windows applications include only the code required for the current activities they are performing, thus decreasing the amount of RAM required.

Using Windows

Windows for Workgroups provides the user with a pleasing, graphical desktop to take advantage of the new products available for Windows. The proper implementation of Windows brings a new level of function to the user. Combine this with NetWare, and you have a winning combination of systems.

In the next few chapters, we will review the other components of a networked Windows system.

2

Novell NetWare

Now that we have looked at Microsoft Windows, the next step is to investigate Novell NetWare. If you have an existing local area network, the choice of NetWare versions may be limited. If you are building a new system, selecting the right version of NetWare will be crucial for the operation of the network.

Novell is truly one of the great success stories in the computer industry. From very small and shaky beginnings in 1983, they have become a dominating force in local area networking, which they helped invent. Headquartered in Provo, Utah, the approximately 3500 employees provide support for their many different products.

Research groups have estimated that Novell has about 65 to 68 percent of the networking market with Microsoft's LAN Manager, Banyan Vines, IBM's PC Server, and other systems, each taking a fraction. Installing a NetWare system does not guarantee automatic success, but their products do have the widest support from third-party hardware and software vendors. Novell's dedication to interconnectivity ensures that you can connect with virtually any other system—midrange or mainframe. What functionality Novell doesn't provide, other vendors will.

Critics have charged that NetWare is an inefficient, nonserious product because it doesn't have many of the "bells and whistles" of other operating systems. While there is room for improvement, NetWare performs its core activities (file serving) without equal.

One of the greatest weaknesses of NetWare is the cost of the base operating system itself. The high performance comes at a price, with some versions costing several times more than their nearest competitors. Unfortunately, price becomes somewhat irrelevant as it is difficult to flip back and forth between operating systems just to save a few dollars.

In this chapter, we will discuss the different versions of NetWare and how to determine which one is most appropriate for a Windows installation.

NetWare 3.12

NetWare 3.0, introduced in the early 1990s, was the first of the new breed of NetWare operating systems. While this version had many technical problems and didn't take the market by storm, subsequent versions (3.10, 3.11, and now 3.12) have become the mainstay of Novell network offerings.

Version 3.12 is a full 32-bit operating system providing client support not only for Windows but also for OS/2, Macintosh, and UNIX. The capabilities of v3.12, when properly installed and configured, can rival a midrange or small-mainframe computer system.

Like other versions of NetWare, v3.12 runs directly on the server and can take advantage of the advanced features of the 386, 486, and Pentium CPUs. The features include

Between 5 and 250 simultaneous users

Up to 100,000 open files per server

A maximum of 64 volumes per server

Up to 32 physical disk drives

Maximum total disk space of 32 Tbytes

4 Gbytes of RAM

One of the biggest breakthroughs in server operating system design for NetWare was the NetWare loadable module (NLM). These modules run on the server and provide everything from utilities to full applications and are limited only by the developer's imagination. Novell uses NLM architecture for disk drivers, NIC drivers, monitoring, and repair utilities.

One of the greatest benefits of NetWare is the ability to work in mixed hardware, operating system, and protocol environments. If your current network has mixed network systems [e.g., Ethernet, Token Ring, FDDI (fiber distributed data interface)], the file server can communicate with all protocols by routing communication packets through the file server to the desired network segment. This saves on the cost of expensive dedicated routers to perform the same task.

Version 3.12 includes an NLM that enables IPX packets to be routed through IBM source-routing bridges. There are also NLMs for TCP/IP protocols, SNA, AppleTalk, and OSI TP4, which can run with the NetWare IPX/SPX protocol.

It is imperative that the Windows server have a high degree of reliability and security because of the reliance of users on that system. Version 3.12 has all the safety features found in previous versions while adding some of its own.

Read-after-Write Verification

A basic reliability feature for a network operating system is read-after-write verification. This routine compares the data written out to the disk with the same data still in memory. If they are the same, the data is discarded from memory and the next block is processed; if the data is not the same, another attempt is made to write out the data. If that fails, the disk block is marked "bad" in the file allocation table (FAT) and a spare block is used.

This feature comes with a great impact on performance. After the data is written to a disk block (see Fig. 2.1), the operating system must wait until the block spins around again and is positioned under the disk head before it can be read and compared. If the block is bad, the whole cycle starts over. Failure to free memory quickly can affect the user because it may impair his or her access to data if server memory is low.

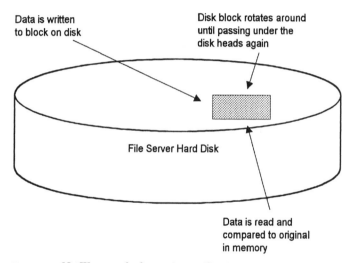

Figure 2.1 NetWare read-after-write verification.

A far better option for this level of data protection is to purchase hard-disk controllers that perform data checks at the hardware level. We have found an approximate 25 percent decrease in speed when NetWare performs the read-after-write verification with little performance impairment when the verification is done in the disk controller.

Hot Fix

The spare block comes from a reserve of blocks called "hot fix" (Fig. 2.2). When the operating system is defined, you have the option of creating many of these blocks so that the operating system can use them when necessary. The default is 2 percent of disk space allocated for these "spares," with the remainder used for the regular volume.

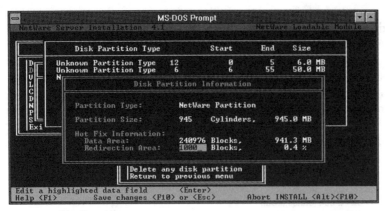

Figure 2.2 Hot-fix setup.

When installing a large disk ($\geq$ 1 Gbyte), accepting the default of 2 percent of disk space will mean a loss of at least 20 Mbytes. This large spare area is not needed because of the high reliability of hard-disk systems. We usually set aside about 1000 blocks for hot fix and leave the remainder for data. If the disk is failing so badly that it needs more than 1000 blocks, the whole system is doomed, anyway, and more spare blocks will only delay the inevitable crash. Frequent inspections of the hot-fix status (found on the monitor screen on the console) will notify you when a disk is failing.

A few hot-fix blocks are taken for internal housekeeping purposes, and it is not uncommon for a few blocks to be used over time. We have found that when a disk fails, the hot-fix blocks are used rapidly, providing a great early-warning system that the hard-disk is failing. By monitoring hot fix carefully, you can prevent one of the network administration nightmares: a hard-disk crash.

Disk Mirroring

If you choose to run Windows from the file server, it becomes imperative that the programs and data on those disks be as safe as possible. The reliability of hard disks has become extraordinary, with some manufacturers listing 250,000 h or more for mean time between failures (MTBF).

However, even though the chances of a disk problem are low, it will be of little help when a disk does crash and you need to restore from a backup. With large disk sizes in use these days, it could take a day or more to replace the hard disk, create the server volume, and restore the data. And that presumes that there is a good backup!

The chances of two disks going bad simultaneously are small so one of the options available on NetWare 3.12 is *disk mirroring,* in which two disks are connected to the same controller and data written out to one is automatically written to the other. If one disk fails, the other disk will take over automatically without the users knowing there was a failure. While you will have to buy two disks to implement this feature, the safety it provides cannot be overemphasized.

Disk Duplexing

Disk duplexing is actually disk mirroring taken one step further. There are not only two disks but also two controllers providing a secondary data channel. We have found that controller failure is equal to hard-disk failures, and while a controller failure is not as catastrophic as a disk failure, it is a major inconvenience.

There is an additional benefit of using disk duplexing. By having the redundant channels in the server, the operating system will write to both disks but will read from whichever disk is idle. Novell claims this feature will speed up disk access by as much as 25 percent. When building a Windows server, which will be handling large files, anything that will give an additional measure of safety *and* increase performance, is well worth the cost. We have had servers where disk duplexing worked so well that the failure of a controller or disk wasn't noticed by the users or us!

Tip: If you are using one of the methods listed here for storing data on two disks simultaneously (mirroring, duplexing, SFTIII), you may want to consider turning off the read-after-write verification. Reading the data twice for safety purposes is good for a single-disk storage system but is seldom needed for dual-disk storage. The only risk you take is that both disks will have bad areas when the data is written out. The odds of both storage locations being bad for the same block of data is quite small—but it is a danger we need to be aware of.

SFTIII

For the ultimate in reliability and safety, Novell has developed a fault-tolerant system that incorporates two servers. These servers mirror each other physically and create one logical server that the user sees.

The disk drives and RAM are mirrored, with one server being the "master" (primary) server and the second server being the "slave" (secondary) (see arrangement in Fig. 2.3). The primary server keeps in constant communication with the secondary server. When the secondary server no longer receives "keep alive" communication from the primary server, it assumes that the primary server is down and takes over the duties of the primary server.

This has solved a problem that has bedeviled those running Windows from the server. The moment that server goes live, the users will have total

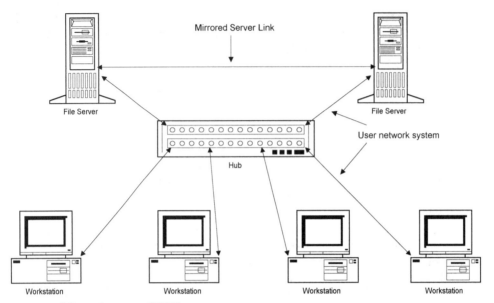

Figure 2.3 Mirrored servers: SFTIII.

reliance on that server for their day-to-day operation. If it goes down, whole departments could be out of business until the server is restored.

You probably wrestle with the problem of finding a convenient time to take a server down for routine maintenance. This becomes even more difficult if your organization runs on a 24-h/day, 7-day/week basis. SFTIII allows the administrator to take a server offline as needed for maintenance.

Whatever your experience with NetWare, installing SFTIII is not something to be taken lightly. While the user functions and utilities are similar, the operations of the consoles are much different from those of the standard version of v3.12.

The consoles on both machines have three main screens. There is one screen for each physical server and one screen for the logical server. This makes three separate servers. Each physical server handles hardware systems, while the logical server (the combination of both machines) becomes the third logical server. Only those NLMs which deal with the hardware should be loaded on each server, with the remainder of the NLMs loaded on the mirrored (logical) server.

Other precautions include mirroring the disk drives between servers. This requires some care as they can easily be matched with the wrong disk drive on the other server and problems will never end. Also, the allocation of primary versus secondary server is based on which one comes up first.

We recommend installing and testing SFTIII thoroughly first before providing it live for users. You will need to get experience with the system before making it available for users.

Hardware Protection

The methods of data protection described above are not, however, the answers for all problems. Frequently data protection is sold to management and users as a total answer to the end of downtime and data problems. SFTIII reduces downtime but does not eliminate it totally. That distinction is critical because if users don't understand the protection, they will lose faith in the new system.

Disk mirroring, disk duplexing, and SFTIII provide only a level of *hardware* protection. If the application destroys the database through bad programming or other software problems, the data will be ruined on both disks or servers, requiring restoration and perhaps lengthy downtime.

NetWare 4

This next generation of NetWare servers is designed for a system where more than one server is on the network. While it will work very well in single server sites, we are convinced that its true abilities don't become obvious until it is used in a multiserver environment.

Unfortunately, this next generation of server operating systems is the most radical departure from the standard NetWare systems. Gone is the familiar bindery (a type of database), PCONSOLE, SYSCON, SLIST, and other utilities we have memorized through the years. All items in the server system are now classified as objects. The computer, hard disks, volumes, printers, queues, users, etc. are all classified as objects and are essentially handled similarly.

NetWare Directory Services (NDS)

The biggest change from previous versions is the introduction of directory services. NDS changes how users log in and access the servers. In previous versions, each server stored information about valid users in a database called a *bindery,* and an administrator had to set up each user on all servers that the user might need to reach. On large networks this became a massive task, sometimes taking hours to add just a few users. Users had to specify which server they wanted to log in to and attach to other servers as needed. While some of these tasks could be automated, the whole system revolved around individual servers.

Directory services are created on a server and then replicated to the other servers regularly so that all servers are aware of the users. Users can be setup with a "domain" of servers to which they will attach automatically on login. You can think of this system as logging into a large "logical" server regardless of how many physical servers are in place.

Server Memory

The NetWare loadable module (NLM) makes it possible to load drivers and other system utilities in memory. The ability to load and unload these modules in memory without rebooting the server can cause some memory problems. For 3.x servers, the memory is divided into several memory pools that have different functions in the system.

When memory is no longer needed for running NLMs or internal purposes, it may not be available in the future because memory from one pool cannot be reallocated to another memory pool. This is the reason for shutting down a 3.x server periodically, allowing memory allocation to be reset, extra memory to be recovered, and RAM fragmentation to be eliminated.

This problem has been largely solved by version 4.x as there is only one memory allocation pool. Memory used by an application or utility will be returned to the general pool and made available to any application that will be loaded in the future.

NLM Operation

NetWare loadable modules have been used extensively in NetWare 3.x and are still available in NetWare 4. However, in v3.12 the NLMs operate in ring 0 of the CPU, which makes it run very quickly, but the operating system is susceptible to problems. If the NLM has an error, it will not only stop but will also, most likely, abend the server. This feature has been a source of trouble for network administrators. We have experienced problems with an optical disk NLM abending the server when unloaded and a backup NLM that abended the server when the backup was stopped during the first minute of operation.

NetWare 4 has added some new options when running NLMs to eliminate some of these problems. You have the choice of running the NLM in the original ring 0, or you can move it to ring 1, 2, or 3 for greater safety. In these protected rings (1 to 3), an NLM can malfunction but will most likely not cause the server to crash. There is a performance penalty for running the NLMs in levels 1 to 3, as the levels of safety require more overhead. For those wanting maximum security, all NLMs can be run in the higher rings so that the server will not abend as a result of NLM errors. If you want the maximum in speed and security, run the NLMs in ring 3 until you are sure that they are stable, and then move them to ring 0.

Disk Storage

NetWare 4 adds functionality to the disk system, thus providing additional efficiency. These enhancements are optional and can be used or ignored. Versions 3.x and 4.x allow you to choose the size of the disk blocks when the operating system is installed. This was always a dilemma for administrators because choosing the wrong block size would have a great impact on the performance of the server.

Previous versions allow block sizes between 4 and 64 kbytes. If 4 kybtes were chosen, large files would be broken into hundreds or thousands of blocks. When retrieving a file spread across thousands of blocks, the operating system must undertake a tremendous amount of work to copy the file into RAM and then send it to the workstation. On the other hand, setting the block size to 64 kbytes, a large amount of disk space would be lost to slack space. A 1-kbyte file stored in a 64-kbyte block would mean a loss of 63 kbytes of space (called "slack" space). Most administrators set the block size to 4 kbytes to avoid this potential loss of space.

Version 4.x overcomes this problem with a new method of storage that uses block suballocation. This method divides the blocks into 512-byte subblocks that can store more than one file if needed. Therefore, the 1-kbyte file stored in a 64-kbyte block would not waste the remaining 63 kbytes but would use two of the 512-byte blocks, and the remainder of the 512-byte blocks would be available for other files.

Disk Compression

To increase disk space, some or all files and directories can be set for automatic compression. If the compression attribute is set, the files are compressed automatically in the background and decompressed as needed.

Although this is a great space saver, there is a speed penalty for decompression that may be noticeable to the users. With the greatly decreased price of hard disks, the speed loss is significant, and we have not found the compression feature useful but have just added more disks as needed.

Data Extension

There probably isn't a network administrator alive who isn't always on the lookout for additional storage space. NetWare 4 has a couple of utilities that will help the administrator reach those goals. The first utility migrates unused data from the file-server hard disk to an alternate storage medium.

The administrator can set an inactivity threshold time span for each file where the file will be moved from the hard disk to the alternate storage medium (like an optical disk jukebox). If no one accesses a marked file during the time specified, it is moved to an alternate site. The file name stays in the file allocation table (FAT), so the users cannot tell the difference between a migrated or nonmigrated file.

To access a migrated file, the user moves the file back from the alternate storage media to the hard disk. This resets the timer, and the file will be moved to the alternate storage when the inactive time has been reached.

High-Capacity Storage System (HCSS)

This system extends the hard-disk storage space by integrating optical disk jukeboxes into the file server and making it part of the overall file storage system. These jukeboxes can be as large as 100 Tbytes for high-capacity storage needs. The optical disk systems connect to the server through a standard data communications system such as the small computer systems interface (SCSI).

When used with the file migration utility, HCSS can provide a unique method of large disk storage systems, thus extending the file storage.

Server Auditing

In keeping with the enterprisewide services of NetWare 4, sophisticated auditing is available to monitor the network properly. An auditor who does not normally have access to the server can be set up with special rights to view the audit files. The audit files contain information about logins and logouts, who created or modified directories and files, NDS activities, and modifications to trustee rights.

Packet Burst

NetWare 3.x and 4.x support the packet-burst protocol, greatly increasing communication performance by decreasing the overhead of the normal IPX/SPX protocol. This feature becomes critical with Windows as most program and data files under Windows are larger than standard DOS applications.

The IPX/SPX protocol is very "chatty," with an acknowledgment packet being sent for every packet received, thus effectively doubling the communications traffic. It is not uncommon for data to be sent in ≥500-byte packets, and transmitting a 2-Mbyte file in 515-byte packets with an acknowledgment for each packet requiring a large amount of network communication resources.

With packet burst, the server and the client negotiate a transmission and then send a series of packets with only one acknowledgment returned. This greatly affects the communications system because many packets are eliminated from the large file transmission cycle. A reason for an acknowledgment for each packet sent is to enable retransmission of a packet if there is a problem. If a packet fails in a packet-burst transmission, only the failed packet is retransmitted, avoiding the need to resend the whole series of packets.

Just implementing packet burst is not enough, because this high level of transmission could cause problems for a network with heavy traffic. During high-volume traffic, packet burst will adjust the number of packets in the burst, smaller packet sizes, and more acknowledgments.

Packet burst is enabled by loading the PBURST.NLM at the server (on version 3.12) and enabling packet burst at the client by adding a line to enable packet burst in the NET.CFG file. This selective implementation is handy because it can be turned on for only those clients who need it and the other stations would run normally.

There is a price to pay for packet burst. For stations that have light communications needs, packet burst can impair performance slightly because of the extra overhead to run it. On networks that are very busy, packet burst may slow overall network communications because of the high level of throughput.

The packet-burst NLM is included with the operating system in version 3.12 and is built into version 4.x. The clients need to run VLM client software to use packet burst.

Large Internet Packet

Another method of increasing network communications is to increase how much data is sent in each packet. This is assisted by the *large internet packet* (LIP) system, where the size of the packet is adjusted according to transmission needs. Normally, the packet size is set to 512 bytes of data and 64 bytes of overhead information. With LIP, the client and the server negotiate the largest optimal packet size. The packet sizes can be as large as 4202 bytes but will depend on the maximum physical size the server can send.

Frame Type

For NetWare 3.12 and 4.x servers, NetWare offers a choice of frame types for those running Ethernet. In previous versions, the only choice was Ethernet 802.3, which is a nonstandard version of the IEEE description of Ethernet packets. This frame type is limited because it supports only the IPX protocol. To support a variety of protocols, you need to switch over to the 802.2 frame type which is standard.

Fortunately, both frame types can be installed on a server that will allow clients running either frame to connect. This is very handy because you don't have to convert every workstation simultaneously. Over time you can change the clients to the new frame type.

To add the 802.2 frame type to the server, a second command must be issued as follows:

```
load NE2-32 slot=5 frame=Ethernet_802.2
bind IPX to NE2-32 net=1234
```

If you want these loaded all the time, remember to add that to the AUTOEXEC.NCF. On the client station, modify the NET.CFG file by adding the following line to the LINK DRIVER section:

```
FRAME Ethernet_802.2
```

See also Fig. 2.4.

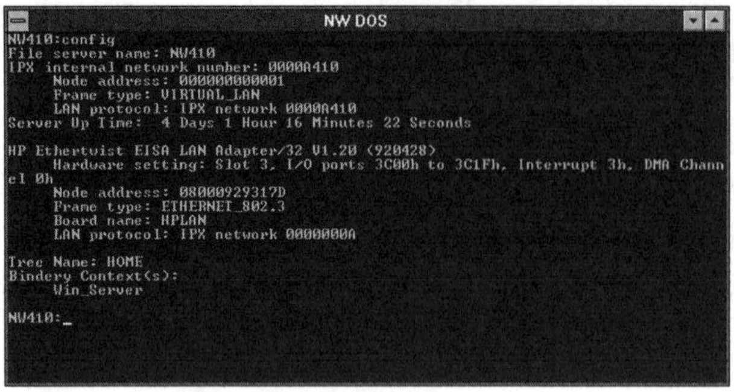

Figure 2.4 Config Console command.

Enhanced Security

In an attempt to enhance security, Novell has added a feature called *NCP packet signature,* which helps prevent packet forgery. This system requires the server and workstation to sign each packet with the security key negotiated on login. Every packet that is not correctly signed is ignored with an alert sent to the server console.

When a workstation logs onto a 3.x or 4.x server, the server and station negotiate a shared key for that session. Each workstation has a unique key. The packet has a unique signature added to it so that the recipient will know whether it is a valid packet from that station. The recipient checks the signature and will process the packet if the signature is correct.

You can choose to enable NCP packet signature or not depending on the need to implement security. This feature does affect performance negatively because of the extra work required by the server. However, a network that has high-speed servers, a good communication system, and high-performance workstations should not be impacted too heavily.

If you decide to implement NCP packet signature, there are several levels from which you can choose. If set to level 1, the server will sign and check signatures only if the client requests it. Level 2 instructs the server to always sign the packet if the client can transmit a signature. Level 3 is the highest level of security, in which the server will not communicate with a client unless NCP packet signature is used.

NCP packet signature is enabled at the server by the command shown here:

```
File Server:
SET NCP PACKET SIGNATURE OPTION = (0, 1, 2, 3)

Client:
SIGNATURE LEVEL = (0,1,2,3)
```

At the client station, the line shown above should be added to NetWare DOS requester section of the NET.CFG file. For security reasons, the NCP signature level can be increased dynamically at the file-server console, but it cannot be decreased unless the server is brought down and restarted.

Enhanced Printing

NetWare 4 has increased the functionality of the print server and printing queues by changing them from bindery objects to individual objects. This allows users to access printers without needing to know to which server the print queue is connected.

The new printing system will allow multiple print servers to run on the same server, and the maximum number a print server can service has been increased from 16 to 256.

Version Comparisons

Today, network administrators are faced with the choice of installing version 3.12 or 4.1. While this may seem like a simple decision, new advances and features in NetWare 4 make the decision much more difficult.

The traditional description of NetWare 4 is for an enterprise network operating system involving hundreds of users, many file servers, and a complex operating system. However, many network managers are revising their thinking because of the additional features available in NetWare 4.

The architecture of a NetWare 3.12 server is best suited for a single-server system. The biggest barrier to using 3.12 for multiserver large installations is the bindery, which is a small database that contains all the critical information about each user including the login name, password, account restrictions, security, and other information.

The biggest change in NetWare 4 is the replacement of the bindery with directory services. This has been a welcome change in the architecture of NetWare, making it much more compatible with an enterprisewide system. Even if you have a single-server network, there are many additional features in NetWare 4 that may make it worth upgrading.

For the first time, a NetWare server is aware of other servers and will communicate with the other servers frequently. A large amount of additional information is stored in the NetWare 4 server, which makes the directory services a handy employee-user directory tracking phone numbers, e-mail (electronic-mail) addresses, station information, and other items.

In NetWare 4, everything is considered an object. The server operating system, the server itself, hard disk, network card, NLMs, printers, printer queues, and users are all considered objects and are treated in the same manner. Passwords can be applied to these objects and are tracked in the directory services database.

When a user or any object is set up on a server, information about that object is transmitted to all other servers. The user is not forced to remember which server has an object such as a printer but can reference the printer name only, and each server knows where the printer is located and how to reach it.

Because of the object technology, a user can log in to any server and be connected to the correct server immediately. This interserver communication eliminates the need to set up a user on each server several times. You do it just once on a server, and the information will be replicated to the others automatically.

After reviewing the differences between NetWare 3.12 and NetWare 4 and our in-depth experiences with both systems, we have come to the conclusion that for small networks, NetWare 4 is a viable choice.

3

NetWare File-Server Parameters

NetWare 3.x and 4.x provide a variety of parameters that can be set to fine-tune the server for maximum efficiency. Most people accept the defaults when the system is installed, and those parameters are never touched again. Leaving those parameters set to default values may not be the best for your network. When Windows is installed, many more files are open at one time, much more traffic is generated than normally, and the server gets much busier.

Execution of Set Parameters

Most parameters can be set at the file console dynamically (while the server is running), and the changes become effective immediately. However, this setting is in effect only while the file server is running. Down the file server and the next time the server starts, it will revert to the default conditions.

To avoid this problem, all settings must be placed in either the AUTOEXEC.NCF or SETUP.NCF file. This will ensure that the same settings take place every time the file server is started. AUTOEXEC.NCF and STARTUP.NCF can be modified at the file-server console with the INSTALL.NLM (under System Parameters, Edit AUTOEXEC.BAT), or with the EDIT.NLM. From a workstation, change into the SYSTEM directory and use a standard text editor (e.g., EDIT.COM) to modify the file.

The STARTUP.NCF is a standard ASCII text file located on the DOS partition of the hard disk (or on a floppy disk) and can be edited with a standard text editor. It also can be edited through the INSTALL.NLM on the file-server console like the AUTOEXEC.NCF.

Nondynamic Settings

There are some settings that are global and cannot be changed while the file server is running. These settings involve memory configuration, and changing them while the file server is operational could cause problems for the users or cause the file server to crash. The following list shows the parameters that can only be set in SETUP.NCF.

Autoregister memory above 16 Mbytes

Auto TTS backout flag

Cache buffer size

Maximum physical receive packet size

Maximum subdirectory tree depth

Minimum packet receive buffers

Reserved buffers below 16 Mbytes

If you try to set these parameters on the file server, you will get an error message and the parameter will not be changed.

Set Menu

The set parameters can be accessed on the file-server console by typing set at the console prompt and pressing <Enter>. You will get a menu which lists the main categories of the set parameters (see Fig. 3.1).

Default Settings for NetWare

The parameters listed here are for NetWare versions 3.12 and 4.1. Parameters that are found in both NetWare 4.1 and 3.12 are shown with a bullet (•). If 3.12 parameter values are different than 4.1, the value for version 3.12 is shown in parentheses.

```
Settable configuration parameter categories:
        1. Communications
        2. Memory
        3. File caching
        4. Directory caching
        5. File system
        6. Locks
        7. Transaction tracking
        8. Disk
        9. Time
       10. NCP
       11. Miscellaneous
       12. Error handling
       13. Directory services
Which category do you want to view?
```

Figure 3.1 Set parameter menu.

Alert message nodes = 20

Alloc memory check flag – OFF

- Allow change to client rights = ON

Allow deletion of active directories = ON

Allow invalid pointers = OFF

- Allow LIP = ON

- Allow unencrypted passwords = OFF

Allow unowned files to be extended = ON

- Autoregister memory above 16 Mbytes = ON

- Auto TTS backout flag = OFF

Automatically repair bad volumes = ON

Cache buffer size = 4096 bytes

Compression daily check starting hour = 0

Compression daily check stop hour = 6

- Concurrent remirror requests = 4 (2)

- Console display watchdog logouts = OFF

Convert compressed to uncompressed option = 1

Daylight Savings Time offset = +1:00:00

Daylight Savings Time status = ON

Days untouched before compression = 7

Decompress free-space warning interval = 31 min, 18.5 s

Decompress percent disk space free to allow commit = 10

Default time server type = SINGLE

- Delay before first watchdog packet = 4 min, 56.6 s

- Delay between watchdog packets = 59.3 s

Deleted files compression option = 1

Developer option = OFF

- Directory cache allocation wait time = 2.2 s

- Directory cache buffer nonreferenced delay = 5.5 s

- Dirty directory cache delay time = 0.5 s

- Dirty disk cache delay time = 3.3 s

Display disk device alerts = OFF (3.12 only)

- Display incomplete IPX packet alerts = ON

- Display lost interrupt alerts = ON

Display NCP bad component warnings = OFF

Display NCP bad length warnings = OFF

- Display old API names = OFF

- Display relinquish control alerts = OFF

- Display spurious interrupt alerts = ON

- Enable disk read-after-write verify = ON

Enable file compression = ON

Enable IPX checksums = ON

- Enable packet-burst statistics screen = OFF

End of Daylight Savings Time = (OCTOBER SUNDAY LAST 2:00:00 AM)

- File delete wait time = 5 min, 29.6 s

Garbage collection interval = 15 min

Global pseudo-preemption = OFF

Halt system on invalid parameters = OFF

- Immediate purge of deleted files = OFF

IPX NetBIOS replication option = 2

Maximum alloc short-term memory = 8388608 (3.12 only)

Maximum concurrent compressions = 2

- Maximum concurrent directory cache writes = 10

- Maximum concurrent disk cache writes = 50

- Maximum directory cache buffers = 500

- Maximum extended attributes per file or path = 16 (8)

- Maximum file locks = 10,000

- Maximum file locks per connection = 250

Maximum interrupt events = 10

Maximum number of internal directory handles = 100

Maximum number of directory handles = 20

- Maximum outstanding NCP searches = 51

- Maximum packet receive buffers = 100 (400)

- Maximum percent of volume used by directory = 13

- Maximum percent of volume space allowed for extended attributes = 10

- Maximum physical receive packet size = 1514

Maximum record locks per connection = 500

- Maximum record locks = 20,000
- Maximum record locks per connection = 500
- Maximum service processes = 40 (20)
- Maximum subdirectory tree depth = 25
- Maximum transactions = 10,000

Minimum compression percentage gain = 2

Minimum directory cache buffers = 20 (3.12 only)

Minimum file cache report threshold = 20 (3.12 only)

Minimum file cache buffers = 20

Minimum file cache report threshold = 20

Minimum file cache buffers = 20 (3.12 only)

- Minimum file delete wait time = 1 min, 5.9 s

Minimum free memory for garbage collection = 8000

- Minimum packet-receive buffers = 50 (10)

Mirrored devices are out-of-sync message frequency = 30

- NCP file commit = ON
- NCP packet signature option = 1

NDS backlink interval = 780

NDS client NCP retries = 3

NDS external reference life span = 192

NDS inactivity synchronization interval = 30

NDS janitor interval = 60

NDS servers status = UP/DOWN

NDS synchronization restrictions = OFF

NDS trace file name = SYSTEM\DSTRACE.DBG

NDS trace file length to zero = OFF

NDS trace to screen = OFF

NDS trace to file = OFF

- New packet-receive buffer wait time = 0.1 s
- New service process wait time = 2.2 s

New time with Daylight Savings Time status = ON

Number of watchdog packets = 10

Number of frees for garbage collection = 5000

Number of watchdog packets = 100 (3.12 only)

Pseudo-preemption count = 10

Pseudo-preemption time = 2000 (3.12 only)

- Read ahead enabled = ON
- Read-ahead LRU sitting time threshold = 10 s

Read fault notification = ON

Reject NCP packets with bad lengths = OFF

Reject NCP packets with bad components = OFF

Remirror block size = 1

- Replace console prompt with server name = ON
- Reply to get nearest server = ON
- Reserved buffers below 16 Mbytes = 200 (16)

Server log file overflow size = 4,194,304

Server log file state = 1

Sound bell for alerts = ON

Start of Daylight Savings Time = (APRIL SUNDAY FIRST 2:00:00 AM)

Time zone = PST8PDT

TIMESYNC ADD time source = <name of server>

TIMESYNC configuration file = SYS:SYSTEM\TIMESYNC.CFG

TIMESYNC configured sources = OFF

TIMESYNC directory tree mode = ON

TIMESYNC hardware clock = ON

TIMESYNC polling count = 3

TIMESYNC polling interval = 600

TIMESYNC REMOVE time source = <name of server>

TIMESYNC RESET = OFF

TIMESYNC restart flag = OFF

TIMESYNC service advertising = ON

TIMESYNC synchronization radius = 2000

TIMESYNC time adjustment = none scheduled

TIMESYNC time source = <name of server>

TIMESYNC type = SINGLE

TIMESYNC write parameters = OFF

TIMESYNC write value = 3

- TTS abort dump flag = OFF
- TTS backout file truncation wait time = 59 min, 19.2 s
- TTS unwritten cache wait time = 1 min, 5.9 s
- Turbo FAT reuse wait time = 5 min, 29.6 s

Upgrade low-priority threads = OFF

Volume log file overflow size = 4,194,304

Volume log file state = 1

- Volume low, warn all users = ON
- Volume low warning threshold = 256
- Volume low warning reset threshold = 256

Volume TTS log file state = 1

Volume TTS log file overflow size = 4,194,304

Worker thread execute in a row count = 10

Write fault emulation = OFF

Write fault notification = ON

Parameter Values

The items marked with an asterisk are ones you should evaluate closely as they may need adjustment for Windows. If you are running Windows from the file server, many of these parameters will need adjustment (usually increased).

Communications Parameters

These are the parameters for versions 3.12 and 4, and those that are important to Windows are marked with an asterisk (i.e., each item with an asterisk may need adjusting for Windows). Pay careful attention to these parameters because they may need adjustment. Windows increases network traffic and puts extra strain on the file server, and adjusting certain parameters may help the efficiency of your system.

*Maximum packet-receive buffers

This is the maximum number of packet-receive buffers that can be allocated. Windows will increase the communications traffic which may require increased buffers to handle the higher level of packets coming to the file server.

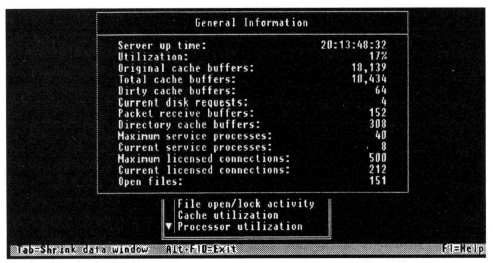

Figure 3.2 Console monitor utility.

To determine whether you need to increase the number of packet-receive buffers, follow this formula:

One packet-receive buffer per simultaneously attached workstation

Five additional buffers for each bus master board in the file server

After making these adjustments, view the packet-receive buffers in MONITOR (see Fig. 3.2) to determine whether there is an adequate number of buffers. If the server has reached the maximum, increase this amount. The default is set to 100 buffers, and values can range from 50 to 2000.

Tip: Increasing the maximum number of service processes parameters will decrease the need for packet-receive buffers because the additional processes will handle the packets faster.

Tip: Check LAN information in MONITOR to see if there are any event control block (ECB) errors. If there are, increase the number of packet-receive buffers until the errors stop. ECBs are used for sending and receiving packets and control the sequence of packets in the network drivers, and errors of this type usually mean that there are too many packets for the number of buffers allocated.

Minimum packet-receive buffers

This is the opposite of the maximum settings. Usually this does not have to be modified because the default of 10 (3.12) and 50 (NetWare 4) is seldom adequate for a busy network. We have found that setting this value to 100 gives a much better response. The allowable values are 10 to 1000 and can be set only in the STARTUP.NCF.

*Maximum physical receive packet size

This is the value of the physical packet size that can be transmitted and received by the file server. With Windows, it is imperative that large packets be transmitted to increase the speed of operation. The default is 2 kbytes (2048), but the values can be set from 618 to 4202. For Token Ring and Ethernet networks, the default is fine, but for other networks, check the documentation for the network boards you are using and set this value to the value in the documentation. This can be set only in STARTUP.NCF.

Maximum interrupt events

These are the interrupt events that can occur before a switching of the thread switch is guaranteed to occur. The values range from 1 to 1,000,000 with a default of 10. Don't set this value too high, as you want the server to switch to different threads to handle all processes.

*Number of watchdog packets

Because there are no direct connections between a file server and the workstation, the file server must have some mechanism to ensure that the workstation is still operational. This is done through watchdog packets that are sent out to a silent station "asking" if it is still alive. If the workstation doesn't answer, additional watchdog packets are sent and after a specified amount of time, a lack of reply will indicate the workstation is turned off or disconnected from the network. This setting determines how many watchdog packets are sent to the workstation before the workstation is determined to be nonoperational. The default number of watchdog packets is 10 with a range of 5 to 100. If the network has become busy because of additional Windows traffic, you may need to increase this value.

Delay between watchdog packets

This next parameter is part of the watchdog trio. It determines the amount of time the workstation should wait after sending out additional watchdog packets. For reasons beyond logic, the default is 4 min, 56.6 s. The values can range from 1 s to 10 minutes, 26.2 s. If the workstation doesn't reply in this time, then the watchdog system starts its procedure to drop the connection. Setting this value too low may cause some stations to be dropped prematurely, while setting the value too high may place an unnecessary burden on the file server.

Delay before first watchdog packet

The first watchdog packet is sent out when the file server hasn't heard from a workstation for a specified time. This value determines how long the file server should wait until it hears from the workstation. The default is also 4 min,

56.6 s with ranges from 0.1 to 20 s. Usually this value doesn't need to be adjusted.

*New packet-receive buffer wait time

When packets are received at the file server, additional buffers need to be allocated to handle the load, which takes up additional memory. If there are spikes in usage, the file server may create additional buffers when they won't be needed on a long-term basis. If a delay is set, the file server won't allocate additional buffers needlessly. This parameter determines how long the increased level of traffic lasts before additional buffers are created.

If the delay is too short, additional buffers may be allocated needlessly, whereas waiting too long will impair the performance of the file server because additional buffers aren't available. If the server has a large amount of RAM, set this value low because there is no need to worry about waiting memory for buffers. The default is 0.1 s, with acceptable ranges between 0.1 s and 20 s.

Reply to get nearest server

On a multiserver network, a workstation broadcasts a "get nearest server" message to the network to find out where there are file servers. This attachment gives access to the login directory to enable users to log in to the server using their login name and password. The client shell (NETX or VLM) will attach to the first server that answers the request. If this value is set to OFF, the server will not respond to the "get nearest server" request. The acceptable values are OFF and ON.

Console display watchdog logouts

This feature determines whether a message should be displayed on the console when a connection is cleared. The value can be set to OFF or ON. Default is OFF.

Memory Parameters

Alloc memory check flag

This value does not affect a Windows system. This parameter determines whether servers will do corruption checking in alloc memory. The values are ON or OFF with the default being ON.

Autoregister memory above 16 Mbytes

This determines whether the server will automatically register memory above 16 Mbytes. This is for EISA (extended industry-standard architecture) machines and is designed for backward compatibility with older peripheral boards that cannot address memory above 16 Mbytes. Since you will probably need more than 16 Mbytes of RAM to run the Windows file server correctly, leave this set to ON and replace the older cards with new EISA cards.

Garbage collection interval

One of the more interesting parameters, this determines the maximum time between garbage collections. "Garbage collection" is an interesting name given to a process to increase efficiency. It is a method of taking defragmented memory, gathering it up and placing it in larger blocks. The longer the server is up, the more defragmented the memory tends to get.

In NetWare 3.x, this occurs only when an NLM calls a Free routine, which may happen on an irregular basis. In NetWare 4, this procedure takes place at specified times. The more frequently NLMs are loaded and unloaded, there can be a high amount of memory defragmentation. During the garbage collection routine, an NLM's allocation list of memory is reviewed, if possible, and the blocks are combined into a larger block and placed in a linked list showing the new location of the data. The memory freed up by this routine is made available to cache buffers. Default value is 15 min, with time values from 1 min to 1 h allowed.

Number of Frees for garbage collection

This is the minimum number of Free commands issued by an NLM before garbage collection will occur. NLMs have the ability to use memory and return it back to the system after use. The command to perform this release is called a "Free." The Free values is the number of times the memory is freed and does not indicate how much memory was freed. The range is 100 to 100,000, with a default of 1000.

Minimum Free memory for garbage collection

This is the minimum number of bytes needed before garbage collection begins. The default is 8000 bytes, with values from 1000 to 100,000 bytes allowed.

Allow invalid pointers

This does not have a direct effect on Windows. It sets the environment to allow a nonexistent page to be mapped in with only one notification. The default is OFF.

Read fault notification

This is another value that does not have a direct impact on Windows. It establishes whether there is a message to the console and error log whenever there are emulated read page faults. The value defaults to ON.

Read fault emulation

Again, this is a value that doesn't impact Windows directly. It determines whether a read that occurs from a nonpresent page is emulated. The default is ON.

Write fault notification

This is another value that does not have a direct impact on Windows. It establishes whether there is a message to the console and error log whenever there are emulated write page faults. The value defaults to ON.

Write fault emulation

Again, this is a value that doesn't impact Windows directly. It determines whether a write that occurs to a nonpresent page is emulated. The default is OFF.

File Caching Parameters

Read-ahead enable

During a sequential file read, if this value is set to ON, the file server will do background reads in advance of the user requesting the data. The default is OFF.

Read-ahead LRU sitting time threshold

This value sets the minimum cache least recently used sitting time for reading data in advance of requests. The default is 10 s, with values allowable from 0 s to 1 h.

Reserved buffers below 16 Mbytes

For older peripheral cards that cannot access memory above 16 Mbytes, this feature reserves buffers below 16 Mbytes to communicate with the cards. The default is 16, with values from 8 to 200 supported.

Minimum file cache buffers

This is the minimum number of buffers set aside for file caching. Memory allocation in NetWare divides up memory for system processes first, and then all leftover memory is allocated for file caching. This value determines the minimum number of buffers for file caching regardless of system needs. Setting this value too high may mean system failure. It is better to keep it low. The default is 20, with accepted values ranging from 20 to 1000.

Maximum concurrent disk cache writes

NetWare uses a technique called "elevator seeking" to perform I/O operations on the hard disk. This brings a great level of performance as reads and writes are done on an organized basis. All actions are stored in memory and as the hard-disk heads sweep across the disk and perform operations. This value determine how many write requests are placed in the queue for writing to the disk during the next sweep.

Because of the high activity Windows will bring to the file server, you may need to make an adjustment to this value. If you are doing mostly write request to the file server, then set this value high. If there are mostly read requests, then set this value low for the best performance. The default is 50 items, with values ranging from 10 to 4000 accepted.

Dirty disk cache delay time

This value is how long the file server will keep a write request before sent to the disk. When a cache buffer is filled, it becomes available for writing to disk. The problem arises when a cache buffer doesn't have enough data to fill it completely. A decision has to be made to write that data to the disk before it gets too old. This value sets the time in seconds as to how long a file server will hang onto the dirty unfilled cache buffer. The default is 3.3 s, with acceptable values ranging from 0.1 to 10 s.

Tip: Check MONITOR for total number of buffers and dirty cache buffers. If the value of dirty cache buffers is 50 percent or higher of total cache buffers, then you should increase this value.

A general rule is to keep the data in memory as long as you dare before writing it to disk. This results in better performance but also can be dangerous, as a server crash during this time could cause data to be lost. The application thinks that the data has been written to disk; in reality, it hasn't, and data corruption will occur.

Minimum file cache report threshold

This is a warning value as to when the warning for low number of cache buffers takes place. This is a warning to the file server console. When the cache buffers get too low, file-server connections will be dropped and users will not be able to log in again. The default is 20.

Directory Caching Parameters

Dirty directory cache delay time

The directory cache buffers hold directory entries and will stay in the buffer as long as it is being accessed. This determines how long the file server will keep a directory table write request in memory before writing it to disk. The default is 0.5 s, with acceptable values ranging from 0 to 10 s.

Maximum concurrent directory cache writes

This is similar to the file cache settings. It determines how many write requests from the directory cache buffers can be put in the elevator before the disk head starts the write sweep across the platter. As with file caching, setting this value high is more efficient for write requests, while this value needs to be lowered for read requests.

Directory cache allocation wait time

This value determines the amount of time the system has to wait before another directory buffer can be allocated. Setting this value too low will allocate more resources than necessary during heavy access. If a high value is set, directory searches may be slow. The default is 2.2 s, with a low permissible value of 0.5 s and a high of 2 min.

Directory cache buffer nonreferenced delay

When a directory entry is cached, this value determines how long the system can wait until it can be overwritten by another directory entry. The time the system needs to wait is specified here. If you increase this value, directory access will be faster, but more memory is taken up. Decrease this value if the server memory is low. The default is 5.5 s, with acceptable values ranging from 1 s to 5 min.

Maximum directory cache buffers

This feature determines how many cache buffers can be allocated by the file server for directory caching. If the file server seems to run slow, increase this value. If the file server is low on memory, decrease this parameter. The default is 500, with acceptable values ranging from 20 to 4000.

Minimum directory cache buffers

This value determines the minimum number of cache buffers that can be allocated for directory caching. When running Windows, this value should not be lowered. Don't raise it, either, because you may be wasting memory unnecessarily. The default is 20, with acceptable values ranging from 10 to 2000.

File System Parameters

*Minimum file delete wait time

This parameter deals with the salvage feature of NetWare. When a file is deleted, it is kept (out of sight) on the disk and is deleted only when the purge command is run or when the disk is full and needs new space. This parameter determines how long the files can be held until they are eligible for overwriting when the disk is full. Since Windows creates many temporary files, it is a good idea to make them eligible for deletion as soon as possible. The default is 1 min, 5.9 s, with acceptable values ranging from 0 s to 7 days.

*File delete wait time

This is the time when a deleted file can be deleted and the space used for a new file. This parameter determines the time when files will be marked eligible for deletion. NetWare tries to keep a little more than 3 percent of disk space free for new files. Like the previous parameter (minimum file delete wait time), this can help take care of temporary Windows files. The removal of these deleted files occurs in a three-step process.

1. All files marked "purgeable" are deleted—these are the ones older than the value in this parameter.
2. All files greater than the minimum file delete wait time but less than the file delete wait time.
3. All files with a deletion date less than that specified in minimum file delete wait time.

The default is 5 min, 29.6 s, with acceptable values ranging from 0 s to 7 days.

*Allow deletion of active directories

Because of the multiuser nature of NetWare, the actions by one user can have great effect on other users. If you allow a user to delete a directory when another user has a drive letter mapped to it, other users may be unable to use their applications until they log in again. If you don't allow a directory to be deleted until there are no users mapped to the directory, it may be impossible to delete a directory until all users are logged out.

Because of the file manager and how easy it is to delete files and whole directories, a user may select deletion of a directory by accident. By setting this value to OFF, you may help prevent a directory from being deleted accidentally. The default is ON.

Maximum percent of volume space allowed for extended attributes

This is not needed for Windows operation. It is used for extended attribute storage (foreign systems name space) and is configured when the volume is mounted. The default is 10 (percent), with acceptable values ranging from 4 to 512.

Maximum percent of volume used by directory

This value determines how much of a volume should be used for directory space. A default of 13 is usually adequate for most operations. Some Windows applications may create a large number of directories, and this value may need to be increased. Accepted values range from 5 to 50.

*Immediate purge of deleted files

To circumvent the problems of saving deleted files, this attribute can be set to ON. There is a performance penalty when the file server saves the deleted files for possible recovery at some later date. Tracking all those files slows down operation of the server. Windows creates a large number of temporary files that are deleted whenever print jobs are closed or the user exits from Windows. These temporary files add up very quickly, and soon there can be thousands of temporary files in some directories. Setting this parameter to ON will remove the file from the disk when it is deleted by the user and cannot be recovered.

If you don't want the entire disk purged immediately, leave this parameter to OFF and set the individual directories to immediate purge through FILER. The default is OFF.

Maximum subdirectory tree depth

This value is designed to limit the number of levels of subdirectories that can exist on the disk. The default is 25, with acceptable ranges from 10 to 100. Some Windows applications require a number of subdirectory layers. However, we have not seen more than 25 levels required in any of the hundreds of Windows applications we have used or tested. This parameter must be set in STARTUP.NCF.

Volume low, warn all users

This determines whether users will see messages on their screens when a volume on the file server runs low on space. This can be a great inconvenience to users and will cause them to worry needlessly. The default is ON, but it is better to set it to OFF. Don't forget to put this line in the AUTOEXEC.NCF so that it will be enacted each time the file server is started.

Volume low warning threshold

The previous parameter dealt with who should see the warnings about when a volume runs low on free space. The next logical question is when that warning should take place. This parameter will set that value. This information is valuable because Windows can take up much more disk space than you ever imagined and it is important to warn the users in time to solve the problem.

The value given here is in blocks which must be calculated in megabytes to give you a more recognizable reading of disk space. When determining how much warning you want, calculate the free space in megabytes and then divide by the block size. For example, if the block size is 4 kbytes and you want to be notified when 5 Mbytes of disk space is free, the calculation would be

$$\frac{5,120,000 \ (5 \ \text{Mbytes of free space})}{4096 \ (4\text{-kbyte block size})} = 1250 \ \text{blocks}$$

The default is 256 blocks, with acceptable values ranging from 0 to 100,000 blocks.

Volume low warning reset threshold

This is the "second" level of warning that will be issued about low-volume free space. The first warning came from the two parameters shown above. It is designed to prevent the constant issuing of messages when the volume hovers around the full level. This parameter will specify the minimum amount of space available above the threshold before users will be warned again. If you have specified 10 Mbytes as the amount of space as low level, then the server would have to free up another 10 Mbytes of disk space and then use up that new 10 Mbytes of space before the warning would be issued again.

The default is 256 blocks, with acceptable values of 0 to 100,000 blocks.

Turbo FAT reuse wait time

The value specified here will set how long a turbo FAT (file allocation table) buffer remains in memory after an indexed file is closed. After this time value has passed, the file server will create another buffer for the indexed file. If your Windows data files are large, the turbo FAT feature will allow faster access to the files. This value can be increased if the server has plenty of RAM, and you will get additional speed to access the large files.

The default is 5 min, and 29.6 s, with acceptable values of 0.3 s to 1:05:54.6.

Compression daily check stop hour

One feature of NetWare 4.1 is the ability to compress files at the operating system level transparently to the user. This can save a great amount of space with little trouble. This parameter determines what hour of the day the compression utility stops scanning the volumes for files that need to be compressed. This saves the file server from working every hour of the day when it doesn't need to. The default is 6 (6:00 P.M.), and values range from 0 (midnight) to 23 (11:00 P.M.).

Compression daily check starting hour

This is the partner to the stop hour value and determines the hour of the day when compression will start. The default is 6 (6:00 P.M.) and values range from 0 (midnight) to 23 (11:00 P.M.).

Minimum compression percentage gain

What is the purpose of compressing files if you don't gain much from the compression? Some types of files compress much better than others. This value sets a standard for the amount of compression that must be realized before it is to stay as a compressed file. If the gain is less than specified, the file is uncompressed and left in an uncompressed state.

The default is 5 (percent), and acceptable values range from 0 to 50 (percent).

Enable file compression

This determines whether file compression will be turned on or off. If the value is set to OFF, any request for compression will be held until compression is turned on again. The default is OFF.

Maximum concurrent compressions

This determines how many concurrent compressions are allowed across multiple volumes. The default is 4, with acceptable values of 1 to 8.

Convert compressed to uncompressed option

This parameter determines what happens to the file after it has been uncompressed. Should it be uncompressed, leave it uncompressed for a specified period, or compressed. The value of 0 means to leave the file compressed. A value of 1 indicates that the file should be left compressed until another user accesses it, assuming that it is read only once during the time specified in the "days untouched before compression" parameter. If the value is 2, always leave the file uncompressed. The default is 1.

Uncompress percent disk space free to allow commit

This parameter determines how much free space is required on a specified volume for file compression to permanently change compressed files into an uncompressed state. One problem with compression is that when files are uncompressed, they can fill the disk volume suddenly, causing the server to halt operations. The default is 10 (percent), with acceptable values of 0 to 75.

Uncompress free-space warning interval

This is the time interval between system alerts when disk space gets so low the file server cannot uncompress the files into a normal state. The default is 0:31:18.5, while acceptable values are 0 s to 29 days and 15:50:3.8.

Deleted files compression option

The value here determines when compression will take place for deleted files. A value of 0 sets compression for deleted files. If deleted files are to be compressed the next day after they are deleted, set this value to 1. A value of 2 will compress the deleted files immediately after deletion. The default value is 1.

Days untouched before compression

This is probably the most important parameter for compression. It determines the number of days from the time the file was last accessed until it is compressed. The default is 7 days, but acceptable values can range from 1 to an incredible 100,000 days (or a whopping 274 years!).

Lock Parameters

*Maximum record locks per connection

This value determines the number of record locks each user can have. There are different types of record locks. Logical record locks are created by the programmer to prevent two users from accessing the same piece of data in the file. Locking can be done by the application or by NetWare when a physical location in the file is specified. Each lock takes up file-server memory, and this setting controls how many locks each user can have. The default is 500, with acceptable values of 10 to 1000.

Maximum file locks per connection

File locks are a poor method of controlling multiple access. When there is a physical file lock, only one user can access the entire file at a time. This value determines how many open files can be locked at the same time. Under a few circumstances, you may need to increase this value when running Windows applications. The default is 250, with acceptable values of 10 to 1000.

*Maximum record locks

While the two previous parameters deal with locks per connection, this parameter is the number of the record locks for all users on the server. This may need to be increased if you have a large number of Windows users logged in simultaneously. The default is 20,000, with acceptable values ranging from 100 to 200,000.

Maximum file locks

This is the same as the previous parameter, except it determines the number of file locks rather than record locks. The default is 10,000, and values can range from 100 to 100,000.

Tip: Problems with too few record locks can show up in strange ways. We have found errors claiming that the disk was full when, in fact, it was a record or file lock problem. If you ever receive a message that the disk is full but there is still free space, check the number of file locks.

Transaction Tracking Parameters

Auto TTS backout flag

If a NetWare server crashes, there will be files left in an incomplete state. Transaction tracking is a part of NetWare and is accessed through code written into applications. If a single transaction is written out to several files (e.g., in a database), the files may not be totally synchronized at the time of the crash. On resumption of service, some files may have part of the transaction while others may not have the transaction. This is a great problem for files that depend on other files for maintain a complete record about a transaction. When this value is set to ON, the incomplete transactions will be backed out on startup of the server. The default is OFF.

TTS abort dump flag

When a transaction is backed out of a file (see Fig. 3.3), what happens to the data that was removed from the file(s)? If this parameter is set to ON, the data is removed from the files when the file server shuts down prematurely and is saved to a test file TTS$LOG.ERR (in the SYS: volume root directory). The default is OFF.

Maximum transactions

A value here specifies how many transactions can occur at the same time. The default is 10,000, with acceptable values ranging from 100 to 100,000. You don't need to change this except under the rarest of circumstances.

```
Monday, May 1, 1995  11:24:54 am
Initializing Transaction Tracking System

Monday, May 1, 1995  12:01:21 pm
Initializing Transaction Tracking System
Scanning TTS Backout File

Monday, May 1, 1995   1:35:16 pm
TTS has been shut down.

Monday, May 1, 1995   1:35:58 pm
Initializing Transaction Tracking System

Monday, May 1, 1995   1:36:55 pm
TTS has been shut down.

Monday, May 1, 1995   1:40:59 pm
Initializing Transaction Tracking System

Monday, May 1, 1995   1:46:05 pm
TTS has been shut down.

Monday, May 1, 1995   1:48:15 pm
Initializing Transaction Tracking System

Monday, May 1, 1995   1:49:30 pm
Initializing Transaction Tracking System
Scanning TTS Backout File
```

Figure 3.3 Transaction tracking log file.

TTS unwritten cache wait time

When using transactions, there may be a need to write out data in a certain time or order. This parameter will determine how long a block of transactional data will be held in memory. NetWare will write out the blocks at the end of this time limit regardless of any queuing or order. The default time is 0:01:05.9 with values from 11 s to 0:10:59.1.

TTS backout file truncation wait time

This value specifies how long the blocks will be available for the TTS backout file when these blocks are not being used. The default is 59 min, 19.2 s.

Disk Parameters

Enable disk read-after-write verify

When data is written to disk, the system has no way of knowing that the data was written properly. When setting this parameter to ON, the data is written to disk and then read back when the disk makes another revolution. The data is read from the disk and then compared to the original block in memory. If the two values are the same, the memory copy of the data is discarded. If they are not the same, the data is then written out to another block, where the whole process is started again. The default is ON.

Tip: While performing read-after-write verification in the operating system is better than nothing, it is much more efficient to purchase a disk subsystem that does this verification in the hardware. You get the same amount of data protection but without a great speed penalty.

This parameter can also be set in the install utility when setting up hard disks.

Remirror block size

The size of the remirror block is determined in 4-kbyte steps. The values can be from 1 to 8, with a default of 1.

Concurrent remirror requests

This value is the number of remirror requests per logical partition. The default is 4, and values from 2 to 32 are allowed.

Time Parameters

TYMESYNC ADD time source

This is from the NetWare 4 system, where the servers all need to be in time synchronization before they can communicate with each other under NetWare Directory Services. This value specifies another NetWare 4 server that will be added to the configured time source list. There is no default and the value is a valid server name.

TIMESYNC configuration file

The previous parameter determined that a file server will be added to the configuration list. This value determines where the file that contains this information will be stored. The maximum length is 255 bytes.

TIMESYNC configured sources

If this value is set to OFF, the server will listen to any time source advertised on the network. There should be only one time source (reference server), so this shouldn't be a problem. If there is, setting this to ON means the server will pick up time only from servers that are configured in the *TIMESYNC time source* parameter. The default is OFF.

TIMESYNC directory tree mode

This parameter determines the use of service advertising protocol (SAP) packets. If this parameter is set to OFF, the server will received SAP packets from any time source on the network, while setting it to ON will cause the server to ignore the SAP packets that do not originate from the directory tree. The default is ON.

TIMESYNC hardware clock

This determines how the server will handle the hardware clock synchronization. If you are setting the server time through an external time source (e.g., modem calls to a time source) that is not constant, then set this parameter to ON. It will enable both the reference server and the secondary servers to set the hardware clock (with the reference server doing it at the beginning of each polling interval). If you are using a constant time source such as a radio clock where the time is constantly being input into the server, set this to OFF. The default is ON.

TIMESYNC polling count

When using NetWare 4 on a large network, this value determines the number of times polling takes place between servers. If the interval is too long, the servers will not be updated properly; if the interval is too short, excessive traffic will slow down the network and users may complain. Set this parameter in seconds with values from 0 to 160,704,000 (31 days!).

TIMESYNC REMOVE time source

This is the opposite of the TYMESYNC ADD time source parameter. It removes a server name from the TIMESYNC.CFG file.

TIMESYNC RESET

This configures the method of resetting time synchronization. If this parameter is set to ON, the values in the TIMESYNC.CFG is reset and configured server list is cleared.

TIMESYNC restart flag

Since time synchronization is so critical between servers, setting this parameter to ON means that time resynchronization will restart when the TIMESYNC.NLM is reloaded without rebooting the server. The default is OFF.

TIMESYNC service advertising

This value controls the time source advertisement as an OFF setting means that there is a list of the time sources you have set up. A parameter of ON means that a single server will supply time signals through SAP. The default is ON.

TIMESYNC synchronization radius

This feature determines how long of a time difference there can be between servers (reference and secondary) before the system considers it as being out of synchronization (out of sync). If the time difference is excessive, operator intervention may be required rather than automatic resetting of the values. Setting this value too low may cause false synchronization errors when the network is busy, while setting it too high will result in true synchronization errors not being noted. The value is in milliseconds with values from 0 to 2,147,483,647 (24.85 days). The default is 2000.

TIMESYNC type

This is the type of time source that will be noted in the TIMESYNC.CFG file. The values in this parameter are reference, primary, secondary, and single. The default is secondary.

TIMESYNC write value

These are the parameters written by the *TIMESYNC write parameters* set parameter. Specifying a 1 here will write internal parameters only, a 2 will write out configured time sources only, and a 3 will write both parameters and configured time sources. The default is 3.

TIMESYNC write parameters

This value is applied only for determining whether parameters are written to the configuration file. The default is OFF.

Time zone

For those networks that span time zones, this parameter determines which time-zone indicator will be used. The difference between Universal Time (previously known as Greenwich Mean Time) and local time or abbreviated time-zone names can be used. Either value determines Universal Time from the value specified here. There is no default.

Start of Daylight Savings Time

This is the start of Daylight Savings Time, if it is observed in your area. The default is APRIL SUNDAY FIRST 2:00:00 AM.

End of Daylight Savings Time

This is the same as above, except it specifies when Daylight Savings Time reverts back to Standard Time. Default is OCTOBER SUNDAY LAST 2:00:00 AM.

Daylight Savings Time offset

This is the amount of time to change when Daylight Savings Time is in effect (usually one hour). The default is + 1:00:00.

Daylights Savings Time status

This shows whether Daylight Savings Time is in effect. If you are creating the server during Daylight Savings Time, enter the value of ON and then use the actual time. At the end of Daylight Savings Time, time will revert properly. The default is OFF.

New time with Daylight Savings Time status

This will determine adjustment of local time when Daylight Savings Time is in effect. By setting this to ON, the server time will be added or subtracted from the *Daylight Savings Time offset*. The default is OFF.

NetWare Core Protocol (NCP) Parameters

*NCP file commit

If this value is set to ON, applications will be able to flush pending file writes to disk. This is done through a special command rather than waiting for the file server to write it to the disk as part of its normal operation. Letting NetWare decide when data is written from RAM cache to disk means a great efficiency of operation. However, there may be some applications where writing data to the server hard disk cannot wait until a normal write occurs. The default is ON.

Display NCP bad component warnings

This entry will determine whether NCP bad component messages are seen on the console. The default is ON.

Reject NCP packets with bad components

What happens to an NCP packet that fails component checking? With this parameter, you can decide whether or not to reject these packets. The default is OFF.

Display NCP bad length warnings

If an NCP packet is not correct, this value determines whether or not to display the warnings. The default is ON.

Reject NCP packets with bad lengths

If a packet that fails the boundary check is rejected, are they in fact rejected? The default is OFF.

*Maximum outstanding NCP searches

How many NCP directory searches can be processed simultaneously? We have found the default of 51 to be too low when certain activities are running under Windows. For example, programmers running compiles of their programs may run into too few NCP searches. Since little RAM is used for each search value, setting this to 100 or 200 will solve many NCP problems.

The default is 51 with acceptable values ranging from 10 to 1000.

NCP packet signature option

This is part of the new security on the NetWare servers, and a packet signature is set at the workstation and decoded at the server. Both the server and the workstation place a signature on the packet which changes for each packet. This makes it more difficult for someone to break into the system with network packet utilities.

Watch out for this parameter because workstations will not be able to find the server if their NCP packet signature value in NET.CFG is not set to an equal level of that in the server. In the NET.CFG place the line SIGNATURE LEVEL = # under the NetWare DOS requester section with the # replaced by the desired level.

Setting this to 0 is the most open as the server will accept any packets. There are no settings for this required at the workstation. A value of 1 means that the server will sign the packets only if the workstation requests it. A value of 2 turns on signing automatically if the workstation can handle it, and a value of 3 means all workstations *must* sign each packet. The only drawback is that NCP can mean a slight performance degradation while it is running. NCP packet signature values can be increased while the server is running but cannot be lowered unless the server is brought down.

Enable IPX checksums

This is a method of determining whether the packets coming from a workstation to the server are complete and have not been changed or corrupted. The data bits are fed through an algorithm, and a checksum is computed and stored with the data. The same calculation is performed when the server receives the data, and if the same number is calculated, it is assumed the data has not been changed.

The values for this parameter are similar to NCP signature. Place a 0 for no checksums, 1 for using checksums if the client is using it, and a value of 2 to force the use of checksums. A significant drawback to using checksums is reduction in processing speed because every packet has to be examined and a checksum calculated. We have found this feature useful on networks where there are communication problems. On a network that is running properly, this parameter is not needed. For normal communication errors, there is no problem as IPX communications can catch most errors. If there are errors internally in the server operating system or client shells, then the IPX checksum will help ensure that the correct data is sent and received.

Allow change to client rights

Some job servers and other utilities may need to have the same rights of the client to perform their work. The programming code written into the utility may emulate the client rights automatically. To increase security, set this value to OFF, and a potential security hole is plugged. However, that may render a job server or other utility unable to complete its job. The default is ON.

*Allow LIP

The default packet in IPX carries only 576 bytes of data. This was fine a few years ago when DOS applications were quite small. Now, Windows applications are getting bigger and bigger, and it sometimes takes thousands of packets to deliver the program code for one program. For example, it takes over 7100 packets to load Excel from the file server! Remember that one acknowledgment packet is sent back to the sender for each packet received. In the Excel example, over 14,200 packets would be sent because of the acknowledgment packets.

The small size of data in the packets was due to older bridges and routers that couldn't handle larger size packets. Now, larger packets can be handled, and it is a good idea to increase the size of the packets when Windows is being run on the network. With LIP set on the file server, the workstation will request the largest packet size and the server will respond with a value that corresponds to the type of drivers and network topology being used. While we have found LIP to be useful, it can overload a network because it is so efficient. A few users can maximize a 10-Mbits network system.

Miscellaneous Parameters

Replace console prompt with server name

When running more than one file server, it can become confusing as to which file server you are working on. We have mistakenly brought down the wrong file server as a result of this confusion. It's becoming more common to have a number of servers in a common area (e.g., data center), and a number of identical machines side by side makes a mistake easy. When the server name is not shown on the screen, it is easy to be careless and issue the down command on the wrong server. By placing the name on the command prompt, you are constantly reminded which server you are working on. Now, you can replace the console prompt with the file server name. The default is ON.

Alert message nodes

This is the number of alert message nodes that have been previously allocated. The default is 20, with an acceptable range of 10 to 256.

Worker thread execute in a row count

This is a rarely modified parameter. It indicates the number of times the operating system scheduler will dispatch new work before allowing other threads to run. The default is 10, with acceptable values ranging from 1 to 20.

Display disk device alerts

When the file server is running under heavy load, or there is a lot of system activity, it is imperative to monitor the system constantly. These disk device alerts will display information about disk activity anytime there is a change in the disk driver or server, or if there are problems with a disk drive. The default is OFF.

Halt system on invalid parameters

When the operating system comes across an invalid parameter or condition, what should happen? Set this value to OFF if you want NetWare to display a message and continue operating. If you set this to ON, NetWare will shut down when encountering a problem. The default is OFF.

Upgrade low-priority threads

There is a rare condition in which some NLMs can cause problems with low-priority threads, which can cause system problems. By upgrading low-priority threads to a higher value, some of these problems can be avoided. If you find intermittent problems that just can't be explained, try setting this value to ON and see if that solves those unexplained problems. The default for this parameter is OFF.

Display relinquish control alerts

When this parameter is set to ON, information about CPU controls is sent to the console. NLMs must give up control to the CPU on a frequent basis. If this parameter is set to ON, you will see all the alerts. Usually, there is no need to set this to ON except when you suspect that an NLM is causing problems. The default is OFF.

Display incomplete IPX packet alerts

If the server receives an incomplete IPX packet, do you want the server to display the message on the screen? The default is ON.

Display old API names

This is a transition parameter that has been a source of concern for many people because they see the old API messages and worry needlessly. There was a great change in APIs between NetWare 3.0 and 3.1. Some NLMs could run on v3.1 just fine, while others run into problems. For compatibility reasons, the old API calls are supported but do not run efficiently as the new APIs.

Set this parameter to ON and contact the vendor who supplied the NLM as there probably is a new NLM available. The default is OFF.

Pseudo-preemptions count

This determines how many times an operating system thread can make a file read-or-write call before it is forced to relinquish control to another thread. Set the value too low, and the system will be switching threads frequently and be less efficient; set the value too high, and other threads will have to wait too long before being processed. The default is 10, with acceptable values ranging from 1 to 4,294,967,295.

Global pseudopreemption

Setting this value to ON will force all threads to use pseudopreemption. The default is OFF.

Developer option

This value is used only when developing NLMs or other network programs. It enables some additional functionality. The default is ON.

Display spurious interrupt alerts

If NetWare creates an interrupt that has been reserved for another device, NetWare perceives this as a potential problem and displays an error on the screen. This problem can be corrected by viewing the setup configuration or by eliminating one peripheral board at a time to determine which one is causing the problem. Trying to find the problem can be a long and tortuous process. The default is ON.

Display lost interrupt alerts

A bad peripheral board or driver can cause this problem. If the driver initiates a service request with an interrupt call and then loses the service request before the server can respond, NetWare will display the message "Interrupt controller detected a lost hardware interrupt." The easiest method of solving this problem is to load NLM drivers one at a time to determine which one is causing the problem. If no interrupt is detected, this could mean lost packets or missed disk I/O requests. The default is ON.

Maximum service processes

This parameter can help out when the server is low on memory or very busy. If RAM is low, decrease this number to help conserve memory. That, however, is only a short-term fix, and you will need to increase RAM to make the server run properly. If the server is very busy, increasing this number will help the server handle service requests more efficiently. Watch the disk I/O dirty cache buffers, and if these are high, increase this number to see if it helps. The default is 20, with an acceptable range of 5 to 40.

New service process wait time

If you want to be alerted when a problem occurs on the server, set this value to ON. Sometimes, there are alerts on the screen that you are already aware of, and you don't want to keep being reminded of the problem. Then you set this parameter to OFF. The default is ON.

*New service process wait time

How long will the file server wait following a request for another service process before making an allocation for a new service process? Setting the value too low will potentially cause a new service process to be allocated prematurely, while setting the value too high will affect the performance of the server. The default is 2.2 s, with an acceptable range of 0.3 to 20 s.

Automatically repair bad volume

When starting a server, a check is made of the copies of the FAT and other parameters to ensure that the volume is in good shape and can be mounted. If not, you can run VREPAIR automatically by setting this value to ON. However, we find that it is useful only when running the server remotely. We like to run VREPAIR manually when encountering these problems. The default is ON.

Allow unencrypted passwords

One of the greatest security problems of previous versions of NetWare was the passing of passwords in clear text on the network. Anyone with a utility such as Sniffer or Lanalyzer could view the packets that contained the password and see it without any difficulty. Now, you have a choice of the workstation encrypting the password before it is sent to the server. The only time you should use unencrypted passwords is when working on a network with old servers or network resources (e.g., printing devices) that require unencrypted passwords to operate. The default is OFF.

Bindery context

This is exclusively for NetWare 4 and is used for backward compatibility to NetWare 2.x and 3.x systems. By setting the bindery to a certain NetWare 4 NDS container, users can log in and use the server in the same method as they did with a NetWare 3.x server. This is a life saver to many because it is impossible to cut over to NDS right away.

To set the bindery context, you must include all containers that the users need to access. For example, if user objects are in one container and the group objects are in another container, then the command would look like this:

```
SET BINDERY CONTEXT=OU=USERS.OU=WEST.O=ABC_Company;
OU=USERS.OU=WEST.O=ABC_Company.
```

The command will appear on one line with a semicolon (;) separating the different bindery contexts. You can have up to 16 contexts set on the same server, but you cannot use more than 256 characters to list those contexts.

Server log file state

The system error log file created in the SYS: volume is named SYS$LOG.ERR and, over time, can grow to be quite large. You can specify the largest size possible for the error log in the *server log file overflow size* parameter. The question does arise as to what happens when the file exceeds the value specified in that parameter. This parameter allows you to specify the disposition of the file. By entering a 0, no action will take place and the file will grow larger unchecked. A 1 means that the file will be deleted when it grows too large, and a 2 will mean that the file will be renamed and a new file started. You could end up with several files on the disk under this option, but none would be larger than you specified. The default for this parameter is 1.

Volume TTS log file state

The system error log file created in the SYS: volume is named TTS$LOG.ERR and, over time, can become quite voluminous. You can specify the largest size possible for the error log in the *TTS log file overflow size* parameter. You may wonder, however, what happens when the file exceeds the value specified in that parameter. This parameter allows you to specify the disposition of the file. If you enter a 0, no action will take place and the file will grow larger unchecked. Enter a 1, and the file will be deleted when it grows too large; enter a 2, and the file will be renamed and a new file started. You could end up with several files on the disk under this option, but none would be larger than you specified. The default for this parameter is 1.

Volume log file state

The system error log file created in the SYS: volume is named VOL$LOG.ERR and, over time, can become quite large. You can specify the largest size possible for the error log in the *volume log file overflow size* parameter. What happens when the file exceeds the value specified in that parameter? This parameter allows you to specify the disposition of the file. A 0 indicates that no action will take place and the file will grow larger unchecked. A 1 means that the file will be deleted when it becomes too voluminous, and a 2 will indicate that the file will be renamed and a new file started. You could end up with several files on the disk under this option, but none would be larger than you specified. The default for this parameter is 1.

Server log file overflow size

This parameter sets the maximum size of the SYS$LOG.ERR before any action is taken as specified in the *server log file state* parameter. It is a good idea to set a limit on this file, or it could grow large enough to take away a substantial portion of your server volume. The default is 4 Mbytes with a potential range of 64 kbytes to 4 Gbytes.

Volume TTS log file overflow size

This parameter sets the maximum size of the TTS$LOG.ERR before any action is taken as specified in the *volume TTS log file state* parameter. You should set a limit on the expansion of this file, or it could consume a substantial portion of your server volume. The default is 4 Mbytes, with an acceptable range of 64 kbytes to 4 Gbytes.

Volume log file overflow size

This parameter sets the maximum size of the VOL$LOG.ERR before any action is taken as specified in the *volume log file state* parameter. Again, this file could consume a significant portion of your server volume unless you limit its growth. The default is 4 Mbytes, with acceptable values ranging from 64 kbytes to 4 Gbytes.

Set time

This command is used to set the date and time on the file server. You can set the date, the time, or both. They must be in the M/D/Y format or written as *month_name / day / year* for date and H:M:S for time. If seconds are not specified, the value defaults to :00 seconds. If the date is not specified, the date remains the same. If the time is not specified, the time remains the same. Issuing the time command by itself indicates the server current date and time.

If you are using a NetWare 4 server on a multiserver network, you cannot change the server time if it is a secondary server. It must be a single or master time server before the time can be changed.

Set time zone

This value is used for creating the time zone as offset from Universal Time (previous known as Greenwich Mean Time). The time will change automatically for Daylight Savings Time if your location uses it and it is a critical parameter for those organizations that have a global network.

The format is SET TIME ZONE code hours. For Pacific Time, the command would be SET TIME ZONE PST8PDT.

Geographic area	Standard Time code	Daylight Savings Time code	Hours west from UCT
Eastern Standard Time	EST	EDT	5
Central Standard Time	CST	CDT	6
Mountain Standard Time	MST	MDT	7
Pacific Standard Time	PST	PDT	8

European users east of London should place a plus (+) sign in front of the number.

Server Tuning

Setting file server parameters is not one of the more exciting tasks in networking. However, adjusting parameters on the file server can make a great difference in performance when running Windows on the network. Becoming familiar with these parameters is well worth the time.

4

Workstation Memory Configuration

The workstation is a key element in a local area network, and the configuration of this system is critical to success with Microsoft Windows. There are two ingredients in the workstation that need some careful attention: memory and the network shells.

Memory Fundamentals

One of the major problems of PC systems is the limitation of memory that can be addressed directly by DOS. There is some confusion about the 640-kbyte memory limit that the DOS system can directly address. In 1981, when PCs were first introduced, 1 Mbyte of memory was far beyond the typical 64 kbytes of RAM found in most systems. Few of us knew what a limitation this would turn out to be.

Out of the 1 Mbyte of RAM, 384 kbytes is used for purposes such as the monitor display, BIOS, and other internal systems. Figure 4.1 shows a diagram of memory in a PC.

Memory banks

Memory banks are areas of memory starting at addresses that are a multiple of 64 kbytes. Logical banks of memory provide a range of memory for applications regardless of whether there is actual memory at these addresses. Physical memory is a grouping of memory chips accessed when reading data from memory.

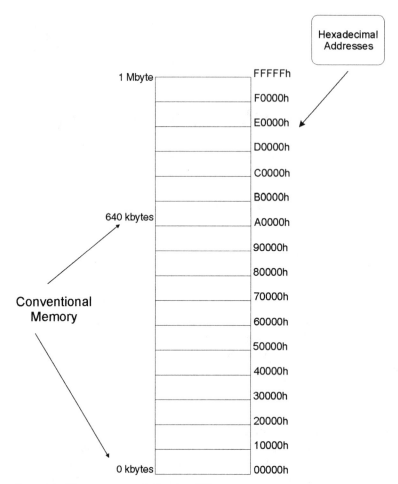

Figure 4.1   Memory segmentation in a PC.

Pages

For efficiency in operation, memory must be arranged in logical groups that can be accessed together. In the context here, a *page* is a section of memory that can be read or written to in one operation. For most PCs, the page size is 4 kbytes, although computers using the Pentium chip can have much larger pages for greater efficiency.

There are some entries in the Windows SYSTEM.INI file involving memory pages. If you add the line Paging = no under the [386Enh] section, this will effectively turn off the swapping to disk. Another strange problem that may arise if you create a temporary swap file of less than 512 kbytes is that out-of-memory error messages may appear.

Conventional memory

This a common name given to the first 640 kbytes of memory which is used by DOS for loading programs and data when they are run. DOS applications require contiguous blocks of memory for running and while there may be other blocks of memory available, they cannot be used because they are not located adjacent to the conventional memory.

Upper memory

This is one of the least understood sections of memory as many people have wrong ideas about how it operates. The term *upper memory* refers to the space between 640 kbytes and 1 Mbyte (hexadecimal addresses A0000h to FFFFFh). In this space you will find BIOS, video displays, and other system information. Sprinkled through the system use of memory are empty areas that are above 640 kbytes. Unfortunately, it cannot be used by DOS applications because of the need for contiguous memory.

A strange problem is that early PCs barely used this memory but later models have begun to use it increasingly for system activities. In the last few years, we have been able to place terminate-and-stay-resident (TSR) utilities into upper memory, thus freeing up conventional memory for running DOS applications. The most logical TSRs to place in upper memory are network shell files (e.g., LSL.COM, MLID driver, IPXODI.COM, VLM.EXE). Some of these shell files can take up as much as 80 kbytes of conventional memory if they are not placed in upper memory.

Loading utilities in upper memory

Unfortunately, many people view the process of loading drivers and utilities into upper memory as a combination of luck and black magic. However, there is actually a method to this madness, and you can have some control over what happens when loading these drivers.

Although an extended memory manager must be present before the upper-memory blocks become available, you must also set DOS = UMB to enable DOS to control these areas. Therefore, if an application asks the memory manager directory for space in upper memory, it will be available, but if the same application requests upper blocks from DOS, it will be unavailable.

Loading TSRs

A bit of trivia for those who like to get into the internals of a system. When a TSR is loaded from a disk into memory, it goes through several different phases and there are different memory needs. While TSRs are written to take up little space when running, they need larger RAM amounts when loading because of the setup required. It is theorized that there is no memory crunch when loading these TSRs—only after they are loaded.

The first phase is when the TSR is stored on the disk. Do not look at the file size and figure that it will be the actual loaded and running size. The next phase is setting up the TSR in memory (called the *load size*). After TSR is loaded, it goes through an initialization size which sets up the TSR, creates any environmental changes, and then goes into the final phase where it discards all excess memory and creates the resident size. These size changes can fool a UMB (upper-memory block) manager because the initialization size may be seen as a resident size and placed in a larger memory block than needed.

The memory block sizes will vary in upper memory because this is fragmented, leftover memory. TSRs are like DOS applications in that they cannot be split across more than one memory block—all memory must be contiguous. Therefore, placing a TSR of 48-kbyte size in a 64-kbyte block of memory will mean that 16 kbytes of memory will be wasted unless you have a TSR that is smaller than 16 kbytes to be loaded. A similar problem occurs if you have a small TSR that loads into a large block area. If the TSR is 16 kbytes in size and is loaded into a 64-kbyte block of memory, the next TSR you try to load that may be 52 kbytes in size will not load. However, if you loaded the 52-kbyte TSR first into the 64-kbyte block, then there might be another location where the 16-Mbyte TSR will fit. Therefore, if possible, make sure that you load the largest TSRs first down to the smallest which will most likely give you the best fit. Unfortunately, loading the TSR by size is not always possible.

High memory

The high-memory area (HMA) is not the same as upper memory. It is a special location above 1 Mbyte in hexadecimal address 0FFFF0h to 10FFEFh. It is an area that can still be accessed even though it is beyond the 1-Mbyte range. This 64-kbyte area can be used to place some TSRs and can make a great amount of difference between success and failure in freeing up enough conventional memory for running some large DOS applications.

You need to have an extended memory driver that conforms to the *extended memory specification* (XMS) to gain access to the HMA. The most common method is through the HIMEM.SYS utility that is supplied with DOS and Windows disks.

Even though the HMA has 64 kbytes of space available, only one application at a time can gain access to it. This has changed because some vendors such as Microsoft *have* written DOS and mouse drivers to exist in the same HMA area. The XMS says that the A20 gate (that controls access to the HMA) should be closed whenever a utility is placed in the HMA. However, the latest versions of DOS don't close that gate, and now other vendors are starting to place their utilities in the same space.

Extended memory

The XMS was designed to give access to upper memory, high memory, or any memory beyond 1 Mbyte. While this sounds great, it still does not make that memory directly available to DOS. However, Windows can take great advantage of it. When the HIMEM.SYS driver is loaded in memory, it checks to see what memory has not been allocated already. It will convert all unclaimed memory for its own use and then give access to the HMA to the first program that asks for it.

Expanded memory specification

The *expanded memory specification* (EMS) is a method of giving DOS applications that have special code written for it to have access to memory beyond 1 Mbyte. The original purpose of expanded memory was to allow early computers to address extra memory. One of the original needs came from financial experts who were creating huge spreadsheets on Lotus 1-2-3 that quickly overwhelmed the 640 kbytes of memory space available for program and data. Even though there were more than 2000 rows available in Lotus 1-2-3, it was impossible to fill more than just a fraction.

It makes sense that the first companies to join forces to create the EMS were Lotus and Intel, who developed the EMS v3.0 (which happened to be the first version—the version number was added for marketing purposes). The biggest problem with this first expanded memory standard was that there were few specifications on add-in memory cards.

The Lotus-Intel consortium was joined later by Microsoft, and the resulting version was a much more stable expanded memory version that didn't set any specifications about hardware memory cards. The new expanded memory standard was known as LIM-EMS v3.2.

A further modification to the standard came from other vendors who developed the *enhanced expanded memory* specification. While the changes were not earth-shattering, they nonetheless helped make life easier for those configuring systems. Later the Lotus-Intel-Microsoft consortium created version 4.0 of the expanded memory standard and brought a new level of flexibility with a higher amount of RAM supported, reduced block sizes, etc.

The next question is: Because expanded memory was designed for use with DOS applications who cannot access more than 1 Mbyte of RAM, how is expanded memory used in Windows? The main purpose of running an expanded memory manager is to manage the allocation of upper-memory blocks (Fig. 4.2). To better explain how all the different memory managers work together, we need to examine the CONFIG.SYS file and how it should be tweaked for Windows.

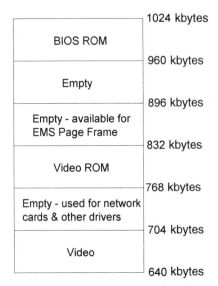

Figure 4.2 Typical upper-memory allocation—not drawn to scale.

CONFIG.SYS

The CONFIG.SYS file is critical to the operation of your computer and Windows as it creates the memory and driver environment to access hardware systems on the computer. The wrong entries here could have great consequences in the operation of the computer. We need to optimize hardware drivers through the CONFIG.SYS file.

A big mistake all of us make is to forget to document our work as we go along. If you have DOS 5 or higher (and you should), you can place remarks in the CONFIG.SYS file for documenting certain lines or for disabling a line during testing.

DEVICE

The device statements in the CONFIG.SYS file are designed to load hardware drivers for memory or other peripherals. This is the only method for adding new hardware devices to the system and have DOS recognize them. Of course, you will need a driver file supplied by the hardware manufacturer that has to be copied to your hard disk.

The device statement can also be a problem when starting the computer, as the wrong driver or the wrong settings could cause the computer to hang.

There are a couple of methods for solving this problem. By pressing the <F8> key will cause DOS to ask if you want to execute each line of the CONFIG.SYS and AUTOEXEC.BAT files. Pressing <F5> will bypass them altogether. If you don't want to go through answering the prompt for each line, place a question mark behind the device line (e.g., DEVICE?=), and you will be prompted for only that line and not the whole file.

DEVICEHIGH

Each one of those drivers you load take memory to run. Some take very little, while others take a good chunk. Unfortunately, they all like to live in conventional memory, which means more pressure on that precious space below 640 kbytes. By using the DEVICEHIGH command rather than DEVICE, DOS will try to load the drivers in the upper-memory blocks first and, if there isn't enough room, will load them in lower memory. You will not suffer any penalty for using DEVICEHIGH as it will act just like DEVICE if it cannot load the driver in upper memory.

Buffers

Note: We have observed occasional problems between EMM386.EXE and HIMEM.SYS when running Windows on a network. Frequently, these problems have been solved by using those utilities supplied with Windows rather than with the ones that came with DOS. The buffers statement in CONFIG.SYS is to hold all the data from disk reads and writes temporarily before it is passed on. This is like a simple caching program as it will leave the last reads and writes in memory until the capacity of the buffers are reached. Each buffer takes about 550 bytes of RAM, so reducing the buffers will not have a great impact on free memory.

There are a couple of things to keep in mind about buffers. Since this is a pseudo-disk caching feature, it will give you some efficiency but not the type of performance you need for Windows. You should always use SMARTDRV.EXE as it is optimized for Windows-type performance. With SMARTDRV.EXE, you can set the buffers at 1 (don't leave this line out of CONFIG.SYS as it may default to a higher number). Then SMARTDRV will be the only caching utility, and you will not have this double caching.

Also, be aware that some programs running on the computer (e.g., WordPerfect DOS versions) will complain if the buffers are too low. Some will not even run at all if there are not enough buffers.

If you need to use buffers and you are concerned about losing conventional memory for buffers, keep the number below 40, and it will load automatically in the HMA along with DOS. That number is not precise because it depends on how much space DOS takes.

Files

The Files statement in the CONFIG.SYS file indicates the number of file handles that can be used at one time. Each file handle takes around 55 bytes, so it will not hurt to increase this number to make sure all applications can be opened.

When DOS loads an application, it creates a job file table with a size equal to the number you have set for files in the program segment prefix (PSP). Programmers can extend this table with internal application code, but frequently they take the number set in Files and use that. That is why you see some applications requiring file handles to be as high as 99.

DOS high

This command will cause DOS to load itself in the HMA if it is available. It will be available only if the HIMEM.SYS driver is loaded that will make that area accessible to DOS. DOS can take as much as 30 kbytes of conventional memory and move it up to the HMA; this 30 kbytes might be just enough to enable an application to run that otherwise wouldn't be able.

DOS upper-memory blocks

The DOS UMB command (which can be combined with the HIGH command) is enabling DOS to manage upper RAM. While this command does not take any memory, if DOS cannot take control of upper RAM, then you will not be able to load device drivers and shells into that location. The amount of available conventional RAM will be greatly reduced. As with the DOS = HIGH command, this command requires that an extended memory driver be installed before you run the command.

Lastdrive

The Lastdrive command tells DOS how many disk drives to handle. This command has become a problem for NetWare users. If you are using NETX, you need to leave this out as DOS. Despite what some people think, the NetWare shells do not allocate F: as the first network drive automatically. It allocates the first available drive letter. Since DOS allocates five drives as a minimum, then F: becomes the next available letter. If you partitioned your disk drive into several portions or had CD-ROM drives and RAM drives setup, you may need to set a Lastdrive setting to G:. This would mean that the NetWare shell would allocate H: as the first network drive.

This all changes when using VLMs as you need to allocate the maximum number of disk drives you want to allocate for the local computer and the file servers. So, set the Lastdrive equal to Z: and then in the NET.CFG set the first network drive to F:.

The NET.CFG file now defines which letter will be allocated for the first network drive, and then all drives can be allocated later.

File control blocks

The file control blocks are not used much any more but were used in the past for referencing disks. Most applications now use file handles to access files rather than control blocks, but there may be some DOS applications you run that need file control blocks to be allocated. The memory requirements are modest as each block allocation takes about 60 bytes.

Shell

The shell statement is designed for making modifications to the current environment or for changing the command interpreter used in DOS. This was used for command interpreter replacements such as the shareware 4DOS. The shell statement can be used to expand the environment to 1204 bytes to allow enough room to add a number of DOS environment variables set in the login statement. The default value is only 160 bytes, and that is not near enough to handle most network situations where you may be using a number of environment variables.

The statement SHELL = C:\COMMAND.COM /E:1024 /P specifies the file to use for the command interpreter (in this case COMMAND.COM). The /E specifies the size of the environment space, and the /P makes this shell permanent (cannot be unloaded with the exit command).

Stacks

This feature of DOS is usually not noticed by most people (except programmers) and is used to store internal information for short periods of time when running applications and by DOS. Normally, application programs create stacks for themselves, but the ones created in the CONFIG.SYS are general stacks available to DOS and any applications that need it.

Despite what some believe, Windows does not need any stacks allocated to it. That is why some people recommend setting the stacks equal to 0,0. It is required for the utilities associated with Windows: SMARTDRV.EXE, mouse drivers, EMM386.EXE, etc. They all need stack space for proper operation. If you set the stack to 0,0, you will most likely receive stack overflow error messages. Unfortunately, because this is so critical to the operation of DOS, a stack overflow usually means you have to reboot the computer.

The default stack assignment (if you don't specify it in CONFIG.SYS) is 9,128. Windows will change the line to 9256. The first number is the amount of stacks to be created, and the second number is the size in bytes each stack will be.

Other statements can be placed in the CONFIG.SYS file but do not have any impact on Windows, so we will not cover them here.

Install

This command is not widely used but has a couple of interesting properties. When you load a TSR through the AUTOEXEC.BAT file, the utility is also loaded by a copy of the current DOS environment it created. Not every program or utility needs to have its own copy of the environment.

Granted, the amount of RAM saved is minor, but there are also other reasons for using this command. Some TSRs need to get loaded as soon as possible, and loading in the CONFIG.SYS ensures it will be in place before any other utilities are loaded. For example, the SHARE command is critical to the operation of many programs, and loading it in the CONFIG.SYS will ensure that it be in place.

Of course, there are some TSRs that should never be loaded with the Install command. If the utility looks to DOS for an environmental variable (e.g., a directory for creation of temporary files) or if it runs another utility from inside its code, then it will have to be loaded from AUTOEXEC.BAT. If you don't need these, then it is a candidate for loading in the CONFIG.SYS file.

CONFIG.SYS statement positions

For some configuration files it does not matter where a statement resides because the file will be read and then work will be performed after all lines have been read. In CONFIG.SYS it is different. While more than one pass is made through the file, order does become important.

The first pass looks for the DOS statement to see if it is being loaded high or if control of upper-memory blocks are being made. This makes sense because DOS has to position itself correctly first before any other activities can occur.

After DOS is loaded high, the second pass is made through the file. If you are using a disk compression utility (e.g., Double Space), it is loaded first in memory, and device drivers get loaded next. Even though device drivers are loaded next, they load according to where they occur in the file. That is why it is so critical to have HIMEM.SYS as the first line in the CONFIG.SYS, as subsequent devices may not get loaded properly if HIMEM is not operational.

The next item to be read is the files statement so that the system file table can be created. This is followed by the *file control blocks* (FCBS) and then buffers. The memory set aside to track drive assignments are created after buffers and the size is determined by the drive letter you specify in the Lastdrive entry.

Next, the memory area for stacks is created unless you specify STACKS = 0,0. Then those utilities are loaded through the INSTALL command and, finally, the area of memory set aside for the command interpreter through the SHELL command.

Diagnosing Memory

It is one thing to talk about memory problems and how to solve them; it is something else to actually do it. But, if you don't know what the problem is, how can you make changes? There are a number of utilities available that can let you "see" memory. The most common one is Microsoft Diagnostics (MSD) (Fig. 4.3), which is shipped with every copy of Windows.

Another tool useful for diagnosing memory problems or just viewing the current status of your machine is Manifest from Quarterdeck. This utility gives clear information and recommendations on how to make your memory as efficient as possible.

Figures 4.4 to 4.6 show process information on Windows utilities running in the background.

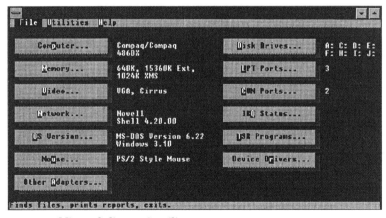

Figure 4.3 Microsoft diagnostic utility.

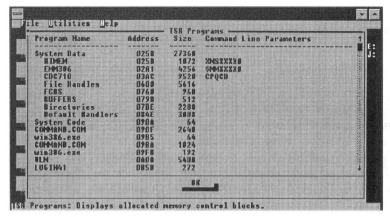

Figure 4.4 TSR memory locations.

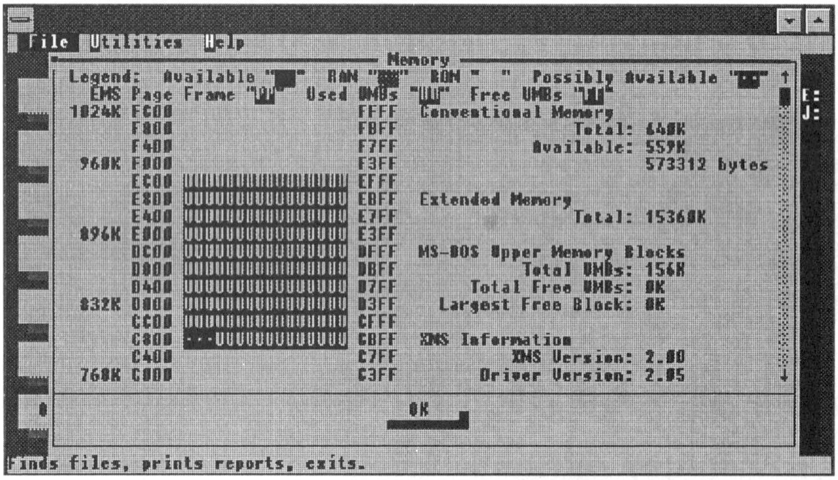

Figure 4.5 MSD memory map.

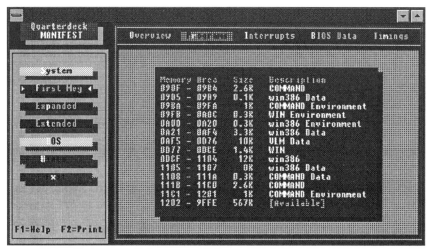

Figure 4.6 Program memory addresses.

5

Workstation Network Configuration

In the previous chapter, we looked at the memory configuration of the workstation. In this chapter, let's take a look at the NetWare shells and how to configure the NetWare communications for a workstation.

Novell NetWare Client Software

There are a number of files required to connect a client system with Novell NetWare and for Windows to communicate with NetWare. First, the NetWare client software needs to be installed and the user logged into the file server (Fig. 5.1).

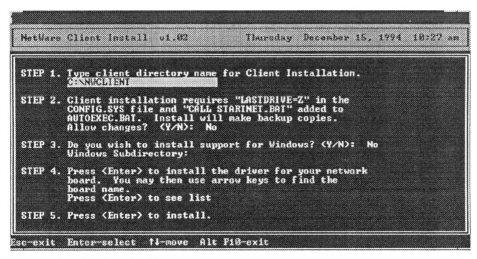

Figure 5.1 NetWare install utility.

The NetWare client software should be the latest version to take advantage of certain utilities (e.g., network dialog boxes). The first step is to gain access to the desired files for the client system and the Windows NetWare files.

Obtaining Access to NetWare File Servers

There are two main sources for the NetWare client software: the NetWare operating system disks and CompuServe. When using the disks that came with the operating system, run the install utility to install client network files automatically.

Step 1 allows you to designate the directory to install the client files on the workstation hard disk. The changes required to CONFIG.SYS and AUTOEXEC.BAT can be done automatically by the install routine. The only problem here is that the line added to the AUTOEXEC.BAT file is added at the end of the file, which may not work properly. Our recommendation is to let the install routine make the changes and then edit the files later. Step 3 is a critical point in the install routine because it will install Windows files for NetWare connectivity in the Windows directory.

The problem with using the client files from the operating-system installation disks is that they may not be the latest versions. To make sure you have the latest version of drivers, download the latest files from CompuServe. The files are located in the Novell Files directory (GO NOVFILES) (listed below).

```
Novfiles Download + NOVFILES

 1 About this Area
 2 311PTD.EXE (8/2/93)
 3 UPD311.EXE (1/10/94)
 4 LANDR3.EXE (11/1/93)
 5 DOSUP9.TXT, VLMUP1.EXE, or NET33X.EXE (10/5/94)
 6 WINUP9.TXT, (WINVLM.EXE), WINDR1.EXE, or NWDLL1.EXE (10/5/94)
 7 CERT3 Files(9/26/94)
 8 Client Kits
 9 NetWare Lite Utility
10 NetWare 3.12 Operating System Patches (47k)
```

NetWare shell update files:

```
WINDR1.EXE
NWDLL1.EXE
NWDLL1.EXE
VLMUP1.EXE
```

The two main sections of NOVFILES on CompuServe you will need to access are menu items 5 and 6, which will give you the latest DOS and Windows client files. Previously, there were only two files with the version names DOSUP9.EXE and WINUP9.EXE.

DOSUP9.EXE was replaced with VLMUP1.EXE and NET33X.EXE while VLMUP1.EXE has all the updated virtual loadable modules (VLMs), updated LSL.COM and IPXODI.COM, the updated MLIDs, and other associated files.

There is another file called NET33X.EXE that contains the latest NETX.EXE. While Novell makes this file available, they have abandoned this client file and replaced it with VLM files.

For Windows utilities, WINUP9.EXE was separated into two files: WINDR1.EXE and NWDLL1.EXE. WINDR1.EXE contains the updated Windows drivers and Windows network utilities. These files can be used with VLM or NETX utilities except for NETWARE.DRV. If you are using the old NETX file, use the NETWARE.DRV contained in the NETX33.EXE file, while the VLM drivers require the NETWARE.DRV from the WINDR1.EXE file.

It is a good idea to check the NOVFILES area every month or two to ensure that you have the latest network driver files. NWDLL1.EXE is not required unless you are running NWADMIN.EXE for NetWare v4.1.

Recommendation: Because of the additional functionality available with VLM files, we recommend only VLM files should be installed and not the older NETX.EXE. The old monolithic driver IPX.COM is also not recommended because Novell hasn't supported that version for a couple of years. It was replaced by the open data-link interface (ODI) technology files.

NET.CFG File

A NET.CFG file needs to be created containing the hardware settings and other configuration information about the NetWare shell drivers. This file will most likely look like that listed below.

```
NET.CFG File Entries:

FILE HANDLES = 100
SHOW DOTS = ON

Link Driver NE2000
        Int 5
        Port 300
        Frame Ethernet_802.3
        Protocol IPX 0 Ethernet_802.3
```

Link Driver

Under the ODI and VLM shells, the NET.CFG file becomes much more important as it contains hardware settings for the network card. Previously, the hardware information was integrated into the IPX.COM file. Now, everything can be changed easily through the NET.CFG file.

The Link Driver section has several settings for identifying the address or other settings for the network card. We have not had occasion to use all settings at once, but you will have to use several options together. The first line of this section starts over on the left-hand side of the line. All other lines that pertain to the Link Driver section should be indented at least one space so that the LSL and other shell drivers know that these items are modifiers to the Link Driver. The Link Driver line gives the name of the network card driver. We will use the EXP16ODI driver as an example of how this works.

The network communications shells that need to be loaded are

```
LSL.COM
EXP16ODI
IPXODI
VLM
```

In the NET.CFG the Link Driver line will read (examples of all the options available for Link Driver will be listed below this line)

```
Link Driver Section of NET.CFG:

LINK DRIVER EXP16ODI
     SLOT 2
     INT 10
     PORT 300
     DMA 1
     MEM 300
     NODE ADDRESS A33005B58A11
     ALTERNATE
     FRAME ethernet_802.2
     LINK STATIONS 1
     MAX FRAME SIZE 1024
     PROTOCOL NEWPROT 320A
     SAPS 3
```

Slot. The *slot* number is used for EISA-based computers that can identify boards through scanning the slots or when the slots are identified specifically. Whenever you have a chance to use the slot identification rather than interrupt and port settings, you have an easier time identifying the board.

Hardware addresses. If you can't identify the card through the slot number, then you will have to specify the interrupt number and the memory address through the MEM or PORT commands. The DMA (direct memory address) channel can also be specified if required by the card. Check the documentation supplied with the card to see if it uses a DMA channel.

Node address. The NODE ADDRESS setting allows you to specify a node address number (in hexadecimal notation) if the network card allows it (e.g., Token Ring network cards).

ALTERNATE. The ALTERNATE setting (without parameters) is required for some token-based network cards to use an alternate board rather than the primary network board.

FRAME. The FRAME setting allows you to identify what frame types you want to enable on this network card. There can be more than one of these in the Link Driver section. The frame types that can be used here are

```
Ethernet_802.3
Ethernet_802.2
Ethernet_II
Ethernet_SNAP
Token-Ring
Token-Ring_SNAP
IBM_PCN2_802.2
IBM_PCN2_SNAP
NOVELL_RX_NET
```

Link Stations. The Link Stations option is intended for LANSUP when using the IBM LAN support program to connect to a midrange or mainframe system.

Maximum frame size. There are a number of choices when specifying the maximum size of data in a network packet. Generally the larger the size of data in a network packet, the more efficient communication will be. This value is highly dependent on the type of network card you have installed in your computer. Check the documentation for your network card to see the largest packet size possible. A warning about the VIPX drivers follows here.

   Warning: Regardless of the maximum packet size possible for your card, the VIPX.386 driver in Windows cannot handle more than 8000 bytes in a single packet.

Protocol. This setting is used with protocols that have different frame types. The format is

```
Protocol name ID frame
```

The name is the protocol name (e.g., IPX, IP, ARP). The ID field is a hexadecimal number of the protocol that specifies the frame type listed in the frame parameter. The following table lists the common protocols and their hexadecimal equivalents.

Protocol	Hexadecimal number	Frame type
IPX	0	Ethernet 802.3
	e0	Ethernet 802.2
	e0	Token Ring
	e0	IBM PCN2 802.2
	8137	Ethernet II
	8137	Ethernet SNAP
	8137	Token Ring SNAP
	8137	IBM PCN2 SNAP
	fa	Novell RX-Net
IP	800	Ethernet II
	800	Ethernet SNAP
	800	Token Ring SNAP
	d4	Novell-RX-Net

SAPs

The SAPs parameter is the number of service access points required for the IBM LANSUP driver for loading the IBM PC support utility.

Link Support

This section of the NET.CFG also has a header line that starts out in the first column of the file and has a number of options below it. This section is used to configure communications with the network card. As the name implies, this section configures options for the LSL.COM driver.

```
Link Support Parameters in NET.CFG:

LINK SUPPORT
    BUFFERS 3 1500
    MAX BOARDS 8
    MAX STACKS 16
    MEMPOOL 5 3
```

Buffers. This feature sets the number and size of the buffers to receive data for the LSL driver. It is seldom required unless specified in the documentation for a card. The default is 0. The first value is the number of buffers, and the second value is the size of each buffer. The only limitation is that the combination of buffers and size of each buffer must not exceed 59 kbytes.

Max boards. You can configure the LSL to handle more than one logical board for the LSL. If you wanted to have the workstation communication on several different frame types, you would specify the number of boards equal to or higher than the number of frame types you were implementing. Each frame type is called a *resource,* and each logical board uses one resource.

Max stacks. This value is rarely specified until you receive an error message that indicates a problem with resources. Sometimes a protocol stack will not load because of a lack of resources. Setting this value above the default will solve this problem. Of course, increasing the stack size also increases the amount of memory required. The default value is 4, with a maximum of 16 possible.

Mempool. Some protocols need to adjust the memory pool buffers the LSL will maintain. This option specifies the number and the size (in kilobytes) of each buffer. If you are having problems communicating, check the document supplied with the network to see if you have to adjust the Mempool values.

NetBIOS parameters

If you will be using NetBIOS in addition to IPX/SPX for communication on your network, you may need to adjust the parameters to ensure the most efficient communication. NetBIOS parameters that can be used in NET.CFG files are

```
NETBIOS
      NETBIOS ABORT TIMEOUT 540
      NETBIOS BROADCAST COUNT 4
      NETBIOS BROADCAST DELAY 36
      NETBIOS COMMANDS 12
      NETBIOS INTERNET ON
      NETBIOS LISTEN TIMEOUT 108
      NETBIOS RECEIVE BUFFERS 6
      NETBIOS RETRY COUNT 20
      NETBIOS RETRY DELAY 10
      NETBIOS SEND BUFFERS 6
      NETBIOS SESSION 32
      NETBIOS VERIFY TIMEOUT 54
      NPATCH
```

NetBIOS abort timeout. This entry determines the amount of time (in CPU ticks) that NetBIOS will wait without a response from the receiving station before terminating the session. The default is 540 ticks. Use 18.2 ticks per second as the basic value for calculation.

NetBIOS broadcast count. This value will determine the amount of time it takes to broadcast a name resolution packet on a network. If you have a large network, this number will have to be increased as it will take longer to send a broadcast packet. The default when the NetBIOS Internet value is ON is 4 or 2 when the NetBIOS Internet value is OFF. The value can be as high as 65,535.

NetBIOS broadcast delay. This value compensates for the delay in sending a NetBIOS packet across a network. The default is 36 with the NetBIOS Internet value set to ON and 18 when it is set to OFF. If the network is busy (and Windows can make it busy), you may need to increase the count.

NetBIOS commands. These are NetBIOS commands that may be called from applications running on the network. If the network shell drivers report an error of 22, increase this value. The default is 12, with a maximum of 450.

NetBIOS Internet. Set this value to OFF if you are running a NetBIOS application and there is only one NetWare server and network. If you have a large enterprise with a network divided by routers or packet switchers, then set it to ON. The default is ON, which runs slower than when it is set to OFF (assuming that there isn't a large network in place).

NetBIOS listen timeout. This is similar to the watchdog feature of NetWare. This is the time (in ticks) that the shell will wait before it requests a keep-alive packet from the responding station. The default is 108 ticks, with up to 65,535 possible.

NetBIOS receive buffers. This is the number of IPX receive buffers that may be needed by NetBIOS. If you are running peer-to-peer networking or gateways, it may be necessary to increase this from the default of 6 to a higher number (maximum of 20).

NetBIOS retry count. This is used when communicating with another computer running a NetBIOS session, and indicates the number of times another packet will be sent when establishing a session with another system. You may have to increase this from the default of 20 if you have a large or very busy network.

NetBIOS retry delay. This is a close partner to the previous command. It determines the amount of delay between packets when trying to establish a session. If you have a large or busy network, there may be a need to increase the count from the default of 10 ticks.

NetBIOS send buffers. This is the number of IPX send buffers used by NetBIOS. Same criteria as the receive buffers mentioned earlier. The default is 6 buffers.

NetBIOS session. This parameter determines how many virtual circuits can be supported at the same time. The default is 32.

NetBIOS verify timeout. This parameter determines how frequently a keep-alive packet is sent to another computer to keep a communications session alive. The default is 54 ticks.

Npatch. This is a unique value for network shell commands that allows dynamic patching of the shell with additional code to be added later. Some hardware vendors could use this to create their own addition to the communication code.

Protocol IPXODI

This section of the NET.CFG file modifies the IPXODI.COM driver to tune the communications to your specific needs.

```
IPXODI Protocols in NET.CFG:

PROTOCOL IPXODI
     BIND EXP16ODI
     CONFIG OPTION
     INT64 ON
     INT7A ON
     IPATCH
     IPX PACKET SIZE LIMIT 1500
     IPX RETRY COUNT 20
     IPX SOCKETS 20
     MINIMUM SPX RETRIES 20
     SPX ABORT TIMEOUT 540
     SPX CONNECTIONS 15
     SPX LISTEN TIMEOUT 108
     SPX VERIFY TIMEOUT 54
```

Bind. This parameter is seldom required as binding takes place to the first board found. If you have more than one network card in the workstation, this parameter will identify which board you want to bind.

CONFIG option. This allows you to temporarily override the configuration options when installing the drivers through WSGEN.

INT64. NetWare now uses Interrupt 64h to communicate with IPX services. Older systems may not be able to operate reliably if this option is present. The problem will manifest itself through applications that hang when running on NetWare versions 4.x and 3.x. By specifying this to OFF, you will ensure compatibility with those older systems.

INT7A. As with the previous parameter, some older system may use interrupt 7Ah to communicate on the network. This ensures backward compatibility with older systems (e.g., v2.0).

IPATCH. This parameter is similar to the NPATCH option in NetBIOS in that you can specify a byte offset value to modify the IPXODI.COM driver. This value will be supplied by Novell or a vendor when needed.

IPX packet size limit. Many parameters in NetWare are a balance between two competing benefits. There are two factors when deciding packet size limit. A LAN driver in NetWare can have packet sizes of up to 16 kbytes, but if you cannot use that full size, the amount of memory required to handle packets of that size may not be beneficial. This value can be set from 576 to 6500 bytes.

IPX retry count. This value determines how many times a packet is retransmitted. If the network is very large or busy, you may need to increase this value, which will be passed on to SPX. However, be aware that some network functions may be delayed on a busy network by increasing this value too high. The default is 20.

IPX sockets. This value determines how many IPX sockets are available at the same time. If you are using certain network diagnostic or monitoring programs, you may need to increase this value to accommodate their background communication requirements. The default is 20.

Minimum SPX retries. With connectionless networks, the user might not know whether the other station or file server is still on the network and communicating. If you are seeing errors about lost connections or similar errors, then try setting this value and see if the problems go away. We recommend starting at 20 and steadily increasing that value until the problems are solved. The maximum value is 255.

SPX abort timeout. This is the amount of SPX wait time before a connection is terminated. Since SPX is responsible for the delivery of data to the receiving station, it also needs to know whether the receiving station is operational. The problem is that too short a wait time will mean a busy network. If you delay response from a station, communication to that station could be dropped prematurely. Too long a wait means a delay in determining whether a station has been turned off or has otherwise stopped communicating with the network. The default is 540 ticks.

SPX connections. Some network communication and monitoring programs (e.g., RConsole) use SPX for their communication and may need more SPX simultaneous connections. The default is 15.

SPX listen timeout. Similar to the abort timeout parameter, the listen timeout parameter is the time that SPX will wait to receive a packet from the other station before it will request a response packet from the other side. The default is 108 ticks.

SPX verify timeout.   As with the previous parameter, this one determines how often to send a packet to the other station to determine whether it is still communicating on the network. The default is 54 ticks.

NetWare DOS requester section.   This section of the NET.CFG file controls parameters for the VLM shell. These options will modify a specified VLM file.

```
NetWare DOS Requester Options in NET.CFG:

NETWARE DOS REQUESTER
     AUTO RECONNECT = ON
     AVERAGE NAME LENGTH = 48
     CACHE BUFFERS = 5
     CACHE BUFFER SIZE = 512
     CACHE WRITES = ON
     CHECKSUM = 1
     CONNECTIONS = 8
     DOS NAME = MSDOS
     FIRST NETWORK DRIVE = F
     HANDLE NET ERRORS = ON
     LARGE INTERNET PACKETS = ON
     LOAD LOW CONN = ON
     LOAD LOW IPXNCP = ON
     LOCAL PRINTERS = 3
     LONG MACHINE TYPE = IBM_PC
     MAX TASKS = 31
     MESSAGE LEVEL = 1
     MESSAGE TIMEOUT = 0
     NAME CONTEXT = "OU = SALES.OU = WEST.O = ABC COMPANY"
     NETWORK PRINTERS = 3
     PB BUFFERS = 3
     PREFERRED SERVER = FS1
     PREFERRED TREE = ABC COMPANY
     PRINT BUFFER SIZE = 64
     PRINT HEADER = 64
     PRINT TAIL = 16
     READ ONLY COMPATIBILITY = 1
     SEARCH MODE = 1
     SET STATION TIME = ON
     SHOW DOTS = ON
     SHORT MACHINE TYPE = CMPQ
     SIGNATURE LEVEL = 1
     TRUE COMMIT = OFF
     USE DEFAULTS = ON
     VLM = RSA.VLM
```

Auto Reconnect.   One of the most frustrating problems with network activities is the sudden loss of connection to a file server. By setting this parameter to ON, any disruption to a session will be reconnected (provided the server is available) and the environment rebuilt. These services are provided by AUTO.VLM, NDS.VLM, and PNW.VLM. The default is ON if the AUTO.VLM is loaded.

This feature is truly incredible because the reconnection becomes automatic and it reduces the calls for support when a problem occurs. The only problem we have seen with this feature is in a communication failure on a large network. If a router or switch goes down, the resumption of service will mean that all stations are trying to reconnect simultaneously, and this can greatly delay the resumption of service.

Average name length.   The maximum number of characters in a NetWare server name is 48 and space has to be set aside to allow storage of these names for the number of simultaneous connections. If your server names are shorter, you can set this value to the longest name and save some memory for the VLM driver. The parameter modifies CONN.VLM.

Cache buffers.   This feature sets the number of cache buffers allocated for the local caching of nonshared files from the network. You will need to allocate one buffer for each file you want to cache. It will also increase the speed of reads and writes under certain conditions. The default is 5 cache blocks, with a maximum of 64 blocks. This parameter modifies the values of FIO.VLM.

Cache buffer size.   This is related to the previous parameter but allocates buffer size for caching. By increasing this value, you can increase the speed of network access even though it will mean more memory to handle disk accesses. The default is 512 bytes, with a maximum of 4096 bytes. Be careful—if you allocate a size larger than the maximum size of the protocol packet, you will not gain any efficiency, but it will take up more memory—all pain, no gain. This will modify the FIO.VLM file.

Cache writes.   You can control the caching of write requests to the file server which will increase speed of access. Of course, any time you cache write requests, there is a danger that a server failure will result in loss of data before the data is written to the disk. The default is ON and modifies FIO.VLM.

Checksum.   If you have a network that is subject to problems, you may want to validate each packet received to ensure that it wasn't corrupted during transmission. By setting this parameter to 0, you can disable the checksum. A value of 1 enables a check, but it is not preferred. A value of 2 means that checksum is enabled and preferred, and a value of 3 means that checksums are required. The default is 1, and this parameter modifies IPXNCP.VLM and NWP.VLM.

Connections.   For those who have large networks, this feature is available only under NetWare Directory Services and enables connection to more servers than were available under the NETX shell. The default is connection to 8 servers simultaneously, with a maximum of 50 possible. Do not use this with the NETX.EXE shell; it works only with VLMs. The VLMs responsible for connections are CONN.VLM and FIO.VLM.

DOS name. This parameter is used to identify the type of DOS running on the workstation. It can be used in login scripts for a variety of purposes. The default value is MSDOS; the value must be a maximum of 5 bytes, and if you set this parameter, the autodetect feature for DOS name is not available.

First network drive. In our earlier discussion of parameters in CONFIG.SYS we discussed the Lastdrive command, which specifies how much space DOS should allocate for disk drives. This works only with the VLM shell in conjunction with the Lastdrive command. This parameter defines the first letter that will be assigned to the network file servers. You can specify any letter, but the most commonly used one is drive F:. This parameter is used only for the drive letter and not for the colon following the drive letter. This modifies GENERAL.VLM.

Handle net errors. This parameter determines how network errors will be handled and is used mainly for the workstation when it doesn't respond to the file server. If you set this parameter to ON (the default), Interrupt 24h will be used to handle network errors or you can specify OFF to return the NET_RECV_ERROR value. This modifies IPXNCP.VLM.

Large Internet packets. This parameter will allow the workstation and file server to communicate on the largest packet size that each can support and set the packet size to the largest possible size. This size change can take place even though it is communicated through routers and bridges. However, if the router or bridge cannot handle a large-size packet, then this parameter will have no effect. The default is ON and modifies IPXNCP.VLM.

Load low conn. The IPXNCP.VLM will load in conventional memory if this value is set to ON (the default), which is faster, but there is a loss of conventional memory. If you set this value to OFF, the VLM will load in upper memory but will have decreased performance. This parameter modifies the IPXNCP.VLM module.

Local printers. On a workstation, BIOS defines how many local printers are available (one for each parallel port). If you set this value to 0, it will eliminate all local printers, and if capture wasn't loaded, the print job will not hang the computer. The default is 3, with a maximum of 9 possible. This parameter modifies PRINT.VLM.

Long machine type. This parameter will pass the type of computer used and can be read by the machine variable in a NetWare login script. You are limited to a maximum of 6 bytes, and the default is IBM_PC. It modifies NETX.VLM and GENERAL.VLM.

Max tasks. This is the maximum number of tasks that can be running simultaneously. When more than one application runs at a time, there will be several tasks running from each application. This parameter is critical for Windows because if you open too many applications at once, there may be problems because not enough memory was allocated for tasks. The default is 31, with a maximum of 128 allowed. If you are running more than four or five applications simultaneously on the workstation in Windows at the same time, you probably should increase this value to 50. It modifies CONN.VLM.

Message level. When a problem occurs, this value will determine what messages will be sent to the screen when loading VLMs. The levels of messages are as follows, with each level displaying all messages defined previous to that number. The default is 1, and it modifies NWP.VLM.

Message level	Messages
0	Copyright and critical errors
1	Warning messages
2	Program load information for VLMs
3	Configuration information
4	Diagnostic information

Message timeout. If leaving broadcast messages on the screen is a problem for users, you can limit the time that the message is displayed on the screen. The default is 0, which means that the message will be displayed indefinitely until the user presses a key. If you set a value for this (in ticks), the message will clear after that time. The maximum is 1000 ticks.

Name context. This value is used with NetWare Directory Services to specify the location in the directory tree you wish to default to. If you don't specify this value, the user will have to specify the tree structure to determine where their login name is located. In bindery-based systems, there was only one location where a user login name was stored, but in NDS it can be stored in any container, and there is no way of knowing automatically where that is located. However, by specifying this value, the user doesn't have to worry about the tree structure. This modifies the NDS.VLM driver.

Network printers. This is the number of printers that the DOS requester shell can capture and redirect to the network file-server print queues. The default is 3, with a maximum of 9. This parameter modifies the PRINT.VLM driver, but if you specify 0 for this parameter, PRINT.VLM will not load.

PB buffers. This controls the number of buffers available for packet burst to increase speed of communication between file server and workstation. The default is 3, with a maximum of 10. Increase this value if the network is busy.

Preferred server. This is used to ensure that you gain access to a specified server regardless of how many servers there are on the network and whichever one answers first. This is especially useful when you have a mixture of NetWare 4.x and 3.x servers on the network. If you want to attach to a 3.x server, this parameter will ignore all other servers and just attach to the desired server for login. If you want to attach to NDS in a NetWare 4 environment, use the next parameter rather than the preferred server. This parameter modifies BIND.VLM.

Preferred tree. This is very similar to the preferred server, except it is for an NDS tree rather than a specific server. This one modifies the NDS.VLM. Don't specify both preferred server and preferred tree because the shell will be confused about which to attach to. In the event you do specify both parameters, the VLM shell will attach to the first server or tree that meets the conditions specified in one of the parameters.

Print buffer size. You can set the size of the print buffer to increase the speed of printing by changing this parameter from the default of 64 bytes to a maximum of 256 bytes. It modifies PRINT.VLM. We have found little benefit from this parameter when printing standard documents, although you may gain some speed if you are printing graphics.

Print header. If you are using standard dot-matrix or laser printers for printing documents, you will probably not need to use this parameter. If, however, you are using a printer where you are changing emulation modes or a large amount of control codes, then you may need to enlarge the print header to contain the control codes for the printer. The default is 64 bytes, with a maximum of 1024 bytes possible. This parameter modifies PRINT.VLM.

Print tail. After each print job is sent to the printer on a network, it is a good idea to reset the printer back to default status so the next user won't get a bad printout. If the printer is not resetting to default codes, change the size of the print tail beyond the default 16 bytes and see if that doesn't resolve the problem. This parameter modifies the PRINT.VLM driver.

Read-only compatibility. This parameter deals with one of the most confusing aspects of the NetWare operating system. When setting the file attributes with the Flag command or in Filer, you can mark a data file "read only," which means it will honor all requests for reads from the file but will not allow any attempts to write to the file.

In the first versions of NetWare (prior to v2.1), an application could open a file (e.g., database data file) that was marked "read only" with write access calls and not get an error until it actually attempted to write data to the file. This was designed to solve a problem where you wanted a data file for reading only even though the database program tried to open it in write mode. Since those applications created for old versions of NetWare might still be operating in that mode, you may need to set this to ON to solve a database problem. The default is OFF, and this parameter modifies the REDIR.VLM driver.

Note: We have seen strange error codes involved with files that are marked "read only." The problems usually arise with single-user DOS programs running on the file server but can be applicable to any application. Sometimes when attempting to write to a file marked "read only," the application will report on out-of-disk space error. When you look at the file server volume, there will most likely be a large amount of free space. Check the rights and file attributes, and that will most likely solve the problem.

Search mode. This is similar to the SMODE (now an option in the FLAG utility for NetWare 4.x) command except that it is set in the NetWare DOS requester rather than on a per executable-file basis. You can set executable files to search for data along the path just the same as it works for running .EXE and .COM files. When setting the search mode here, the search mode settings work for all .COM and .EXE files that are run by the workstation.

The following table shows the different search modes possible.

Mode	Description
0	Disables the search mode by not providing any search methods.
1	If the application has a directory location for the data file, no data file searches are made. If the application does not specify a directory, then the operating system searches the current directory first and then the path for the correct data file. This option is the default.
2	Only the default directory and directories specified in the application are searched.
3	If the application has a directory location for the data file, no data file searches are made. If the application does not specify a directory and the application opens a file flagged "read only," only the current directory and then the path are searched for the correct data file.
4	This mode is not available to users.
5	The application searches the default directory and file-server search drivers regardless of whether the path is specified in the executable code. The shell will search for files with any extension.
6	This mode is not available to users.
7	If the application accesses data files flagged as "read only," the application searches the current directory and search drives regardless of the path specified in the application code.

Set station time. This is a handy feature for large networks especially in those areas where time is changed in spring and fall (i.e., to Daylight Savings Time or Standard Time). This parameter will set the workstation clock time to that of the file server each time the workstation attaches to a file server (i.e., when the VLM.EXE file is loaded). Previously, this had to be done with the SYSTIME.EXE utility. This parameter modifies the VLM.EXE file.

Show dots. The directory structure in NetWare is different from that in DOS. NetWare is commonly mistaken for a DOS system. It is not, and it only emulates the file structure of DOS for compatibility purposes. Sometimes, a few discrepancies creep in, and the dots are just one of those problems. DOS uses a hierarchical directory structure in which a single dot represents the current directory and double dots represent the parent directory. This allows a number of shortcuts as you can issue the DIR .. command and get a listing of the files in the parent directory. Or, you can issue the DEL . command and delete all files in the current directory.

Because NetWare does not have these dots in its directory system problems can surface when you use Windows. If you are using a mouse and click on the double dots to move up one directory level, you must set the SHOW DOTS = ON to ensure that they are displayed in the file manager. This parameter modifies REDIR.VLM.

Tip: When on a NetWare drive, you can move backward through the directory tree easily by using dots with the CD command. To move backward one directory level (the same as in DOS), issue the CD .. command. To move back two directories, use the CD ... command. Use the command CD with one more dot than the number of levels you want to move up in the directory tree. DOS does not recognize this command, other than the two dots.

Short machine type. This is the same parameter as used with the NETX shell. It is used to set a value for the %MACHINE variable in the login script and also for loading screen overlay files. The default is IBM, and there can be a maximum of 4 bytes for this value. This modifies NETX.VLM and GENERAL.VLM.

Signature level. This is the level of security required for data being passed over the network. This must be set at each workstation in coordination with values on the file server. If you set this to a 0, it disables all signature security. A 1 enables the signature but only if needed. A value of 2 prefers using this security if it is available on the file server, and a value of 3 forces the workstation to use the signature in its communication. If the file server cannot handle that level of security, then the workstation cannot communicate with the file server. The default is 1, and the NWP.VLM is modified.

Use defaults. Because VLM.EXE loads the drivers as needed, it is necessary to specify each VLM that is required. Take time to create a list in case the NET.CFG is not efficient. It is possible to miss a crucial VLM and not be able to attach to a file server. There are default VLM files that are loaded automatically unless you set this parameter to OFF. The VLMs that are loaded automatically are listed below.

```
BIND.VLM
CONN.VLM
FIO.VLM
GENERAL.VLM
IPXNCP.VLM
NDS.VLM
NETX.VLM
NWP.VLM
PRINT.VLM
REDIR.VLM
SECURITY.VLM
TRAN.VLM
```

VLM. This can be used when you don't want to use the default loading of VLMs. It allows you to specify each individual driver to load. Be aware that you need to set USE DEFAULTS = OFF if you want to specify the loading of each individual driver.

VLM options

When running the VLM.EXE shell, there are several command-line options that can help in the administration of your system.

Unload. The /U switch allows you to unload VLM.EXE only if it was the last TSR loaded. Because of DOS memory design, you must unload TSRs in the reverse order they were loaded. There is an undocumented problem with the VLM utility that can cause you momentary confusion. VLM.EXE is only a TSR manager because it loads the other files with a .VLM extension by default or as specified in the NET.CFG. If you cannot attach to a file server because it is down or because there is a hardware problem (network card, cabling, hubs, routers, etc.), then VLM.EXE still loads in memory even though it cannot find a file server.

Before attaching to the network again, most people reboot the computer, which reloads everything and attaches to the network. If you want a shortcut, just issue the command VLM /U, and the shell will unload, and then you can run VLM again normally to load up in memory and attach to a file server.

Configuration file. If you don't specify a configuration file to load, the VLM driver looks to the current directory for a file named NET.CFG. For most people, this is more than satisfactory. However, if you want to run multiple configurations, you can create different configuration files and use them with the

/C command. You need to enter the command in this format: VLM /C = C:\NWCLIENT\NET2.CFG. You can specify configuration files in different directories, or you can give them different names.

This is frequently used with LAN WorkPlace for DOS for testing when you want to load the TCP/IP drivers only at certain times. By specifying different configuration files, you can have precise control over what is being loaded and the parameters required for each driver.

Information display. For those of us who are technical, we like to see a great amount of information on the screen, but frequently the users don't want their screens cluttered. For users we redirect the screen information to NULL when loading shells. This keeps a clean startup, and users aren't bothered by all the information on the screen. For example, for the VLM the command would be VLM>NULL:. This keeps all information about the VLM hidden from the user.

If you want more information about the shells in a permanent form, you can redirect the output to a file with this command: VLM>VLM.TXT. This ASCII text file will contain the output normally seen on the screen in the file. If this is in the batch file that loads the shells, it will replace the text file each time. If you want to keep a log of each time it started, place two redirect symbols in the command, which will append those screen outputs to the file: VLM>>VLM.TXT.

There are several switches that can be used to display various amounts of information about the VLM driver. The format is a /V#, with the # specifying the option for displaying various levels of information about the shell. The switch /V0 shows only a copyright and errors about VLM files that don't load:

```
VLM.EXE - NetWare virtual loadable module manager v1.20 (941108)
© Copyright 1994 Novell, Inc. All Rights Reserved.
Patent pending.

The VLM.EXE file is pre-initializing the VLMs.............
The VLM.EXE file is using extended memory (XMS).
You are attached to server FS1
```

Option /V1 is the default and is the same as /V0 except it displays an error whenever an individual .VLM file doesn't load:

```
VLM.EXE - NetWare virtual loadable module manager v1.20 (941108)
© Copyright 1994 Novell, Inc. All Rights Reserved.
Patent pending.

The VLM.EXE file is pre-initializing the VLMs...........

NETX-120-58: The PRINT.VLM file has not been loaded. The NETX.VLM file will
load successfully without print services. To enable printing services,
load the PRINT.VLM file before loading the NETX.VLM file.
.
The VLM.EXE file is using extended memory (XMS).
You are attached to server FS1
```

The switch /V2 is the same as /V0 and /V1, except it provides module names when they load:

```
VLM.EXE     - NetWare virtual loadable module manager v1.20 (941108)
© Copyright 1994 Novell, Inc. All Rights Reserved.
Patent pending.

The VLM.EXE file is pre-initializing the VLMs...........

NETX-120-58: The PRINT.VLM file has not been loaded. The NETX.VLM file will
load successfully without print services. To enable printing services,
load the PRINT.VLM file before loading the NETX.VLM file.
.
The VLM.EXE file is using extended memory (XMS).
CONN.VLM     - NetWare connection table manager v1.20 (941108)
IPXNCP.VLM   - NetWare IPX transport module v1.20 (941108)
TRAN.VLM     - NetWare transport multiplexor module v1.20 (941108)
SECURITY.VLM - NetWare security enhancement module v1.20 (941108)
NDS.VLM      - NetWare directory services protocol module v1.20 (941108)
BIND.VLM     - NetWare bindery protocol module v1.20 (941108)
PNW.VLM      - Personal NetWare protocol module v1.20 (941108)
NWP.VLM      - NetWare protocol multiplexor module v1.20 (941108)
FIO.VLM      - NetWare file input-output module v1.20 (941108)
GENERAL.VLM  - NetWare general purpose function module v1.20 (941108)
REDIR.VLM    - NetWare DOS redirector module v1.20 (941108)
NETX.VLM     - NetWare workstation shell module v4.20 (941108)
You are attached to server FS1
```

Switch /V3 has all of the information in previous switches and adds information about parameters from the NET.CFG file:

```
VLM.EXE - NetWare virtual loadable module manager v1.20 (941108)
© Copyright 1994 Novell, Inc. All Rights Reserved.
Patent pending.

The VLM.EXE file is pre-initializing the VLMs...........

NETX-120-58: The PRINT.VLM file has not been loaded. The NETX.VLM file will
load successfully without print services. To enable printing services,
load the PRINT.VLM file before loading the NETX.VLM file.
.
The VLM.EXE file is using extended memory (XMS).
CONN.VLM     - NetWare connection table manager v1.20 (941108)
IPXNCP.VLM   - NetWare IPX transport module v1.20 (941108)
TRAN.VLM     - NetWare transport multiplexor module v1.20 (941108)
SECURITY.VLM - NetWare security enhancement module v1.20 (941108)
NDS.VLM      - NetWare directory services protocol module v1.20 (941108)
BIND.VLM     - NetWare bindery protocol module v1.20 (941108)
PNW.VLM      - Personal NetWare protocol module v1.20 (941108)
NWP.VLM      - NetWare protocol multiplexor module v1.20 (941108)
FIO.VLM      - NetWare file input-output module v1.20 (941108)
GENERAL.VLM  - NetWare general purpose function module v1.20 (941108)
FIRST NETWORK DRIVE F
REDIR.VLM    - NetWare DOS redirector module v1.20 (941108)
SHOW DOTS ON
FIRST NETWORK DRIVE F
SHOW DOTS ON
NETX.VLM     - NetWare workstation shell module v4.20 (941108)
FIRST NETWORK DRIVE F
You are attached to server FS1
```

The /V4 switch provides the most information of all:

```
VLM.EXE     - NetWare virtual loadable module manager v1.20 (941108)
© Copyright 1994 Novell, Inc. All Rights Reserved.
Patent pending.
```

```
The VLM.EXE file is pre-initializing the VLMs............

NETX-120-58: The PRINT.VLM file has not been loaded. The NETX.VLM file will
load successfully without print services. To enable printing services,
load the PRINT.VLM file before loading the NETX.VLM file.
.
The VLM.EXE file is using extended memory (XMS).
CONN.VLM      - NetWare connection table manager v1.20 (941108)
IPXNCP.VLM    - NetWare IPX transport module v1.20 (941108)
TRAN.VLM      - NetWare transport multiplexor module v1.20 (941108)
SECURITY.VLM  - NetWare security enhancement module v1.20 (941108)
NDS.VLM       - NetWare directory services protocol module v1.20 (941108)
BIND.VLM      - NetWare bindery protocol module v1.20 (941108)
PNW.VLM       - Personal NetWare protocol module v1.20 (941108)
NWP.VLM       - NetWare protocol multiplexor module v1.20 (941108)
FIO.VLM       - NetWare file input-output module v1.20 (941108)
GENERAL.VLM   - NetWare general purpose function module v1.20 (941108)
FIRST NETWORK DRIVE F
REDIR.VLM     - NetWare DOS redirector module v1.20 (941108)
SHOW DOTS ON
NETX.VLM      - NetWare workstation shell module v4.20 (941108)
FIRST NETWORK DRIVE F
You are attached to server SERVER1
```

Memory locations

The VLM shell can run in extended or expanded memory. It will try to load in extended memory first and then expanded memory before residing in conventional memory as a last resort. You can issue the VLM /MX and VLM /ME commands to force the VLM to try to load in extended or expanded memory first, but usually letting it load by itself is more than adequate.

VLM diagnostics.   The VLM /D option (Fig. 5.2) gives in-depth technical information about where the VLM files are being loaded. Unless you are a programmer or want to understand VLMs in great depth, this information will not be that helpful.

Loading VLMs

When loading VLMs, you can use the defaults or specify the specific VLMs you want to load. If you are using VLMs with NetWare 3.x only, then there are a number of VLMs that do not need to be loaded, thereby freeing up more space. If you are attaching to a NetWare 4.x server for bindery emulation only or a NetWare 3.x server, the following list shows the VLMs you need to load.

```
BIND.VLM
CONN.VLM
FIO.VLM
GENERAL.VLM
IPXNCP.VLM
NETX.VLM
NWP.VLM
PRINT.VLM
REDIR.VLM
TRAN.VLM
```

```
VLM.EXE      - NetWare virtual loadable module manager  v1.20 (941108)
© Copyright 1994 Novell, Inc.  All Rights Reserved.
Patent pending.

The VLM.EXE file v1.20 is currently loaded
VLM transient switch count : 147
VLM call count             : 286
VLM current ID             : 0040h
VLM memory type            : XMS
VLM modules loaded count   : 13
VLM block ID (0 if CON)    : A8F8h
VLM transient block        : E2E1h
VLM global seg (0 if CON)  : D99Fh
VLM async queue (h, t, s)  : 0000:0000, 07D2:0030, 0
VLM busy queue (h, t, s)   : 0000:0000, 07D2:003C, 0
VLM re-entrance level      : 1
VLM full map count         : 145

VLM diagnostic information            Address      Memory Sizes (decimal)
NAME     ID   Flag Func Maps Call TSeg GSeg Low  High  TSize  GSize  SSize
-------- ---- ---- ---- ---- ---- ---- ---- ---- ----  -----  -----  -----
VLM      0001 A000 0005 0000 0053 07D2 0941 FFFF 0000   5408      0      0
CONN     0010 B000 0011 0000 0055 D99F DA6A FFFF FFFF   3248    384   6704
IPXNCP   0021 B000 000B 0000 000B DA82 DBBC FFFF FFFF   5024   2912   2032
TRAN     0020 E000 000B 0001 0010 DA82 DBBC FFFF FFFF    314    182   2032
SECURITY 0061 A000 0005 0005 0004 E2E1 DC72 0000 0000   4192      0   3280
NDS      0032 A000 0010 0014 000A E2E1 DC72 1060 0000   6112    896    992
BIND     0031 A000 0010 0007 0006 E2E1 DCAA 2840 0000   3008    448    720
PNW      0033 A000 0010 0008 0006 E2E1 DCC6 3400 0000   5680   2528   1376
NWP      0030 A000 0011 000E 0008 E2E1 DD64 4A30 0000   3040   1840   1248
FIO      0041 A000 000B 0005 0004 E2E1 DDD7 5610 0000   7008  10240    480
GENERAL  0043 A000 000A 000A 0008 E2E1 E057 7170 0000   1760    720   1536
REDIR    0040 A000 0009 0033 0020 E2E1 E084 7850 0000  10256   2688   1328
PRINT    0042 A000 000F 0009 0006 E2E1 E12C A060 0000   3952   2864   1520
NETX     0050 A000 0007 0011 0008 E2E1 E1DF AFD0 0000  10080   4112   2224
Total                                                  68768  29632
Maximum                                                10256  10240   6704
```

Figure 5.2 VLM diagnostic function.

VLM modules

It is not enough to tell you which VLM modules to load under certain circumstances. We need to explore what each VLM driver does and when it is appropriate to use it. The common VLM drivers and their functions are described in the following paragraphs (arranged alphabetically).

AUTO.VLM. This driver provides a functionality that has been greatly lacking in networks for some time. Whenever a server goes down or communication between the file server and workstation is not available, this driver will reconnect to the server, when possible, open files that were in place when the connection was lost and will re-create other settings such as drive mappings and printer connections.

BIND.VLM. This driver enables the user to access bindery emulation services in NetWare 4.x and the network system in previous server versions.

CONN.VLM. One of the most critical drivers, this VLM maintains the information about connections to file servers and Directory Services. This is where space is set aside to track up to 50 simultaneous server connections under NDS.

Warning: Even though the connection table manager will let you set CONNECTIONS = to a number larger than 8 for bindery-based systems, some utilities may not be able to handle more than eight servers at a time and will cause no end of problems on your system.

FIO.VLM. When accessing files on a file server, this VLM tracks all activities that involve communication with the file server. It is called the *file input/output module.*

GENERAL.VLM. We wonder whether this name was assigned because its originators couldn't think of another. It handles a wide variety of chores but is dedicated mostly to tracking connection information, search drive mappings, search modes, etc.

IPXNCP.VLM. This is required in the VLM drivers to build packets with proper information before passing it on to the IPXODI driver for transmission on the network.

NDS.VLM. The NetWare Directory Services equivalent of BIND.VLM. It provides access to the Directory Services and makes it available to the user.

NETX.VLM. A holdover from the NetWare 3.x systems and bindery databases, this driver is kept in for compatibility purposes when attaching to a non-NetWare 4.x server, or there may be certain calls required for specific applications. If you are having problems with certain applications (e.g., Btrieve database applications), you can check to make sure this has been loaded.

NMR.VLM. NMR is required for compatibility with Windows utilities. It is a responder and can provide diagnostic utilities on the workstation and the network shells. It is not required for access to the network.

NWP.VLM. A critical piece of the network driver, this driver handles logins and logouts and other user connection services.

PRINT.VLM. This driver is required when network printing is desired. If this is not loaded, you will still be able to attach to the file server and run applications, but you will not be able to run the capture utility in DOS or use the capture utility in NetWare Tools.

REDIR.VLM. There are some DOS requests that NetWare can take over and handle. This VLM provides the connection between NetWare and these services.

RSA.VLM. This can be loaded if you want a high level of security for your system. It provides support for AUTO.VLM so that security can be maintained while reconnecting to the network file server.

SECURITY.VLM. This driver provides packet-level security for data being transferred between workstation and file server. However, when using signatures on packets, you will see some decrease in performance.

TRAN.VLM. The transport driver provides IPXNCP services to the workstation. It is required for communication to the file-server operating system.

Efficient Communication

Windows imposes a strain on the network system because of the large files that are accessed. For example, the main executable file for Microsoft Excel is over 2.5 Mbytes in size. Whenever a user runs the spreadsheet, this file has to be sent from the file server to the workstation. Depending on the version of Microsoft Excel, there are at least 5 executable files that have a total size of almost 4 Mbytes and 12 DLL files that total almost 1 Mbyte in size. This means that each user will download most, if not all, of these files whenever running this application.

Even if your network is running fine now, there may be problems once you install Microsoft Windows. Let's take a look at some of the methods for making the network communications more efficient.

High-speed networks

It wasn't too long ago that we all felt that the 10-Mbit/s Ethernet and the 16-Mbit/s Token Ring transmission speeds on networks were more than adequate for any activities on the network. Windows has now proved that notion wrong. With the large number of files being sent across the network, the system may slow to unacceptable levels.

Today, there are the Ethernet Fast and Ethernet-VG protocols that all run at 100 Mbits/s. These systems run on standard Level 5 copper wiring and do provide a good throughput. However, there are not many network cards, hubs, routers, etc., available for these standards yet, and until the industry settles on a couple of high-speed systems, we will not have too many products supporting these standards.

Other high-speed systems usually involve fiber-optic cabling where transmission speeds are greater than 100 Mbits/s. ATM, FDDI, TCNS, and other systems can provide from 100 Mbits/s to 2 Gbits/s and can handle the high loads that Windows imposes on the network.

Network segmentation

Before you take on the high cost of changing the transmission system on the network, you may want to investigate breaking up the network into segments. Through the use of hubs, bridges, and routers, we have been able to increase the speed of network operations without incurring a huge cost.

Of course, segmenting networks takes some work and may require the help of an outside group, but it can be a great help.

Packet burst

One of the drawbacks of the IPX/SPX protocol used by NetWare is that it is very "chatty." For every packet sent from a workstation to a file server, there will be a returned packet acknowledging the receipt of the first packet. So, for every user on the network only half of the number of packets are actually containing data to be sent between a file server and a workstation.

For instance, if you are running a network that has a packet size of 512 bytes (Ethernet), it will take almost 2000 packets to transmit only 1 Mbyte of data. However, with the IPX/SPX protocol, there will actually be 4000 packets transmitted (2000 packets of data and 2000 packets for acknowledgment).

The packet-burst protocol reduces some of the traffic by only sending an acknowledgment for a group of packets that are sent rather than for each packet. This can have a great effect on network communication speed. (Compare Figs. 5.3 and 5.4.)

When a connection is made between the file server and a workstation, the maximum size of packet burst is negotiated between those two systems. Once

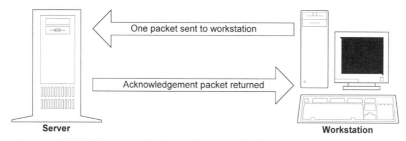

Figure 5.3 IPX/SPX communication without packet burst.

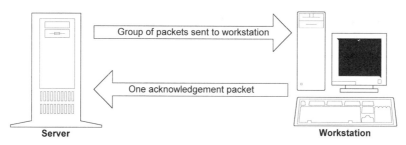

Figure 5.4 IPX/SPX communication with packet burst.

these sizes are determined, the packets are sent in groups. If a packet arrives damaged or doesn't arrive at all, the returning packet advises the sending system that the packet did not arrive. The sender will resend the missing packet, which is then inserted and reassembled at the other end.

If you set the PB BUFFERS = 0 in the NET.CFG file, the packet burst is disabled for that station. Packet burst must be enabled at the file server and at each workstation.

Large Internet packet (LIP). This is the companion to packet burst as it changes the efficiency of the packets themselves regardless of whether they are sent in groups or singly. The default packet size for IPX/SPX is 576 bytes, of which approximately 512 bytes are used for data, with the remainder of the packet containing address and other system information.

Let's return to our example of sending 1 Mbyte of data through the network. With an average of 512 bytes in each packet, it will take 2000 packets to send the 1 Mbyte of data between a file server and a workstation, plus another 2000 packets returned for acknowledgment. With these large files, it doesn't make sense to have such low packet size.

Warning: Before attempting to use LIP, make sure that all routers, bridges, and switches can handle the larger sizes. Some cannot handle packet sizes larger than 576 bytes, although that is becoming rare today.

With LIP enabled, the server and the workstation negotiate the largest packet size, and communication can end up with a size of 2 kbytes, 4 kbytes, or higher. Even if the 2-kbyte packet size is used, only 505 packets will be needed to transmit a 1-Mbyte file and, if packet burst is used, 8 packets will be returned for acknowledgment. Tables 5.1 and 5.2 show the calculations for LIP and packet burst. All sizes shown in these calculations are approximate and can vary depending on the protocol used and other factors. Calculations for packet burst and LIP are shown in these tables regarding total packets, packet size, etc. As with packet burst, LIP is enabled at the workstation by

TABLE 5.1   Data transmission with packet burst

Packet size	4096 bytes
Data size	4032 bytes
Packets transmitted	254
Packet-burst group size	64
Acknowledgment packets	4
Total packets	68

**TABLE 5.2   Data transmission of a
1-Mbyte file without packet burst**

Packet size	576 bytes
Data size	512 bytes
Packets transmitted	2000
Acknowledgment packets	2000
Total packets	4000

the command under the NetWare DOS requester section of NET.CFG or LARGE INTERNET PACKETS set to ON, or is disabled by setting it to OFF.

Warning: When setting the size of packets, make sure that the protocol you use does not transmit packets of a size greater than 8000. Windows cannot handle any packets larger than that size, and any packets received will be accepted by the network interface card but not handled in Windows. This can cause Windows to hang or the applications to start generating strange errors. Also remember that it is a good idea to make a backup of the Windows files before installing these new drivers. There is always a possibility that some of the new files may not work properly with your system.

Network Messages

NetWare's SEND command allows users and administrators to send messages from the console or another station that will appear either on the first line or the 25th line of the screen (depending on version of NetWare client software). If a message is sent through this method to a station running Windows, it will not be seen until the user starts a DOS session or exits Windows.

Some messages are critical and need to be seen by the user immediately. The NWPOPUP.EXE file should be added to the LOAD line of the WIN.INI file so that it will be started whenever Windows is loaded.

Installation of Client Files

The next task is to copy the files found in the directories to the appropriate Windows directories. To install the Unicode files (found in the VLMDRVS directory), create a directory under Windows (if it doesn't exist already) named NLS and copy the Unicode files to that directory.

Novell Technical Support Windows Diagnostic (NTSWD)

It is not uncommon to have minor problems when running Windows and NetWare software. For example, a broadcast message may not be seen in the NWPOPUP.EXE dialog box. The problem may be utility files that aren't loaded properly or a similar problem.

This utility will report on which dynamic link libraries are loaded (Fig. 5.5), what VxDs are loaded (Fig. 5.6), which NetWare modules are running in memory, and which programs are running in Windows.

This information can be printed out or saved to a file, and was originally used by Novell Technical Support. To install this utility, copy to the Windows directory and then create an icon for it (see Fig. 5.7) in program manager with the parameters listed. Figure 5.8 shows a sample output from the utility.

Figure 5.5 NTSWD dynamic link libraries descriptions.

Figure 5.6 NTSWD program description.

Figure 5.7 NTSWD icon setup.

```
Loaded Program Info:
PROGMAN          C:\WINDOWS\PROGMAN.EXE
Handle: 627      Usage Count: 1
3:11 AM 11/1/1993
CHKSUM: 2B02

CLIPSRV          C:\WINDOWS\CLIPSRV.EXE
Handle: 1407     Usage Count: 1
3:11 AM 11/1/1993
CHKSUM: 28B6

NTSWD            C:\WINDR1\NTSWD\NTSWD.EXE
Handle: D1F      Usage Count: 1
1:32 PM 10/6/1994
VERSION: 1.04 Novell Technical Support Windows Diagnostics
CHKSUM: 5331

Loaded DLL Information:

KERNEL           C:\WINDOWS\SYSTEM\KRNL386.EXE
Handle: 10F      Usage Count: 26
3:11 AM          11/1/1993
CHKSUM: 5B1A

SYSTEM           C:\WINDOWS\SYSTEM\SYSTEM.DRV
Handle: 13F      Usage Count: 17
3:11 AM          11/1/1993
CHKSUM: 95DD

KEYBOARD         C:\WINDOWS\SYSTEM\KEYBOARD.DRV
Handle: 147      Usage Count: 19
3:11 AM          11/1/1993
CHKSUM: 711

MOUSE            C:\WINDOWS\SYSTEM\LMOUSE.DRV
Handle: 15F      Usage Count: 17
11:16 AM         3/11/1993
CHKSUM: E903

DISPLAY          C:\WINDOWS\SYSTEM\CPQAVGA.DRV
Handle: 1BF      Usage Count: 18
12:00 PM         4/28/1993
CHKSUM: AFA2

SOUND            C:\WINDOWS\SYSTEM\MMSOUND.DRV
Handle: 1DF      Usage Count: 17
3:11 AM          11/1/1993
CHKSUM: 60D

COMM  C:\WINDOWS\SYSTEM\COMM.DRV
Handle: 22F      Usage Count: 17
3:11 AM          11/1/1993
CHKSUM: B63D
```

Figure 5.8 Sample printout of NTSWD.

6

Installing Microsoft Windows for Workgroups

Installing Windows for Workgroups requires some forethought and planning because decisions made here will have a great impact on the future operation of Windows. If you are installing Windows on a stand-alone system, the decisions are quite simple. Add a network to the mix, and decisions become more complex. Of course, adding a network also gives much more flexibility than does a stand-alone system.

There are five main methods of installing Microsoft Windows on a network. We will explain each method of installation in this chapter.

Everyone wants to know which is the "right" method of installation. Just like many choices in computers, the installation method chosen depends on a variety of factors, including type of network installed, user needs, and type of workstation and file-server hardware.

In this chapter, we will take an in-depth look at each of these installation methods to determine which is the best method for you. We will assume that you are installing Windows for Workgroups v3.11 as it is the best version for network connectivity.

Before deciding which method of installation you want to employ, there is a fundamental decision required. These methods fall into two categories: convenience for the network administrator or convenience for the user. Some installation methods are easy, require little maintenance, and are very reliable. However, these methods usually result in user dissatisfaction or users returning to the DOS system to run their non-Windows applications. If the resources are available, minimizing user problems is far preferable to making it convenient for technical staff.

Installing Windows is similar to the construction of a house. If the workers take the time to install the front door properly, putting a high-quality lock on the door, it will take them longer to complete the job. If a lock is not installed in the door, the residents of the house will have to go to a lot of trouble each night to ensure that their house is secure by using other methods to secure the front door. Installing the lock will inconvenience the construction workers once, but not installing the lock will inconvenience the residents every night.

Enterprise Windows Installation

When installing Windows in an organization, it is imperative to make the installation as efficient as possible. You will want to be able to start the installation at the workstation and run uninterrupted without further work. Regardless of which method you want to use for installation, there are several steps you should take to prepare the file server for these multiple installations (see also Fig. 6.1).

Windows master copy setup

1. Check file-server volume to see if there is at least 75 Mbytes of free disk space.
2. Create a directory in the root named WFW (or any other directory name you choose).
3. Copy all files to this directory from the floppy disks using the /a parameter (e.g., SETUP /A).

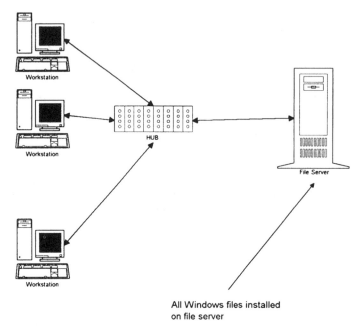

All Windows files installed
on file server

Figure 6.1 Windows installed on file server.

4. Copy NetWare shell drivers to the WFW directory. You can place these files in another directory if you choose as the SETUP program will ask you for the location of the NetWare files during installation.
5. Modify .SRC, .SHH, and .INF files as desired (described later).
6. Copy special drivers (e.g., printer or video drivers) to WFW directory.
7. Set rights for users or technicians who will be installing Windows.

You now have a basic set of Windows files on the file server. Now, to install WFW, go to any workstation, log in to the file server, and run SETUP.

Local Hard Disk

Installing Windows on the local hard disk is the simplest and most reliable. All executables, DLLs, and configuration files are placed on the local hard disk and can be run from that location. (See Fig. 6.2.)

Even though Windows is installed on the local hard disk, it is still possible to access a NetWare file server without any impairment. Windows and DOS applications can be run from the local hard disk whether they are located on the local hard disk or on the network file server.

Installing on the local hard disk means there are no performance problems as all files to run Windows are located on the hard disk. If the network is

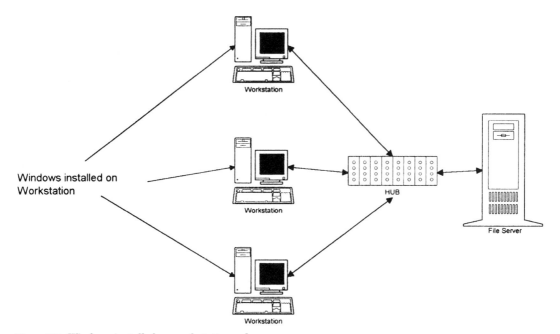

Figure 6.2 Windows installed on workstation only.

down or the communication system not running properly, the user can continue operation because everything is self-contained.

The major drawback to a local installation is the lack of flexibility. All groups, items, colors, drivers, and other unique configurations are available only on the local hard disk. A user who moves to another computer will lose all the modifications to Windows and may not have access to applications and may also encounter a different configuration that makes it difficult to run the application(s).

One benefit of a local area network is the ability to move from workstation to workstation as needed or to log in simultaneously to run different applications at the same time. Users will be happy with this method of access because it is flexible.

Because everything is contained on the local hard disk, it is imperative that a backup system be installed to include the local drive.

Installation is simple by running the SETUP program without any switches, and the express installation method will work just fine. The directory can be the standard C:\WINDOWS or any other name you want.

File-Server Installation

This is in contrast to the local installation, where all the files are placed on the file server rather than the local hard disk. Installation is also quite simple because rather than specifying drive C: as the location for installation, it can be drive F: or some other network drive letter.

The benefit of installing everything on the file server is for each user to run their own version of Windows from any workstation at any time. This is the ultimate in flexibility because the installation of Windows is separated from any workstation on the network.

There are a few things to be aware of in this installation method. First, there will be a heavy penalty to pay in network performance. Windows consists of many different executable files and dynamic link libraries (DLLs) that are loaded and unloaded frequently. Each time one of these files is loaded, it must be copied from the file server over the network communications system to the workstation. Frequent transmission of these files will impair performance of the network.

While installing all files on a server is simple for a network installation, the price of impaired network communication may be too high, and another method must be developed to handle network needs. The network communications traffic problems with a file-server installation must be evaluated against the potential problem of low disk space on a client station.

Split Installation

In an effort to avoid the network performance penalty in the previous installation, we can split the installation of Windows between the file server and

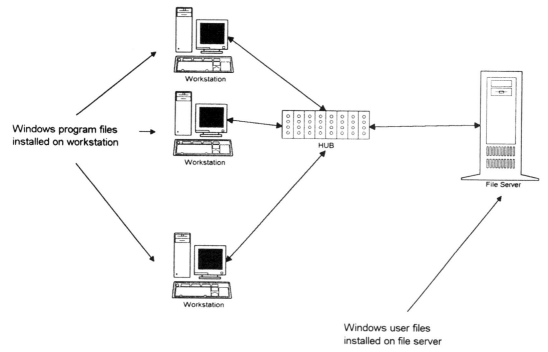

Figure 6.3 Split installation of Windows.

the workstation (see Fig. 6.3). This splitting will give us the flexibility we need but not impair network performance.

To do this, we need to combine the network installation mode of Windows SETUP with a complete installation of files on the local station. The first step is to create a copy of all Windows files on the workstation hard disk. This is done by installing WFW with the switch: SETUP /A. This method is not a true installation but just expands the files from the floppy disks and stores them on the workstation or network file-server hard disk.

Now, there is a complete set of every file on the hard disk that will be able to support any configuration the user wants to run. This is important because we don't know what executable files the user needs to access, and so we place every file on the disk. When expanded, these files will take over 30 Mbytes of disk space. This is approximately double the size of a normal installation, but it ensures that there won't be any problems later.

For purposes of this example, we will assume an installation in drive F:. While it is not necessary to install user files in a specific set of directories, we will choose several directory names for examples.

A master directory containing a unique directory for each user and their customized Windows files must be created. Figure 6.4 shows the structure of these directories.

```
F:\-----    |LOGIN
            |SYSTEM
            |PUBLIC
            |WINUSER---   |JROBB
                          |LFINE
                          |WROBERTSON
                          |EKOOP
```

Figure 6.4 File-server directory structure.

To install the user files, use the network switch: SETUP /N. This only installs the files that are directly related to the customized needs of the user.

SYSTEM.INI	_DEFAULT.PIF
WIN.INI	DOSPRMPT.PIF
SPART.PAR	REG.DAT
WIN.COM	MAINO.GRP
WININI.W31	AUTOEXEC.WIN
SYSINI.W31	CONFIG.WIN
BOOTLOG.TXT	ACCESSOO.GRP
PROGMAN.INI	NETWORKO.GRP
NCDINFO.INI	GAMESO.GRP
SERIALNO.INI	WFWSYS.CFG
IFSHLP.SYS	SHARES.PWL
EMM386.EXE	NET.EXE
CONTROL.INI	NET.MSG
HIMEM.SYS	NETH.MSG
MSCDEX.EXE	STARTUP1.GRP
RAMDRIVE.SYS	WINFILE.INI
SMARTDRV.EXE	SYSTEM.CLN
WININIT.EXE	WIN.CLN
WINVER.EXE	DIR.LST

These files are the .INI files for user or system preferences and WIN.COM that is customized to display a certain opening screen for a specific type of monitor. The original files will take only approximately 140 kbytes of space, which could grow to 300 kbytes over time with the addition of other user files for applications and utilities.

To use this configuration, you need to start Windows with a batch file that looks like the one in Fig. 6.5. The first step is to map a search drive to the

```
@echo off
cls
f:
map ins s1:=sys:windows
cd\winuser\%!
win.com
map del s1:
f:
cd\
```

Figure 6.5 Sample Windows batch file.

hard drive of the workstation so the generic executable files will be run from the local drive. Redirecting the command to NULL prevents the map command from being shown on the screen. We change directories by creating an environmental variable in the system login script that may look like DOS set login=%LOGIN_NAME.

After running Windows, we can delete the search path to clean up the mappings and return the user to their original state. As long as each workstation is set up the same way, this system will work just fine. If additional user convenience is required, the batch file could be changed as shown in Fig. 6.6.

These changes to the batch files check for the existence of a user environmental variable, key Windows file on the local drive, and the starting file on the file server. If any one of these elements is missing, Windows will not start.

Now users can gain access to their own Windows setup from any workstation on the network. This gives the best combination of communication efficiency and flexibility.

Installation Issues

Now that we have looked at the overview of a Windows installation, let's take a look at some specific issues. Before starting the installation, check to ensure that these requirements have been met.

DOS and Windows Versions

While Windows will run with a variety of DOS versions, it will not run with versions older than 3.3. Windows for Workgroups can be installed over the top of Windows 3.1, which will keep the groups intact. If the current version is v3.0 or older, it cannot be upgraded to Windows for Workgroups and must be installed as a new system.

```
@echo off
cls
f:
if not exist f:\windows\gdi.exe goto error1
if not exist f:\winuser\%1\win.com goto error2
map ins s1:=sys:windows>NUL:
cd\winuser\%!
win.com
map del s1:>NUL:
f:
cd\
goto end

:error1
cls
echo Windows users files not found - please contact system administrator
pause
goto end

:error2
cls
echo Windows user not setup - please contact system administrator
pause
goto end


:end
```

Figure 6.6 Expanded Windows batch file.

Disk space

When calculating the space needs of a local or network installation, refer to Fig. 6.7 to determine the approximate space required.

Installation Type	Windows for Workgroups 3.11	Windows 3.1
Full (normal)	18MB	9.5MB
Upgrade (additional disk space)	9MB	5.2MB
Network Master (all files - /A)	21MB	15.3MB
Network user setup (/N)	1.2MB	.3MB

Figure 6.7 Windows file sizes.

Setup Alternatives

There are a number of options available for installation in addition to the /n parameter mentioned earlier.

/a

This is a simple yet important option that uncompresses each file and copies it to the directory you have specified. This does not create the .INI files or the WIN.COM file; it just copies all the files from the floppy disks to a network or local hard disk.

The compressed files are named on the floppy disks with an underscore as the last character of the extension. This process copies the files (usually to a file server), and creates a new name by replacing the last character with the proper character (e.g., GDI.EX_ is renamed GDI.EXE). After the files are renamed, they are flagged as "read only." This copy of all files gives you the option of using it for installation or for running Windows in conjunction with the /n setup described earlier.

/b

By specifying this parameter, you can install Windows on a computer that has a monochrome monitor (which is rarely used these days).

/h

When you want to have full control over the installation of Windows, the /h parameter allows you to specify default settings. If you are installing Windows on a number of machines, you are much more efficient to use this option and automate the installation.

```
[sysinfo]
showsysinfo = yes
[configuration]
machine = ibm_compatible
display = vga
mouse = ps2mouse
network = wfwnet/00026000
keyboard = t4s0enha
language = enu
kblayout = nodll

[windir]
c:\windows

[userinfo]
; If you are setting up Windows across a network, the [userinfo] section
; will be ignored.
;
"John Q. Public"              ; User Name (30 chars MAX) (required)
"Microsoft Corporation"       ; Company Name (30 chars MAX) (optional)
xx-xxx-xxxx-xxxx              ; Product No. (16 chars MAX) (optional)
```

```
[network]
; Network = wfwnet/00026000
MultiNet =
UserName =
WorkGroup =
ComputerName =
ShowNames = yes
MakeProtocol = no

[protocol.ini]
; Sections to be deleted from the .shh file in order to make protocol.ini
sysinfo =
configuration =
windir =
userinfo =
network =
protocol.ini =
dontinstall =
options =
printers =
endinstall =

[dontinstall]
accessories                    ; Do NOT install accessories
readmes                        ; Do NOT install readme files
games                          ; Do NOT install games
screensavers                   ; Do NOT install screen savers
bitmaps                        ; Do NOT install bitmaps

[options]
setupapps                      ; Setup applications already on hard disk
autosetupapps                  ; Set up all applications on hard disk
tutorial                       ; Start Windows Tutorial at the end of Setup

[printers]
"HP LaserJet III",LPT1:
[endinstall]
configfiles = save
endopt      = exit
```

This file can be modified as long as you follow the rules. You can customize it any way you want.

/I

This option is used when there are hardware problems that prevent Windows from installing properly. Normally, when Windows setup is running, a check is made of the hardware to detect what is currently connected. However, sometimes this check may cause the computer to hang and prevent installation. As a last-ditch effort, use this switch and perform the installation. Sometimes, installing Windows with this switch will circumvent the problem and therefore Windows will still run properly. Be aware that if you use this option, hardware incompatibility may result in the future.

/n

This option is the companion to the /a command. While the administrative option copies all the Windows files to a network server, this option sets up the user portion of Windows to be run in conjunction with the full copy on the file server.

/o

This switch specifies the SETUP.INF file and where to find it. The format is /o:setup.inf.

/s

This switch specifies the SETUP.INF file on the Windows installation disks and where to find it. The format is /s:a:\setup.inf.

/t

This parameter is not an installation option but performs a scan of the computer checking for TSRs that are incompatible with Windows.

Installation setup files

Windows uses a number of files as reference for the installation and setup process. These files all have the extension of .INF and can be modified for your own use. The first file used by the setup program is SETUP.INF. It is on disk 1 and is used by both the DOS and Windows setup utilities.

SETUP.INF

The SETUP.INF file is the main file that the setup program uses to load and configure Windows. There are a number of changes you can make to this file to customize it to your needs. We will look at each section and describe how it operates and how you can modify it. Although it is not possible to show the entire file here, a few entries will be shown in each section. To see the whole file, just bring the ASCII text into an editor of your choice.

When modifying any of these files, make sure the editor isn't a word processor, as formatting (e.g., line wrap) will ruin the file. Of course, making a backup copy of this and any file you modify is a good practice.

Setup

This setting determines where the online help is located so that you can press <F1> and get more information about the installation steps.

```
[setup]
    help = setup.hlp
```

Run

If you have your own installation programs or want to install a Windows application automatically at the end of the setup program, place the executable file names here, and they will run in the order shown. One minor word of warning: Windows applications, because they can run in conjunction, will all load first before they will run. You will see the application load, the screen will clear, and then the next application will load. It looks very confusing at first but is not an error or problem.

```
[run]
app1.exe
app2.exe
```

Dialog

The dialog section of this file is just a series of captions and text settings during the installation process. You can modify these virtually any way you want to customize them for your organization. We have introduced some modifications to these entries (shown in bold).

```
[dialog]
    caption   = "Windows Setup for ABC Company"
    exit      = "Exit Windows Setup"
    title     = "Installing Windows for Workgroups 3.11 for ABC Company"
    options   = "In addition to installing Windows, you can:"
    printwait = "Please wait while Setup configures your printer(s)..."
copywait = "Welcome to Microsoft Windows for Workgroups 3.11!\n\n   - If
you're new to Windows, see 'A Guided Tour of\n Microsoft Windows' in the
User's Guide."
copywait5 = "Make sure you register your copy of Microsoft Windows
for\nWorkgroups 3.11. When you register, Microsoft will:\n\n   - Notify you
of product updates and new product releases.\n\n   - Send you a FREE Windows
newsletter."
```

A modified version of copywait is

```
copywait = "Welcome to Microsoft Windows for Workgroups 3.11!\n\n Please call
extension 5000 if you have any questions or problems with Microsoft Windows."
copywait5 = "Training for Microsoft Windows will be held in the employee annex
on Tuesday\n\n and Thursday afternoons for the next six weeks - please call
extension 2100 to reserve a seat."
```

Data

This section determines how much disk space is required for the different methods of installation and other parameters involved with installation. The first value on the left-hand side of the column is the type of installation selected by the user. The first value to the right of the equal sign is the maximum amount of disk space required for installation. The next value is the minimum amount of disk space required.

```
[data]
; Disk space required
; <type of setup> = <Full install space>, <Min install space>

upd2x386full = 19000000,14000000 ; 19.0 Mb, 14.0 Mb   2.x -> WFW 3.11
upd30386full = 14500000,10500000 ; 14.5 Mb, 10.5 Mb   3.0 -> WFW 3.11
upd31386full = 10500000, 7500000 ; 10.5 Mb,  7.5 Mb   3.1 -> WFW 3.11
updWW386full =  6000000, 3500000 ;  6.0 Mb,  3.5 Mb   WFW 3.1  -> WFW 3.11
updW1386full =  3000000, 2000000 ;  3.0 Mb,  2.0 Mb   WFW 3.11 -> WFW 3.11
new386full   = 19000000,14000000 ; 19.0 Mb, 14.0 Mb

netadmin    = 29000000           ; 29.0 Mb
netadminupd = 29000000           ; 29.0 Mb
upd2x386net = 1300000            ;  1.3 Mb
upd30386net = 1300000            ;  1.3 Mb
upd31386net = 1300000            ;  1.3 Mb
new386net   = 1300000,1300000    ;  1.3 Mb, 1.3 Mb
```

Options. The values shown here are defaults, and some of the items can be modified. We recommend only changing the following parameters:

dafter. This is the default installation directory that is shown on the setup screen. It can be changed by the user, so if you know a standard directory name you want for Windows, make the change here.

defdevdir. This directory contains device drivers (in WFWG only) for networking and you can specify another directory without any problems.

Welcome. The welcome screen is just text and can be changed as desired.

Tutor. The tutor entry determines which file will be run at the end of the setup, where setup asks if you want to run the tutorial or skip it. The file specified will be the tutorial file executed. If you want another tutorial run at this point, then enter the executable path and file name.

NetSetup. This variable can be set to TRUE and will force users into a network (/n) installation no matter what they specify when running SETUP. It is not a foolproof method of security, but it can slow those who want to circumvent the setup process. If you have stored all the Windows files on the file server (with the SETUP /A command), you can flag the rights to this file as "read only" and "file scan," which makes it available for setup, but the user cannot change it.

Mousedrv. If you want the mouse to be available during the setup, then leave this value to TRUE. If there are problems running the mouse during setup, then set it to FALSE.

```
startup   = WIN.COM
dafter    = C:\WINDOWS
defdevdir = C:\NET
shortname = Windows
welcome   = "Microsoft Windows for Workgroups 3.11"
```

```
deflang    = enu
defxlat    = 437
defkeydll  = usadll
register   = "regedit /s /u setup.reg"
tutor      = "wintutor.exe "
winsetup   = "winsetup.exe"
NetSetup   = FALSE
MouseDrv   = TRUE
partial    = FALSE
Version    = "3.11.050"
dosmemK    = 410
```

DOS utilities. This is simply a list of the DOS driver utilities and their version numbers that are being shipped with Windows.

```
himem.sys.hi  = 0x0310
himem.sys.lo  = 0x0300
smartdrv.exe  = 0x0500
ramdrive.sys  = 0x18F5
emm386.exe    = 0x0430
```

Windows setup. There are two phases to the setup: DOS and Windows. The DOS setup runs long enough to install the base Windows system and then start Windows. It then runs the remainder of the installation inside Windows. This section determines what to load and the best method of starting Windows. There is no need to change this section. For example, neatness freaks are convinced they need to remove the space between the quotation mark and the "k" in the execcmd command. That will only result in problems with starting Windows during installation because the space is there for separation between calling an executable and this kernel.

```
[winexec]
    execstd   = "dosx.exe "
    execcmd   = " krnl386.exe /b /q:"
    exechimem = "xmsmmgr.exe"
    himemcmd  = ""
    Krnl386   = 1:krnl386.exe
    dosx      = 2:dosx.exe
```

Setup disks. Because Windows can't be shipped on one floppy disk (obviously), there is a need to identify each of the six disks and where certain files are located so that the installation routine doesn't get confused. This section lists the disks and search information. The first number is the disk number and corresponds to the number on the floppy disk.

```
; Names of the disks Setup can prompt for.
[disks]
    1 =. ,"Microsoft Windows for Workgroups 3.11 Disk 1",disk1
    2 =. ,"Microsoft Windows for Workgroups 3.11 Disk 2",disk2
    3 =. ,"Microsoft Windows for Workgroups 3.11 Disk 3",disk3
    4 =. ,"Microsoft Windows for Workgroups 3.11 Disk 4",disk4
    5 =. ,"Microsoft Windows for Workgroups 3.11 Disk 5",disk5
    6 =. ,"Microsoft Windows for Workgroups 3.11 Disk 6",disk6
```

```
    7 =. ,"Microsoft Windows for Workgroups 3.11 Disk 7",disk7
    8 =. ,"Microsoft Windows for Workgroups 3.11 Disk 8",disk8
```

The dot to the right of the equal sign is included for searching purposes. Because Windows can be installed from floppy disks or a network server, this dot signifies the current directory so that setup will look there first and then to the floppy disk if not found in the current directory.

The string inside the quotes is just a text identifier that is displayed on the screen when the next disk is prompted for. We have seen some people create their own installation disks for users, and this string could be modified to show other information.

The disk1..disk6 entries at the end of the line reference small files contained on the disks with those names as file names. When the setup program finds these files on the disk, it knows there is a good probability that the files are there also and looks for the selected files. The number for each of these disks is important because the files listed below are preceded by a number that shows what disk it is on.

```
[disks]
    1 =. ,"Microsoft Windows for Workgroups 3.11 Disk 1",disk1
    2 =. ,"Microsoft Windows for Workgroups 3.11 Disk 2",disk2
    3 =. ,"Microsoft Windows for Workgroups 3.11 Disk 3",disk3
    4 =. ,"Microsoft Windows for Workgroups 3.11 Disk 4",disk4
    5 =. ,"Microsoft Windows for Workgroups 3.11 Disk 5",disk5
    6 =. ,"Microsoft Windows for Workgroups 3.11 Disk 6",disk6
    7 =. ,"Microsoft Windows for Workgroups 3.11 Disk 7",disk7
    8 =. ,"Microsoft Windows for Workgroups 3.11 Disk 8",disk8
```

Windows files.   This section shows the files that will be copied to the Windows and system directories. The number that precedes each section is the disk on which it can be found. If you want to add your own files, create an entry in the section above and then add your own files listed below.

```
[windows]
    1:setup.hlp
    1:setup.txt
    2:win.src,    Net
    2:system.src, Net
    1:winsetup.exe
    1:winhelp.exe
    1:control.hlp

[windows.system]
    1:gdi.exe
    1:user.exe
    1:win.cnf
    2:lzexpand.dll
    2:ver.dll
    2:shell.dll
    1:wfwsetup.dll
    1:commdlg.dll
    2:commctrl.dll
    1:ncdw.dll
```

```
        2:sconfig.dll

[windows.system.386]
        2:cpwin386.cpl

[386max]
        2:386max.vxd
        2:windows.lod

[bluemax]
        2:bluemax.vxd
        2:windows.lod
```

Default shell. Almost everyone uses the program manager as the default shell for Windows, but if you wish to use another one, you must supply the name and the disk information listed above for it to be copied. TabWorks and other shells are available to replace the program manager. You can also change it later in SYSTEM.INI by changing the shell command (see Fig. 6.8).

```
[shell]
        progman.exe, "Program Manager"
```

Video drivers. This section references the drivers used for the monitors according to the type of video standard you will be using. By default, the standard drivers are installed, and if you want a nonstandard monitor installed, you will have to add a line for the codes yourself. Some installation routines from manufacturers will do it for you. For many, it is a do-it-yourself project. Contained in these lines are the video driver name (e.g., VGA.DRV), the grabber files (used for importing data from DOS programs), and drivers to provide virtual displays while in enhanced mode. The lines for these drivers are shown below. Each line is a different driver, but because of the page-width limitations of this book, we cannot show them to you on one line. Each line

```
[boot]
 .
 .
 .

;shell=progman.exe
shell=tabworks.exe
network.drv=netware.drv
language.dll=
 .
 .
```

Figure 6.8 SYSTEM.INI file specifying default shell.

adheres to the following format: driver type = driver file for Windows, description of driver, resolution, 286grabber, logo code, Virtual Display Driver, 386 grabber, file name for EGA drivers, Microsoft logo, additional information.

Notes: The driver resolution is actually an aspect ratio that uses three numbers to specify what resolution will be used. The logo code is the LGO file, which determines how to display the logo, and the logo data is the RLE (run-length encoded) file where the actual logo resides. Be aware that under certain conditions, changing the description of the drive can cause problems because it might not match up with other descriptive strings and the wrong driver may be installed.

```
[display]
.
.
.
vga =2:vga.drv,"VGA","100,96,96", , 2:vgalogo.lgo,
x:*vddvga,2:vga.3gr,,2:vgalogo.rle
vga30=2:vga.drv,"VGA (version 3.0)","100,96,96",,
2:vgalogo.lgo,2:vddvga30.386, 2:vga30.3gr,,          2:vgalogo.rle
svga=2:supervga.drv,"Super VGA (800x600, 16 colors)","100,96,96",,
2:vgalogo.lgo, x:*vddvga,      2:vga.3gr,,2:vgalogo.rle
8vga480=1:svga256.drv,"Super VGA (640x480, 256 colors) ","100,96,96",,
2:vgalogo.lgo,2:vddsvga.386,  2:vgadib.3gr,,2:vgalogo.rle, svga640
.
.
.
```

Existing monitors. The current monitor will be detected during installation and an attempt made to match it to the appropriate drive. This section has a listing of a wide spectrum of video standards. If yours is not in this list, a warning will be displayed on the screen.

```
[display.old]
8514     = "8514/a"
cga      = "CGA"
egahibw  = "EGA Black and White (286 only)"
egahires = "EGA"
egamono  = "EGA Monochrome (286 only)"
hercules = "Hercules Monochrome"
hpmulti  = "HP CGA Display"
mcga     = "IBM MCGA (286 only)"
olibw    = "Olivetti/AT&T Monochrome or PVC Display"
plasma   = "Compaq Portable Plasma"
tiga1    = "TIGA"
v7vga    = "Video 7"
vga      = "VGA"
vgamono  = "VGA with Monochrome display"
xga16    = "XGA"
```

Optional video descriptions. This section is not required but can contain other information about the video drivers including file name to be copied, where it will be copied, whether an .INI file is to be created, etc. Rarely will you have to change anything in this section.

```
[8514]
,,system.ini,8514.DRV,"dpi=","dpi=120"
```

Selecting keyboards. If you have a different type of keyboard or if you want a language different from English, then use these drivers, which bring different options to Windows. Normally, you won't have to change this unless you want to add a driver for your installation on more than one machine. By inserting the code for the keyboard driver here, installation becomes much easier. The codepages determine what codes the keyboard will be translated into and enable you to buy any system and make it work in almost any language.

```
[keyboard.drivers]
kbd   = 2:keyboard.drv
kbdhp = 2:kbdhp.drv

[keyboard.types]
.
.

.
t4s0enha = "Enhanced 101 or 102 key US and Non US keyboards"   ,nodll
t3s0hp1  = "Hewlett-Packard Vectra keyboard (DIN)"              ,nodll
t4s40oliv = "Olivetti 101/102 A keyboard"                       ,nodll
.

.
.

[keyboard.tables]
.
.

.
bridll = 2:kbduk.dll , "British"
cafdll = 2:kbdfc.dll , "Canadian Multilingual"
dandll = 2:kbdda.dll , "Danish"
dutdll = 2:kbdne.dll , "Dutch"
gerdll = 2:kbdgr.dll , "German"
icedll = 2:kbdic.dll , "Icelandic"
itadll = 2:kbdit.dll , "Italian"
.

.
.
nodll  =            , "US"
usadll = 2:kbdus.dll , "US"
usddll = 2:kbddv.dll , "US-Dvorak"
usxdll = 2:kbdusx.dll, "US-International"
.

.
.

[codepages]
863 = 2:xlat863.bin, 2:vga863.fon, 1:dosapp.fon, "Canadian-French (863)"
861 = 2:xlat861.bin, 2:vga861.fon, 2:app850.fon, "Icelandic (861)"
865 = 2:xlat865.bin, 2:vga865.fon, 2:app850.fon, "Nordic (865)"
850 = 2:xlat850.bin, 2:vga850.fon, 2:app850.fon, "Multi-Lingual (850)"
860 = 2:xlat860.bin, 2:vga860.fon, 1:dosapp.fon, "Portuguese (860)"
437 =              ,              , 1:dosapp.fon, "English (437)"
```

Mice. While the official generic term for this section is *pointing devices,* most often it is a mouse. Since Windows handles drivers internally for mice and other pointing devices, this section determines what will be used. Information includes the internal device name, what driver will be used, description of the device, what driver will be used for DOS applications in the enhanced mode, and a section for other information about the mouse setup. Below this section are additional setup items that can be used to fine-tune the mouse drivers; these items are referenced by the name given in the last field (optional section). Below that are driver listings for mouse drivers in DOS.

```
[pointing.device]
lmouse   = 2:lmouse.drv,   "Logitech",                           2:lvmd.386,
lmouse
ps2mouse = 2:mouse.drv,    "Microsoft, or IBM PS/2",          x:*vmd
genius1  = 2:mscmouse.drv, "Genius serial mouse on COM1"    , 2:mscvmd.386
genius2  = 2:msc3bc2.drv,  "Genius serial mouse on COM2"    , 2:mscvmd.386
msmouse2 = 2:mscmouse.drv, "Mouse Systems serial or bus mouse", 2:mscvmd.386
msmouse1 = 2:msc3bc2.drv,  "Mouse Systems serial mouse on COM2",2:mscvmd.386
nomouse  = 2:nomouse.drv,  "No mouse or other pointing device", x:*vmd

[lmouse]
2:lmouse.com,0:,,,,

[dos.mouse.drivers]
;mouse.sys   = !:mouse.SYS,    "MS Dos Mouse driver .SYS ver 7.XX"
;mouse.com   = !:mouse.com,    "MS Dos Mouse driver .COM ver 7.XX"
```

Fonts. The fonts listed here are used for the screen display and are built around the selection of video drivers.

```
[sysfonts]
2:vgasys.fon,"VGA (640x480) resolution System Font", "100,96,96"
2:8514sys.fon,"8514/a (1024x768) resolution System Font", "100,120,120"
  .
  .
  .
```

File copy. Virtually everything in this file involves copying files from the installation disks to the Windows directory. This section is designed for the express purpose of copying program and utility files to the directory. It is an extremely simple format. The files are listed From (including a disk number) and To, with the To field showing a 0: (copy to the Windows directory) or a 0:system (copy to system directory below Windows directory) entry.

The win.copy.net.win386 and win.copy.win386 are intended for workstations on the network that have a 386 CPU or higher; the win.devices is a copy for all workstations. The items referenced in the win.copy.net.win386 and win.copy.win386 are not files but sections later on in the file that are to have file names in them. This multilayered method of copying and referencing is common throughout Windows, which makes following the logic very difficult. (Maybe Microsoft purposely made it that way!)

```
[win.copy.net.win386]
; copy this section for network setup on 386 machines
   #net,      0:

[win.copy.win386]
```

```
; copy this section for full setup on 386 machines
    #net,       0:
    #win.shell, 0:
    #pwin386,   0:system
    #mapi,      0:system
    #win.other, 0:system

[net]
    6:CONTROL.SRC,      "Windows User Files"
    6:WINVER
    6:WININIT.EXE,      "Setup System-Initialization Utility"

[win.devices]
; These devices will be copied on all machines
    6:HIMEM.SYS,        "XMS Memory Manager"
    6:SMARTDRV.EXE,     "Disk Caching Program"
    6:RAMDRIVE.SYS,     "RAM Drive Program"
    6:IFSHLP.SYS,       "File System Manager"

[win.devices.win386]
; These devices will be copied on 386 machines only
    6:HIMEM.SYS,        "XMS Memory Manager"
    4:EMM386.EXE,       "LIM Expanded Memory Manager"
    6:SMARTDRV.EXE,     "Disk Caching Program"
    6:RAMDRIVE.SYS,     "RAM Drive Program"
    6:IFSHLP.SYS,       "File System Manager"

[win.other]
    6:WIN87EM.DLL,      "Windows System Component"
    6:SYSEDIT.EXE
    6:NDDEAPI.DLL
    .
    .
    .

[mapi]
    4:AB.DLL,           "Windows Mail System Component"
    5:DEMILAYR.DLL
    .
    .
    .

[win.shell]
    4:PROGMAN.EXE,      "Program Manager"
    6:TASKMAN.EXE,      "Task Manager"
    3:WINFILE.EXE,      "File Manager"
    4:CLIPBRD.EXE,      "ClipBook Viewer"
    6:CLIPSRV.EXE,      "ClipBook Server"
    6:CONTROL.EXE,      "Control Panel"
    .
    .
    .
```

File deletion. If there are files on the hard disk of the local station you want deleted, you can place the executable file names of these files here. This feature is designed to remove files from older version upgrades, but you can also use it for your needs.

```
[DelFiles]
    tmsr?.fon
```

```
helv?.fon
swapfile.exe
kernel.exe
```
.
.
.

Miscellaneous files.   Yet another section for copying files from the installation disks to the Windows directories. The format is disk number, file name, description (for icon), size, and reference to other sections below.

```
[win.apps]
   5:CALC.EXE,        "Calculator"                   ,  43072, calc
   4:CARDFILE.EXE,    "Cardfile"                     ,  93184, cardfile
   6:CLOCK.EXE,       "Clock"                        ,  16416, clock
   5:NOTEPAD.EXE,     "Notepad"                      ,  32736, notepad
   3:PBRUSH.EXE,      "Paintbrush"                   , 190142, pbrush
   3:TERMINAL.EXE,    "Terminal"                     , 148160, terminal
   6:CALC.HLP,        "Calculator Help"              ,  18076
   6:CARDFILE.HLP,    "Cardfile Help"                ,  24810
   .
   .
   .

   diskspace=4143890

[win.dependents]
pbrush   = 6:PBRUSH.DLL
recorder = 6:RECORDER.DLL
   .
   .
   .


[win.games]
   4:SOL.EXE,         "Solitaire"                    , 180688, sol
   6:WINMINE.EXE,     "Minesweeper"                  ,  27776, winmine
   .
   .
   .

   diskspace=509187

[win.scrs]
   6:SCRNSAVE.SCR,    "Default Screen Saver"         ,   5328
   6:SSMARQUE.SCR,    "Marquee Screen Saver"         ,  16896
   6:SSSTARS.SCR,     "Stars Screen Saver"           ,  17536
   6:ssflywin.scr,    "Flying Windows Screen Saver", 16160
   diskspace=55920

[win.bmps]
   6:ARCADE.BMP,      "Arcade Wallpaper"             ,    630
   3:ARGYLE.BMP,      "Argyle Wallpaper"             ,    630
   6:CASTLE.BMP,      "Castle Wallpaper"             ,    778
   .
   .
   .

   diskspace=121797
```

Groups.   This section creates the groups and icons within the groups. It is a convenient place for you to create your own groups or remove ones you don't want installed. The format is group number = name of group, and display status. The display status is 1 if you want the group maximized on startup and nothing in this field if you want it minimized. Below the group names are the files that are to be installed in those groups with the format: icon name and executable file name.

```
[progman.groups]
group3 Main,1
group4=Accessories
group8=Network
group5=Games
group1=StartUp
[group3]
"File Manager",    WINFILE.EXE
"Control Panel",   CONTROL.EXE
"Print Manager",   PRINTMAN.EXE
"ClipBook Viewer", CLIPBRD.EXE
"MS-DOS Prompt",   DOSPRMPT.PIF, PROGMAN.EXE, 9
"Windows Setup",   WINSETUP.EXE
"PIF Editor",      PIFEDIT.EXE
"Read Me"
"Read Me",         README.WRI,,,                    readme
"Clipboard"
"Clipboard Viewer"
"DOS Prompt"
"Tutorial"

[group4]
"Write",           WRITE.EXE
"Paintbrush",      PBRUSH.EXE,,,                     pbrush
"Terminal",        TERMINAL.EXE,,,                   terminal
"Notepad",         NOTEPAD.EXE,,,                    notepad
"Recorder",        RECORDER.EXE,,,                   recorder
"Cardfile",        CARDFILE.EXE,,,                   cardfile
"Calculator",      CALC.EXE,,,                       calc
"Clock",           CLOCK.EXE,,,                      clock
"Object Packager", PACKAGER.EXE,,,                   packager
"Character Map",   CHARMAP.EXE,,,                    charmap
"Media Player",    MPLAYER.EXE,,,                    mplayer
"Sound Recorder",  SOUNDREC.EXE,,,                   soundrec
"PIF Editor"
; Remove old network icons
"Chat"
"WinMeter"
"Net Watcher"
"WinPopup"
"Virtual Disk Status"
"Fast Mail"
"Password List Editor"
"Message Popup Utility"

[group5]
"Solitaire",       SOL.EXE,,,                        sol
"Minesweeper",     WINMINE.EXE,,,                    winmine
"Hearts",          MSHEARTS.EXE,,,                   hearts
; Remove old icons
"FreeCell"

[group2]
"Object Packager", PACKAGER.EXE,,,                   packager
"Character Map",   CHARMAP.EXE,,,                    charmap
"Media Player",    MPLAYER.EXE,,,                    mplayer
```

```
"Sound Recorder",    SOUNDREC.EXE,,,                          soundrec
"PIF Editor"
"Write", WRITE.EXE
.
.
.

[group6]
"Solitaire",         SOL.EXE,,,                               sol
"Minesweeper",       WINMINE.EXE,,,                           winmine
"Hearts",            MSHEARTS.EXE,,,                          hearts
; Remove old icons
"FreeCell"

[group7]
"Clipboard"
"Clipboard Viewer"
"ClipBook Viewer",   CLIPBRD.EXE
"Windows Setup",     WINSETUP.EXE
"PIF Editor",        PIFEDIT.EXE
"Read Me"
"DOS Prompt"
"MS-DOS Prompt",     DOSPRMPT.PIF, PROGMAN.EXE, 9
"Read Me",           README.WRI,,,                            readme
"Tutorial"

[group8]
"Network Setup",     "WINSETUP.EXE /Z",,,
"Mail",              MSMAIL.EXE,,,                            msmail
"Mail",              MSMAIL.EXE,,,                            msfax
"Schedule+",         SCHDPLUS.EXE,,,                          schdplus
"Remote Access",     RASSTART.EXE,,,                          rasmac
; Remove old network icons
"Message Popup Utility"
```

Fonts.   The next section lists the fonts to be installed for display and printing uses. Rarely will you need to modify these sections.

```
[fonts]
    5:SSERIFE.FON, "MS Sans Serif 8,10,12,14,18,24 (VGA res)", "100,96,96"
    5:SSERIFF.FON, "MS Sans Serif 8,10,12,14,18,24 (8514/a res)", "100,120,120"

    6:COURE.FON, "Courier 10,12,15 (VGA res)", "100,96,96"
    6:COURF.FON, "Courier 10,12,15 (8514/a res)", "100,120,120"
.
.
.


[ttfonts]
5:ARIAL.FOT,   "Arial (TrueType)",              5:arial.ttf, ""
5:ARIALBD.FOT, "Arial Bold (TrueType)",         5:arialbd.ttf, "Arial0100"
5:ARIALBI.FOT, "Arial Bold Italic (TrueType)",  5:arialbi.ttf, "Arial1100"
5:ARIALI.FOT,  "Arial Italic (TrueType)",       5:ariali.ttf, "Arial1000"
.
.
.
```

Compatibility.   This section contains names of drivers and TSRs that have been found to be incompatible with Windows. Usually these are disk drivers of some type that are not designed to exist with Windows. If you find these files, remove them from the CONFIG.SYS file. You can also add your own file names here.

```
[compatibility]
icache.sys
ibmcache.sys
cache.sys
cache.exe
mcache.sys
fast512.sys

[incompTSR1]
ep.exe       = "Norton Desktop/Windows Erase Protect TSR"
qmaps.sys    = "QMAPS Memory Manager"
qcache.exe   = "386 Max Disk Cache Utility"
cache.exe    = "Disk Cache Utility"
flash.exe    = "Flash Disk Cache Utility"
hyper386.exe= "Hyper Disk Cache Utility"
hyperdkx.exe= "Hyper Disk Cache Utility"
.
.
.

[incompTSR2]
ndosedit.com  = "Command Line Editor"
doscue.com="DOSCUE Command Line Editor"
datamon.exe="PC Tools Datamon"
subst.exe="MS-DOS SUBST Utility"
join.exe="MS-DOS JOIN Utility"
.
.
.

[block_devices]
tscsi.sys
tcscsi.sys
atdosxl.sys
dmdrvr.bin
drdrive.sys
[Installable.Drivers]
; key         = filename,       type(s),        description, VxD(s), Default
Params
msadlib       = 5:msadlib.drv,  "MIDI",         "Ad Lib", 5:vadlibd.386,
lapc1         = 6:mpu401.drv,   "MIDI",         "Roland LAPC1",,
midimapper    = 4:midimap.drv,  "MidiMapper",   "MIDI Mapper",,
mpu401        = 6:mpu401.drv,   "MIDI",         "Roland MPU-401",,
sequencer     = 6:mciseq.drv,   "Sequencer",    "[MCI] MIDI Sequencer",,
soundblaster  = 5:sndblst.drv,  "Wave,MIDI",    "Creative Labs Sound Blaster
1.0", :vsbd.386,, msadlib
soundblaster2 = 5:sndblst2.drv, "Wave,MIDI",    "Creative Labs Sound Blaster
.5", 5:vsbd.386,, msadlib
timer         = 5:timer.drv,    "Timer",        "Timer", 5:vtdapi.386,
thunder       = 5:sndblst2.drv, "Wave", "Media Vision Thunder Board",
5:vsbd.386,, msadlib
wave          = 6:mciwave.drv,  "WaveAudio",    "[MCI] Sound",, "4"
cdaudio       = 6:mcicda.drv,   "CDAudio",      "[MCI] CD Audio",,
```

Computer brands. Certain computers have known problems with Windows or need special drivers. This section specifies those computers and what drivers to load for them. Usually you do not need to access this section. At the end of the line is a special "cookies" section that points to another section down below containing special instructions on how to modify .INI files to accommodate these computers.

```
[machine]
ibm_compatible  =  "MS-DOS
System",system,kbd,t4s0enha,nomouse,vga,sound,comm,,ebios,
ast_386_486     =  "AST Premium 386/25 and 386/33
(CUPID)",system,kbd,t4s0enha,nomouse,vga,sound,comm,,ebios,ast_cookz
at_and_t        =  "AT&T  PC",system,kbd,t4s0enha,nomouse,vga,sound,comm
,,ebios,
everex_386_25   =  "Everex Step 386/25 (or ;
.
.
.


[apm_cookz]
specialdriver,,,2:power.drv
system.ini,386enh,"device=vpowerd.386",2:vpowerd.386
,,,2:power.hlp

[apm_sl_cookz]
specialdriver,,,2:power.drv
system.ini,386enh,"device=vpowerd.386",2:vpowerd.386
,,,2:power.hlp
system.ini,power.drv,"OptionsDLL=sl.dll",2:sl.dll
,,,2:sl.hlp

[ast_cookz]
system.ini,386enh,"emmexclude=E000-EFFF",

[everex_cookz]
system.ini,386enh,"8042ReadCmd=A2,1,F",
system.ini,386enh,"8042ReadCmd=A3,1,F",
system.ini,386enh,"8042WriteCmd=B3,8,F",
```

APPS.INF

Several text files are used to install Windows. The APPS.INF file has information about the DOS applications that are set up when it scans the system for *.EXE and *.COM files. Among the items are base program information files, which are used when no other PIF files are specified for a DOS system.

When the setup program finds a file that matches the description in the [pif] section, there are several parameters. The last item in the line identifies the section to create the PIF file from information provided in the corresponding data items located further in the file.

The dialog section provides a title for the Windows dialog box to be shown when the DOS files are being set up in Windows. You can change this string at any time.

```
[dialog]
   caption="Set Up Applications"
```

The Base_PIFs section is information about what is to be created for a default

PIF file. Since every DOS application needs a PIF file, there has to be a PIF file when a user runs DOS commands directly from the File Run command. When running a DOS program directly, the _DEFAULT.PIF file is used.

```
[base_pifs]
_DEFAULT.BAT = _DEFAULT,"",,cwe
COMMAND.COM  = DOSPRMPT,"MS-DOS Prompt",,cwe,,,,enha_dosprmpt
```

The format for the PIF settings here and also in the PIF section that follows is a series of values separated by a comma: executable file = pif name, window title, startup directory, close-window flag, icon filename, icon number, standard pif, 386 pif, ambiguous exe, optimized pif. All entries must conform to this format, and if you don't have an entry for a value, just leave it blank by putting another comma in the next space.

For purposes of example, we will show a setup in this file for automatic setup of Windows and the same file created manually with the PIF editor. We will look at the EDIT.COM text editor in DOS and set that in a PIF file. Figure 6.9 shows the first screen of the setup.

```
C:\dos\edit.com=dosedit,DOS Text Editor, c;\dos, cwe,
moricons.dll ,9,std_EDIT,enha_EDIT,amb_edit,,
```

Executable file.   The *executable file* is the term used in DOS when running the application. This corresponds to the program file name of the PIF editor.

PIF name.   The *PIF name* is the file name used to store the PIF file on disk.

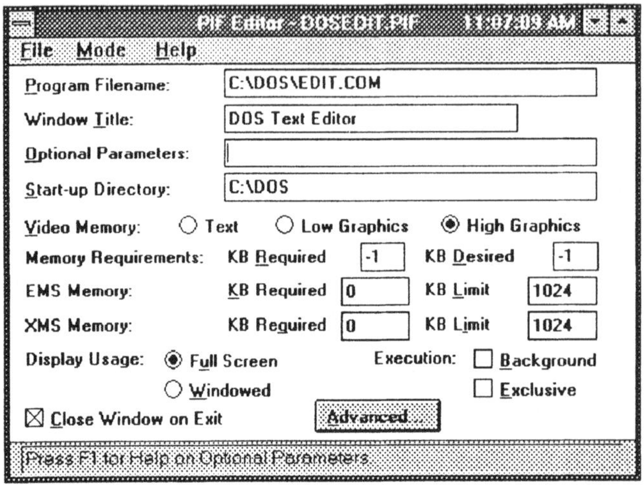

Figure 6.9   DOS text editor PIF file.

Window title. *Window title* is what will display on top of the window when the DOS application is being executed.

Startup directory. The *startup directory* is the directory of the application that will be used for data when the application starts. It is not necessary for the operation of the DOS application to specify this value, but it can be used for those applications that don't default to a directory for data.

Close window. The "close window" flag is the equivalent of the "close window on exit" command in the PIF editor. When the application exits, what happens to the DOS session that was running? If you put the value cwe (current working environment parameter) in this value, the window will close on exiting from the DOS application. If you leave it blank, the user will drop down to the command line in DOS after the DOS application closes.

Icon file name. Since there isn't any icon associated with a DOS file, you will need to pull an icon from some other file. The default file is PROGMAN.EXE (Fig. 6.10), where a number of icons are available for use. Another file is MORICONS.DLL (Fig. 6.11), which you can access to obtain icons. You are

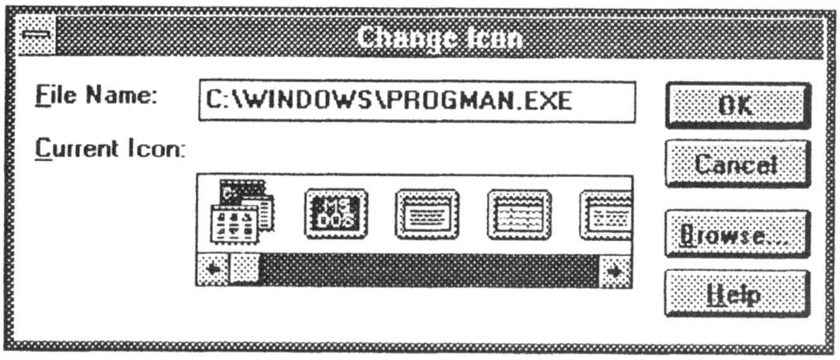

Figure 6.10 PROGMAN.EXE icons.

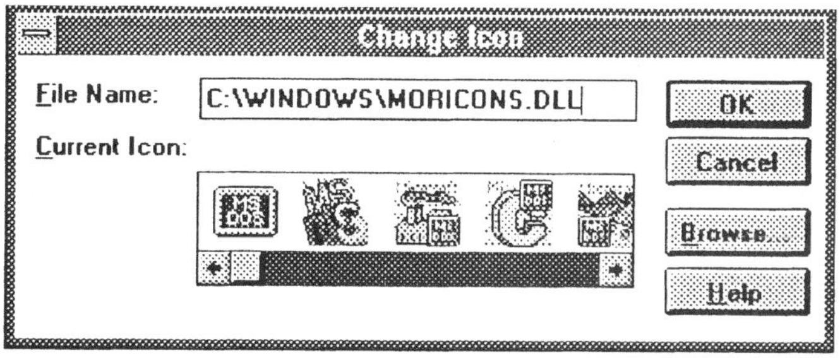

Figure 6.11 Program icons in MORICONS.DLL.

not limited to these files as you can get icons from any Windows executable file, DLL file, or ICO file that contains icons.

Icon number.   When choosing a file for icons, there may be more than one icon stored in the file. If you do not specify a value here, then it will default to 0 (or in the case of PROGMAN.EXE it will be 1).

Standard PIF.   The information in this section is for the PIF file in standard mode. For a discussion of the differences between the standard and enhanced mode of PIF files, see Chap. 8.

386 enhanced.   This entry is for special settings for the PIF file running in enhanced mode.

Ambiguous EXE.   This value points to a section in the APPS.INF that has the same name as specified in the executable file section (the first entry). This is used in the event that two or more programs have the same executable name. By creating a section in the APPS.INF file that has the heading [amb_*identifername*], you can separate the entries.

Optimized PIFs.   This is where you can make minor changes to the PIF file based on optimizing the PIF.

Enha_dosprompt

This is the memory requirement for MS-DOS when running in the 386 enhanced mode of Windows. A -1 setting for memory signals the PIF to provide all memory required to the application.

```
[enha_dosprmpt]
convmem      = -1,-1
```

Don't find

Because there are bound to be executable files other than DOS files or there are files you don't want set up in Windows, any executable files found on this list will be ignored by the setup program and will not be installed. The default list contains mainly Windows files, but you can add any others you want.

```
[dontfind]
  apm.exe
  calc.exe
  calendar.exe
  cardfile.exe
  charmap.exe
  clipbrd.exe
  .
  .
  .
```

```
          wintutor.exe
          winver.exe
          wordart.exe
          wpcdll.exe
          wpwinfil.exe
          write.exe
          zoomin.exe

[pif]
;
; It is VERY important that this list remain and be maintained in
; lexicographical order (by exe name, no extension)
;
; Description strings that contain more than one word (i.e. contain blank
; space) must be enclosed in quotes (").
;
; Parameter order
;
; (0)  Exe file =
; (1)  PIF name
; (2)  Window Title
; (3)  Startup Directory
; (4)  Close Window on Exit flag
; (5)  File from which to extract icon (default is Progman.exe)
; (6)  Icon number (default is 0)
; (7)  Standard PIF settings section (default is [std_dflt])
; (8)  Enhanced PIF settings section (default is [enha_dflt])
; (9)  Ambiguous EXEs section (Other applications with same EXE name)
; (10) Optimized PIFs section
;
123.COM    = 123    ,"Lotus 1-2-3",,cwe,,3,std_gra_256,enha_123c
123.EXE    = 123    ,"Lotus 1-2-3
3.1",,cwe,moricons.dll,50,std_123,enha_123,amb_123
ABPI.COM   = ABPI   ,"ACCPAC BPI",,cwe,moricons.dll,30,,enha_BPI
 .
 .
 .

Rabbit",,cwe,,2,std_WRABBIT,enha_WRABBIT,amb_wrabbit
WRITE.COM  = WRITE  ,"IBM Writing Assistant 2.0",,cwe,
,2,std_WRITASST,enha_WRITASST,amb_writasst
WS.EXE     = WS     ,"WordStar Professional 6.0",
,cwe,moricons.dll,68,std_WS6,enha_WS6,amb_ws
WS2.EXE    = WS2    ,"WordStar 2000",,cwe,,2,std_WS2,enha_WS2

[amb_123]
123.EXE    = 123    ,"Lotus 1-2-3 2.2 to
2.4",,cwe,moricons.dll,51,std_123R23,enha_123R23
123.EXE    = 123    ,"Lotus 1-2-3 2.3
WYSIWYG",,cwe,moricons.dll,51,std_123WYSIW,enha_123WYSIW
 .
 .
 .

[std_dflt]
; default is text mode app which does not directly modify COM ports
;
; Other Possible options are given for reference
; ( (or) means entry corresponds to radio button group)
;
minconvmem    = 128
videomode     = txt    ; (or) gra
xmsmem        = 0,0    ; ##,, ## (min, max)
```

```
checkboxes    =              ; c1,c2,c3,c4,kbd,nse,pps,ata,aes,ces,psc,aps,nss

[enha_dflt]
; default is as follows
;
; Other Possible options are given for reference
; ( (or) means entry corresponds to radio button group )
;
convmem       = 128,640 ; ##,## (Required, Limit)
emsmem        = 0,1024   ; ##,## (Required, Limit)
xmsmem        = 0,1024   ; ##,## (Required, Limit)
dispusage     = fs       ; (or) win
execflags     =          ; bgd, exc
multaskopt    = 50,100   ; ##,## (Bgd Pri, Fgd Pri)
procmemflags  = dit,hma  ; eml,xml,lam
dispoptvideo  = txt      ; (or) lgr,hgr
dispoptports  = hgr      ; txt,lgr
dispflags     = emt      ; rvm
otheroptions  = afp      ; cwa,ata,aes,ces,psc,aps,asp,aen

[enha_123c]
convmem       = 256,640
    .
    .
    .

[std_dm]
params        = "/nf /ngm"
minconvmem    = 330
videomode     = txt
checkboxes    =
[enha_dm]
params        = "/nf /ngm"
dispoptvideo  = txt
convmem       = 330,640
emsmem        = 0,1024
dispusage     = fs
execflags     =
multaskopt    = 50,100
procmemflags  = dit,hma
dispoptports  = txt
dispflags     =
otheroptions  = asp

[std_view]
params        = "/nf /ngm"
minconvmem    = 300
[enha_view]
params        = "/nf /ngm"
dispoptvideo  = txt
convmem       = 300,640
dispoptports  = txt
dispflags     =
otheroptions  = asp

[std_express]
minconvmem    = 320
checkboxes    = c1,c2,c3,c4
[enha_express]
dispoptvideo  = txt
convmem       = 320,640
dispusage     = win
execflags     = bgd
multaskopt    = 100,100
```

```
procmemflags = lam
dispoptports =

[enha_procomm1]
execflags    = bgd ; background execution
procmemflags = dit,hma,lam

[enha_r2call]
procmemflags = dit,hma,lam
```

CONTROL.INF

The CONTROL.INF file provides information to the SETUP program for printers and international settings. You can copy in setup information from vendors' disks for special printers that you may be installing. Rather than having to insert the floppy disk from the vendor by copying these files from their OEMSETUP.INF disk and the drivers to the network directory that you are using as a master copy of Windows, you can avoid the "floppy shuffle" when installing Windows on workstations.

```
[io.device]
; (printers, plotters, etc.)
; The filename is followed by
;
; - the descriptive string which will appear in Control Panel and
; which will appear in WIN.INI
; - 1 or 2 strings indicating the scaling for this device
;
; There may be more than one line for a driver, corresponding to different
; printers.

6:TTY.DRV,"Generic / Text Only","DEVICESPECIFIC"
6:PSCRIPT.DRV,"Agfa 9000 Series PS","DEVICESPECIFIC"
6:PSCRIPT.DRV,"Agfa Compugraphic 400PS","DEVICESPECIFIC"
7:HPPCL.DRV,"Agfa Compugraphic Genics","DEVICESPECIFIC"
  .

  .

6:PSCRIPT.DRV,7:phiipx.WPD,"Tektronix Phaser II PX","DEVICESPECIFIC"
6:PSCRIPT.DRV,7:tkphzr21.WPD,"Tektronix Phaser II PXi","DEVICESPECIFIC"
6:PSCRIPT.DRV,7:tkphzr31.WPD,"Tektronix Phaser III PXi","DEVICESPECIFIC"
6:PSCRIPT.DRV,7:TIM17521.WPD,"TI microLaser PS17","DEVICESPECIFIC"
6:PSCRIPT.DRV,7:TIM35521.WPD,"TI microLaser PS35","DEVICESPECIFIC"
7:HPPCL.DRV,"Toshiba PageLaser12","DEVICESPECIFIC"
7:HPPCL.DRV,"Unisys AP9210","DEVICESPECIFIC"
6:PSCRIPT.DRV,"Varityper VT-600","DEVICESPECIFIC"
6:PSCRIPT.DRV,"Wang LCS15","DEVICESPECIFIC"
6:PSCRIPT.DRV,"Wang LCS15 FontPlus","DEVICESPECIFIC"
7:HPPCL.DRV,"Wang LDP8","DEVICESPECIFIC"
[io.dependent]
  pscript.drv = 7:pscript.hlp, 7:testps.txt
  tty.drv = 6:tty.hlp
  ibm4019.drv = 6:sf4019.exe
  lbpiii.drv = 6:can_adf.exe
  lbpII.drv = 6:can_adf.exe
  hppcl.drv = 7:finstall.dll, 7:finstall.hlp, 7:BP1CP2.PCM,, 7:DD1CP1.PCM
  hppcl5ms.drv = 7:finstall.dll, 7:finstall.hlp, 7:BP1CP2.PCM,, 7:DD1CP1.PCM
```

```
hppcl5e.drv = 7:hppcl5e.hlp, 7:hppcl5eo.hlp, 7:finstall.dll,
7:finstall.hlp, 7:hppcl5e1.dll, 7:hppcl5e2.dll, 7:hppcl5e3.dll, 7:hppcl5e4.dll
hpdskjet.drv = 7:finstall.dll, 7:finstall.hlp
paintjet.drv = 6:dmcolor.dll
epson9.drv = 6:dmcolor.dll
epson24.drv = 6:dmcolor.dll
oki24.drv = 6:dmcolor.dll
nec24pin.drv = 6:dmcolor.dll
panson24.drv = 6:dmcolor.dll
panson9.drv = 6:dmcolor.dll

[country]
"Australia", "61!1!0!2!0!0!0!2!0!0!AM!PM!$!,!.!/!:!,!d/MM/yy!dddd, d MMMM
yyy!ENG"
"Austria", "43!2!2!2!1!1!0!2!9!1!!!!S!.!,!-!:!;!yyyy-MM-dddd!dddd, dd. MMMM
yyyy!DEU"
    .
    .
    .
"United Kingdom", "44!1!0!2!1!1!0!2!1!1!1!!!ú!,!.!/!:!,!dd/MM/yy!dd MMMM
yyyy!ENG"
"United States", "1!0!0!2!0!1!1!2!0!0!AM!PM!$!,!.!/!:!,!M/d/yy!dddd, MMMM dd,
yyyy!ENU"
"Other Country", "1!0!0!2!1!0!1!2!0!0!!!$!,!.!/!:!,!M/d/yy!dddd, MMMM dd,
yyyy!ENU"
```

NETWORK.INF

The NETWORK.INF file has information about network adapter cards that will be used for the operation of Windows. There are four distinct sections in this file: general installation, network adapter drivers, network protocol drivers, and secondary network drivers.

The general installation contains default settings for network setup in the [nwsdata] section, some common Windows network driver files in the [workgroup], protocol manager driver files in the [progman_install] section, and information for the protocol manager PROTOCOL.INI section.

The network adapter driver section contains data for the network adapters that are directly supported by Windows. You can find this data in the [netcard] section. The [netcard_install] section has settings for network drivers files for a specific network card. There is information for the PROTOCOL.INI about network cards to be placed in the PROTOCOL.INI file.

In the network protocol drivers section, there is information about the protocols to be used in the setup of the network drivers. The [transport] section gives a list of default protocols supported by Windows. The [transport_install] section contains information about a specific driver, and the [transport_protocol] section provides data for the PROTOCOL.INI file.

The last section has secondary network driver information in the event you want to install support for more than one network system. The [multinet] section is a list of secondary network drivers supported by Windows. The [multinet_install] section is provided for specific network drivers. A portion of the NETWORK.INF file is shown below.

```
;; Windows for Workgroups 3.11
;; NETWORK.INF
;; Copyright © Microsoft Corporation, 1991–1993
[data]
type=network
version="3.11.060"
autoexec_anchor="net start"
config_anchor=""
transport_hook=ms$ndishlp
defNDIS2_transport=ms$netbeui
defNDIS3_transport=ms$netbeui
defNDIS3_transport2=ms$netbeui,ms$nwlinknb
defODI_transport=ms$nwlinknb
defNW_transport=ms$netbeui,ms$nwlinknb
defNWipxmono_card=ms$nwsupnb
defODI_arcnet_trans=ms$nwsupnbt

[common]

; Protman Install and Protocol Sections
[protman_install]
netdir=8:protman.dos,8:protman.exe

[protman]
drivername=PROTMAN$
param=PRIORITY,,static,MS$NDISHLP

; NDIS3 manager
[ndis3]
device386=7:ndis.386
```

OEMSETUP.INF

There is a file by each name on each vendor drive disk that is supplied with printers, network cards, video displays, and other equipment. Whenever you choose unlisted or "Other" devices, Windows looks in the directory that you have specified for the OEMSETUP.INF file to find the driver information and any setup parameters. (See Fig. 6.12.)

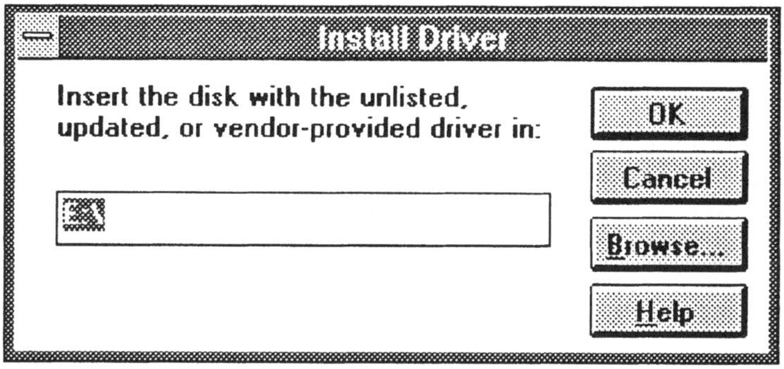

Figure 6.12 Driver installation dialog box.

Here is a sample OEMSETUP.INF file used for the installation of drivers for HP LaserJet 4 printers:

```
; HP LaserJet 4 family driver installation file for Windows 3.1
; Copyright Hewlett-Packard 1994
;
; Version 31.V1.50
;
; /*
_____

*\
; |
; | hppcl5e.drv  = HP LaserJet 4 Printer Drivers
; | hppcl5e.hlp  = Help file for HP LaserJet 4 Printer Drivers
; | hppcl5eo.hlp = Help file for common dialog box
; | hppcl5e1.dll = DLL for HPGL2 graphics
; | hppcl5e2.dll = DLL for raster graphics
; | hppcl5e3.dll = DLL for text
; | hppcl5e4.dll = DLL for building PCLETTO's
; | finstall.dll = Font Installer for HP LaserJet 4 Printer Drivers
; | finstall.hlp = Help file for Font Installer for HP LaserJet 4
; | Printer Drivers
; |
; \*
_____

*/

[disks]
    1 =. ,"HP LaserJet 4 Drivers 31.V1.50 Disk"

[io.device]
    1:HPPCL5E.DRV,"HP LaserJet 4V/4MV","DEVICESPECIFIC"
    1:HPPCL5E.DRV,"HP LaserJet 4/4M","DEVICESPECIFIC"
    1:HPPCL5E.DRV,"HP LaserJet 4Si/4Si MX","DEVICESPECIFIC"
    1:HPPCL5E.DRV,"HP LaserJet 4P/4MP","DEVICESPECIFIC"
    1:HPPCL5E.DRV,"HP LaserJet 4ML","DEVICESPECIFIC"
    1:HPPCL5E.DRV,"HP LaserJet 4L","DEVICESPECIFIC"
    1:HPPCL5E.DRV,"HP LaserJet 4 Plus/4M Plus","DEVICESPECIFIC"

[io.dependent]
hppcl5e.drv=
hppcl5e.hlp,hppcl5eo.hlp,finstall.dll,finstall.hlp,hppcl5e1.dll,h
ppcl5e2.dll,hppcl5e3.dll,hppcl5e4.dll
```

Windows .INI Files

In addition to copying network shell files and making changes to workstation files, Windows .INI files are changed to reflect the network connection.

WIN.INI file. The installation program adds the NWPOPUP.EXE entry to the LOAD parameter. This utility handles all broadcast and send messages as a dialog box.

SYSTEM.INI. The majority of the entries are made in this file because the system needs to be modified to handle Novell NetWare.

```
[Boot]
Network.drv=Netware.drv

[386Enh]
Network=*vnetbios,vnetware.386, vipx.386
OverlappedIO=off
TimerCriticalSection=10000
ReflectDOSInt2A=True
UniqueDOSPSP=True
PSPIncrement=5
```

PROGMAN.INI. Inside the PROGMAN.INI file the [Groups] section is modified to include a new group for NetWare Tools Group 5: = C:\nwclient\nwuser.exe. The number following the Group variable will be different on your system because it is defined in terms of how many other Windows groups are already installed.

Windows driver files. The installation program will copy a number of driver files to the Windows directory that are referenced in the .INI files: NETWARE.DRV, NETWARE.HLP, NWPOPUP.EXE, VIPX.386, VNETWARE.386.

Multiple Configurations

When you install Windows for Workgroups 3.11 on a version of DOS that supports multiple configurations (v6.0 or higher), the setup routing changes slightly. Normally, Windows setup will modify the CONFIG.SYS file automatically (if you choose).

However, if you use the multiple configuration options in CONFIG.SYS, then Windows setup does not know what to do when modifying the file. It will create a file called CONFIG.WIN with some recommended settings and let you make them yourself. An example CONFIG.SYS file is shown in Fig. 6.13. The results of that file are shown in Fig. 6.14.

Critical Windows Files

The file which almost everyone sees, and many think contains the code for Windows, is WIN.COM. Actually, this is just a starting utility that calls other core files and performs a couple of other tasks. It checks out the hardware system and any device drives that may be loaded and makes a decision as to whether Windows can start and the best mode in which to start it in. It also checks for HIMEM.SYS and determines what type of CPU is on the computer.

Once these items are checked and decisions made, it then starts up the appropriate files and loads what we know as Windows. It also brings up the opening screen (Windows logo), which you can bypass by starting Windows with WIN :. The colon disables the opening logo screen. Some people feel that it is a good idea to not run this as it will take time to load up the opening graphics. However, we have tested this feature and found little difference in

```
[common]
DEVICE=C:\WINDOWS\HIMEM.SYS
DEVICE=C:\WINDOWS\EMM386.EXE NOEMS
BUFFERS=10,0
FILES=100
DOS=UMB
DEVICEHIGH /L:1,12048 =C:\DOS\SETVER.EXE
DOS=HIGH
REM BUFFERS=20

[menu]
menuitem=office,Office Setup
menuitem=remote,Away from Office

[office]
LASTDRIVE=Z
FCBS=16,8
DEVICE=C:\DOS\CDC710.SYS /D:CPQCD
SHELL=C:\DOS\COMMAND.COM C:\DOS\ /E:1024 /p
STACKS=9,256

[remote]
```

Figure 6.13   CONFIG.SYS multiple configuration file.

```
MS-DOS 6.22 Startup Menu
======================

        1. Office Setup
        2. Away from Office

Enter a choice: 1




F5=Bypass startup files F8=Confirm each line of CONFIG.SYS AND AUTOEXEC.BAT
```

Figure 6.14   CONFIG.SYS menu.

the time it takes to start Windows. Therefore, disabling the beginning logo will not make any difference in terms of operation, except that you will be staring at a blank screen.

Windows system files

WIN.COM calls up the system files of Windows, which create the environment and at the same time brings up the graphical interface that we are all acquainted with. The first file is KRNL386.EXE (KRNL286.EXE for starting Windows in standard mode). It sets the environment and controls all access to memory, loads applications, and takes care of scheduling program execution.

The next file, USER.EXE, takes care of the Windows on the monitor; handles the creation, deletion, or adjustment of the Windows; and takes care of icons and virtually anything else involving the graphical user interface. In addition to graphical duties, it also handles any input from the user, whether from the keyboard, mouse, or other pointing or input device (e.g., bar-code reader).

GDI.EXE handles all graphics operations that may be displayed on the screen. This ensures that graphics are handled properly inside Windows.

An interesting note is that the system resources we talk about later tie in directly to these files. These files are so critical to the operation of Windows that the removal or corruption of any one of them will mean an inability for Windows to run. If you see an error after the beginning logo is displayed on the screen such as "Error loading USER.EXE," you will know the file is missing or has been corrupted. You may have to reinstall the file if it has been damaged or has been deleted by accident.

Rather than trying to install Windows all over again, you can copy the missing file from the floppy disks and then uncompress it with the EXPAND.EXE utility. The format is EXPAND.EXE USER.EX_ USER.EXE, or you can copy it from the file server.

Changing the logo screen

Microsoft has provided a simple method for personalizing the first logo screen in Windows for your organization or some other purpose. If you look on the setup disks, there are three files: WIN.CNF, VGALOGO.LGO, and VGA-LOG.RLE. The LGO has some of the start code of the banner, and the RLE file contains the actual graphic.

If you want to change the default logo file, use a graphics editor that supports run-length encoded (RLE) graphics, import the file, and add or remove any of the default information you want. Save the file and issue the following DOS command: copy WIN.CNF+VGALOGO.LGO+VGALOGO.RLE WIN.COM /B. You must use the copy command with the /B (binary) switch to copy these three files together into one called WIN.COM. Look as you might, you will not find WIN.COM on the installation disks; it is created by SETUP during the installation process.

Initialization Source Files

The .INI files are created at the time of Windows installation. Because there are a number of variables when installing Windows, it is not possible for Microsoft to provide a standard set of initialization files. However, some of the initialization files have a template provided by Microsoft for standard entries. These files are used as the basis for the initialization file, and you can provide your own entries to be built into the final initialization file.

These files have the name of the initialization file with the extension .SRC. Each heading corresponds to the final section of the initialization file, and many of the entries are blank as they will be filled out on the basis of the settings you have specified during installation or hardware detection.

```
[A] WIN.SRC
[windows]
load=
run=
Beep=yes
Spooler=yes
NullPort=None
device=
BorderWidth=3
CursorBlinkRate=530
DoubleClickSpeed=452
Programs=com exe bat pif
Documents=
DeviceNotSelectedTimeout=15
TransmissionRetryTimeout=45
KeyboardDelay=2
KeyboardSpeed=31
ScreenSaveActive=1
ScreenSaveTimeout=600
SetupWin=1
CoolSwitch=1

[Desktop]
Pattern=(None)
wallpaper=cpq256.bmp
GridGranularity=0
TileWallpaper=1
IconSpacing=75

[Extensions]
cal=calendar.exe ^.cal
crd=cardfile.exe ^.crd
trm=terminal.exe ^.trm
txt=notepad.exe ^.txt
ini=notepad.exe ^.ini
pcx=pbrush.exe ^.pcx
bmp=pbrush.exe ^.bmp
wri=write.exe ^.wri
rec=recorder.exe ^.rec
hlp=winhelp.exe ^.hlp
```

```
[intl]
sCountry=United States
iCountry=1
iDate=0
iTime=0
iTLZero=0
iCurrency=0
iCurrDigits=2
iNegCurr=0
iLzero=1
iDigits=2
iMeasure=1
s1159=AM
s2359=PM
sCurrency=$
sThousand=,
sDecimal=.
sDate=/
sTime=:
sList=,
sShortDate=M/d/yy
sLongDate=dddd, MMMM dd, yyyy
sLanguage=enu

[ports]
; A line with [filename].PRN followed by an equal sign causes
; [filename] to appear in the Control Panel's Printer Configuration dialog
; box. A printer connected to [filename] directs its output into this file.
LPT1:=
LPT2:=
LPT3:=
COM1:=9600,n,8,1,x
COM2:=9600,n,8,1,x
COM3:=9600,n,8,1,x
COM4:=9600,n,8,1,x
EPT:=
FILE:=
LPT1.DOS=
LPT2.DOS=

[FontSubstitutes]
Helv=MS Sans Serif
Tms Rmn=MS Serif
Times=Times New Roman
Helvetica=Arial

[TrueType]
[Sounds]
SystemDefault=ding.wav, Default Beep
SystemExclamation=chord.wav, Exclamation
SystemStart=tada.wav, Windows Start
SystemExit=chimes.wav, Windows Exit
SystemHand=chord.wav, Critical Stop
SystemQuestion=chord.wav, Question
SystemAsterisk=chord.wav, Asterisk

[mci extensions]
wav=waveaudio
mid=sequencer
rmi=sequencer

[Compatibility]
NOTSHELL=0x0001
```

```
WPWINFIL=0x0006
CCMAIL=0x0008
AMIPRO=0x0010
REM=0x8022
PIXIE=0x0040
CP=0x0040
JW=0x42080
TME=0x0100
VB=0x0200
WIN2WRS=0x1210
PACKRAT=0x0800
VISION=0x0040
MCOURIER=0x0800
_BNOTES=0x24000
MILESV3=0x1000
PM4=0x2000
DESIGNER=0x2000
PLANNER=0x2000
DRAW=0x2000
WINSIM=0x2000
CHARISMA=0x2000
PR2=0x2000
PLUS=0x1000
ED=0x00010000
APORIA=0x0100
EXCEL=0x1000
GUIDE=0x1000
NETSET2=0x0100
W4GL=0x4000
W4GLR=0x4000
TURBOTAX=0x00080000

[Microsoft Word 2.0]
HPDSKJET=+1
[A] SYSTEM.SRC
[boot]
shell        =
display.drv  =
system.drv   =
comm.drv     =
network.drv  =
oemfonts.fon =
fonts.fon    =
fixedfon.fon =
386grabber   =
286grabber   =
mouse.drv    =
keyboard.drv =
sound.drv    =
language.dll =
taskman.exe  =
drivers=mmsystem.dll
SCRNSAVE.EXE = C:\WINDOWS\SSSTARS.SCR

[keyboard]
type         =
subtype      =
keyboard.dll =
oemansi.bin  =
[boot.description]

[386Enh]
```

```
display=*vddvga
keyboard=*vkd
mouse=*vmd
network=*vnetbios, *dosnet
device=vtdapi.386
device=*vpicd
device=*vtd
device=*reboot
device=*vdmad
device=*vsd
device=*v86mmgr
device=*pageswap
device=*dosmgr
device=*vmpoll
device=*wshell
device=*BLOCKDEV
device=*PAGEFILE
device=*vfd
device=*parity
device=*biosxlat
device=*vcd
device=*vmcpd
device=*combuff
device=*cdpscsi
local=CON
FileSysChange=off
DEVICE=C:\DOS\VFINTD.386

[standard]

[NonWindowsApp]
localtsrs=dosedit,ced

[mci]
WaveAudio=mciwave.drv
Sequencer=mciseq.drv
CDAudio=mcicda.drv

[drivers]
timer=timer.drv
midimapper=midimap.drv

[A] CONTROL.SRC
[current]
color schemes=Windows Default

[color schemes]
Arizona=804000,FFFFFF,FFFFFF,0,FFFFFF,0,808040,C0C0C0,FFFFFF,4080FF,C0C0C0,0,
C0C0C0,C0C0C0,808080,0,808080,808000,FFFFFF,0,FFFFFF
Black Leather
Jacket=0,C0C0C0,FFFFFF,0,C0C0C0,0,800040,808080,FFFFFF,808080,808080,0,10E0E0
E0,C0C0C0,808080,0,808080,0,FFFFFF,0,FFFFFF
Bordeaux=400080,C0C0C0,FFFFFF,0,FFFFFF,0,800080,C0C0C0,FFFFFF,FF0080,C0C0C0,0
,C0C0C0,C0C0C0,808080,0,808080,800080,FFFFFF,0,FFFFFF
Cinnamon=404080,C0C0C0,FFFFFF,0,FFFFFF,0,80,C0C0C0,FFFFFF,80,C0C0C0,0,C0C0C0,
C0C0C0,808080,0,808080,80,FFFFFF,0,FFFFFF
Designer=7C7C3F,C0C0C0,FFFFFF,0,FFFFFF,0,808000,C0C0C0,FFFFFF,C0C0C0,C0C0C0,0
,C0C0C0,C0C0C0,808080,0,C0C0C0,808000,0,0,FFFFFF
Emerald
City=404000,C0C0C0,FFFFFF,0,C0C0C0,0,408000,808040,FFFFFF,408000,808040,0,C0C
0C0,C0C0C0,808080,0,808080,8000,FFFFFF,0,FFFFFF
Fluorescent=0,FFFFFF,FFFFFF,0,FF00,0,FF00FF,C0C0C0,0,FF80,C0C0C0,0,C0C0C0,C0C
```

0C0,808080,0,808080,0,FFFFFF,0,FFFFFF
Hotdog
Stand=FFFF,FFFF,FF,FFFFFF,FFFFFF,0,0,FF,FFFFFF,FF,FF,0,C0C0C0,C0C0C0,808080,0
,808080,0,FFFFFF,FFFFFF,FFFFFF
LCD Default Screen
Settings=808080,C0C0C0,C0C0C0,0,C0C0C0,0,800000,C0C0C0,FFFFFF,800000,C0C0C0,0
,C0C0C0,C0C0C0,7F8080,0,808080,800000,FFFFFF,0,FFFFFF
LCD Reversed -
Dark=0,80,80,FFFFFF,8080,0,8080,800000,0,8080,800000,0,8080,C0C0C0,7F8080,0,C
0C0C0,800000,FFFFFF,828282,FFFFFF
LCD Reversed -
Light=800000,FFFFFF,FFFFFF,0,FFFFFF,0,808040,FFFFFF,0,C0C0C0,C0C0C0,800000,C0
C0C0,C0C0C0,7F8080,0,808040,800000,FFFFFF,0,FFFFFF
Mahogany=404040,C0C0C0,FFFFFF,0,FFFFFF,0,40,C0C0C0,FFFFFF,C0C0C0,C0C0C0,0,C0C
0C0,C0C0C0,808080,0,C0C0C0,80,FFFFFF,0,FFFFFF
Monochrome=C0C0C0,FFFFFF,FFFFFF,0,FFFFFF,0,0,C0C0C0,FFFFFF,C0C0C0,C0C0C0,0,80
8080,C0C0C0,808080,0,808080,0,FFFFFF,0,FFFFFF
Ocean=808000,408000,FFFFFF,0,FFFFFF,0,804000,C0C0C0,FFFFFF,C0C0C0,C0C0C0,0,C0
C0C0,C0C0C0,808080,0,0,808000,0,0,FFFFFF
Pastel=C0FF82,80FFFF,FFFFFF,0,FFFFFF,0,FFFF80,FFFFFF,0,C080FF,FFFFFF,808080,C
0C0C0,C0C0C0,808080,0,C0C0C0,FFFF00,0,0,FFFFFF
Patchwork=9544BB,C1FBFA,FFFFFF,0,FFFFFF,0,FFFF80,FFFFFF,0,64B14E,FFFFFF,0,C0C
0C0,C0C0C0,808080,0,808080,FFFF00,0,0,FFFFFF
Plasma Power
Saver=0,FF0000,0,FFFFFF,FF00FF,0,800000,C0C0C0,0,80,FFFFFF,C0C0C0,FF0000,C0C0
C0,808080,0,C0C0C0,FFFFFF,0,0,FFFFFF
Rugby=C0C0C0,80FFFF,FFFFFF,0,FFFFFF,0,800000,FFFFFF,FFFFFF,80,FFFFFF,0,C0C0C0
,C0C0C0,808080,0,808080,800000,FFFFFF,0,FFFFFF
The
Blues=804000,C0C0C0,FFFFFF,0,FFFFFF,0,800000,C0C0C0,FFFFFF,C0C0C0,C0C0C0,0,C0
C0C0,C0C0C0,808080,0,C0C0C0,800000,FFFFFF,0,FFFFFF
Tweed=6A619E,C0C0C0,FFFFFF,0,FFFFFF,0,408080,C0C0C0,FFFFFF,404080,C0C0C0,0,10
E0E0E0,C0C0C0,808080,0,C0C0C0,8080,0,0,FFFFFF
Valentine=C080FF,FFFFFF,FFFFFF,0,FFFFFF,0,8000FF,400080,FFFFFF,C080FF,C080FF,
0,C0C0C0,C0C0C0,808080,0,808080,FF00FF,0,FFFFFF,FFFFFF
Wingtips=408080,C0C0C0,FFFFFF,0,FFFFFF,0,808080,FFFFFF,FFFFFF,4080,FFFFFF,0,8
08080,C0C0C0,808080,0,C0C0C0,808080,FFFFFF,0,FFFFFF

[Custom Colors]
ColorA=FFFFFF
ColorB= FFFFFF
ColorC=FFFFFF
ColorD=FFFFFF
ColorE=FFFFFF
ColorF=FFFFFF
ColorG=FFFFFF
ColorH=FFFFFF
ColorI=FFFFFF
ColorJ=FFFFFF
ColorK=FFFFFF
ColorL=FFFFFF
ColorM=FFFFFF
ColorN=FFFFFF
ColorO=FFFFFF
ColorP=FFFFFF

[Patterns]
(None) = (None)
Boxes= 127 65 65 65 65 65 127 0
Paisley=2 7 7 2 32 80 80 32
Weave=136 84 34 69 136 21 34 81
Waffle=0 0 0 0 128 128 128 240

```
Tulip=0 0 84 124 124 56 146 124
Spinner=20 12 200 121 158 19 48 40
Scottie=64 192 200 120 120 72 0 0
Critters=0 80 114 32 0 5 39 2
50% Gray=170 85 170 85 170 85 170 85
Quilt=130 68 40 17 40 68 130 1
Diamonds=32 80 136 80 32 0 0 0
Thatches=248 116 34 71 143 23 34 113
Pattern=224 128 142 136 234 10 14 0

[Screen Saver.Stars]
Density=25
WarpSpeed=5
PWProtected=0
```

Network Connections

In addition to Novell NetWare, Windows for Workgroups 3.11 supports a number of network systems. Of course, it has its own built-in peer-to-peer network operating system and can connect with other systems. Figure 6.15 shows the different networks to which Windows for Workgroups can connect.

Windows SETUP /A Doesn't Install Properly

The SETUP /A parameter is designed to uncompress all the files on the installation disks and place them on the file server. This enables you to access all files on the server without having to load the Windows installation disks again.

At the end of the installation of files with the /A option, a message may appear informing you that the properties of the SETUP.INI file or other files cannot be changed. The SETUP utility in Microsoft Windows will try to open the file in a read/write mode. If the open procedure does not succeed, then it determines that the file is flagged "read only."

◊ Novell NetWare (3.x, 4.x)
◊ Artisoft LANtastic (3.x, 4.x, 5.x)
◊ Banyan VINES 4.11, 5.0, 5.52)
◊ DEC Pathworks (4.0 and later)
◊ IBM OS/2 Lan Server (1.2, 1.3, 2.0)
◊ Microsoft Workgroup Client (all versions)
◊ Microsoft LAN Manager (2.1)
◊ Microsoft Windows NT (3.1 and higher)
◊ Sun Microsystems PC-NFS
◊ TCS 10Net (4.1x, 4.2, 5.0)

Figure 6.15   Local area networks supported by Windows for Workgroups.

Figure 6.16 Install utility main menu.

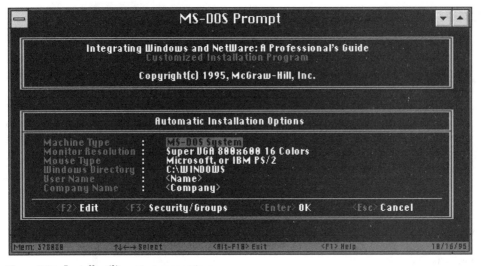

Figure 6.17 Install utility setup parameters.

However, some versions of NETX and VLM allow files to be opened in read/write mode even though the file is flagged "read only." This, in turn, fools the SETUP program into thinking that the file is available for writing. When writing takes place on these files, the error message appears because the file is set to "read only" and cannot be modified. To remedy this problem, insert the line READ ONLY COMPATIBILITY = OFF in the NET.CFG file under the NetWare DOS requester section. This should solve the problem. The latest versions of NETX and VLM have the read-only compatibility set to OFF as a default.

Install Utility

We have created an installation utility (see Figs. 6.16 and 6.17) to assist you in installing Windows in your organization. This utility enables you to customize your installation in several ways easily.

7

Configuration Files

Meeting the needs of everyone is a very difficult job. It is almost impossible to build a computer program that will make everyone happy. The complaint about "canned" software is that it doesn't meet the needs of the user. This is because everyone needs slightly different screens and computations to get their work done. This is one of the strongest reasons for the continuing popularity of custom software. It gives users exactly what they want.

However, it is not economically viable to create a new application for every company or group of users just because they want a slight modification from a standard computer application. For practical and economic reasons, it is not possible for developers to include source code with the program. This leaves users in quite a quandary because they don't want to reinvent the programs but yet want a customized system.

Early software provided the ability to modify minor items such as default printers, directories, and maybe some user options. This wasn't good enough. Users need the ability to configure almost every facet of the system. This is the idea in Microsoft Windows.

Windows is more than just a software application—it is an operating environment. Configuration becomes critical to the successful operation of Windows. This is done through ASCII (American Standard Code for Information Interchange) files called .INI (for files initialization). These files are read when Windows is first started or when running certain utilities in Windows. Developers have used the same idea, and many will include their own .INI files for configuring their application.

These .INI files give us some level of standardization as they are in the format of a heading (denoted by brackets around a name; e.g., [windows]) and individual items with the variable on the left, or a value on the right with an equal sign in the middle (e.g., NetMessage = Yes).

Two main files are required by Windows: WIN.INI and SYSTEM.INI. These (and all other .INI) files are in ASCII format and can be edited by any text editor. In addition, many values inside the .INI files can be changed by utilities contained in Windows.

Searching for .INI Files

The .INI files are critical to the operation of Windows, and if Windows can't find one or more of these files, partial or total failure may result. If Windows can't find critical files like WIN.INI or SYSTEM.INI, you will be aware of the problem. Ensuring that .INI files are in the correct location is a critical part of troubleshooting Windows problems.

WIN.COM looks in the current directory for the .INI files (see Fig. 7.1) first, if they are not found there, a search is made through the DOS path. There are so many .INI files that can be installed once you start installing applications, that it gets to be a problem quickly.

Whether Windows is installed on a file server or on the local drive, WIN.COM, WIN.INI, PROGMAN.INI, and SYSTEM.INI should be in the same directory (see Fig. 7.2).

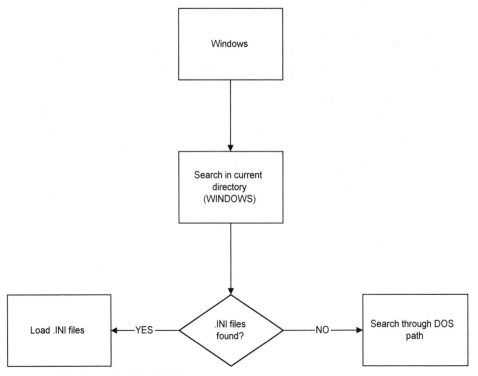

Figure 7.1 Windows search for .INI files.

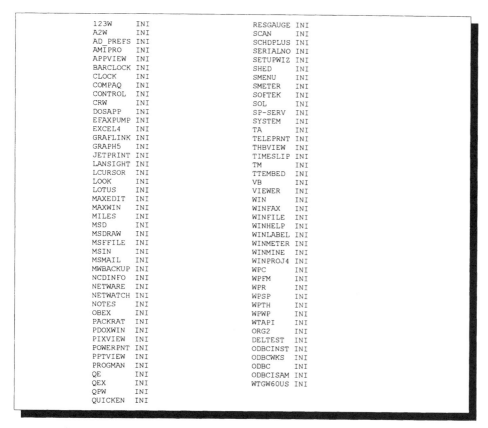

```
            123W     INI              RESGAUGE INI
            A2W      INI              SCAN     INI
            AD_PREFS INI              SCHDPLUS INI
            AMIPRO   INI              SERIALNO INI
            APPVIEW  INI              SETUPWIZ INI
            BARCLOCK INI              SHED     INI
            CLOCK    INI              SMENU    INI
            COMPAQ   INI              SMETER   INI
            CONTROL  INI              SOFTEK   INI
            CRW      INI              SOL      INI
            DOSAPP   INI              SP-SERV  INI
            EFAXPUMP INI              SYSTEM   INI
            EXCEL4   INI              TA       INI
            GRAFLINK INI              TELEPRNT INI
            GRAPH5   INI              THBVIEW  INI
            JETPRINT INI              TIMESLIP INI
            LANSIGHT INI              TM       INI
            LCURSOR  INI              TTEMBED  INI
            LOOK     INI              VB       INI
            LOTUS    INI              VIEWER   INI
            MAXEDIT  INI              WIN      INI
            MAXWIN   INI              WINFAX   INI
            MILES    INI              WINFILE  INI
            MSD      INI              WINHELP  INI
            MSDRAW   INI              WINLABEL INI
            MSFFILE  INI              WINMETER INI
            MSIN     INI              WINMINE  INI
            MSMAIL   INI              WINPROJ4 INI
            MWBACKUP INI              WPC      INI
            NCDINFO  INI              WPFM     INI
            NETWARE  INI              WPR      INI
            NETWATCH INI              WPSP     INI
            NOTES    INI              WPTH     INI
            OBEX     INI              WPWP     INI
            PACKRAT  INI              WTAPI    INI
            PDOXWIN  INI              ORG2     INI
            PIXVIEW  INI              DELTEST  INI
            POWERPNT INI              ODBCINST INI
            PPTVIEW  INI              ODBCWKS  INI
            PROGMAN  INI              ODBC     INI
            QE       INI              ODBCISAM INI
            QEX      INI              WTGW60US INI
            QPW      INI
            QUICKEN  INI
```

Figure 7.2   Sample list of system and application .INI files.

Editing .INI Files

Almost every Windows user eventually ends up modifying .INI files by hand as there are some variables that cannot be changed with any other method. Here are some guidelines to note before editing any of these files.

Text editors

Be careful in the selection of editors to use with .INI files. The editor must not insert any formatting codes at all into the file, and it must not have a right margin of less than 255 characters. If there is a right-hand margin, the line will wrap, and as a result that variable will not work and potential error messages will be seen on the screen. Most lines are very short, but some can be quite long, and it is a good idea to be prepared for this problem. Do not use a word processor to edit .INI files as most will wrap the lines and cause many problems in these files.

Backup copies

Always make a safety backup copy of any .INI files you are modifying directly with a text editor. It is very easy to make a seemingly minor change that will result in Windows not starting. The backup copy gives you a reference and can be restored in the event of a major problem.

Changing variables

Whenever changing variables, never delete the original line. Make a copy of the line (by selecting and copying it into the clipboard) and the identical copy just below it. Place a semicolon at the start of the first line to turn it into a comment, and make the modifications to the second line. This allows you to reference the original setting whenever further changes are needed. (See also Fig. 7.3.)

Comments

It is almost impossible to put too many comments in an .INI file. Whenever a change is made to a file, there has been some reasoning behind it. If you don't create a comment describing the reason why this change was made, it is likely you will forget the reason a few months later.

You can place anything in the .INI files as comments as long as the first character is a semicolon. We also apply the idea of an identification of the person making the change along with the date and time the variable was changed (see Fig. 7.4).

Separating sections

Windows does not require any blank lines between sections in any .INI files. All items can be slammed together, and everything will run fine as long as each variable or heading item is on its own separate line. If it makes it easier to read the entries by separating sections or even variables, with lines—go ahead and set blank lines wherever you want.

```
;NetMessage=YES
NetMessage=NO
```

Figure 7.3 Duplicate variables with original line commented out.

```
;run=
;Display of clock utility on window title line - Wayne Robertson & Ed Koop 10/3/95-12:19
run=c:\clock\barclock.exe
```

Figure 7.4 Documentation of changes in .INI files.

Headings

Heading names are case-insensitive as you can put any combination of upper- and lowercase characters you want. However, inside the brackets that surround the heading names, spaces become critical.

For example, the heading [386Enh] is designed to be spelled exactly that way, and changing it to [386 Enh] will ensure that all items in that section will be ignored by Windows. Missing the variables in the [386Enh] section is a method of making Windows fail.

Variable values

When searching for variables and their values, Windows looks for integers (zero, positive, or whole numbers) or strings (alphanumeric characters). This is not a big problem, but sometimes strange things can occur. A value that would be ignored when Windows is looking for an integer (e.g., 9.1—only the whole number 9 would be used) would be read as a string (e.g., the complete number 9.1 would be evaluated).

There are some other rules for variables that are a big help in diagnosing problems with variables that are read properly by Windows. When parsing across the variable, Windows looks to the left of the equal sign for the variable name, then looks to the right of the equal sign for the value.

For variables that have strings for their value, Windows inputs the entire string to the right of the equal sign and then trims off spaces, tabs, and any single and double quotes that are at the beginning and end of the value. Some have reported that if a tab is between a pair of quotes along with alphanumeric characters, everything is stripped out of the value, leaving only the first quote.

Windows treats variables that have integers as their value the same as it would a character value by trimming off spaces, tabs, and quotes. If the first character is a minus sign, Windows evaluates the next character to see if it is a number. Windows looks at all numbers in the integer and accumulates those values in memory for use later. If there are no numbers, it returns a value of zero.

This brings up some bizarre results when evaluating values. The number 16.6 comes back as 16, −16alpha comes back as −16, and +16 comes back as 0 because the plus sign is not a valid value and renders the whole value invalid.

Critical .INI Files

There are many .INI files found in Windows; some are critical and others are not as important. Figure 7.5 lists a critical .INI file you will need in your Windows installation.

Review of .INI Files

Before we can install Windows and make the configuration changes for high performance, it is necessary to understand some of the critical items in these

```
CLOCK.INI              NETWARE.INI              WIN.INI
COMPAQ.INI             PROGMAN.INI              WINHELP.INI
CONTROL.INI            SYSTEM.INI
MSMAIL.INI             VB.INI
```

Figure 7.5 Sample of .INI system and application files.

files. The following discussion reviews these configurations and what effect they have on Windows operation. There are two basic components in WIN.INI file settings: the Windows section and .INI file structure.

Windows section

This section (see Fig. 7.6) sets up some screen parameters plus a few other minor settings.

Spooler =. First a couple of words about spoolers. Using a spooler, either in Windows or on a file server, makes the printing time much slower. Printing directly to an attached printer will be the fastest method of printing. What spooling provides is the ability to return to the application as quickly as possible. Printing will take place in the background as CPU time allows.

This variable determines whether the Windows print spooler should be used. The spooler can be activated by changing this variable in the WIN.INI file or checking the box in the control panel printer setup (see Fig. 7.7).

Using the Windows spooler introduces a problem when running with a network, especially Windows. If the spooler is used, this means that the print job is spooled twice—once in Windows and a second time on the NetWare file server. The obvious answer is to set this value to No and not use the Windows print spooler. Of course, there are other considerations.

If the print spooler is turned off, print jobs go directly to the file server spooler and are printed from there. The NetWare spooler doesn't have many features such as the ability to pause or easily cancel print jobs. If you are printing from a Windows application and want to cancel the print job, the

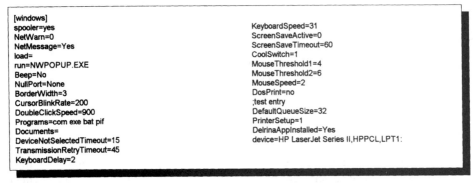

Figure 7.6 Windows section of WIN.INI.

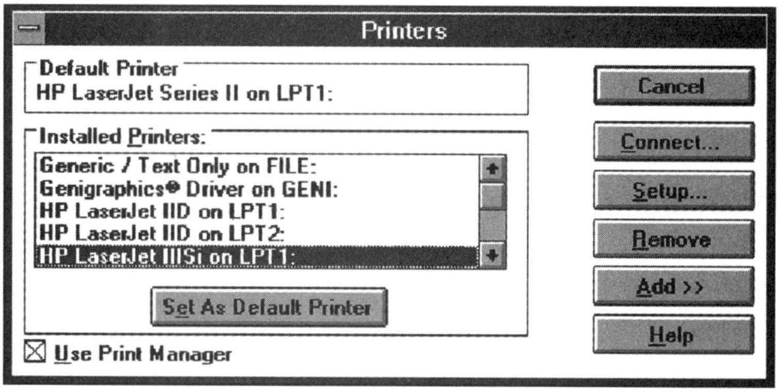

Figure 7.7   Activating spooler in print manager.

data is already in the NetWare spooler and cannot be removed except by switching to a NetWare utility.

NetWarn = 0.   This value determines whether Windows will check for a valid network connection. If this value is set to 1 (enabled), you will be warned as to whether the ODI drivers and NETX.EXE or VLMs are not loaded. (Since this is a book on NetWare, we will ignore other network systems.)

This feature is important because if NetWare shells are not loaded and you start Windows, once you discover the problem it will be necessary to exit Windows, load the drivers, and start Windows again. This warning will save you some time. If, however, you have a laptop computer that is connected to the network only some of the time, having this feature will be a life saver.

NetMessage.   For an example of NetMessage, see Fig. 7.8.

[network].   The network section of WIN.INI (Fig. 7.9) is reserved for connection information to printer queues, port settings, and drive mappings. If you want permanent drive letter mapping to specified servers, then the information will

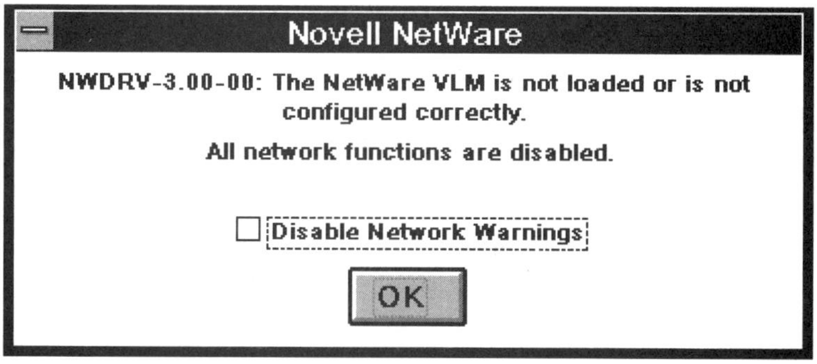

Figure 7.8

```
[Network]
LPT1:=FILE_SERVER_1/PRINTER1
LPT1-OPTIONS=128,1,8,0,0,LST:,SUSAN
LPT2:=FILE_SERVER_1/PRINTER2
LPT2-OPTIONS=128,1,8,0,0,LST:,SUSAN
```

Figure 7.9 Sample network section of WIN.INI.

be placed in this section. Regardless of what drive letters are mapped on the workstation, the new drive letters will be installed when Windows starts.

.INI file structure

The files you will be spending most time worrying about are the *SYSTEM.INI* and the *WIN.INI* files. The SYSTEM.INI is concerned mainly with the hardware setup of the computer; WIN.INI contains mostly application information and user preferences. PROGMAN.INI controls the program manager shell, while CONTROL.INI handles the settings for the control panel. In addition to Windows .INI files, many applications have their own .INI files which can be placed in their own directories or in the Windows directory.

Many of the settings in these files can be modified through a dialog box in Windows itself. However, to be successful in implementing Windows in your organization and on a network, it is important to understand many settings in these files to ensure that you are getting the best out of your system. We will now look at these files and the settings that are available.

The .INI file is the main configuration file for user preferences. by controlling most of what you see in Windows. Fonts, groups, icons, and a variety of other settings are defined in here. Many changes can be made within Windows, but advanced configuration changes of Windows sometimes requires changes be made directly in the file.

All initialization files (denoted by the .INI extension) have a structure that is flexible, but certain rules must be followed. A comment can be placed in any initialization file as long as it starts with a semicolon (;). Rather than deleting a line, you can use the semicolon to turn a command into a comment which identifies any changes you may have made in the file. WIN.INI file sections are listed in Fig. 7.10.

Now that we have seen the major sections of WIN.INI, let's take a look at each section and what individual choices there are and how we can tune the system to our needs. The sections are a word or words inside brackets that give you a hint as to what the sections are all about. While these section names are not descriptive, they are better than a numeric value that could have been used.

Section Names

A section names can contain virtually any printable character inside the brackets. It is limited to what the programmer will call the sections. Case is not a significant factor; while most section names are lowercase, some names are a combination of upper- and lowercase, and in a few rare instances, some application installation routines will create a section with all-uppercase names.

A section name can appear in any position on a line (centered, flush left, etc.), so location is not an important factor. About the only rule is that it appear on the line by itself (i.e., as a stand-alone heading) to ensure that Windows understands the heading title. What appears inside the section name brackets is, however, very important. Back in the days when typewriters ruled offices, we came to learn that a space was nothing, i.e., an absence of typed characters. In computers, spaces constitute a character, and placing a space inside the brackets will change the name of the section and cause untold problems with the Windows operation. Don't try to "clean up" the section headings by putting spaces between words that are joined together.

The section names define each area of variables for Windows, and it is assumed that all variables are tied to the preceding section name. Therefore, putting variables before any section names would result in neither Windows nor applications being able to get access to those variables! The order of sections is irrelevant as Windows scans through the WIN.INI file to find the correct section. (See Fig. 7.10)

Variable Standards

You can use virtually any character in variable names with the exception of brackets. These symbols are not case-sensitive and, similar to the section names, spaces inside the variable names do make a difference. Spaces can occur around the equal signs but cannot occur inside the variable names or values.

[windows]

This section usually appears as the first section of the file and holds a variety of items that don't easily fit into other areas.

SYSTEM.INI

This file controls the setting of the Windows system resources. It controls very little of the appearance of Windows but handles the hardware aspects of Windows. Most of the items in this file can be changed through the control panel in the main group. However, there may be a need to change the items by hand (manually) to solve specific problems.

Section	Purpose
[windows]	Defines the basic parameters of the desktop
[desktop]	Appearance of backgrounds and spacing
[extensions]	Maps files extensions to applications
[intl]	International settings (e.g. currency, language, etc.)
[ports]	Definition of output ports
[fonts]	Defines screen font files will be loaded upon startup
[fontSubstitutes]	Fonts that are interchangeable
[TrueType]	TrueType options
[mci extensions]	Setup of Media Control Interface devices
[network]	Network connection initial settings and options
[embedding]	Server objects for Object Linking and Embedding
[Windows Help]	Initial placement settings of the help files
[sound]	What sound files will play for each type of event
[printerPorts]	Active and inactive output devices
[devices]	Defines devices providing compatibility with earlier versions
[programs]	Directory paths are stored here which indicates where to look when opening an application. If you click on a data file that has a recognized extension in the registration file, Windows will look in these directories for the associated executable.

Figure 7.10 Standard sections of WIN.INI file.

Tip: When you change any current entry in the initialization files, it is not hard to put in the wrong entry and cause major problems with Windows operation. To help get around that problem, copy the original line just below the current line so you have two entries the same. Place a semicolon in front of the first line and make your modifications to the second line. This way you will have saved the original entry and can easily go back to that value if a problem occurs.

The SYSTEM.INI file is shown in Courier font, and comments are shown in a **_bold, italicized font._** Your SYSTEM.INI file will not look exactly like this as it changes depending on applications loaded and selections made during setup or in the Control Panel.

```
[boot]
shell=progman.exe
mouse.drv=lmouse.drv
```
***This line determines what driver will be used for the network communication.
If this file is not located in the SYSTEM directory, then the path for the
driver needs to be installed.***
```
network.drv=NETWARE.DRV
language.dll=
drivers=mmsystem.dll power.drv
sound.drv=mmsound.drv
comm.drv=comm.drv
keyboard.drv=keyboard.drv
system.drv=system.drv
386grabber=cpqvga.gr3
oemfonts.fon=vgaoem.fon
286grabber=cpqvga.gr2
fixedfon.fon=vgafix.fon
fonts.fon=vgasys.fon
display.drv=cpqavga.drv
SCRNSAVE.EXE=(None)

[keyboard]
subtype=
type=4
keyboard.dll=
oemansi.bin=

[boot.description]
```
***This description shows up in the Windows setup options. You can put a specif-
ic description in here to communicate with a user who is changing their
setup.***
```
keyboard.typ=Enhanced 101 or 102 key US and Non US keyboards
mouse.drv=Compaq Mouse
network.drv=Novell NetWare (shell versions 3.26 and above)
language.dll=English (American)
system.drv=MS-DOS System with APM
codepage=437
woafont.fon=English (437)
aspect=100,96,96
display.drv=COMPAQ AVGA, 640x480, 256 color, 6-bit DAC

[386Enh]
32BitDiskAccess=off
mouse=lvmd.386
network=*vnetbios, vnetware.386, vipx.386
device=vpowerd.386
ebios=*ebios
woafont=dosapp.fon
display=cpqvdd.386
EGA80WOA.FON=EGA80WOA.FON
EGA40WOA.FON=EGA40WOA.FON
CGA80WOA.FON=CGA80WOA.FON
CGA40WOA.FON=CGA40WOA.FON
keyboard = *vkd
device=vtdapi.386
device=*vpicd
device=*vtd
```

```
device=*reboot
device=*vdmad
device=*vsd
device=*v86mmgr
device=*pageswap
device=*dosmgr
device=*vmpoll
device=*wshell
device=*BLOCKDEV
device=*PAGEFILE
device=*vfd
device=*parity
device=*biosxlat
device=*vcd
device=*vmcpd
device=*combuff
device=*cdpscsi
local=CON
FileSysChange=off
OverlappedIO=off
PermSwapDOSDrive=D
PermSwapSizeK=6000

[standard]

[NonWindowsApp]
localtsrs=dosedit,ced
CommandEnvSize=1536

[mci]
WaveAudio=mciwave.drv
Sequencer=mciseq.drv
CDAudio=mcicda.drv

[drivers]
timer=timer.drv
midimapper=midimap.drv
Wave=speaker.drv

[LogiMouse]
Release=2.23
LockSetting=No
Type=PS/2
ConnectedModel=MouseMan
Port=4
DragLock=None

[speaker.drv]
CPU Speed=33
Volume=1000
Version=774
Enhanced=1
Max seconds=0
Leave interrupts enabled=0
```

Network Variables

There are several variables in the SYSTEM.INI file that are critical to network operation. Here is a detailed list:

Section	Variable	Description
[boot]	CachedFile Handles	Must be edited directly as there is no Windows setup available. Indicates the number of program files that can remain open at any time. The default value is 12. If you are short of memory on the file server, reduce this number so that the server doesn't run out of memory. Reducing this number will slow down Windows but may make the difference between operation and nonoperation.
	Network.drv	Can be set from the Windows setup icon in the main group or edited directly. It must be the file NETWARE.DRV to communicate with the server properly.
[Standard]	Int28Filter	Must be edited manually—this is the number of INT 28h interrupts (used for task switching) available for memory-resident software loaded before Windows starts. A value of 2 means that every second interrupt will be available to memory-resident software. The default value is 10 (every 10th interrupt 28h is available) but should be adjusted if you are having problems with network communications while running Windows.
		Setting this value too low may cause very slow Windows operation and problems with modem or terminal communications. A value of 0 disables INT 28h.
	NetHeapSize	This is the size of data-transfer buffers Windows allocates in conventional memory for transferring data over a network. Used only in standard mode. Default is 8.
[NonWindows-Apps]	NetAsynch Switching	Use only if you are running in standard mode and using NetBIOS in addition to IPX/SPX. Determines if you can switch away from a running application after it has made a network BIOS call. If the application that made the call isn't in the foreground, the application could hang and cause Windows errors.
[386enh]	FileSys Change	To manage all segments of the computer, Windows needs to know about all activities. Unless noted otherwise, Windows running in enhanced mode will be notified whenever a non-Windows application creates, renames, or deletes a file. In standard mode this variable defaults to OFF.
	Network	Same function as DEVICE variable.
	InDOS Polling	If this variable is ON, it prevents Windows from running applications when memory-resident software is performing a critical operation.
	PSP Increments	If this variable is ON, it specifies the amount of additional memory Windows should reserve for each successive virtual machine. Values represent 16-byte increments, and valid entries range from 2 to 64. Default is 2.

Section	Variable	Description
	Int28Critical	Needed for network shells to ensure vital access to INT 28h. If you are not using any network shells, setting this entry to OFF will improve Windows task switching.
[386enh]	NetAsynchFallback	Needed only if running NetBIOS.* Allocates additional memory buffers when large amount of data received in a short period of time. Default is OFF.
	NetAsynchTimeout	Used for NetBIOS and in conjunction with NetAsynchFallback. Value is a timeout period to handle a NetBIOS request. Default is 5.0.
	NetDMASize	Size of DMA buffer. Default is 0 for non-Micro Channel machines and 32 for Micro Channel systems.
	NetHeapSize	The size (in 4-kbyte increments) of the data-transfer buffers that Windows in enhanced mode allocates in conventional memory for transferring data over the network. Default is 12.
	ReflectDOS Int2A	See text.
	TimerCriticalSection	See text.
	TokenRing Search	Set to ON if using a Token Ring Network Interface Card on AT type machines.
	UniqueDOS PSP	See text.

*While NetWare uses IPX/SPX to communicate between server and workstation, there may be times when you need to run NetBIOS in addition to IPX/SPX.

PROGMAN.INI

This file controls the optional settings for program manager and defines groups and look of that application. While changing values here is not difficult, there is nothing that cannot be changed in program manager.

The file displayed here is shown in Courier font, and comments are shown in a ***bold, italicized font.*** Your PROGMAN.INI file will not look exactly like this as it changes depending on applications loaded and selections made during setup or in the control panel.

```
[Settings]
This is the location and order of the windows in program manager.
AutoArrange=1
Window=64 48 576 384 3
```

Tip: Don't be stingy with comments in the initialization files. You may forget why you changed a setting when you look at it again several months later. A good comment on the line above the changed entry will help explain why you made those changes.

```
display.drv=cpqavga.drv
Order= 2 10 1  6 5 11 3 4 7 8 9
[Groups]
Group1=C:\WINDOWS\MAIN.GRP
Group2=C:\WINDOWS\ACCESSOR.GRP
Group3=C:\WINDOWS\GAMES.GRP
Group4=C:\WINDOWS\STARTUP.GRP
Group5=C:\WINDOWS\COMPAQUT.GRP
Group6=C:\WINDOWS\MICROSOF.GRP
Group7=C:\WINDOWS\STACKER.GRP
Group8=C:\WINDOWS\WORDPERF.GRP
Group9=C:\WINDOWS\GRAMMATI.GRP
Group11=C:\WINDOWS\MICROSO0.GRP
```

Program manager security

The default settings of PROGMAN.INI work fine for a single-user system but may cause problems on a network. There are two schools of thought about how much freedom to give the user.

The first group want to give users the maximum amount of freedom to change the setup of Windows any way they want. To achieve this goal, users will need to be trained on the use of Windows and how to set up and adjust the program manager.

If the users aren't highly trained in the use of Windows or don't want to learn about Windows, giving them access to certain functions can be a source of great frustration to network support staff. Users will be calling frequently asking for help when they have deleted a group or have created other problems. To help solve the second problem, you can modify the PROGMAN.INI file to restrict user access to the file menu. To set up the restrictions, use a text editor (like Notepad in the Accessories group) to add another section called [restrictions]. There are several variables that can be added: NoRun, NoFileMenu, NoClose, or NoSaveSettings (see Figs. 7.11 and 7.12).

The values for these entries follow standard programming convention, in which 0 is false and 1 is true.

Variable	Actions
NoRun	A value of 1 changes the Run command to gray and does not allow the user to run applications in the File... Run... commands.
NoClose	A value of 1 disables the Exit command either in the File menu or with <Alt-F4>.
NoSaveSettings	A 1 disables the Save Settings on Exit where changes in open groups or arrangement of windows will be the same the next time windows starts.
	Setting this variable to 1 overrides the SaveSettings entry in PROG-MAN.INI (see text).
NoFileMenu	A 1 completely disables and removes the File menu from program manager. All the items on that menu will be unavailable to the user except for Exit, which can still be done with <Alt-F4> (unless NoClose=1).

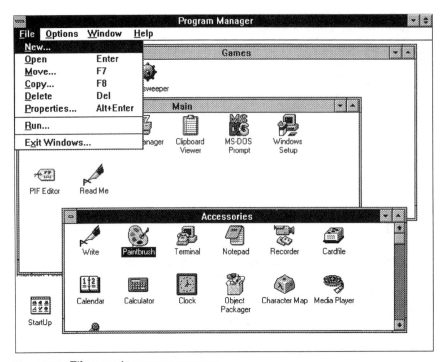

Figure 7.11   File menu in program manager.

```
[restrictions]
NoRun=1
NoFileManager=1
NoClose=1
NoSaveSettings=1
EditLevel=4
```

Figure 7.12   Edit levels in PROGMAN.INI file.

Variable	Actions
Edit Level	A value of 1 does not allow the user to create, delete, or rename groups. New, Move, Copy, and Delete options in the File menu are disabled.
	A value of 2 has the restrictions in 1 plus the inability to create or delete program items.
	A value of 3 has the restrictions in 1 and 2 and disables the ability to change the command lines for program items.
	A value of 4 has the restrictions in 1, 2, and 3 and disables all items in the Properties dialog box of File menu except Cancel and Help.

PROTOCOL.INI

The PROTOCOL.INI file is created when Windows is installed from information in the NETWORK.INF file, from OEMSETUP.INF files (if needed), and according to the choices you make during installation.

The PROTOCOL.INI file is not one you can easily change by hand. The settings are modified through the network setup icon (Fig. 7.13). The PROTOCOL.INI file contains all the information about the network protocols and adapters. The network shells and drivers are given the information located in this file through the protocol manager PROTMAN.DOS on the type of network communication desired. (See also Figs. 7.14 to 7.16.)

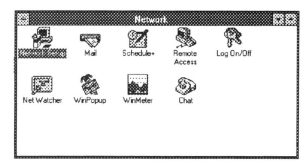

Figure 7.13 Network setup icon in network group.

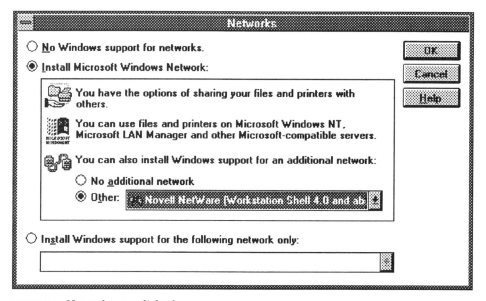

Figure 7.14 Network setup dialog box.

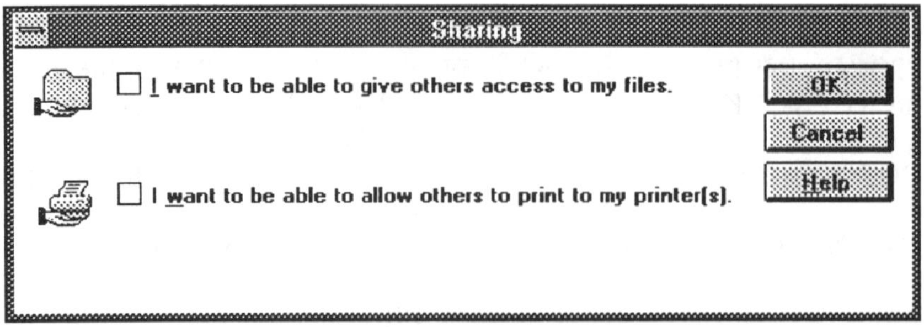

Figure 7.15 Sharing options for workgroups network.

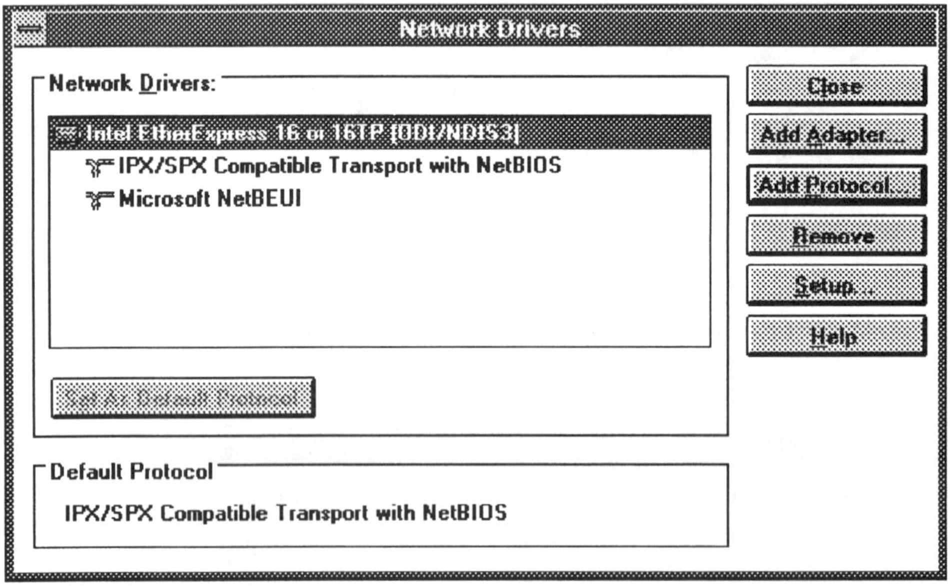

Figure 7.16 Network adapter and protocol setup.

There are several sections in the PROTOCOL.INI that define information about the hardware drivers and network communication protocols. These sections are discussed below (see also Fig. 7.17).

[network.setup]

This is used for setup purposes when you want to change the network setup. This saves you from reinserting the installation disks each time you want to make a change on your Windows system. The version variable determines the

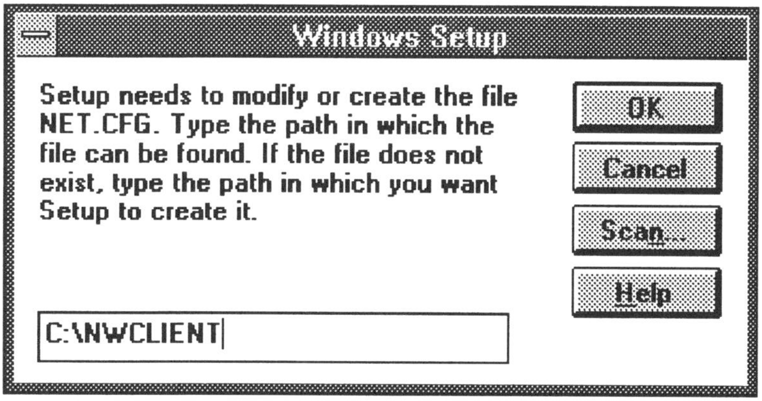

Figure 7.17 Modifying network parameters in NET.CFG.

current Windows version number. The netcard variable defines the network adapter information which came from the NETWORK.INF file during setup or modification. The transport value determines which protocol(s) will be used, and the lana# value is used to identify the binding between the network adapter and the network protocol.

```
[network.setup]
version=0x3110
netcard=ms$ee16,1,MS$EE16,4
transport=ms$nwlinknb,NWLINK
transport=ms$netbeui,NETBEUI
lana0=ms$ee16,1,ms$nwlinknb
lana1=ms$ee16,1,ms$netbeui
```

[protoman]

These values used are for PROTOMAN.DOS (the protocol manager) to provide instructions to the network card drivers on what data will be passed to it (the protocol format). The values are drivername for the driver entry in the protocol manager. The priority value is the order in which the data network frames will be processed.

```
[protman]
drivername=PROTMAN$
priority=MS$NETBEUI
```

[netcard]

These values involve the NDIS network adapter to provide information about the network card and its hardware address. The netcard word is replaced by the corresponding name for the network card inside the brackets.

```
[MS$EE16]
drivername=EXP16$
IRQ=11
IOADDRESS=0x360
```

[Link driver]

The link driver section determines what type of data frames will be used in the protocol. This value should correspond with the values found in NET.CFG under the link driver section there.

```
[Link Driver EXP16ODI]
data=Frame Ethernet_SNAP
data=Frame Ethernet_802.2
data=Frame Ethernet_II
data=Frame Ethernet_802.3
```

[protocol]

The protocol section lists the protocol defined in the protman section and provides additional information about the protocol. In the example below, there is an entry for NWLINK, the identifier for IPX/SPX communication, and one for NetBEUI. There will be an entry for each protocol installed.

```
[NWLINK]
BINDINGS=EXP16ODI

[NETBEUI]
BINDINGS=EXP16ODI
LANABASE=1
SESSIONS=10
NCBS=12
```

Troubleshooting PROTOCOL.INI

We have found several problems to be frustrating when one makes a number of changes to the network setup. You will need to make some changes with a text editor (e.g., Notepad) to make the network connections work.

After running the network setup (Fig. 7.13) several times, there may be so many changes to the PROTOCOL.INI file that nothing will work. Here is a quick method for solving this problem: delete the PROTOCOL.INI file and run network setup again to rebuild this file. That makes sure you have a clean start.

Another problem that can surface with this file is network card drivers not in the default list. Here is a list of the network card drivers Windows for Workgroups has in the install files:

3Com EtherLink 16

3Com EtherLink II or IITP (8- or 16-bit)

3Com EtherLink III

3Com EtherLink/MC

3Com EtherLink Plus

3Com TokenLink

Advanced Micro Devices

Amplicard AC 210/XT

Amplicard AC 210/AT

ARCNET Compatible

Artisoft AE-1

Artisoft AE-2 or AE-3

Artisoft AE-2 (MCA) or AE-3 (MCA)

Artisoft AE-3

Cabletron E2000 Series DNI

Cabletron E2100 Series DNI

Cabletron E3000 Series DNI

Cabletron E3100 Series DNI

Cabletron T2015 Token Ring DNI

Cabletron T3015 Token Ring tokenring

Compaq NE3200

DCA 10 Mb

DCA 10 Mb Fiber s

DCA 10 Mb s

DCA 10 Mb Twisted Ethernet

DEC Ethernet (all types)

DEC DEPCA

DEC EE101 (built-in)

DEC (DE100) EtherWorks Ethernet

DEC (DE101) EtherWorks is

DEC (DE102) EtherWorks 237

DEC (DE210) EtherWorks Ethernet

DEC (DE211) EtherWorks dis

DEC (DE212) EtherWorks

DEC (DE200) EtherWorks s

DEC (DE201) EtherWorks

DEC (DE202) EtherWorks C

DECpc 433 WS (built-in)

Everex SpeedLink /PC16

HP Ethertwist MCA Adapter ndis

HP Ethertwist EISA LAN Adapter/32 (HP27248 or 0

HP PC LAN Adapter/8 TL 3

HP PC LAN Adapter/8 TP 1

HP PC LAN Adapter/16 TL Plus 5

IBM PC Network Adapter broadband

IBM PC Network Adapter broadband

IBM PC Network Baseband dis

IBM PC Network Baseband 5

IBM Token Ring

IBM Token Ring (MCA)

IBM Token Ring II

IBM Token Ring II/Short

IBM Token Ring ndis

IBM Token Ring 4/16Mbs dis

Intel EtherExpress 16 or 16TP

Intel EtherExpress 16 (MCA)

Intel EtherExpress/32

Intel TokenExpress EISA token ring

Intel TokenExpress 16/4

Intel TokenExpress MCA token ring

Exos 105

Madge Networks Smart 16/4 XT

Madge Networks Smart 16/4 AT

Madge Networks Smart 16/4 EISA

Madge Networks Smart 16/4 MC

National Semiconductor AT/LANTIC

National Semiconductor Ethernode

NCR StarCard (8-bit)

NCR Token-Ring 4 Mbs token ring

NCR Token-Ring 16/4 Mbs token ring

NCR Token-Ring 16/4 Mbs

NCR WaveLan AT dis

NCR WaveLan MC dis

NE1000 Compatible

NE2000 Compatible

Novell/Anthem NE1000

Novell/Anthem NE2000

Novell/Anthem

Novell/Anthem dis

Novell/Anthem NE/2

Novell/Anthem NE3200

Olicom 16/4 Token-Ring dis

Proteon ISA Token Ring is

Proteon ISA Token Ring is

Proteon ISA Token Ring is

Proteon ISA Token Ring is

Proteon MCA Token Ring is

Proteon ProNET-4/16 is

Proteon Token Ring (P1390)

Proteon Token Ring (P1392)

Pure Data PDI508 + ndis

Pure Data PDI516 + ndis

Pure Data PDI9025-32 (Token s

Pure Data PDuC9025 (Token s

Pure Data PDI90211

Pure Data PDuC90211

Racal-DATACOM ES3210

Racal NI5210/8

Racal NI5210/16

Racal NI6510

RadiSys EXM-10

SMC ARCNETPC

SMC ARCNET

SMC ARCNET PC250

SMC ARCNET

SMC ARCNET PC130/E

SMC ARCNET PC260

SMC ARCNET PC270/E

SMC ARCNET 0W

SMC 3000 Series

SMC EtherCard (All Types except dis

SMC EtherCard PLUS 293

SMC EtherCard PLUS/A (MCA

SMC EtherCard PLUS/A (MCA

SMC EtherCard PLUS 10T/A (MCA) (WD 2

SMC EtherCard PLUS 16 With BootROM)

SMC EtherCard PLUS/A (MCA) (WD 8003E/A

SMC EtherCard PLUS TP

SMC EtherCard PLUS With Boot ROM Socket

SMC EtherCard PLUS With Boot ROM Socket)

SMC EtherCard PLUS Elite

SMC EtherCard PLUS 10T

SMC EtherCard PLUS Elite 16

SMC EtherCard PLUS Elite 16T

SMC EtherCard PLUS Elite 16 Combo (WD/8013EW

SMC StarCard PLUS 291

SMC StarCard PLUS/A (MCA) (WD 1

SMC StarCard PLUS With On Board Hub

Thomas Conrad (All Arcnet is

Thomas Conrad TC6042

Thomas Conrad TC6045

Thomas Conrad TC6142

Thomas Conrad TC6145

Thomas Conrad TC6242

Thomas Conrad TC6245

Tulip NCC-16

UB NIU (All Types)

UB NIC/ps

UB NIUpc

UB NIUpc/3270

UB NIUpc/EOTP

UB NIUps or NIUps/EOTP

UB pcNIU

UB pcNIU/ex 128K

UB pcNIU/ex 512K

Xircom Pocket Ethernet I

Xircom Pocket Ethernet II

Zenith Data Systems dis

Zenith Data Systems NE2000 2

IPXODI Support Driver is

IPXODI Support Driver (Token ring)

IPXODI Support Driver (ArcNet)

IPX Support Driver (Monolithic) with NetBIOS

Generic NDIS2 hernet

Remote Access Service

NDIS2 Mapper

Microsoft is

IPX/SPX Compatible

IPX/SPX Compatible Transport with

ODI ArcNet Support transport with s

Novell IPX

Novell IPX (Token etbios)

Banyan VINES

PC-NFS Protocol

RAS Transport

If you have one of these cards, there should be no problem installing the driv
ers for them. However, if you have another type of network card not included

in this list, the network connection may not work. We have encountered a problem that occurs during setup. In the link driver section, the name of the card is required as a reference point during loading of drivers (at startup of Windows).

```
[Link Driver NE2000]
data=Frame Ethernet_SNAP
data=Frame Ethernet_802.2
data=Frame Ethernet_II
data=Frame Ethernet_802.3
```

Some nondefault card installation routines do not insert the name in the link driver heading on setup and you will receive an error dialog box stating that the network cannot run properly. Edit the PROTOCOL.INI file, and type in the name of the network card. You may need to look in the OEMSETUP.INF file to find the proper name for the card or look at the beginning of the PROTOCOL.INI for the name.

WINFILE.INI

This file controls the optional settings for the file manager and defines groups and look of that application. While changing values here is not difficult, there is no setting here that cannot be done in file manager.

The file displayed here is shown in Courier font and comments are shown in a **bold, italicized font.** Your WINFILE.INI file will not look exactly like this as each file is unique depending on applications loaded and selections made during setup or in the control panel.

```
[Settings]
UNDELETE.DLL=C:\DOS\MSTOOLS.DLL
Window=0,0,640,480, , ,1
```
These are the multiple windows that can be opened showing different directories simultaneously.
```
dir1=13,200,513,409,-1,-1,1,0,201,1905,224,C:\
dir2=71,-7,571,188,-1,-1,3,0,201,1808,196,C:\DOS
[AddOns]
MS-DOS Tools Extensions=C:\DOS\MSTOOLS.DLL
Stacker Extension=C:\STACKER\stacfm.dll
File Size Extension=C:\WINDOWS\FILESIZE.DLL
```

(See also Fig. 7.18.)

Control Panel

The control panel (Fig. 7.19) is the heart of Windows setup, and you can change almost every setup parameter here easily with Windows dialog boxes and menus. These system parameters can also be changed by modifying the CONTROL.INI file (see next section), although it is much more difficult to do it that way.

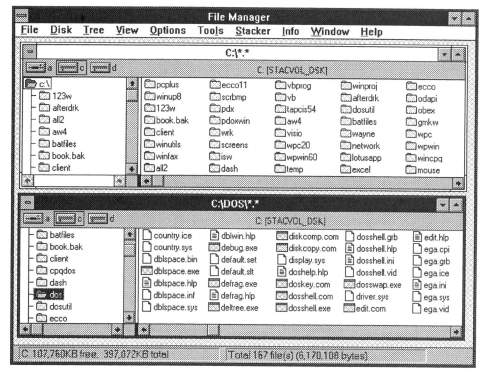

Figure 7.18   File manager multiple directories.

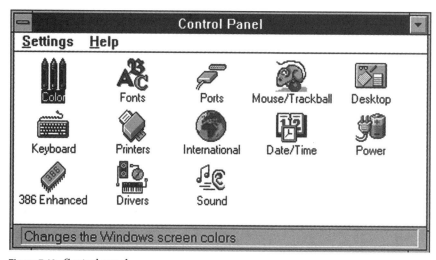

Figure 7.19   Control panel.

Colors

Windows itself and applications written for Windows get their color schemes from settings in the CONTROL.INI file. These settings are in the form of obscure codes (hexadecimal) that are not meaningful. The simple method of creating these codes is to choose the Colors section of the control panel and select the colors.

At the top is a dialog box that shows the currently saved color schemes. Windows includes 23 standard schemes, and you can create and save others. Color is one area where virtually no two people will agree, and thus no two users will have identical systems.

CONTROL.INI

This file controls the setup of the options in control panel and is displayed here in text font and comments are shown in a ***bold, italicized font.*** Your CONTROL.INI file may not look exactly like this as each file is different depending on applications loaded and selections made during setup or in the control panel.

```
[current]
```
This is the color scheme chosen in the Colors dialog box.
```
color schemes=Windows Default

[color schemes]
```
These are the different color schemes available with their code settings. Due to space limitations, each line is wrapped to fit on the page. Each command line starts with an identifying name and an equal (=) sign.
```
Arizona=804000,FFFFFF,FFFFFF,0,FFFFFF,0,808040,C0C0C0,FFFFFF,4080FF,C0C0C0,0,
C0C0C0,C0C0C0,808080,0,808080,808000,FFFFFF,0,FFFFFF
Black Leather
Jacket=0,C0C0C0,FFFFFF,0,C0C0C0,0,800040,808080,FFFFFF,808080,808080,0,10E0E0
E0,C0C0C0,808080,0,808080,0,FFFFFF,0,FFFFFF
Bordeaux=400080,C0C0C0,FFFFFF,0,FFFFFF,0,800080,C0C0C0,FFFFFF,FF0080,C0C0C0,0
,C0C0C0,C0C0C0,808080,0,808080,800080,FFFFFF,0,FFFFFF
Cinnamon=404080,C0C0C0,FFFFFF,0,FFFFFF,0,80,C0C0C0,FFFFFF,80,C0C0C0,0,C0C0C0,
C0C0C0,808080,0,808080,80,FFFFFF,0,FFFFFF
Designer=7C7C3F,C0C0C0,FFFFFF,0,FFFFFF,0,808000,C0C0C0,FFFFFF,C0C0C0,C0C0C0,0
,C0C0C0,C0C0C0,808080,0,C0C0C0,808000,0,0,FFFFFF
Emerald
City=404000,C0C0C0,FFFFFF,0,C0C0C0,0,408000,808040,FFFFFF,408000,808040,0,C0C
0C0,C0C0C0,808080,0,808080,8000,FFFFFF,0,FFFFFF
Fluorescent=0,FFFFFF,FFFFFF,0,FF00,0,FF00FF,C0C0C0,0,FF80,C0C0C0,0,C0C0C0,C0C
0C0,808080,0,808080,0,FFFFFF,0,FFFFFF
Hotdog
Stand=FFFF,FFFF,FF,FFFFFF,FFFFFF,0,0,FF,FFFFFF,FF,FF,0,C0C0C0,C0C0C0,808080,0
,808080,0,FFFFFF,FFFFFF,FFFFFF
LCD Default Screen
Settings=808080,C0C0C0,C0C0C0,0,C0C0C0,0,800000,C0C0C0,FFFFFF,800000,C0C0C0,0
,C0C0C0,C0C0C0,7F8080,0,808080,800000,FFFFFF,0,FFFFFF
LCD Reversed -
Dark=0,80,80,FFFFFF,8080,0,8080,800000,0,8080,800000,0,8080,C0C0C0,7F8080,0,C
0C0C0,800000,FFFFFF,828282,FFFFFF
```

LCD Reversed -
Light=800000,FFFFFF,FFFFFF,0,FFFFFF,0,808040,FFFFFF,0,C0C0C0,C0C0C0,800000,C0
C0C0,C0C0C0,7F8080,0,808040,800000,FFFFFF,0,FFFFFF
Mahogany=404040,C0C0C0,FFFFFF,0,FFFFFF,0,40,C0C0C0,FFFFFF,C0C0C0,C0C0C0,0,C0C
0C0,C0C0C0,808080,0,C0C0C0,80,FFFFFF,0,FFFFFF
Monochrome=C0C0C0,FFFFFF,FFFFFF,0,FFFFFF,0,0,C0C0C0,FFFFFF,C0C0C0,C0C0C0,0,80
8080,C0C0C0,808080,0,808080,0,FFFFFF,0,FFFFFF
Ocean=808000,408000,FFFFFF,0,FFFFFF,0,804000,C0C0C0,FFFFFF,C0C0C0,C0C0C0,0,C0
C0C0,C0C0C0,808080,0,0,808000,0,0,FFFFFF
Pastel=C0FF82,80FFFF,FFFFFF,0,FFFFFF,0,FFFF80,FFFFFF,0,C080FF,FFFFFF,808080,C
0C0C0,C0C0C0,808080,0,C0C0C0,FFFF00,0,0,FFFFFF
Patchwork=9544BB,C1FBFA,FFFFFF,0,FFFFFF,0,FFFF80,FFFFFF,0,64B14E,FFFFFF,0,C0C
0C0,C0C0C0,808080,0,808080,FFFF00,0,0,FFFFFF
Plasma Power
Saver=0,FF0000,0,FFFFFF,FF00FF,0,800000,C0C0C0,0,80,FFFFFF,C0C0C0,FF0000,C0C0
C0,808080,0,C0C0C0,FFFFFF,0,0,FFFFFF
Rugby=C0C0C0,80FFFF,FFFFFF,0,FFFFFF,0,800000,FFFFFF,FFFFFF,80,FFFFFF,0,C0C0C0
,C0C0C0,808080,0,808080,800000,FFFFFF,0,FFFFFF
The
Blues=804000,C0C0C0,FFFFFF,0,FFFFFF,0,800000,C0C0C0,FFFFFF,C0C0C0,C0C0C0,0,C0
C0C0,C0C0C0,808080,0,C0C0C0,800000,FFFFFF,0,FFFFFF
Tweed=6A619E,C0C0C0,FFFFFF,0,FFFFFF,0,408080,C0C0C0,FFFFFF,404080,C0C0C0,0,10
E0E0E0,C0C0C0,808080,0,C0C0C0,8080,0,0,FFFFFF
Valentine=C080FF,FFFFFF,FFFFFF,0,FFFFFF,0,8000FF,400080,FFFFFF,C080FF,C080FF,
0,C0C0C0,C0C0C0,808080,0,808080,FF00FF,0,FFFFFF,FFFFFF
Wingtips=408080,C0C0C0,FFFFFF,0,FFFFFF,0,808080,FFFFFF,FFFFFF,4080,FFFFFF,0,8
08080,C0C0C0,808080,0,C0C0C0,808080,FFFFFF,0,FFFFFF

[Custom Colors]
*If you have identified any custom colors in the Palette section of the Colors
dialog box, these would be identified here.*
ColorA=FFFFFF
ColorB=FFFFFF
ColorC=FFFFFF
ColorD= FFFFFF
ColorE=FFFFFF
ColorF=FFFFFF
ColorG=FFFFFF
ColorH=FFFFFF
ColorI=FFFFFF
ColorJ=FFFFFF
ColorK=FFFFFF
ColorL=FFFFFF
ColorM=FFFFFF
ColorN=FFFFFF
ColorO=FFFFFF
ColorP=FFFFFF

[Patterns]
(None)=(None)
Boxes=127 65 65 65 65 65 127 0
Paisley=2 7 7 2 32 80 80 32
Weave=136 84 34 69 136 21 34 81
Waffle=0 0 0 128 128 128 240
Tulip=0 0 84 124 124 56 146 124
Spinner=20 12 200 121 158 19 48 40
Scottie=64 192 200 120 120 72 0 0
Critters=0 80 114 32 0 5 39 2
50% Gray=170 85 170 85 170 85 170 85
Quilt=130 68 40 17 40 68 130 1
Diamonds=32 80 136 80 32 0 0 0
Thatches=248 116 34 71 143 23 34 113

```
Pattern=224 128 142 136 234 10 14 0

[MMCPL]
NumApps=13
X=44
Y=44
W=430
H=240

[installed]
3.1=yes
HPPCL.DRV=yes
UNIDRV.DLL=yes
FINSTALL.DLL=yes
FINSTALL.HLP=yes
UNIDRV.HLP=yes
```

Disabling Options

You may not want to let users have access to every section of control panel. For example, letting users set their own colors may be fine, but adjusting other settings in 386 enhanced may cause more problems than you anticipated. Control panel is not an application group but is an executable program by itself that looks like a group. You cannot delete an icon in control panel as you can in a regular group. The method of removing options is through modification of CONTROL.INI.

To disable control panel options, edit the CONTROL.INI file and add a section similar to the one found in Fig. 7.20.

```
[don't load]
Color=no
Fonts=no
Ports=no
Desktop=no
Keyboard=no
Printers=no
International=no
Date/Time=no
Network=no
386 Enhanced=no
Drivers=no
Sound=no
```

Figure 7.20 Disabling control panel options.

Application Files

These files control individual applications that may be loaded on your system.
Here are a few sample .INI files from several applications.

```
CLOCK.INI
[Clock]
Maximized=0
Options=0,0,0,0,0,0
Position=132,132,340,358
QPW.INI (Quattro Pro)
[OBEX]
OBEXPath=C:\QPW

[INSTALL]
SamplesPath=C:\QPW\SAMPLES
ODAPIPath=C:\ODAPI

WPWP.INI (WordPerfect)
[Button Bar]
ATTRIBS=003
BARNAME=c:\wpwin\macros\wp{wp}.wwb
PPATTRIBS=113
[LastOpened]
file1=c:\path\filename
file2=c:\path\filename
file3=c:\path\filename
```

8

DOS Applications and Windows

It is impossible to get away from old DOS programs. No matter how hard we try to eliminate the old text-based programs and run only graphical applications, it is virtually impossible to ignore DOS-based systems. The problem is that Windows' graphical applications communicate with Windows as an integrated group, while attempts to accommodate DOS applications must be considered separately.

DOS Application Features

Windows is able to create multiple virtual DOS sessions that enable the user to execute more than one DOS application simultaneously. At first glance, this seems impossible. A DOS application was created to run on a computer by itself. It assumes the standard 640-kbyte conventional memory setup and also assumes that it does not need to contend with other applications for CPU or system hardware. This sets the stage for great problems as it calls for an environment that will emulate the original computer memory setup while running with other DOS or Windows applications.

Windows provides this environment by creating a virtual-memory environment that "fools" the DOS application into thinking that it is running by itself and does not need to worry about interacting with other applications. The virtual session emulates an 8086 computer, has its own video memory area, and can handle applications that write directly to the video or other hardware. Some programmers, in an effort to increase the speed of their applications, bypassed BIOS and wrote directly to the hardware. While this was very helpful for the application, it caused problems when running in DOS sessions. Fortunately, Windows can handle these programs without causing problems with other applications. WordPerfect and Lotus 1-2-3 DOS versions are notorious for bypassing BIOS systems to communicate directly with the computer hardware.

Program Information Files

The environment created by Windows for these virtual DOS sessions is done through *program information files* (PIFs), which instruct Windows on what type of DOS virtual session to create. Since there are so many different types of DOS applications, each may need unique configurations that will create the best environment possible for running DOS applications. These binary files, created by the PIF file editor (see Fig. 8.1), set a variety of environment considerations (discussed below).

Creating PIFs

Each DOS application must have a PIF file created for it to run properly. Even if you try to run a DOS application directly without accessing it through a PIF file, Windows will use the default PIF file. The creation of this file is done through the PIF editor (see Fig. 8.2).

When creating the PIF for an application, you will need to supply a number of items of information through the PIF editor to create the DOS environment. As an example, we will create a DOS PIF for the DOS editor (EDIT.COM) (see Fig. 8.3).

Program file name

This file indicates the name of the DOS application to run and the path to that file.

Windows title

When running a DOS application, the PIF creates a box for the application, and the text you place in this field will appear in the title bar at the top of the box.

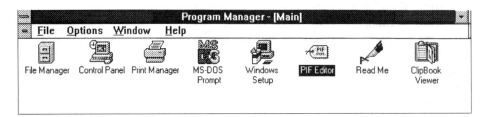

Figure 8.1 PIF editor in main group.

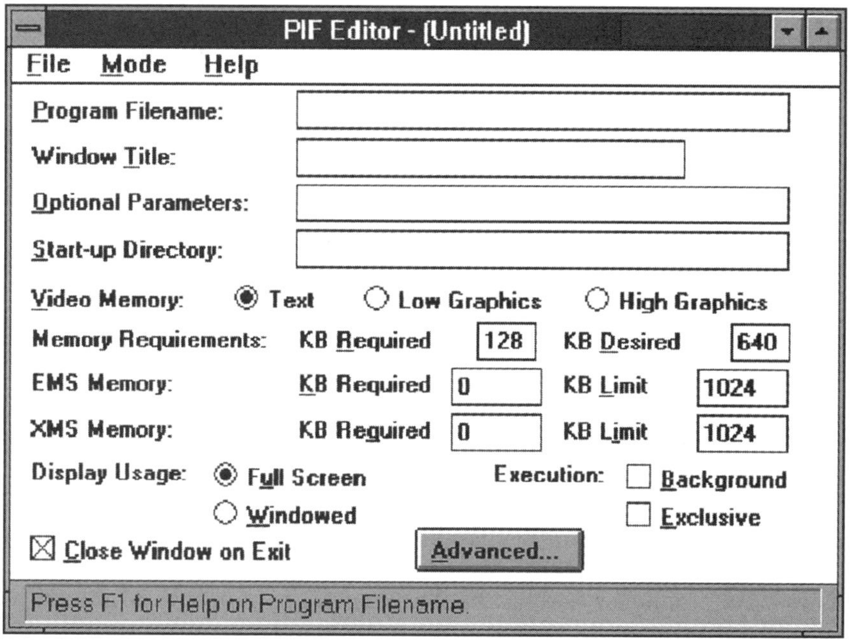

Figure 8.2   PIF editor.

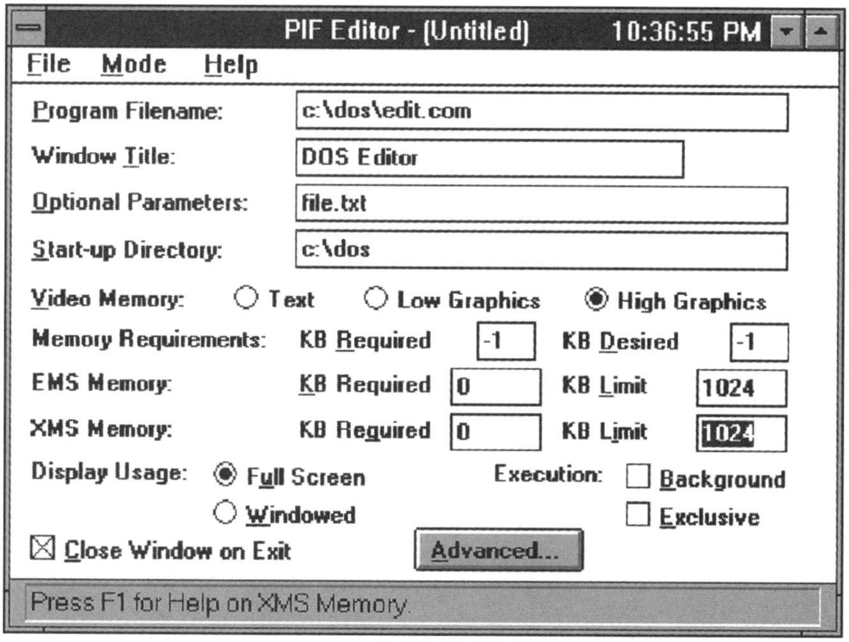

Figure 8.3   Completed PIF screen for DOS text editor.

Optional parameters

This is used for DOS applications that can accept additional information on the command line, such as automatically opening a file when the DOS application is started.

Startup directory

Some DOS applications will run from any directory from which they were started. Usually, Windows is running from the directory where Windows was started and not where the application should be running. Place the drive letter and path to indicate where the DOS application should run from.

Video mode

The term *video mode* might be somewhat of a misnomer, as this mode determines how much memory (rather than the amount or nature of video) will be set aside for screen activity. The lowest amount of memory required used for screen activities is the *text mode,* which is used for applications that use only the standard ASCII text for their screens. The *low-graphics* setting makes more memory available for screen display, and *high-graphics* provides the highest amount of memory.

Memory requirements

This is tough to set, as memory requirements are seldom documented for DOS applications. Placing a value that is too low may cause the program to run not at all or in an impaired state. We suggest a simple solution to this problem. By placing a −1 in this box, Windows will allocate all memory possible up to a maximum of 640 kbytes that the program may need. This ensures that the DOS program will run properly.

EMS (expanded memory specification) memory

This feature allocates memory for the DOS application that emulates the EMS memory that would be available under a standard DOS session.

XMS (extended memory specification) memory

Some DOS programs (especially those created in the last few years) will use extended memory for their operation. If that is the case (usually documented in the manual), Windows will need to allow the DOS program to access extended memory as part of its normal operation.

Display usage

This determines how the DOS application will display the screen when it starts. If you have checked "full screen," it will replace the complete screen, and you will see only the DOS application. If you choose "Windowed," then it will appear in a DOS box among the other Windows and/or DOS applications. This is the startup default size, and you can change it from full-screen to a small window and back with the <Alt-Enter> command.

Warning: When running DOS applications in a DOS box that is less than full-screen, the application will run substantially slower than when running in full-screen. Since DOS applications are text-based, they do not have variable fonts as Windows applications do. Since the DOS program cannot be resized easily, it must be emulated in the small box while it runs in the background. This causes a tremendous slowdown in operation. Use this option only when you absolutely have to.

Execution

If the DOS program is not sensitive to timing, it will be able to run in the background while other DOS or Windows applications run in the foreground. If you are not sure or if the program is sensitive to CPU timing issues, do not check the background box.

Some DOS applications such as communications programs need to have direct access to the CPU and other hardware. If you are having problems running DOS applications, try checking this box.

Close window on exit

When the DOS program is finished, the DOS session needs to be closed, also. If you want the virtual session to be closed at the same time the DOS program is unloaded (e.g., choosing exit on the DOS application menu), then make sure that this box is checked. It is a good idea to mark this box; otherwise the user will be left at the DOS prompt in the DOS session. Figure 8.3 shows the entries for our example of the DOS editor program.

Advanced Options

There is another screen that is used for further tuning of the DOS virtual session and is accessed by clicking on the Advanced button of the first PIF editor screen (shown in Fig. 8.4).

Background/foreground priority

These values determine how much access the CPU will have to resources when the DOS application is in the foreground and in the background. Any application that is time-sensitive (especially those that are dependent on hardware for operation) will require setting the background priority to a higher value.

The numbers here are just ratios and not direct values for the CPU. The actual amount of CPU resource access is determined by the settings for the other DOS applications and for the Windows applications.

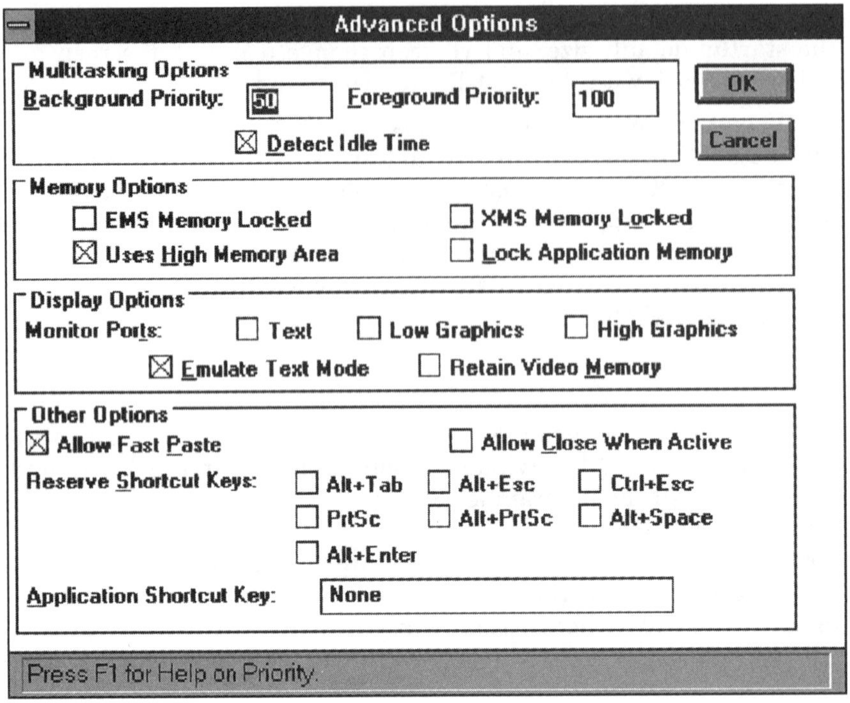

Figure 8.4 PIF advanced options screen.

There are no individual priority settings for each Windows application; instead, there is one setting for all Windows applications in the control panel (Fig. 8.5). The priority setting is for all Windows applications, as they share equal access to the CPU.

Detect idle time

This setting is designed to give additional efficiency in running applications. If the DOS application is idle while waiting for another activity (e.g., user input), the DOS session will give up access to the CPU prematurely to give another application some CPU time to run before it returns to the current application. Leaving the "Detect Idle Time" box checked will not normally cause any problems.

EMS memory locked

This item signals to the system to lock down expanded memory and make sure that Windows does not swap expanded memory to disk. Rarely does this parameter need to be used.

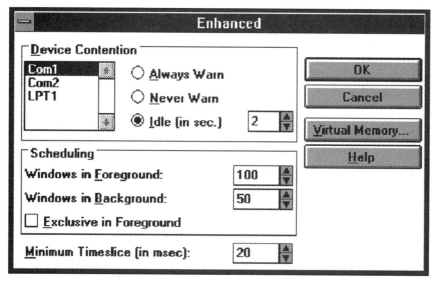

Figure 8.5 Windows setting for CPU resource access.

XMS memory locked

This is similar to the EMS memory-locked parameter; it is designed to prevent any extended memory that an application may use from being swapped to disk.

Uses high-memory area

The *high-memory area* (HMA) will be used if it is not being used for another application. If the memory is available, each application will get its own HMA allocation.

Lock application memory

This is the conventional memory parameter determining whether the standard memory used by an application can be swapped out to disk. Some DOS applications may have problems when memory is swapped to disk because of timing or other problems. This item (box) should not be checked unless there are problems with the DOS application.

Monitor ports

When switching from a DOS application to another DOS or Windows application, returning to the original DOS application may present problems. Graphical DOS applications are especially prone to problems when this item is not checked. When switching back to the application, portions of the screen may be flashing random colors, or the DOS application may have locked up. A simple rule to remember is to check the same box as you did for video memory on the previous screen.

Retain video memory

When a DOS application starts, memory is allocated on the basis of its current needs. It is not uncommon for a DOS program to start out in a text mode and then switch to a graphic mode later on. This is a problem because the allocation of memory is based on the original needs of the programs. When switching to the graphics mode, memory may not be available, the application may lock up, or the screen may not display properly. By checking this box, you can solve some problems in running DOS applications.

Allow fast paste

The paste mentioned here is bringing information to the Windows clipboard. This information can be moved from a DOS application to the clipboard. Keep this option checked unless you are running into problems when moving information to the clipboard.

Reserve shortcut keys

There are a number of keys used by Windows as shortcuts to running the system (e.g., <Alt-Tab>, <Alt-Space>, and <Ctrl-Esc>). While most programs don't use these keys, a DOS application might on rare occasions. Check the keys you don't want used while running the DOS application, and Windows will allow the key combinations to pass through to the DOS program rather than intercept them and use them for itself.

Allow close when active

This is a controversial setting. Most commentators say this is a dangerous option because it will destroy DOS applications. They are only partially right. For a DOS application that has a data file being modified, closing the DOS session before exiting the program can cause loss of data. However, if the application does not have a data file, there will be no problem with closing the program prematurely.

For example, a DOS program that monitors the battery status of a laptop computer will not cause problems if this box is checked and the box is closed prematurely. Checking this box will enable the "close" menu item to become operative, allowing you to close the DOS session without exiting the program (see Figs. 8.6 and 8.7).

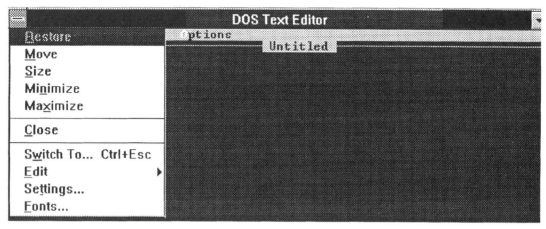

Figure 8.6 DOS application with "allow close when active" enabled.

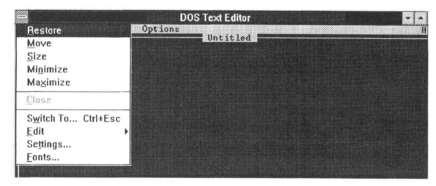

Figure 8.7 DOS application with "allow close when active" disabled.

Application shortcut key

This feature can shorten the running time of DOS applications. Choose an <Alt> or <Ctrl> key combination that will bring up the DOS application whenever pressed. To define a combination, press <Ctrl> or <Alt> and another letter or number which will be entered into this field automatically.

Creating PIFs

There are several different methods of obtaining PIFs.

Application supplied

Because of the popularity of Windows, many DOS applications have PIFs included in their installation routines. The PIF is optimized for that application and can be used immediately after the application is installed.

User-created option

As shown above, you can create your own PIF to run DOS applications.

Windows installation

During the Windows installation routine, the workstation hard disk will be scanned to find any DOS applications and then create PIFs for them. The information for common DOS applications is found in the SETUP.INF (Windows 3.1) or APPS.INF (Windows for WorkGroups 3.11) file.

DOS applications that will be set up automatically, if found, are

ACCPAC BPI
ACCPAC Plus
APPLAUSE II 1.5
Ashton Tate dBase IV
Autocad (batch file)
Autocad
Autosketch 3.0 (batch file)
Autosketch 3.0
Borland C++ IDE
Brief 3.1
Close-Up 4.0
Comm Server 3270
CP Anti-Virus
Crosstalk-XVI 3.71
DataEase
DataPerfect
Decnet Job Spawner
DisplayWrite 3
DisplayWrite 4
DisplayWrite 5
DisplayWrite Assistant
DrawPerfect
DWDOS286
DWDOS386
DWINFO2
DWINFO3
Extra! for MS-DOS

Flight Simulator 3.0
Flight Simulator 4.0
Formtool
Foxbase Plus
FoxPro (maximum configuration)
Framework III
Freelance Plus 4.0
FTP FTPSRV utility
FTP LPQ utility
FTP LPR utility
FTP PCMAIL utility
FTP PING utility
FTP RLOGINVT utility
FTP RSH utility
FTP TN utility
FTP VMAIL utility
Generic CADD
GraphWriter
GW BASIC
Harvard GeoGraphics
Harvard Graphics 2.3
Harvard Graphics 3.0
Harvard Project Manager
Harvard Total Project Manager
HotWire

IBM Filing Assistant
IBM Personal Editor
IBM Professional Editor
IBM Writing Assistant 2.0
Insight
Interleaf 5 for MS-DOS
Kid Pix
KnowledgePro (MS-DOS)
LapLink Pro
Learning Microsoft Works
Learning MS-DOS Quick Reference
Learning MS-DOS 3.0
LetterPerfect
Lotus Access System
Lotus Agenda
Lotus Express
Lotus 1-2-3
Lotus 1-2-3 3.1
LotusWorks 1.0
Magellan 2.0
Managing Your Money
Manifest
Microrim R:Base 5000
Microrim R:Base Clout
Microrim R:Base 3.0
Microsoft Advanced Basic

Microsoft Basic
Microsoft Bookshelf
Microsoft C Compiler 7.0
Microsoft Chart
Microsoft FORTRAN
 Compiler 5.1
Microsoft Game Shop
Microsoft Macro
 Assembler
Microsoft Mail
Microsoft Mail—Admin
Microsoft Make Utility
Microsoft Multiplan
Microsoft Online 1.0
Microsoft Pascal Compiler
Microsoft Project
Microsoft QBASIC
Microsoft QuickBASIC
Microsoft QuickBASIC
 Extended
Microsoft Quick C
Microsoft Quick Pascal
Microsoft Spell
Microsoft Word 4.0
Microsoft Word 5.0
Microsoft Works 2.0
MS-DOS Editor
MultiMate 4.0
Network Control Program
Norton Utilities 4.5
Norton Utilities 5/6.0
Now!
OPTune
Paradox

Paradox 3.0
Paradox 3.5
PC Config 7.x
PC Paintbrush IV Plus
PC3270
PCTools Desktop 5.5
PCTools PCShell 5.5
PCTOOLS—Directory
 Maintenance
PCTOOLS—View
PFS: Access
PFS: First Choice 3.0
PFS: First Choice 3.1
PFS: First Graphics
PFS: First Publisher
PFS: Plan
PFS: Professional Network
Procomm
Procomm Plus 1.1B
Prodigy
Professional File
Professional Write
Programmer's WorkBench
Q&A Report Writer
Q-DOS 3
QModem
Quick Verse 2.0
Quicken
Ready!
Reflection 1
Reflection 2
Reflection 4
Reflection 7
Reflection 8

Reflex 2.0
Relay Gold
Remote 2 call
RightWriter
SAS 604
Scheduler
SEDT Editor
Sethost Terminal Emulator
Sidekick 1.0
Sidekick 2.0
Sidekick Plus
Smartcom II
Soft Kicker
SPSS/PC+
Supercalc 4.0
Supercalc 5.0
Symphony 2.2
TeleMate
Turbo Pascal 6.0
Turbo Tax
Ventura Publisher
Volkswriter 3.0
WordPerfect
WordPerfect Office
WordStar Professional 6.0
WordStar 2000
WPMail
WPOffice Calculator
WPOffice Editor
WPOffice File Manager
WPOffice NoteBook
Writer Rabbit
XTree Gold
XyWrite

9

Printing in NetWare and Windows

Multiple Systems

You will have to set up and maintain both Windows for Workgroups (WFW) and NetWare printing systems to ensure that the user can print successfully to network printers. You can have a number of options, and it is important to modify the settings in these systems to ensure the greatest performance.

Windows for Workgroups Printing

Microsoft helped out users and developers tremendously by providing for a seamless system of printing. In DOS, developers have to include a printer driver for every printer that the user may use. This was seen demonstrated with the DOS versions of WordPerfect word processor. A number of disks were shipped with each copy of the word-processing program containing over 250 printer drivers, and several optional disks were available for those that had uncommon printers. This was a terrible problem for both users and developers.

To simplify the problem of drivers for each different printer, Microsoft created a common set of printing application programming interfaces (APIs) that Windows applications could use. Each application has to create only a common set of commands which are translated by the Windows printer driver. After installing the specific printer driver, all Windows applications can use that same driver. This makes printing much simpler.

When you install Windows or want to add another printer after WFW is installed, the printer dialog box lets you install one of the listed printers, or other printers from a manufacturer printer driver installation disk (see Fig. 9.1).

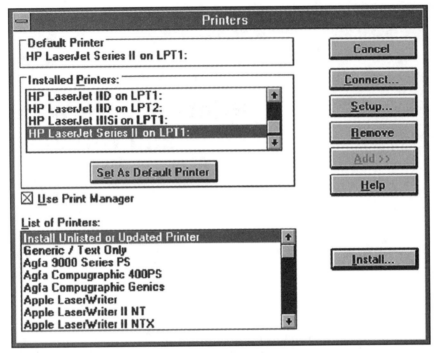

Figure 9.1   Installing printers in Windows for Workgroups.

If you choose to install a printer that requires a driver you don't have installed already, you will be asked for a disk containing the driver file (see Fig. 9.2).

After the printer is installed, you need to assign it to a hardware port, whether the printer is directly connected to the workstation or on the network (see Fig. 9.3).

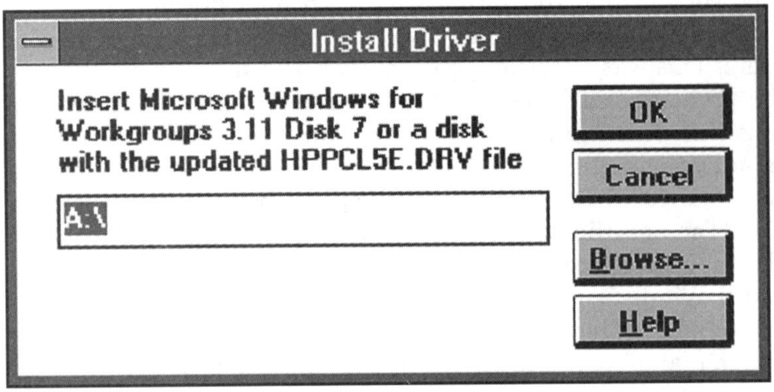

Figure 9.2   Adding a printer driver in Microsoft Windows for Workgroups.

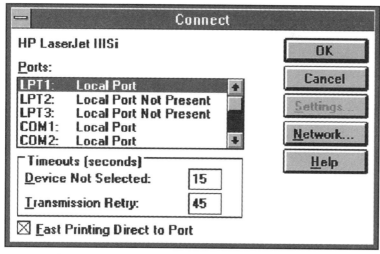

Figure 9.3   Assigning printer to computer port.

The only thing left to do in WFW is to make a connection to the NetWare printing system. Click on the Connect button in the printer dialog box and then the Network button. Figure 9.3 shows the connection box where you assign a printer to the hardware port.

The resources box lists the print queues available in print servers on the network. To assign a NetWare queue to a parallel port, click on the printer icon at the top, select a queue in the resources box, and then select a port you wish to assign. Click on the Capture button to make the printer assignment. This assignment lasts only for the current Windows session. When you exit Windows, the capture will end, and the next time you start Windows, that printer assignment will not be there. Click on the Permanent button to enable Windows to reconnect the printer assignment each time Windows is started. See also Fig. 9.4.

Windows for Workgroups Fonts

There are several methods of creating fonts in WFW. The most common are TrueType, Vector, and Raster fonts. Each font type has its advantages and disadvantages.

TrueType fonts

TrueType fonts (Fig. 9.5) are outline fonts that were developed for Windows 3.1 and later. These fonts are very flexible as they can be scaled and rotated and take up a small amount of disk space. TrueType fonts are identified by the notation [TrueType] following the font name.

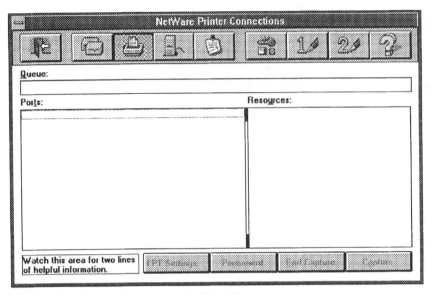

Figure 9.4 Assign printer capture in NetWare Tools.

ARIAL	TTF	65692 11-01-93	3:11a
ARIAL	FOT	1306 11-01-93	3:11a
ARIALBD	TTF	66080 11-01-93	3:11a
ARIALBD	FOT	1308 11-01-93	3:11a
ARIALBI	FOT	1322 11-01-93	3:11a
ARIALBI	TTF	71880 11-01-93	3:11a
ARIALI	TTF	61656 11-01-93	3:11a
ARIALI	FOT	1312 11-01-93	3:11a
ARIALS	TTF	36016 01-07-94	12:00a
ARIALS	FOT	1318 09-23-94	7:57a
SYMBOL	TTF	64516 11-01-93	3:11a
SYMBOL	FOT	1308 11-01-93	3:11a
TIMES	TTF	83260 11-01-93	3:11a
TIMES	FOT	1326 11-01-93	3:11a
TIMESBD	FOT	1328 11-01-93	3:11a
TIMESBD	TTF	79804 11-01-93	3:11a
TIMESBI	TTF	76452 11-01-93	3:11a
TIMESBI	FOT	1342 11-01-93	3:11a
TIMESI	TTF	78172 11-01-93	3:11a
TIMESI	FOT	1332 11-01-93	3:11a

Figure 9.5 TrueType font files included in Windows for Workgroups.

The creation of TrueType is important because, for instance, TrueType fonts can be used for both the screen and the printer. Other fonts cannot do this, and the fonts used on the screen can be quite different from the ones printed out. TrueType fonts can be displayed and printed in virtually any size from 3 points (each point is $\frac{1}{72}$ in) to over 100 points. If there is a Windows driver for your printer, any printer will be able to print these fonts. There won't be much difference in the appearance of documents between printers.

Each TrueType font requires only one .FOT and .TTF file that is quite small. Some other fonts require a large file for each size and type of font (e.g., a file for 8-point and another file for 10-point fonts).

If you want to use only TrueType fonts in your Windows applications, select the TrueType button in the printer dialog box (Figs. 9.6 and 9.7). You can select to enable TrueType fonts and eliminate all other fonts by checking the Show only TrueType fonts in the applications option.

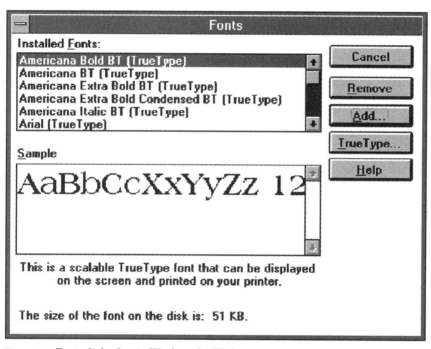

Figure 9.6 Fonts dialog box in Windows for Workgroups.

Figure 9.7 TrueType options dialog box.

Vector fonts

Vector fonts are very popular and are created through a series of lines created into characters. Because these lines are created through mathematical models, the size can be changed easily.

Raster fonts

Raster fonts create each character to form a series of arranged dots. These are the least flexible of the fonts in WFW as they are a form of "pictures" that cannot be scaled or rotated.

Installing Printing Services in NetWare

Printing in NetWare requires some work to set up and maintain properly. There are several decisions you can make about connecting a printer to the system. Here are the methods of connecting a printer to the network.

Direct connection to server

This was one of the first methods of connecting a printer to the server (see Fig. 9.8). The printer can be connected to the file server through a parallel or serial connection. The parallel connection is preferable if the printer is located close to the file server; otherwise a serial connection is required.

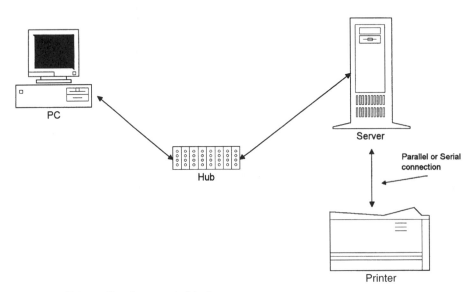

Figure 9.8 Printer directly connected to the server.

The problem with these connections is that they are a slow method of printing compared to current methods. With Windows applications, documents with fonts or graphical applications will be printed, and it is much slower than was possible previously.

Workstation connection

Another method is to connect the printer to a workstation (see Fig. 9.9) and run a *terminate and stay resident* (TSR) utility that will make the network printer available to the stations on the network. The first version was RPRINTER.EXE, which checked the printer queue every 15 s to see if there was a print job ready for printing. As with any TSR, it worked adequately in DOS, but many people had trouble making it work with Windows.

Users encounter two common problems with RPRINTER.EXE. When the video screen changes into graphics mode for Windows, problems can be caused by this change, and occasionally the system will lock up. Also, it is possible to have a garbled print job while running Windows.

In NetWare 4, RPRINTER.EXE was replaced with NPRINTER.EXE, which was more stable in DOS but can still be problematic when run with Windows. Both of these utilities rely on the fact that the TSR will be loaded on the

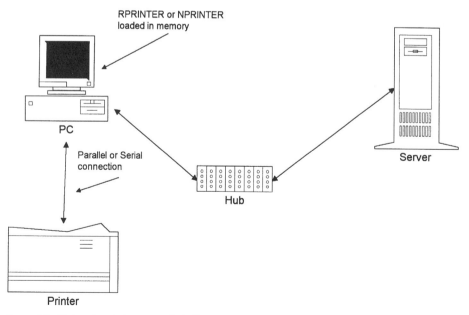

Figure 9.9 Network printer on workstation.

workstation and will operate properly, and that users will leave their machines running so that other network users can print.

While NPRINTER.EXE and RPRINTER.EXE are viable options, we believe that the next method, network connection, is superior.

Network connection

The methods mentioned above all use a serial or parallel connection for printing, which is still a slow method of printing. If the printer is directly connected to the server, you are limited to where you can place the printer. Connecting the workstation to the printer and then running RPRINTER.EXE or NPRINTER.EXE can result in occasional lockups or garbled printing.

By connecting a printer directly to the network (see Fig. 9.10), users can print at high speed ($\geq$10 Mbits/s), and the printer is independent of a workstation connection. The best-known interface card that directly connects a printer to the network is the HP JetDirect. This card fits into the interface slot of the printer and connects directly to the network. This provides a direct path for the print job into the print engine, providing the fastest printing possible on the network.

Configuration is provided by the JetDirect Admin utility (Fig. 9.11), which ties the printer to a NetWare print server queue which it polls on a regular basis to determine whether there is a print job. The card is a node on the net-

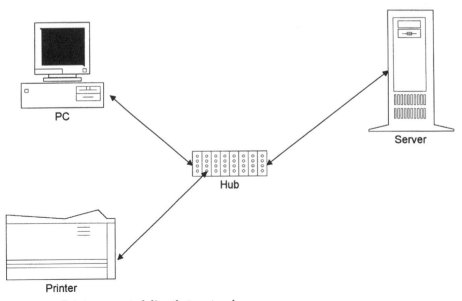

Figure 9.10 Printer connected directly to network.

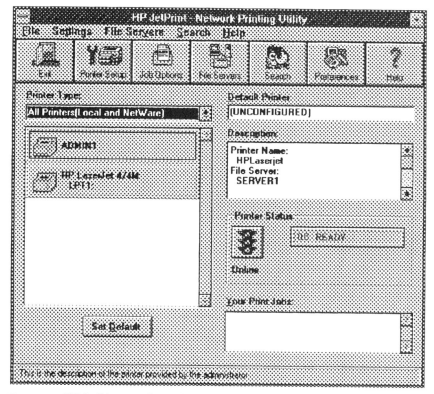

Figure 9.11 HP JetDirect configuration.

work with a unique network address. You can plug the printer interface card into any network connection, and it will be instantly ready for printing. It retains the server and queue information, thus requiring no further configuration.

If you don't use HP LaserJet printers, there are a number of devices similar to the JetDirect that can give you network connectivity (e.g., Intel NetPort). They are separate external boxes that have their own power supply and provide serial or parallel connections from the interface box to the printer. This defeats some of the benefits of a network connection because the printing speed is reduced by the speed of the parallel or serial connection.

Printing graphics

If you will be printing a number of graphical images on a regular basis, you may want to take a look at XiPrint from Xionics. This card works only with the HP LaserJet family of printers and Windows. It compresses the graphic images at the workstation and sends them through the NetWare spooler system to the XiPrint card, which plugs directly into the network and can print full-page graphic images as fast as 17 pages per minute.

By compressing the images before they are sent to the printer, network traffic is greatly decreased yet still giving high throughput. This card has an effect only on graphic images and does not increase or decrease the speed of text print jobs.

NetWare Printing Configuration

NetWare provides the ability to spool print jobs to a printer through the server to enable the user to resume work on the application and not wait for the printing to finish. When setting up a print system, you need to run PCONSOLE on a 3.x system and select "print server information." It will be empty the first time you run this because a print server has not been defined.

Before setting up the print server, it will be faster to set up the logical printing queues first in the server before setting up the print server.

Choose "print queue information" (Fig. 9.12) from the PCONSOLE menu and press <Insert> to create the first print queue. Type the queue name, and press <Enter>. If you have users set up in the server already, press <Enter> again to select options for that print queue and enter the queue operators and queue users. In either of these options, press <Insert> to get a list of users already set up in the server and choose one or more users by either highlighting their name and pressing <Enter> (for selecting just one user) or by highlighting each name you want and pressing the <F5> key, which marks the name for selection. After selecting the last user name, press

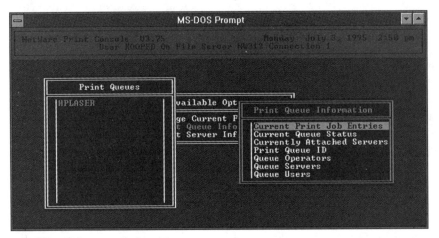

Figure 9.12 Print queue information.

<Enter>, and all users selected will be inserted into the user list for the item you have chosen. For the remainder of the print queue options, you can accept the defaults for the queue for now, although you may want to make some adjustments later.

The PRINT SERVER handles the communication between the printer and the server print queues and passes the print job to the printer as fast as the printer can handle it. This part of the printing setup can be called the *hardware setup*. Press <Insert> to enter a name for the print server you want to create, and then press <Enter> to save the name. If you are going to set up more than one print server, press <Insert> again and enter the new name. Only one print server can be run on the file server at one time as an NLM (see Fig. 9.13), but you can run the PSERVER.EXE on a dedicated workstation and add other print servers to the network.

Press <Enter> again to select information about the print server, and select "printer configuration." This is where you set up and identify the printer connections to the print server. All 16 (256 in NetWare 4) printers are shown in Fig. 9.14, and you can configure the hardware connection to a printer by using the arrow keys to move to the desired printer number and pressing <Enter>. Type a name for the printer, and if you are using a network printing device (e.g., HP JetDirect, Intel Netport, Lexmark, Eagle Technology), choose the "remote/other" choice and take the defaults. If it is a direct connection to the server, choose "parallel" or "serial" from the list.

After you have set up the printer, choose queue assignments and pick a print queue that you previously set up to attach the printer to. This affects the connection between the printer and print queue and can be changed at any time.

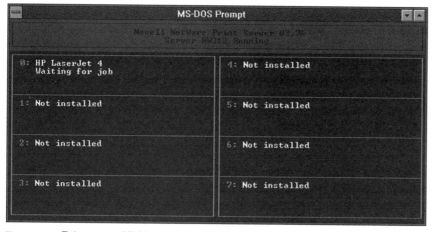

Figure 9.13   Print server NLM console monitoring screen.

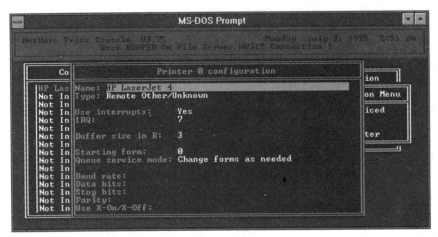

Figure 9.14 Printer hardware configuration.

Printer Modes

There are two types of connections you can make between these network-based printer devices and the print server: the remote and the queue server. The *remote printer mode* is like a workstation running RPRINTER or NPRINTER, as these options function as printer devices while the NLM-based print server handles the print queues and transmission of data to the printer. In NetWare 4, you must set the bindery context for these printers; otherwise they will not work. The remote mode provides a listing of print jobs on the file server where you can monitor them directly.

In the *queue server mode,* the NLM print server is not loaded on the file server or as a stand-alone unit. The printer interface network device communicates directly to the file server and replaces the print server to handle its own print jobs. You have to use the printer utilities that were shipped with the interface cards to view the jobs being printed to determine their status. In NetWare 4, you will have to put the queues, printers, and print server object (interface card) in the same bindery context and preferably in the same container.

Multiple Queues

The most common setup is to have a one-to-one relationship between queues and printers. However, on some occasions, there may be a need to have multiple queues for a printer (Fig. 9.15) or multiple printers for a queue (Fig. 9.16).

If you want to give users different levels of access to a printer you can create more than one queue and attach those queues to the desired network printer. With these different queues you can assign different priority levels

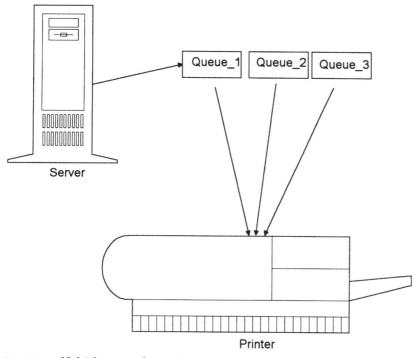

Figure 9.15 Multiple queues for a printer.

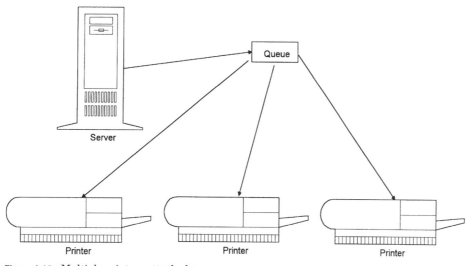

Figure 9.16 Multiple printers attached to one queue.

for printing. For example, to print documents that are not critical, the user can choose the queue with a lower priority while using the queue with the higher priority for printing memos or other documents that are needed in a hurry. Of course, this scheme can be used to separate users. The network administrator can set up a private queue that has higher priority to the printer than others—although we are sure you would never do something like that!

Multiple printers

In some instances one printer cannot handle all the printing. For instance, in a busy office where a number of people may be printing, it may be wise to install several printers. If you set up only one queue to each printer, the user has to decide which printer to capture to. You would probably end up with one or two printers being overloaded and other printers underused. By creating one queue and attaching it to several printers, the print server will choose a printer that is idle to print to, and you can be assured that the printing will be evenly distributed across all the printers (see Fig. 9.16).

Printing Configuration

When configuring the workstation for printing from Windows to a NetWare printer (see Fig. 9.17), the standard recommendation always stands: make

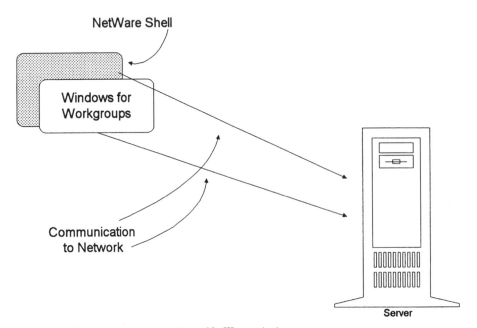

Figure 9.17 Windows communication to NetWare printing.

sure you have the latest client workstation drivers available. Many problems with network communication can be traced to using old network communication drivers or to driver files that are not matched to each other.

Client workstation files can be installed either with Windows support or without Windows support. If you answered "no" to the question of Windows support in the client INSTALL.EXE utility, NetWare drivers for Windows would be installed, providing direct access to the network.

Without Windows support files (including NETWARE.DRV), all network connection and printing takes place outside Windows (see Fig. 9.17). While this still works fine, you lose some functionality from within Windows. Network login and captures for printing must be set up before starting Windows and cannot be changed inside Windows. When a DOS or Windows application prints to a parallel port, it is intercepted by the capture utility and sent to the NetWare print queue for printing. All communication with the network is done through the shell TSR utilities loaded in memory and not through Windows.

When a print job is started in Windows with these drivers present, the print manager will open a file handle and spool the print job to the local workstation disk. It then sends the print job to the parallel port. The NetWare shell intercepts the interrupt calls to the parallel port and opens a file handle to write the print job to a queue file on the NetWare server which is eventually printed. There will be great delays in printing this job because the print data is written to disk twice (see Fig. 9.18).

The other configuration is when you answer "yes" to the Windows drivers question in the INSTALL.EXE utility. When you select Windows support in the Install utility (see Fig. 9.19), the full set of Windows support drivers, including the key file NETWARE.DRV. With the full NetWare support files loaded, print jobs will be sent directly to the NetWare print queue from Windows. After installing these NetWare support files, you will see several new utilities available. In the printer setup utility (in the control panel), click on the Connect button and then the Network button to access the NetWare Tools utility (see Fig. 9.20).

The NetWare Tools utility allows you to modify the current printing setup directly while in Windows. If you hadn't installed these drivers, you would have to exit Windows, change the capture, and then start Windows again.

When you select the printer icon at the top of the NetWare Tools dialog box, the print queues of the servers that you have access rights to and are logged into will be shown. Select a print queue by clicking on a queue, then clicking on a parallel port by clicking on the Capture button at the bottom of the dialog box. If you want the connection to the printer queue to be permanent, click on the Permanent button, and the print queue connection will be reestablished each time Windows starts. If you are not logged into the server that the print queue is on, you will be asked to log in before the connection can be established.

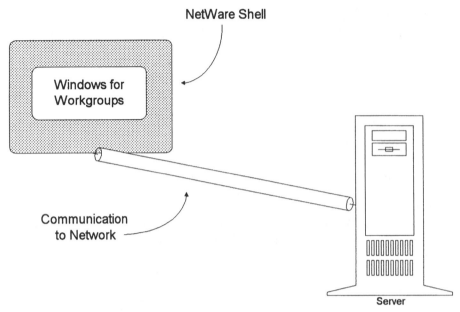

Figure 9.18 Network communication with Windows for Workgroups drivers.

The LPT Settings button at the bottom of the dialog box has a misleading title. It includes options such as banner page, form feed, timeout, and other parameters that correspond with the capture commands in DOS.

```
NetWare Client Install  v1.02          Thursday  December 15, 1994  10:27 am


 STEP 1. Type client directory name for Client Installation.
         C:\NWCLIENT

 STEP 2. Client installation requires "LASTDRIVE=Z" in the
         CONFIG.SYS file and "CALL STARTNET.BAT" added to
         AUTOEXEC.BAT.  Install will make backup copies.
         Allow changes?  <Y/N>:  No

 STEP 3. Do you wish to install support for Windows? <Y/N>:  No
         Windows Subdirectory:

 STEP 4. Press <Enter> to install the driver for your network
         board.  You may then use arrow keys to find the
         board name.
         Press <Enter> to see list

 STEP 5. Press <Enter> to install.


Esc-exit  Enter-select  ↑↓-move  Alt F10-exit
```

Figure 9.19 NetWare install utility.

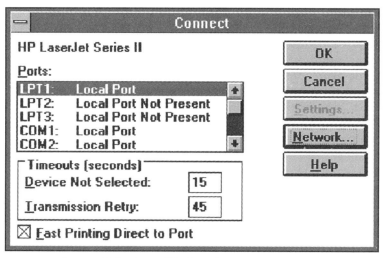

Figure 9.20   Connect dialog box in Windows for Workgroups.

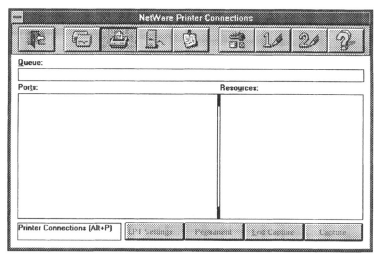

Figure 9.21   Printer resources in NetWare Tools dialog box.

Print Manager

The original Windows-proprietary Print Manager was designed in the early versions of Windows for control of a printer directly attached to the workstation. DOS does not have a built-in spooler, and this was the reason for the delays experienced by users when printing. This a simple concept with a directly attached printer but gets complicated when network printers are introduced.

The NetWare printing system automatically spools print jobs before sending them to the printer; therefore, it would seem that the print manager is irrelevant in Windows. However, we need to examine the whole concept to determine the best configuration for Windows and NetWare.

If you turn off the print manager in the control panel (see Fig. 9.22), printing will go directly to the NetWare print queue from the Windows application.

The decision as to whether to use the print manager when connected to a network print queue is not a simple one. If you do not use it, you lose the ability to monitor print queues much easier than through the NetWare utilities. Since the print manager starts automatically whenever you print, it is always just a couple of keystrokes or mouse clicks away. To monitor a network print job through NetWare utilities, you have to start the DOS PCONSOLE utility. The print manager also gives status information about the percentage of completion not available in PCONSOLE.

In enabling the print manager without installing NETWARE.DRV, you have added another spooling to the print process. This will delay the printing a little, but we have found the additional monitoring ability to be worth the delay in printing. Unless you have a print job that is immediate, the delay in printing is not going to be a problem.

The process of monitoring NetWare print queues does have an impact on the performance of the workstation. It is hard to gauge the performance hit from using the print manager. The delay comes from checking each printer queue on a NetWare server. You can modify how frequently the print manager checks the print queue. By increasing this value, you can reduce the performance impact greatly.

If you have installed and loaded NETWARE.DRV, and you turn off printing net jobs directly in *Windows,* you can use this method of printing to spool the print job to the local disk. NETWARE.DRV then opens a file handle and

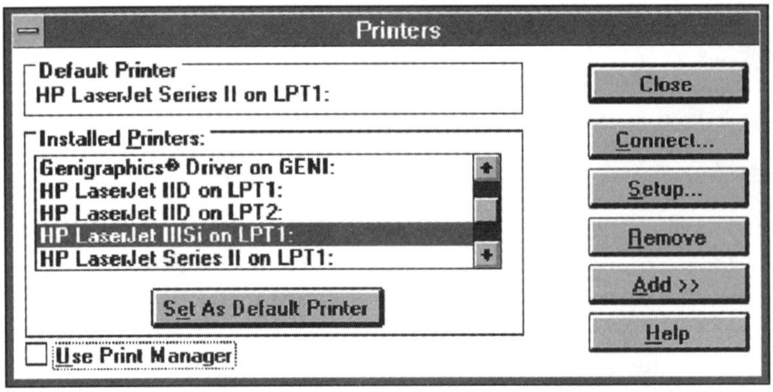

Figure 9.22 Disabling the print manager in Windows for Workgroups.

writes the file to the NetWare server. This is similar to the scenario in which NETWARE.DRV is not loaded as the print job will be double-spooled.

If you choose to print net jobs directly, the internal GDI.EXE module in Windows sends the print job directly to NETWARE.DRV by opening a file handle for the print job. The only work the print manager will do in this method of printing is to monitor the print jobs. The print job is spooled only once—a much better scenario.

There is no quick answer as to whether you need to enable the print manager. The decision comes down to how important it is to have in-depth monitoring of your print jobs. We usually leave it on and have encountered no problems.

Fast printing

One of the most confusing parameters for printing in Windows is the "fast printing direct to port" option (see Fig. 9.23) found in the "connect" dialog box. We have been asked frequently whether this option should be turned off for network printing.

The first step in printing inside Windows is done through an *application programming interface* (API), which makes a call to the network driver (NET-WARE.DRV) to open the network printing activity. If this function is successful, GDI.EXE will write directly to the network port without checking to see if "fast printing direct to port" is enabled. If the NETWARE.DRV is loaded, this parameter becomes irrelevant.

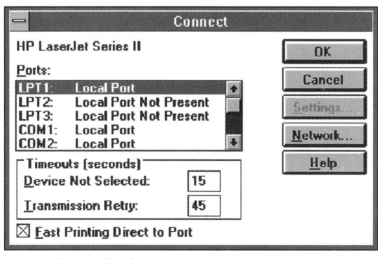

Figure 9.23 Printing directly to port.

10

NetWare 4

NetWare 4 is the general name given to the new generation of the NetWare operating system products from Novell. It includes NetWare 4.00, 4.01, 4.02, and 4.1. For all practical purposes the only viable operating system product is v4.1, as the older versions don't have the functionality and flexibility that this version does.

NetWare Directory Services

The most visible new feature in NetWare 4 is the NetWare Directory Services (NDS) (see Fig. 10.1), which is a fundamental change in the method used to store information about users and other functions in the server operating system. All items in the file server are regarded as objects. This includes users, printers, print queues, servers, hard disks, and similar properties. NDS allows a uniform method of controlling these objects.

All items in the NDS are shown in a graphical format which includes their relationship to the other items in the tree. The tree can contain a number of different items.

Containers

A *container* (in the NetWare context) is an organizational grouping that allows easy division of the company into logical units rather than physical server units as in NetWare 2.x and 3.x. It is a basic method of grouping the different objects. Here are the types of containers that are available.

Country

This occurs at the top of the directory services tree. It is the starting point for most network structures. This is usually used with a global networks where there are several countries that make up the network.

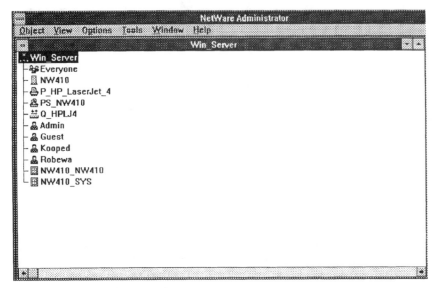

Figure 10.1   NetWare Directory Services.

Organization

Those companies that don't have a global network usually place the organization name as the first container in their network tree. When installing NetWare 4, you will be asked to specify the organization name before directory services can be installed.

Organization unit

This is a generic object for companies, divisions, and departments. It is subordinate to the organization container and is a method of dividing up the organization into logical groups such as engineering, accounting, sales, and administration.

Leaf Objects

While containers provide the general structure of the directory services and contain other objects, leaf objects are the actual items that are users and resources. Applications can modify the directory services and create their own leaf objects (called "snap-in objects"). For example, Groupwise, the Novell e-mail and scheduling application, creates two leaf objects for Groupwise users and groups. These are added to the basic set and used in conjunction with the other leaf objects. The basic objects in directory services are described in the following paragraphs (arranged alphabetically).

Alias

This is a unique type of object that provides a link to an object in different areas of the directory tree. It is seldom needed for small systems where there are only a few servers in the system. The original object may appear in one part of the tree while the users in another portion of the tree may need access to this object. While the user can be given rights to this object, there is a problem of administration and access when the object is contained in another container.

By placing an alias object in the same container the user has access to, it is easier to keep track of what the users have rights to access. It also is more convenient to access items when an alias is present.

AFP server

An Apple file server using AppleTalk Filing Protocol on the network would be shown under this object.

Bindery

When upgrading a NetWare 3.x server to NetWare 4, there will most likely be a number of items that do not have a corresponding function in NetWare 4. These can be queues for backup systems, or some groups or other items that can't be identified. These items will be shown in the directory tree after conversion with a small B in an icon. They are listed for compatibility purposes only and do not have any functionality in the new tree structure.

Computer

This object represents a workstation on the network and holds a variety of pieces of information about the object. You can track the node address, location, department, serial number, and network segment. This is now an easy method of tracking each computer on the network.

Directory map

This object specifies the location of applications and aids in the mapping of application directory locations for users. By defining a directory map object that specifies the location of the application, users can include in their login scripts or access directly this object to map a drive letter or search map. By having users point to this object, it can be changed easily without any further changes to login scripts of users.

Group

This object is roughly similar to groups in NetWare 3.x systems in which users can be associated with the groups for efficiency of administration. Trustee rights, running applications, mappings, and other activities can be handled efficiently by creating groups and making users a member of the group such as, for example, if the e-mail group has rights to the e-mail application directories and needs to load a utility that notifies the users when new messages are received. All of these mappings and loading of the utility can be done in the group object and then users can be added so that they can inherit attributes of the group object you just created.

NetWare server

This is the object that lists the NetWare servers on the network. Each server will have one of these objects, and information about that server is listed here. The information items tracked in this object:

- Name assigned to server
- Description of server
- Location of server
- Network address
- Server trustees (those who can change server properties)
- Server operators
- Server status

Organization role

This is a unique object that is difficult even for experienced NetWare administrators to understand. The organization role object can be given specific attributes such as rights and security equivalency, which can be given to a user, administrator, or temporary user. It helps control who has access to other objects and directories.

Printer

Each printer on the network will have one of these printer objects. The object can be a printer on a file server connected through a print server or a shared printer on the network attached to a workstation.

Print server

The print server can be a print server NLM on a file server, a queue server (e.g., from a device such as an HP JetDirect card), or a print server running on a dedicated PC.

Profile

This object is designed to contain a script for users and groups. A login script is placed in this object, and users are given rights to this object. The login script items in this object are executed following the user's container and before their own personal login script. It is a simple method of creating a generic script for a number of users. There is no system login script in NetWare Directory Services, so the equivalent can be set in container objects or in this profile object.

Queue

Printer queues will be represented by these objects. Users are given rights to these objects to gain access to have the ability to place print jobs in these queues.

User

This object represents the user on the network (see Fig. 10.2). There is one object for each user and it contains these items:

- Personal login script
- User's name

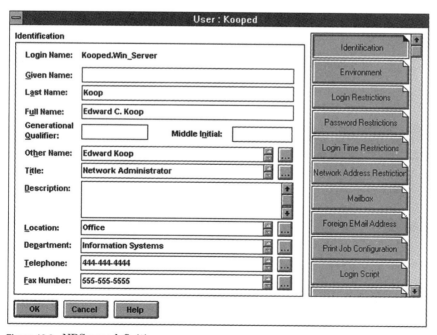

Figure 10.2 NDS user definition.

- Address
- Voice phone number
- Fax phone number
- Account status (amount of available credit, balance, etc.)
- Login restrictions
- Time restrictions
- Password requirements
- Default server for the user
- User group memberships
- Print job configurations
- Printer controls
- Any profile objects the user has access to
- User identification number
- Intruder lockout

Volume

Since every item in the network must be represented by an object, a disk volume is no exception. You can name the volume any name you want when you set up the volume. One of the nice features of this object is the ability to give the volume a name that is different from the actual name of the volume on the disk.

There is a very informative screen that accompanies the volume object. It lists the date and time when the volume was created, the date the information was last updated, and archive information on when the volume was last backed up.

The "user space limits" screen shows how much disk space is available to each user. Limiting the disk space to which users can have access is a great way of maintaining control over the network users.

In the "trustees of the root directory" screen, information is displayed about the users who have trustee rights to the root directory of the volume.

Managing Directory Services

The best method of accessing the NDS objects can be done through the NWADMIN utility. This must be run in Windows because it is graphical and shows all the objects and their relationships to each other. You can use the DOS version of NWADMIN, but it is not as convenient as the Windows graphical version.

The first menu in NWADMIN lists the options for manipulating objects in NDS. The Create command allows you to create a new object; this can also be accomplished by pressing the <Ins> key. The Details option can gives detailed information about any of the leaf or container objects in the tree.

Security

NetWare 4 has a greater focus on security because of the enterprise nature of this version of the network operating system. Also, Windows presents some new security challenges. Users can open a number of windows and load applications or drop to DOS (provided they are given the rights) and potentially cause problems. There are a number of security items in NetWare 4, some of which are inherited from previous versions.

Time restrictions

This is almost the same as previous versions of NetWare. If your users work only from 8:00 A.M. to 5:00 P.M., there is no need for them to have access after a certain time at night. To allow for a user working early or late, you can deny the user the ability to log in from 9:00 P.M. to 6:00 A.M. This will ensure that any hacker who might want to gain access to the network during the night would not be able to gain access through that user login account, even if this hacker were able to determine the correct password.

Unfortunately, the greatest need for security is the administrator account or administrator equivalent. Even though this is the greatest candidate for login protection, you don't want to lock those accounts for time restrictions.

Workstation restriction

The ultimate restriction is to allow the users to log in from only one or more workstations. This is done by entering the network number and node address. A user who wants to log in from another workstation that isn't listed with permission to log in will not be able to successfully log in. We have used this option for polling PCs where we can set up an automatic login from a batch file and we don't want to have a password but yet still want security. Since polling PCs are usually in a data center or secure area, this method of security does not compromise network safety too much.

Account expiration

You may have temporary workers that require access to the network for a limited amount of time. Rather than trying to keep track of the ending date of each account, setting the expiration date for each account will lock the user account automatically.

Changing passwords

Parameters can be set to force users to change their passwords on a specified time basis. The user will be asked to enter a new password on the next attempt to log in.

Unique passwords

If users are compelled to change their passwords and just type the same password back in, the benefit of changing passwords is lost. This function will not allow a user to use the same password again for a year (or other time value you choose).

Login

Login security is similar to the older versions of NetWare but with a heavier emphasis on security. Instead of logging onto a server, users will log in to the directory tree as set up in the system. They do not need any information about physical servers on the network but instead log in to the network. Control of users is much greater with NetWare 4 than with other versions of NetWare.

File and directory security

You can grant rights for a user to any objects, directories, and files on the system. With the Windows administration NWADMIN, it is easy to give rights to users and to monitor which users have rights on the system.

Internetwork security

The biggest complaint about NetWare before version 4 was the independence of servers. All servers existed without any relation to other servers. Administration had to take place individually on all servers, and there was no method of coordinating security across the servers. With NetWare Directory Services, each user can be tracked across all servers, reducing the chance of forgetting to check the user rights on an individual server.

Password encryption

To ensure a higher level of security, all passwords are encrypted at the server and at the workstation to ensure that no one can "see" the passwords on the network communications system.

Bindery Support

While NetWare Directory Services offers a great leap forward, we don't live in a perfect world and may not be able to take advantage of NDS immediately. If you have NetWare 3.x servers on the network or workstations have not been upgraded to the VLM shells, then you will have to use bindery services. This feature makes a NetWare 4 server look like a NetWare 3.x server.

By running SYSCON, you can create a system login script (NET$LOG.DAT) to be accessed by all users logging in under bindery emulation. By placing a /B at the end of the LOGIN command (LOGIN servername/username /B), the user will access the file server, bypassing NDS.

New Console Commands

There are a number of new commands for the server console in NetWare 4. Because of new functionality, there are a number of functions listed (alphabetically) below.

Note: When working with bindery emulation, make sure that you have set bindery context for both the containers that has the user and group objects. If the bindery context is set for both containers, then those items will appear in SYSCON.

Abort remirror

During the mirroring of a partition of the network server hard drives, this command will stop the mirroring. This can be helpful if you want to make changes while the mirroring is taking place. You would stop the mirroring, make the changes, and then start mirroring again.

Note: If you are using the Hewlett-Packard JetDirect network interface card with HP laser printers, make sure the bindery context is set for the container that has the printer object. If the bindery context is not set, the JetDirect card may not be able to connect with the file server.

If the card still does not connect properly, set the bindery context to the company object, and that may solve the problem.

Domain

This is in response to criticism from the computer community about running NLMs in the CPU ring 0. In NetWare 3.x, all NLMs ran in ring 0 that provided fast access to the CPU but there was no safety from an errant NLM. Virtually any error with the NLM will cause the server to crash. Any NetWare 3.x administrator has many horror stories of how servers crashed when an NLM went astray.

The official term for the location where these NLMs run is the "operating system (OS) domain." This command will allow NLMs to run in a protected area (ring 3, also known as "OS-protected domain"). By running the DOMAIN command by itself, install the DOMAIN NLM (LOAD DOMAIN) and then type DOMAIN. A list of NLMs running in rings 0 and 3 will be shown.

If you want to load an NLM in ring 3, run LOAD DOMAIN, then issue the command DOMAIN=OS_PROTECTED, and then load the NLM. Every NLM loaded after the DOMAIN=OS_PROTECTED command is run. To reset the domain back to the normal ring 0, issue the command DOMAIN=OS and then all NLMs loaded after that command will be run in ring 0.

Dsrepair

The NetWare Directory Services database can have problems from time to time. This command will go through each object in the NDS and make any repairs required. If the NDS is damaged, it can prevent all users from gaining access to the network or access to any other objects.

Language

This command will specify the language to be used by NLMs loaded after this command is run.

List device

This command displays all the devices on the server (hard disks, CD-ROMs, etc.).

Media

By running this command, you will cause the screen to display whether media requests to the server are being taken care of.

NSWNUT

This is a utility that provides routines and other functions for other NLMs.

Remirror partition

This is the opposite of the "abort remirror" command. It starts the mirroring process again.

RPL

This is the "remote program load" command to install the RPL protocol stack to enable the remote booting of PC diskless workstations.

Scan for new devices

This utility will show any disk hardware devices that have been added since the server was booted.

Servman

This utility can be used instead of the SET command to configure the parameters for the file server.

NetWare 4 Workstation Utilities

There are a few new commands to be run from the workstation for NetWare 4 (listed alphabetically).

Auditcon

When run from the workstation, this utility audits network transactions to ensure that all network records are accurate and security is maintained.

CX

The CX DOS command (Fig. 10.3) changes the default context inside the NDS tree. If the context is not given, the user has to give the complete address of the object or login user name.

NETADMIN

NETADMIN (Fig. 10.4) is the DOS equivalent of NWADMIN. It controls the configuration and access of all objects in the NDS tree that the user has the rights to see.

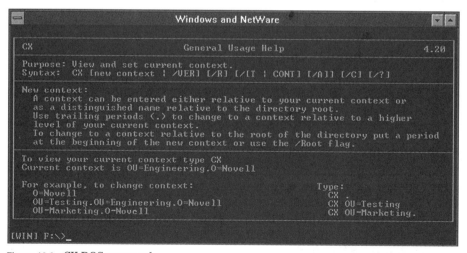

Figure 10.3 CX DOS command.

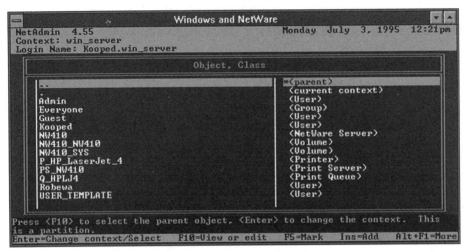

Figure 10.4   NETADMIN utility.

NWADMIN

NWADMIN (Fig. 10.5) is the Windows version of NETADMIN providing a graphical view of the NDS tree and all functionality of the NETADMIN utility. It is an easier utility to use than the DOS version.

PARTMGR

This utility is used to create and maintain partitions in the NDS tree structure.

Installing NetWare 4

The installation procedure for NetWare 4 has changed considerably over the 3.x versions. The screens look different and the operations are unlike any you may have seen before.

Starting the installation

There are several methods of installing NetWare 4 on the file server. You can obtain NetWare 4 on floppy disk or on CD-ROM, or install it from another network drive. The most common method of installation is CD-ROM. You will need to have the DOS device drivers installed in the CONFIG.SYS file and use MSCDEX.EXE to map a drive letter to the CD-ROM drive. Example entries are shown in Fig. 10.6.

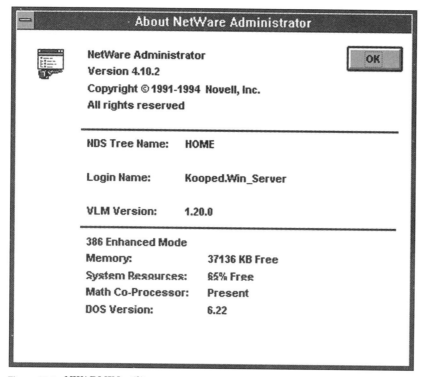

Figure 10.5   NWADMIN utility.

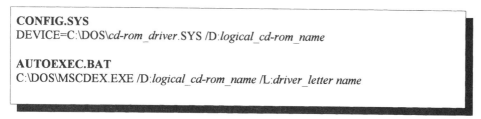

Figure 10.6   CD-ROM driver entries.

Preparing the DOS partition

The DOS partition is used in a manner similar to the setup in NetWare 3.x. It contains the disk drivers and executables to start the file server. We recommend a 20-Mbyte DOS partition which will suffice to handle DOS and NetWare files with a little spare room for other files.

We recommend placing utilities like VREPAIR on this partition also because it will be easy to access if you need to repair the disk NetWare partition.

Starting the installation

After installing the CD-ROM drivers and rebooting the computer, change to the CD-ROM drive (usually the D: drive) and run INSTALL from the root of the CD-ROM. This will start the DOS portion of the installation which copies the drivers for the DOS partition to the directory selected.

Server name

You will be asked to name the server with a name that can contain up to 40 alphanumeric characters.

Internal network number

To facilitate the installation, the IPX internal network number is automatically generated in hexadecimal (hex) format. You can replace it with your own number if you want as long as that number is not already used by any server on the network.

Disk driver

Before a NetWare partition can be created on the hard drive, you need to load the disk driver(s) from the DOS partition where you copied it (them) before starting the installation. The installation program will display the names of all the disk drives it found in the server directory on the DOS partition. Select the appropriate driver(s), and it (they) will be loaded automatically. If the drivers don't load properly, you will be notified on the screen and advised what to do to get the drivers loaded.

NetWare partition

After loading the disk drivers, you then create the NetWare partition(s) either automatically or manually. The automatic selection creates a partition across the entire first physical disk drive free space. If you want to make the partition size less than the free space available, choose the "manual" option. Also, if you want to create mirrored or duplexed drives, or a volume that spans several physical drives.

When choosing to create a NetWare partition, a box will appear listing the partition size (which you can change), and hot-fix information. While the default for the hot-fix size is 2 percent, we have found it a waste of space to set aside that amount of space for redirection blocks. We use 2.0 percent or

1000 blocks, whichever is smaller. This is based on the theory that if you use more than 1000 blocks for redirection, the drive is about to crash.

Data safety

If you want to have data safety by using disk mirroring or duplexing, choose mirror in the "disk partitions" and "options" menu. You will find the disk drives listed with the "not mirrored" notation next to them.

Highlight the first drive listed, and press <Enter>. You will see the drive listed there along with a partition number, a device number, and a drive identification number. Press the <Ins> key to bring up a list of other partitions not set up or mirrored. A quick shortcut to know which drive to match up is to look at the ID number at the end of the partition identification line. By matching each ID number, you will be assured that they are matched up correctly.

Volumes

After the partitions have been set up and mirrored, if desired, you will be asked to create a volume. There must be a SYS: volume on each server, but additional volumes can be named anything you want. When you set up the volume, there are some options you can modify (see Fig. 10.7).

NetWare files

After the volume has been set up, you are given a choice of what files you want to load on the file server, including OS/2 utilities. Each group of files to be loaded on the file server will have an "X" in the box next to it. Use the space bar to turn the "X" on or off.

LAN drivers

After the NetWare files have been loaded, you are asked to select a LAN driver for the network card(s). If the driver for your network card is not listed, press the <Ins> key and change directories of the DOS partition or get a

Volume Information	
Volume Name:	SYS
Volume Block Size:	4 KB Blocks
Status:	New, Not Mounted
File Compression:	On
Block Suballocation:	On
Data Migration:	Off

Figure 10.7 Volume information screen.

driver from the floppy disk. If you are loading an EISA or MCA system, there will be a box to select an interrupt number and memory addresses of the card.

NetWare Directory Services

Before you can initiate NDS, you need to specify at least the first level of the NDS if you are installing the first NetWare 4 server or connect it to an existing tree if installing another NetWare 4 server.

NDS includes time synchronization and server context. Enter a company or organization name and a password for the administrator user object before proceeding. Other items are optional; it is not required to add them.

Startup files

The install routine will create generic information in the AUTOEXEC.NCF and STARTUP.NCF files. You will want to add your own items to these files to customize them to your own needs. Items you might want to include are shown in Fig. 10.8.

Options

The options menu gives you the ability to create a registration diskette to send in to Novell. This is a continuing plan to make registration easier. Another option will upgrade v3.x print services that may have been installed on the server prior to the upgrade to NetWare 4.1. You can also upgrade the bindery from NetWare 4.1 during this upgrade and create users from the

```
AUTOEXEC.NCF
file server name FS1
IPX internal network number=A123
search add c:\server.410
load NE3200
bind IPX TO NE3200 net=AAA
load TLI
load STREAMS
load CLIB
load SPXS
load REMOTE password
load RSPX
load SERVMAN
load MONITOR
```

Figure 10.8 Sample AUTOEXEC.NCF file.

bindery to the NDS. Another option will allow support for other languages, and you can also add support for other protocols. In addition, you can install products like Btrieve by pressing the <Ins> key and selecting the floppy disk or CD-ROM that contains the other files.

You have now installed NetWare 4 and are ready to start the server as a fully installed system. The next step is to set up users and make adjustments to the NetWare Directory Services structure.

Server startup

Starting the server is the same as with the 3.x systems. The SERVER.EXE file starts the operating system, and the options are

- -NA, to skip running the AUTOEXEC.NCF, which is handy when there is a problem with the script or you want the server to have a different name temporarily.

- -NS, which skips using STARTUP.NCF, which is used if you don't want to use the disk drivers when starting. Note that if the disk drivers are not loaded, then the SYS: volume can't mount and then the AUTOEXEC.NCF can't run. You will not need to use -NA and -NS together.

- -C, which will change the block size of the cache buffers. After the -C, place a space and a number that the new blocks should be (e.g., -C 8 would mean change the block size to 8 kbytes).

CD-ROM support

CD-ROMs are used extensively in Windows as you can reference manuals and programs from a variety of sources. Before NetWare v3.12 and 4, you had to load a third-party driver to access a CD-ROM drive from the network. Now, CD-ROM drive support is built in and can be started from the console.

The first step is to load the NetWare disk driver for the CD-ROM. This will be supplied by the manufacturer on a disk that comes with the drive or usually can be obtained from online systems such as CompuServe.

After loading the hardware driver, load the server CD-ROM services with the command LOAD CDROM (NWPA.NLM will autoload when this CDROM.NLM loads). This places the utility code in memory and enables you to access the CD-ROM drives. All commands for the CD-ROM drive need to be prefaced by the CD command.

The first step in mounting a CD-ROM drive is to find out what devices are available. Type the command CD DEVICE LIST to see what CD-ROM drives are recognized by the server. You will see a box that lists the device number, device name, and media volume name and indicates whether the volume is mounted.

A similar command, CD VOLUME LIST, will list only those devices that actually have a CD-ROM drive in them, whereas the CD DEVICE LIST lists all drives connected to the server and recognized by the operating system.

To mount a CD-ROM disk, the command CD MOUNT *device/volumename* is used. This command uses the device number or volume name you discovered in the CD DEVICE LIST or CD VOLUME LIST display on the console screen. NetWare 3.x supported the command CD MOUNT ALL command, but this is not available in NetWare 4.

To dismount the CD-ROM disk, use the command CD DISMOUNT *device/volumename*. This will dismount the CD-ROM disk and release the lock so that you can eject the disk from the drive. A shortcut method of changing disks is the CD CHANGE *device/volumename* command, which will dismount the disk, and prompt you to insert the new disk which it will mount. The same could be done with the CD DISMOUNT command; eject the disk, and then issue the command CD MOUNT on the file server.

At any time when you are unsure of what commands to use, enter the command CD HELP, and you will see a list of the commands you can use.

Server Security

While the best security is to have the file server in a secure, locked room where only authorized people have access, this level of security is the ideal. It is common for more people than necessary to have physical access to the file server. It becomes important to lock the server to minimize the potential for someone causing problems.

NetWare 4.1 has security for the console throughout the secure console command. When this utility has been invoked, the number of actions that can be performed on the file server is limited.

NLMs can be loaded and unloaded but only if they exist in the SYSTEM directory of the SYS: volume. This ensures that only those users who have access to the SYSTEM directory can upload NLMs for loading. Normally, you can load NLMs from the SYSTEM directory, other directories on the file server, the DOS partition on the hard disk, or a floppy disk.

The date and time cannot be changed, which might allow users to gain access to the server during a time when they don't have permission for access. The remove DOS command is automatically issued, thus ensuring that the DOS partition cannot be accessed from the file server.

While this level of security is a good idea, that may not be enough for you. That is why a total lockdown of the file server console is possible. This is done from the "lock file server console" menu choice in the monitor utility. After choosing this option, you will be asked to enter the password twice. Before anything can be done on the console, you will have to enter the password again.

Administration of NetWare 4

One of the first thoughts that come to mind when viewing the administration modules (NWADMIN or NETADMIN) in NetWare 4 is that an overwhelming number of pieces of information can be used in the NDS. We suggest that you use the Windows utility (NWADMIN.EXE) rather than the DOS utility (NETADMIN.EXE).

Filling out these screens of information can be intimidating, so it becomes important to understand the different fields of information and the best information to place in them. The graphical list of objects and containers found in NWADMIN.EXE is very helpful for understanding the structure of the tree. If you have a large number of users or other objects in the system, it can be difficult to see the objects you want through all the other objects. There are several ways you can modify the view to understand it better.

Multiple windows

You can open up several windows (maximum nine) with the browser option found in the NetWare Tools menu. You can view different parts of the NDS tree in these Windows without having to look at the entire tree.

Filtering

Another method of making the view easier is to filter out the objects you don't want to see by selecting the items you want in the include item in the view menu.

Searching

If you know the name of the container or object you want, just start typing the name and the search dialog box will open up automatically. It is a simple method of finding any item.

Eliminating branches

If you will be working at the lower levels of the tree, you can eliminate containers and objects above the areas where you want to work by setting the context to the topmost container you want to see. Choose "set context" from the view menu or use the CX utility in DOS before starting Windows. When setting the context, all items above that context level will not be seen in NWADMIN.

Creating Containers

Containers are used for every object below the company or organization level to hold different types of objects. One of the benefits (and drawbacks) of these objects in NDS is the total flexibility of organization.

One method we have used with great success is to create containers for different types of resources in the organization. We create "organization unit" containers for servers, printers, groups, users, and other categories as needed. This makes it easy to segregate the objects and find them at a future date.

When you want to create a container, click once on the parent container or company object and then press the <Ins> (or click right mouse button and select "create") key to create an object or another container.

Organizational unit

The first container you will create is the organizational unit, which can be used to hold a number of different types of objects such as those mentioned above. There are nine different items of information you can enter information about the container. The items are shown on the right-hand side of the screen as a series of buttons. Clicking on these items opens the section of database fields that relate to that item.

Identification. The NDS is much more than merely a system for logging into the network. It is a database that contains a wide variety of information about the user and other resources. The Identification item contains information about how to reach the group or item.

The name field at the top of the screen is fixed (given at the time you created the container), while the others are optional. Movement around the files (for this and all screens) is by clicking on the field or by pressing the <Tab> key to move forward or <Shift-Tab> to move backward through the fields.

If you would like a longer name for this container, you can use the *other name* field, which is designed to permit a longer name than the official name for the container. This allows short names on the tree but a longer, more descriptive name shown elsewhere.

You can use the *description* container, which can include short textual information about the reason for the container. We find this field important for documenting the network inside the NDS.

The *location* field is designed to describe the physical location of the container. This can include the state, building, city, division, or office.

The *telephone* field is for someone who is responsible for the container (IS staffer or end user). *Fax number* is the same as the telephone field; it is the fax number for the person who is responsible for the container. The *e-mail address* will be for the person who handles this container.

Postal address item. Since these organization units are designed to revolve around departments, divisions, or other workgroups, you can specify an address for that work entity which includes a mailing label that can be used to send out mailings to different groups.

Job configuration item. This item allows you to set up a print job configuration. Any setting like this in the organization container is automatically inherited by all users below this container. A user who has no default job configuration will use this one automatically.

Print forms item. This is similar to the print forms used in NetWare 3.x, which is used to specify page sizes. If the user has no print forms setup, they will use this one automatically.

Print devices item. This is similar to the print devices in 3.x that contain printer control codes for individual types of printers. A user who has no print devices setup will use this one automatically.

Rights to file system item. This is a shortcut to giving rights to a volume or directory in the file server. Once you grant the rights in this item, all users below this container will get the same rights by inheritance except when the rights were blocked explicitly. To add rights to a file system or directory, click on the Include button to display the list of objects available to assign for rights. Click on the appropriate item in the "directory context" box. By double-clicking on an item in this box, you can "drill down" to the level you want to access. The files and directories inside each context will be shown in the box on the left. To select a directory or disk volume, click on the item in the "files and directories" box and then click on OK.

This will take you back to the previous screen and will insert the item you just selected into the volumes box. Click on this box, and then select "add" from the "files and directories" box. Once you have selected the directory or volume, choose the rights in the box below.

This screen also has an "effective rights" selection where you can see the total combination of given trustee rights, rights inherited from previous containers, and security equivalence.

"See also" item. This is an interesting item in that it is a totally open item that can be used to record additional information, or anything about the container that you may want to document. It has no operational functionality but is just there for your needs. Use it for any information you want.

Login script item. Another shortcut item for users is the login script. Any commands entered here in the script will be executed by users when they log in. You should put as many items in these containers as you can rather than placing the same commands in each personal login script.

Intruder limits. A good security system has to build some defense against people who want to break into the network server and cause problems. One of the most common methods of break-in is by guessing the password by entering a number of common names or words for passwords. This means that the password utility must be run a number of times until the right combination of login name and password is found. For each login, the name must be entered a number of times as each password guess is entered.

The intruder limits parameter allows you to set a number of tries the user has to get the right combination of login name and password. For an authorized user, setting the number of tries to four or five is more than adequate. If they can't get it right in those few attempts, then there is some other problem. For a hacker, four or five tries is usually not enough to guess the password.

After the number of attempts has been reached, you can set the utility to lock the account for a specified amount of time. It is common to lock the account for 15 or 30 min. This should discourage an intruder to move on and try to break into another account rather than continue to try that account.

Note: When someone has been denied access to the file server, the LOGIN.EXE utility in NetWare doesn't specifically tell that person what was wrong with the login. It could be the login name, password, intruder limits reached, or other problem. This is for security, because if you are told the reason why you can't access the file server, this could increase the chances of the system being broken into.

User Objects
Templates

Creating a number of new users can be long and tiring. We need to create an environment that allows us to add new users easily and quickly. This can be accomplished by the use of a *user template,* which sets a standard configuration for each new user and allows you to only have to make a few minor changes to meet the needs of the user.

The template looks just like a regular user setup, except it can be used as the master for each user. We will discuss each item of information in the user setup and how it can apply to the template or directly to a user setup.

Identification page

Only the *login name* (which cannot be changed) and *last name* fields are required. All other items on this screen are for internal purposes and tracking in the organization. For example, if you need to contact the user about a problem, this screen will give you the information to contact the user by telephone, e-mail, or fax. Normally, there is little you would fill out on this screen for the template.

Environment

While the identification screen contained biographical and organizational information about the user, the environment screen contains technical information about the user. Here you can specify the language used, the network address of the workstation, a server to whom the user will default, and the file-server volume and directory of the user's home directory. The language and default server are the only fields you can specify in the template. Obviously, specifying the home directory would not be useful.

Login restrictions

The login restrictions screen (see Fig. 10.9) is ideal for a template setting because the settings will be the same for most users. If you want the ultimate security, click on the "account disabled" check box to turn off the account so that no one can access until it is turned on again. If you want the account to expire on a given date, then click the "expiration date" box and set a date for the account expiration. This is used frequently for temporary employees or outside contractors who require access to the network for a specific time.

The "limit concurrent connections" option forces the user to log in only on one workstation at a time. Letting the users log in to more than one workstation at a time could mean a security problem because they couldn't be at two stations at one time and unauthorized users could access data they normally wouldn't have access to.

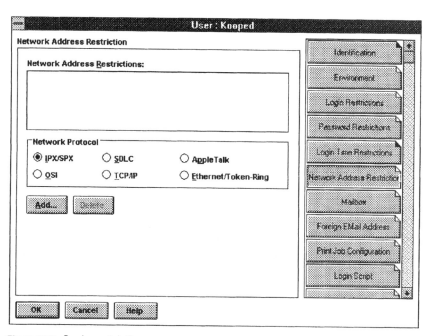

Figure 10.9 Login restrictions.

Password restrictions

A good security plan will create a number of restrictions on the user password to ensure that it cannot be easily guessed or "hacked." If you want to let the user change the password, then check the "allow user to change password" box.

Once the require a password field is checked, you must enter a password for the user (by clicking on the Change Password button), or the user will be asked to enter a password on the next login. To keep the users from entering a one-character password, you can specify the minimum number of characters for the password.

Since users may forget to change their passwords on a regular basis, you can set the number of days the current password will be allowed, thus compelling the users to enter another password. You can specify a number of days or the actual date and time.

The field to require a unique password doesn't allow users to enter the same password again when they are forced to change their passwords. The last eight passwords are remembered.

When users are requested to enter a new password, they will be asked if they want to change the password at this time. Users who choose "no" will be allowed to continue the login but will be limited as to the number of times they can decline the change password request before being locked out of the system. If you do not check this field, there will be no limitation on the number of times users can refuse to change their passwords.

Login time restrictions

This is another feature to help secure the network. You can limit the number of hours that a user can have access to the file server. By default, the user can log in anytime, but if you drag a cursor across the hours, the user will be prevented from logging in during those hours. For example, it might be a good idea to limit login to business hours.

Network address

For a high level of security, you can limit the network address and/or the workstation address in this screen. This will provide good security because it limits the users to one or more workstations or networks and they cannot log in from any other. The "F" character in the fields means that there are no restrictions on the networks or workstations that the user can log in from.

If a network segment was located on one building or on one floor, then restricting the network number would force the user to log in from a computer in that physical location.

Job configuration

This screen will set up and contain the customized print job configurations that can be used when printing to different printers and using a number of forms.

Login script

The *login script* (see Fig. 10.10) is an open page where there are no mandatory items required. You can do anything from running utilities to setting printer capture configurations. It is a good idea to reserve this login script for only those items that are unique to the user. General items (e.g., mapping the public directory search script) should be performed in a container above the users.

Login scripts can occur in an organization object, organization unit object, or profile, or in the user object directly. If you do not want to have a login script for a user, a default script built in the LOGIN utility will run, which creates a default mapping of drive F: to the root of the SYS: volume. If you do not want to have any login script (explicit or default), place the term NO_DEFAULT in the login script of the user or organization unit (user container).

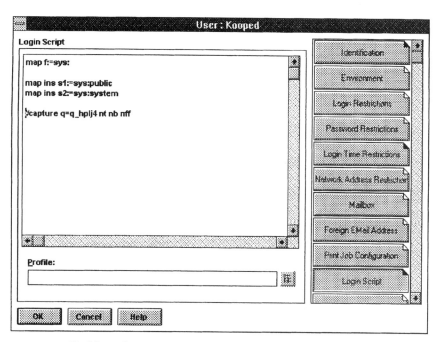

Figure 10.10 NetWare 4 login script.

The commands you can use in the login script are (listed alphabetically):

ATTACH	This command gives you the ability to connect to other NetWare servers if they are bindery-based (versions older than v4.x).
COMSPEC	This command comes from older systems where DOS utilities were run from the file server rather than from the local drive. It is also used for diskless workstations to determine where the COMMAND.COM DOS processor is located.
EXIT	This command is similar to those of other script systems where you can prematurely quit the login script on the basis of certain conditions.
FIRE PHASERS	This command is used only for administrators who want to irritate users by running a grating sound (it doesn't sound like "phasers") that is very irritating.
IF...THEN	This is a necessary command for any script where you want to execute certain applications, utilities, or commands based on logical criteria. It can be used simply for checking for group membership (IF MEMBER OF "ADMINISTRATION") or more complex commands.
MAP	This command creates standard and search drive mappings for different directories or volumes on the file server. The MAP command here works the same as the external command used in DOS.
PAUSE	When you are displaying a variable or message for the user to read, the PAUSE will stop the execution of the login script and then cause the system to wait until the user presses a key to continue.
SET	This command allows the creation of environmental variables from the login script. We use it frequently in conjunction with the IF...THEN command to create environmental variables based on membership or access to certain applications.
WRITE	This command creates a message on the screen for the user to read during the login process. The WRITE command also takes advantage of various internal identifiers listed below.

Type	Identifier	Value returned
Date	DAY	Day of month (01–31).
	DAY_OF_MONTH	Text day of week (Monday, Tuesday, ...).
	MONTH	Month of year (01–12).
	MONTH_NAME	Text name for month (January, February, ...).
	NDAY_OF_WEEK	Number of day in week (Sunday = 1, Monday = 2, ...).
	SHORT_YEAR	The last two bytes of year—century is not shown.
	YEAR	Complete numerical year (e.g., 1996).

Type	Identifier	Value returned
Time	AM_PM	Used to denote morning or evening (can also be used in an IF...THEN statement).
	GREETING_TIME	Full text for before or after noon (morning, afternoon, or evening).
	HOUR	Time in hours (1–12).
	HOUR24	Time in hours (24-h time).
	MINUTE	Current values in minutes.
	SECOND	Current value in seconds.
DOS environmental variable	<variable>	A DOS environment variable created prior to running the LOGIN script. In DOS batch files they must be enclosed in percent signs (%) and just substitute the greater-than (>) and less-than (<) signs. If you want to use an environment variable in a MAP command, use a percent sign in front of the variable (including arrows).
Network	FILE_SERVER	The name of the network server the user is logging into.
	NETWORK_ADDRESS	The hexadecimal physical address of the network where the client workstation is located.
User	FULL_NAME	The value from the full name field in user identification screen.
	LAST_NAME	The last name from the last name field in the user identification screen.
	LOGIN_NAME	The user's login name from the user object.
	MEMBER OF *"group name"*	Used mainly in IF...THEN statement where a group membership is checked. Returns value of TRUE if the user is a member of the designated group. Place the group name in quotation marks (e.g., MEMBER OF "SALES").
	NOT MEMBER OF *"group name"*	Used mainly in IF...THEN statement where a group membership is checked. Returns value of TRUE if the user is not a member of the designated group. Place the group name in quotation marks (e.g., MEMBER OF "SALES").
	PASSWORD EXPIRES	Number of days before the current password expires.
	USER_ID	The unique object ID number automatically assigned for each user.
Workstation identification	MACHINE	Type of computer taken from the MACHINE NAME entry in NET.CFG.
	NETWARE_REQUESTER	The version of the NetWare Requester.
	OS	Which variation of DOS is being used on the workstation (e.g., MSDOS, PCDOS, DRDOS).
	OS_VERSION	The numerical version of the workstation DOS.
	P_STATION	The address of the network card in the user workstation.
	SHELL_TYPE	The version identifier of the workstation shell.
	SMACHINE	The short machine name of the workstation from the NET.CFG.
	STATION	The dynamic ID connection number of the login. This changes for each login.

Type	Identifier	Value returned
Miscellaneous	ACCESS_SERVER	Returns TRUE if the access server is running and FALSE if it is not.
	ERROR_LEVEL	The value of 0 is returned if the previous command is executed properly. The most common usage has been with the attach command: IF "%ERROR_LEVEL" = "0" THEN MAP G: = file server/volume: directory /subdirectory. If the attachment command didn't work properly, the ERROR_LEVEL will equal 1 and then the mapping command will not work.
	%n	This represents the items specified on the command line of the LOGIN. For example, a gateway computer can be identified by the following command-line parameter: LOGIN .email.users.company gateway. The work gateway would be parameter %2 and could be evaluated in a login script.
NDS Objects	*property name*	Any object name in the NDS can be used in the login script. The object and lef names can be used in these arguments.

Group membership

A handy method of handling network administration is to make a user a member of a group. This can help because if there are certain users who need rights to a directory, the ability to run certain applications, printer captures, or other activities, you can make the user a member of the group and set the rights and login script for the group which will be inherited automatically by the user. Removing a user from the group will automatically remove that person from the directory or application.

Where group memberships really come in handy is in the assignment of rights. If additional rights are required or the application has been moved to another directory, it would be a time-consuming task to go to every user and change the rights by hand. By changing the right in a group, all users in that group inherit those rights and the process is handled in just a few minutes.

Security equivalences

This is also a handy method of assigning security to different users by making one user equivalent to another user. This can also be a security hole because if you make user B equivalent to user A and increase the rights to user A, the rights to user B will increase also, but you may forget the relationship between the two and not realize that user B had additional rights.

Postal address

The information on this screen is not required by the system but is part of the user demographic. The information entered here can be used by third-party utilities to create lists or mailing labels for the users.

Account balance

If you want to track the activities of users, the accounting balance is a good method and can also be used for chargebacks. It can give you a good picture of what users are doing and can also limit use of the network by blocking access to an account when the account balance becomes depleted.

See also

This screen contains only one field—a freeform text field that can be used for just about anything. It contains a collection of notes about the container or user.

Group Objects

The group objects are equivalent to groups in NetWare 3.x and can be used to apply common attributes or rights to users who are members of the group. You can create a common login script, rights, or other common activities.

NetWare 4 Utilities

For those experienced in previous versions of NetWare, the utilities used in NetWare have become second-nature. The problem was that there were many different executable files for the utilities and it was confusing for many people. In an effort to make life easier, Novell consolidated the utilities and provided a number of parameters and switches to the utilities that remain behind, providing the same functionality but with fewer utilities.

For other utilities, they have been expanded or modified to provide new features because of additional information available in NetWare 4. We will take a look at some of these utilities now.

NDIR

While the DIR command can be used on NetWare servers, it doesn't give additional information about files stored on the file server (owner, flags, last accessed date, etc.). This problem has been resolved with the NDIR.EXE utility. This utility can be used similarly to the DIR command. When you start using NDIR, you can use the switches to give a large amount of information that can be a great help in controlling the network.

The basic command of NDIR is NDIR *directory or file mask switches.* To find all files that have WPD for the extension, you would type NDIR *.wpd. By adding a /R to the end of this command, you can find out the rights you have to the files listed. If you want to list files by a specific attribute, then you place a slash before the attribute. Some of the attributes to choose from are listed below.

Attributes

A	Archive (has been modified since last backup)
C	Scrolls the information continuously without pausing screen by screen.
CC	The file cannot be compressed (as determined by the operating system).
CI	This file cannot be copied.
CO	File is compressed.
DC	File has been flagged for no compression.
DI	Delete-Inhibit.
DM	This file is not to be migrated from the hard disk to another storage medium.
DO	List directories only.
FI	View drives where a file is located.
HI	File is marked hidden and can be seen only with the NDIR utility.
IC	The file has been marked for immediate compression.
M	The file shown in the directory listing doesn't exist in the directory but has been migrated to another storage medium.
N	The file status is normal.
P	The file is eligible for purging.
RI	The file cannot be renamed ("rename inhibit").
RO	The file has been marked "read only."
RW	The file has been marked "read/write."
S	Search subdirectories for selected files.
SH	The file is sharable and more than one user can have simultaneous access to the file.
SPA	Lists directory space information.
SY	The system file designation is for utilities or data files used by the operating system.
T	A file that has transactional tracking enabled.
VER	The listing will include version information about the files listed.
VOL	Listing of volume information.
X	Used for executable files where the file can only be executed but never copied.

When using these attributes, you can list files that either match the attribute (NDIR *.WPD /A) or don't have the attribute (NDIR *.WPD /NOT A).

Sorting.   The default method of listing files or directories is alphabetical, starting from right to left (file name and then extensions). If you want to change the sorting method, the sort options can be used. The basic format is NDIR *directory or file mask* /SORT *attributes*. This command will sort the files and directories in ascending order. To sort in descending order, modify the command like this: NDIR *directory or file mask* /REV SORT *attributes*. The attributes for the SORT command are

AC	The last date the file was accessed.
AR	The date the file was backed up.
CR	The date when the file was created or copied.
OW	The login name of the owner of the file.
SI	The size of the file.
UP	The last date the file was updated.
UN	The files will be listed in the order they appear in the file allocation table (FAT) (unsorted).

In addition to using these parameters for the sort command, AC, AR, CR, OW, SI, and UP can be used in an operator and value applied to the attribute. The format for applying values to the attributes is NDIR *directory or file mask* /*attributes operator value*. The operator can be

AFT	The value given is after the value of the file.
BEF	Before the given value.
EQ	The value given equals the value of the file.
GR	The value given is greater than the value of the file.
LE	The value is less than the value of the file or directory.

For example, to find out all files created and copied before January 1, 1996, use NDIR *.* /CR LE 01/01/96.

NCOPY

This is another utility that is a companion to a DOS utility. This utility is similar to COPY but is more efficient, and you can use the NetWare volume naming convention rather than using drive letters. The format is very similar to COPY: NCOPY *source destination options*. The source and destination of files can be a path and file mask, or if you simply specify the directory, everything in that directory will be copied. The format for options are a slash (/) before the switch:

```
NCOPY [source path] filename [TO] target path [filename] [/option...]
```

The option switches available for NCOPY are listed here alphabetically:

/A   Copying of files that have the archive bit turned on. This means the file was modified or changed in some way since the file was previously backed up. While NCOPY can be used as a rudimentary backup system, with this switch, you cannot back up hidden or system files. Use NBACKUP to perform backup operations rather than NCOPY.

/C   This switch is designed to emulate the DOS COPY command by copying only the data and basic file information. Additional information available in NetWare (e.g., extended attributes like last accessed and owner) is not copied.

/F   Designed to copy sparse files. A sparse file is one that has empty blocks. The sparse block method of handling files makes the file server system more efficient. Some database systems will create a database file for a total size defined in the setup. This database file will contain only a minimum amount of data at first because the file was just created. If the file was set to 5 Mbytes, there could only be a few bytes of data in the file with the remainder being empty blocks. In this scenario, the last block of the file will most likely have data in it and the remaining 2541 4-kbyte blocks would be empty.

The NCOPY command doesn't write out the spares files automatically. If you give the /F switch, which enables the sparse file operation during a copy process, the DOS commands COPY or XCOPY will copy the empty blocks, and you will lose the sparse file efficiency.

/I   When copying files that have the extended attributes (which is any file stored on NetWare) or any file with name space information (OS/2 or Macintosh files), this switch will warn you when the disk volume you are copying to cannot handle this additional information (e.g., copying to a DOS disk on a workstation).

/M   This is the same as the /A switch, but it turns off the archive bit after the file has been copied to show it has been backed up.

/R   When copying compressed files, this switch will keep the file in a compressed state rather than uncompressing it before copying it to the destination disk. Of course, this will work only if the destination disk can handle compressed files (e.g., another NetWare volume).

By adding /U (e.g., /R/U) to this command, you can copy compressed files to a disk system that doesn't support compressed files. When the compressed file is on a disk system that doesn't support compressed files, it must be copied back to a NetWare volume before it can be uncompressed.

/S   This switch works the same as DOS COPY as it will copy the current directory and all subdirectories that meet the criteria. By adding /E (e.g., /S/E) to the command, you will copy files and empty subdirectories.

/V   When copying the files, how do you know whether it was copied correctly? This verify switch checks whether the file was copied correctly. It does not work on NetWare volumes, just on local workstation drives.

/?   If you forget the switches for NCOPY, run NCOPY /? to see a list.

FLAG

The FLAG command is a necessary command for NetWare as it provides information about the files and their attributes. In addition to viewing the attributes of these files, the FLAG command can change the attributes as required. Since there are so many different switches and options available in the FLAG command, there are different levels of help.

The FLAG /? ALL command will give information on all options for FLAG. FLAG /? FO gives information on file attributes, FLAG /? DO provides directory attributes commands, FLAG /? MODES is for search modes, and FLAG /? OPTIONS will list other commands not included in the previous list.

The format of FLAG is as follows: FLAG *directory/file_specification attributes*. This will replace the directory file attributes with the new set. By replacing the space between the directory/file specification and attributes with a plus (+) sign or a minus (−) sign, you can add or remove the attributes to or from the file or directory.

For example, suppose a file has only an Rw (read/write) attribute set and you want to add sharable attributes to it. You can either (1) replace the current attribute, FLAG *filename* RW S, or (2) add sharable attributes to the current attribute, FLAG *filename* + S. You can use the explicit file name or directory or you can use wildcards as you would in other commands such as NCOPY or NDIR.

The most common use of FLAG is for file attributes:

A   Sets the file to the same attribute if the file had been modified since it was last backed up.

Ci   The copy inhibit command prevents the file from being copied and to help security of files.

Dc   Flags the file to prevent it from being compressed.

Di   The file cannot be deleted even if it was marked Rw.

Hi   The file becomes hidden and can be found only through the NDIR command or by specifying the file name directly.

Ic   Flags the file to be eligible for compression immediately.

P   Marks the file to be purged when deleted.

Ri   The file(s) marked with this attribute cannot be renamed even if the file is marked Rw.

Ro   The files marked with this attribute cannot be modified or deleted. Used for files that are needed for reference only or for executable files.

Rw   Used as the opposite of read-only so that the files can be modified or deleted (assuming the delete-inhibit command is not used).

Sh   Files marked with this attribute will allow more than one user at a time to access the file.

Sy   This attribute marks the file as a system file and is needed only for NetWare operating system operations.

T	Files are marked as transactional in order to fulfill the transactional tracking requirement.
X	The execute-only flag marks the file as the ability to execute only and cannot be changed in other ways. Once assigned, this attribute cannot be removed except by replacing the file and reassigning the attributes.

The directory attributes are similar to the files except, of course, they apply only to directories. The format of the FLAG command for directories is the same as that of the files command.

N	This is the normal command which resets the attributes back to the default of read/write.
Dc	Don't compress the files in the directories.
Dm	Sets the directory to prevent deletion.
Hi	Hides the directory in the same manner as files set to this attribute.
Ic	Compress the files in this directory immediately.
P	Set the files in the directory to be purged when deleted.
Ri	Directories set to this attribute cannot be renamed with the RENDIR command.
Sy	Directories are set to system attribute.

Search mode. The search-mode commands in FLAG are designed to set the search-mode commands. The search-mode command is a unique method of running data in NetWare. This is designed for executable files that do not have a configurable method of searching for data files. For example, some applications look only in the current directory for data files. By setting the search mode to the desired level, you can put the data file in any other directory and set the search directory search path. Now the executable file will look in other directories for the data files.

The format is FLAG *files* /M = *mode_number.*

Mode 0: The search path is set in NET.CFG and is the default mode for all files. The SEARCH MODE parameter in the NetWare DOS requester section of the NET.CFG file applies to all .EXE and .COM files not flagged otherwise by the FLAG command. Mode 0 is a resetting of a file to its default search mode state. The command is in the NetWare DOS requester section of NET.CFG:

```
SEARCH MODE = mode-number
```

Mode 1: The executable file searches the path listed in the file, then searches the default (current) directory and the search drives.

Mode 2: This is a slight modification of mode 1. It searches the file path specified in the executable file and only the search drives (not the default drive).

Mode 3: The executable file searches the path listed in the file; then, if the open request is for read only, the default (current) directory and then the search drives are searched.

Mode 4: This mode is reserved by NetWare.

Mode 5: If there is a patch specified in the application, that path is searched for the requested data file(s), and then there is a search of all search drives for the file(s). This is designed for applications where you may want to move the data file(s) to another directory. If no path is specified for the data files, the current default directory and then the search directories are searched. This mode is the most common one used and is frequently used in the NET.CFG file search mode.

Mode 6: This mode is reserved by NetWare.

Mode 7: The application file searches the path specified first, and if the request is read only, then it searches the search drives. For those executable files that don't have a path specified, the default directory and then all search drives are searched.

Rights

While FLAG creates the file attributes, it is only half of the equation. There is also a need to coordinate the rights of the user with the file and directory attributes. The file and directory attributes can be set properly, but if the user can't gain access to the file, then it is useless. The RIGHTS command has been modified for use in NetWare 4 to provide additional information and replace the TLIST and GRANT commands found in previous versions.

The format for assigning rights for a user is RIGHTS *file/directory_name rights* /NAME=*username, username*. As with the FLAG command, you can use the format show above to assign or replace rights. To add or remove rights, place a plus (+) or minus sign (−) between the file or directory names and rights (e.g., RIGHTS *file/directory_name+rights*).

The following inherited rights can be assigned or removed with the RIGHTS command:

ALL   Will assign all rights (read, write, create, erase, modify, file scan, access control) except supervisory.

A   *Access control*—enables user to assign rights for others to have access to the files.

C   *Create*—the ability to create a file in that directory.

E   *Erase*—to erase the file or, in a directory, to erase all files in the directory.

F   *File scan*—enables the user to do directory listings of specified files or directories.

M   *Modify*—to open the file, modify the contents, and save the file again.

N   *No rights*—removes all rights to the file or a directory. Usually used for taking away inherited rights. This is the same as the command: RIGHTS   *file/directory_name*-S R W C E M F A.

R   *Read*—rights to open up the file and read the contents only.

S   *Supervisor*—assigning this right gives the users access to everything. It is not necessary to give other rights besides this one because the remaining rights are assigned automatically.

W   *Write*—gives users the ability to write to a file to add more information.

User rights.   As the network administrator, it is important that you review users' rights and monitor what the users have on the file system. The RIGHTS command can monitor the rights of users and who has access to the files or directories. The syntax for this command is RIGHTS *directories/files switches.*

/C   Can be used with other switches to scroll the listing continuously.

/I   View where rights were assigned and inherited.

/S   Can be used with other switches to search subdirectories.

/T   This enables you to view trustees of the files or directories. It replaces the TLIST command in previous versions of NetWare.

Inherited rights.   The RIGHTS   command can be used to assign inherited rights for a file or directory for all users who have access to the directory or file.

The format for assigning inherited rights is RIGHTS *file/directory_name rights* /NAME = *username, username.* As with the FLAG command, you can use this format to assign or replace inherited rights. To add or remove inherited rights, place a plus (+) or minus sign (−) between the file or directory names and rights (e.g., RIGHTS *file/directory_name + inherited_rights*).

NetWare Tools

It is important to have the ability to make changes in the configuration and setup for drive mappings, print settings, and other features. This can be accomplished in the login script and after login in DOS, but there is still a need to make adjustments to the settings while inside Windows.

NetWare Tools is the answer which is installed automatically when you run the client install utility found under the SYS:PUBLIC directory. It also creates a NetWare group with the NWADMIN icon. You can access it through clicking on the icon in the group or through the NetWare Hotkey. The Hotkey is set up through the setting screen of NetWare Tools. After you have installed the drivers and related files, click on the NWADMIN icon and then select the sixth icon, which shows a key, and other graphic images.

This brings up the settings screen, where you can set a number of items. In the upper right-hand corner is the NetWare Hotkey setting. Click on the

Enable button to enable the Hotkey. The field below that button is the function key you want to use to bring up the NetWare Tools screen. The default is F6, which can cause problems with some applications. The NetWare Tools Hotkey supersedes application function keys. If the application uses F6 for its own activities, it will be unusable because NetWare Tools will pop up over the application. You can set the values to another function key or turn off the Hotkey altogether.

Across the top of the NetWare Tools window is the *menu bar,* which consists of graphical icons to access different functions of the utility. To select one of the options, click on the button which, when depressed, will tell you which option you are currently using. If the icon button appears grayed out, the option is not active or available.

Note: The NetWare Tools are designed to change the connection or setup once in Windows. For those server connections, drive mappings, and print captures that the user desires to have in place every time, it is better to do it in the login script.

Drive connections

To add or change current drive mappings, click on the drive connection icon, and the drives and resources boxes will appear. The resources on the right-hand size will show what hard-disk drive volumes are available. Click on the volume you want to map, and then click on the drive letter in the left-hand box before clicking on the Map button on the bottom of the screen.

When you choose a volume to map, the mapping will be to the root of the volume. If you want to map a drive letter to a specific directory in the volume, click twice on the volume name and a list of subdirectories will appear, and you can keep on clicking on the directories until you reach the directory you desire to map.

If you want to make the new drive mapping permanent, click on the Permanent button at the bottom of the window, which writes out the drive assignment to the WIN.INI file so that the new assignment will be restored every time you start Windows.

Printing connections

If you don't have a capture assignment or want to change the current assignment, then choose the printer icon on the menu bar. If you understand the capture process already in DOS, then this section is just a Windows version of the same utility. The resources will be on the right-hand box, which lists the NetWare Directory Services (NDS) objects. You need to select the correct container and leaf object before assigning it to a port. Of course, the object you select must be a printer queue object. If you select the wrong object, then the Capture button at the bottom of the screen will not be available. Also, you must be logged into an NDS tree or server before you can make these printer assignments. Current queue assignments currently in effect will be displayed on this screen.

To complete the connection, select the object in the resources box and then select a printer port you want to capture. After both items are selected, click on the Capture button to complete the assignment. After capture is complete, select LPT: settings to set options for these options:

Notify	A message will be sent to the users who sent the print job to notify them it has been completed and that they can go to the printer and pick up the paper printout.
Formfeed	Use this to make sure print jobs end up on different pieces of paper. If "formfeed" isn't enabled and the application doesn't issue its own formfeed, then the next print job may start printing on the same page of the previous job.
Copies	If you need more than one copy of the print job, this option lets you specify the number of copies to be printed.
Enable tabs	You can specify the number of characters in a tab stop if required for printing.
Enable timeout	This is the amount of time where there is no print data sent to the file-server spooler before the print buffer is closed and the job is sent to a printer.
Enable banner	A banner page can be printed at the front of your print job to identify which user sent the print job.
Form name	This allows you to select a print form already set up in the print job database.
Auto endcap	This specifies that the captured printing jobs be closed when the executable file that created the print job unloads.
Hold	The print jobs sent to the queue can be stopped temporarily and then restarted later.

Server connections

This is really the first step in server and NDS connections. You must have the connections in place before drive mappings and printer connections can be made.

Choose the resources and then select the Login button on the bottom of the window. You will be asked to supply a login name and password to attach to the new server or directory tree. If you have already logged into a directory tree, then there is no need to log in again.

You can use this same window to change your existing password. This provides a convenient method of keeping your login secure.

Messages

You can send a message to another user or group of users through NetWare Tools. Select the icon with the note and thumbtack on it to access this option.

Choose the resources, and you can select from a list of groups or users. Type the message, and then just send the message to the user or group. It will appear in a dialog box for the user.

You can block the messages by checking the *broadcasts* box, which is equivalent to the CASTOFF utility. The *network warnings* box will post a message when starting Windows under several conditions:

- When the client shell (VLM) is not loaded.

- The DOS requester configuration is not correctly set up.

- The computer is not connected to the network, and the client shells could not load in memory.

In the *print jobs* section, you can set the parameters for the print jobs. *Maximum jobs* is for setting maximum number of print jobs that can be stored in a print manager queue. This is normally 50 jobs but can be set to a low of 1 or a high of 250. The *update seconds* is used to determine how often the printer manager updates the queue and displays the jobs. The default is 30 s, but the setting can be as high as 65 s or as low as 1 s. Don't set this value too low as it can slow down the operation of Windows.

The resource display has the *bindery* box to determine whether you want bindery servers or just the NDS resources displayed in the resources list. The *personal* section will decide whether to show available Personal NetWare servers in the resources list. *DS object* is to enable display of NetWare directory objects in the resources list of NetWare Tools. *DS containers* is used to determine whether to display the available NDS services in the resources box. The *name sort* will display NDS resources sorted by their name. *Type sort* will show resources sorted by their type (users, servers, printers, volumes, etc.). The *persistent* connection will reconnect a network connection from a previous session.

User-defined buttons.   The buttons marked 1 and 2 on the right-hand side of the menu bar are available for assigning the buttons to starting utilities of your choice. These buttons are commonly used for file or server utilities. The steps for assigning a utility of your choice to the buttons are as follow:

1. Click on the button of your choice if there are no utilities defined. You will be prompted for the path and program file name in the command-line field. Then choose OK to complete the assignment.

2. If a utility has already been defined, press <Alt-1> or <Alt-2> to open up the command line to change the assignment.

3. An icon will appear in place of button 1 or 2 to remind you what has been assigned to those buttons.

11

Windows 95

Windows 95 (Figs. 11.1 and 11.2) is the long-awaited next generation of Windows that moved beyond the current generation of DOS-based Windows systems. Since the first promised delivery date in 1994, there has been much speculation about what this new system will contain.

Figure 11.1   Windows 95 desktop.

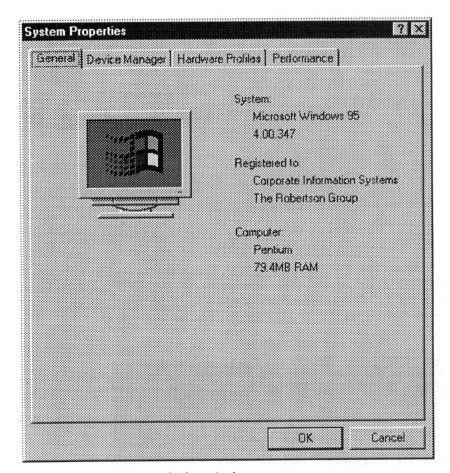

Figure 11.2   Windows 95 general information box.

The information about Windows 95 is based on the general-release beta copies provided by Microsoft in 1995. While we are sure there will be no major changes, it is likely that not every feature will be exactly the same.

Because this is such a major change in the Windows system, we recommend that you investigate and test Windows 95 extensively before implementing it in your organization.

Windows 95 Features

Windows 95 can be run on workstations that are connected to Netware 2.15, 3.x, and 4.x servers. This is critical because many companies cannot change their network systems easily but yet want to take advantage of Windows 95.

Until now, Windows access directly to NetWare has not been possible unless you used the Novell or third-party utilities. Now in Windows 3.1 or Windows for Workgroups 3.11, you can log in to a server, map a network drive, or change printer capture status through NetWare Tools. Before this utility was available, you had to log in and perform drive mappings in DOS before starting Windows.

In Windows 95, all network access and commands are built in and most activities the user wants to perform can be handled inside the system. Since the computer will boot up into Windows 95 and not to DOS, you cannot load DOS drivers and then start the Windows system.

Microsoft has provided the network client services utilities for IPX/SPX plus some administrative tools. The services available in this set of utilities include login to NetWare services or directory services, connection to print queues, plus access to other NetWare services.

The client NetWare utilities by Microsoft provide the best integration with Windows 95. The installation of the Microsoft client utility is performed from the installation routine for Windows 95. Also the Microsoft client provides login and password caching. NetWare servers can also be reached through the "Network Neighborhood" or through the "Save As" or "Open" dialog boxes.

Warning: If you have Windows with one directory (e.g., C:\WINDOWS) already installed and you choose another directory to install Windows 95 (e.g., C:\WIN95), the current version of Windows applications will not be automatically installed. You will need to install those applications all over again in Windows 95. By keeping the same directory as the current 3.x version, all current Windows applications will be automatically installed in Windows 95.

One of the utilities available in Windows 95 is the "Network Neighborhood." After you click on that icon, choose the Map drive button to map an unused drive letter to a NetWare volume. In the next field, you can specify the path you want to use for that drive letter. In this field, you can use the NetWare standard mapping convention (File_server_name/Volume_name:Directories) or the Universal Naming Convention (UNC). The UNC standard uses two backslashes at the beginning of the string and then lists the complete path including server and volume name. For NetWare, the UNC string would be \\File_server_name\Volume_name\Directories.

If you have already logged into the network, your name and password will be authenticated with the server. If Windows 95 can connect with the server, the directories are displayed and you can access the drive. If you are not logged into the network, the "network credentials" will be displayed and you will be asked to enter a login name and password before continuing.

Inside the network neighborhood, you can view a variety of information about the network and file servers, including mapping to a network drive (described previously), properties of the server, your login name (for those who forget!), attachment to another server, and logout from a file server.

HPFS file names

One of the nice features of Windows 95 is its support for long file names on file servers that have the OS/2 name space support. This name space supports the HPFS volume standard, and Windows 95 is able to use this feature. This frees us from the tyranny of the old 8.3 standard for file names in DOS. Each file name can be up to 255 characters long.

No shell memory problems

With Windows 95 and the Microsoft client utility, the 32-bit protocols and other files are a part of Windows 95, and you will not need to hassle with the problem of loading NetWare shells in conventional memory or loading those drivers high in upper memory. Microsoft claims that their utilities are over 200 percent faster than the VLM shell under Windows for transferring a large file on the network.

Server reconnection

One of the most frustrating things in network use is the sudden disconnection of a server during the user's activity. The Windows 95 client system will scan the network and will connect the user to the network again in a manner similar to that in which VLM driver can reconnect with a server.

Large network support

For those that have large networks or large data needs, the Windows 95 NetWare client utility can take advantage of packet burst and large internetwork packet (LIP) protocol. Packet burst enables the client to have file-server communication in bursts of up to 64 packets at a time with only one packet of acknowledgment rather than the standard one-to-one relationship of data packet and acknowledgment packet.

The LIP protocol assistance overcomes the limitation on packet data size of 576 bytes by having the server and client negotiate the largest packet size possible up to a maximum of 4202 bytes.

Remote management

A network administrator can make changes to a Windows 95 system across the network even if Windows 95 is installed on the C: drive on a workstation.

Replacement of .INI files

Windows for Workgroups had the largest amount of .INI files that needed tweaking. With Windows 95, all the configuration is done in the Windows 95 Registry (see Fig. 11.3) rather than the .INI files. Rather than being just one

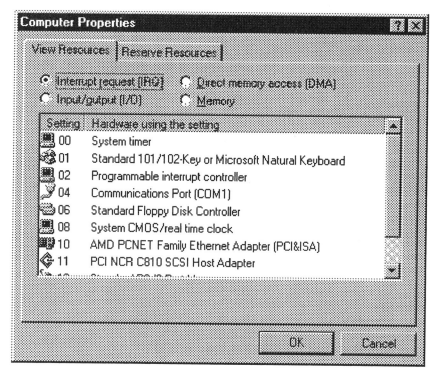

Figure 11.3 System information from Windows 95 Registry.

file, there are three files: USER.DAT, which has configuration items that relate to the user; SYSTEM.DAT, for information about the local computer; and POLICIES.DAT, which handles system activities for the peer-to-peer activities of Windows 95.

In Windows and Windows for Workgroups, the .INI files can grow quickly, but if they exceed 64 kbytes in size, they will not operate properly. There is no limit to registry size, so the Windows 95 Registry can handle a large number of application, hardware, or user information.

Function restriction

The system policy editor enables the administrator to restrict the functions on the desktop by modifying the registry. This utility will change the policies of the entire Windows 95 network, or groups, or of an individual user. These policies can handle security or restrict system items in each Windows 95 setup. From this utility, a network manager can set up configuration and organization names for each workstation.

Graphical network management

If you are frustrated by not being able to handle network administration and connectivity in graphical applications, Windows 95 provides the network neighborhood utility that will give you all the user utilities normally run in DOS (e.g., login, logout, SLIST or NLIST, map). The file servers on the network will be shown as an icon on the screen. In addition to NetWare servers, Windows 95 stations will appear on the screen and can be accessed like a NetWare server.

The system monitor will display a chart of network activities like those involving network stations, or local systems parameters like RAM and network protocols. NetWatcher is a graphical tool that monitors the network like other Windows 95 workstations open files on the network and user information.

Network communication

By using the 32-bit network driver in Windows 95, you can have network communication several times faster than is possible in Windows for Workgroups.

Network protocols and detection

If you try to run multiple protocols in Windows for Workgroups, it will be a frustrating experience. Windows 95 can run 32-bit versions of IPX, TCP/IP, and NetBEUI. The network communications system inside Windows will automatically detect the frame type rather than require manual specification as is required now.

NetWare login

You will be able to accomplish all logins and logouts from inside Windows 95. With Windows for Workgroups and the NetWare Tools, you can log in to a server, but the login scripts are not run during this login. With Windows 95, you will never need to have the users log in and log out from DOS. It supports all the login script commands except for loading TSRs from the login script.

Automatic backups

One problem that network administrators are convinced will never happen is the regular backup of workstations by users. In Windows 95, there are back-up agents that will respond to signals from a compatible backup system that will make a backup of the local hard disk to a centralized backup system.

Network recovery

The failure of a NetWare server will not be noticed by the user except that the user cannot gain access to the file server. The user can still continue to work with the local applications, and when the file server comes back up, network resources will automatically and seamlessly be available again.

Network drivers

All network drivers will be running above the 1-Mbyte boundary, so all DOS-based applications will run with more free memory below 1 Mbyte.

SNMP and inventory support

Windows 95 will work with the Novell Network Management System (NMS), the Microsoft Systems Management Server, and HP OpenView with a built-in SNMP agent. With this agent, a network administrator can keep track of a number of parameters in each Windows 95 system and can be reached through TCP/IP and IPX protocols.

Windows 95 conforms to the *desktop management interface* (DMI) specification by including a DMI agent in Windows 95. Because of the emerging standards of DMI, we can assume that the latest agent will be available in Windows 95, although nothing can be guaranteed.

If you are a network administrator in charge of a large number of workstations, then you will like the ability to gather reports from the registry about each computer and get a complete picture of hardware and user settings for that machine.

Security

Windows had only a very rudimentary level of security. Windows 95 provides a couple of new options for keeping the stations secure. You can set up security for users who want access to a hard disk or printer by requiring them to enter a password—similar to how Windows for Workgroups operates.

The other method of security relies on a NetWare file server to determine access for users and groups. You can grant access to a user or group for full access, read-only access, or custom access (similar to that found in Windows NT).

To gain access through the NetWare-based security system, a special user called WINDOWS_PASSTHROUGH must be set up as a bindery user in the file server. This special user is used to scan the bindery to determine valid users. We have not performed extensive testing to determine how much of a security problem this special NetWare user will be. You cannot have a password on this special user, but you can take away all trustee rights to help ensure security.

This method of security makes it necessary to set up a user in only one place rather than worry about users on the NetWare file server and then on each Windows 95 setup.

Windows 95 Client Limitations

The new Windows 95 client does not provide every service you may be using now. A rule of thumb is that any NetWare utility beyond standard ODI and VLM or NETX shells will not be available in the Windows 95 client.

One of the biggest limitations of the Windows 95 client is the lack of support for NetWare Directory Services. You can access NetWare 4.x servers through bindery emulation only from this Windows 95 client utility.

If you are currently using LAN WorkPlace for DOS to access a UNIX system through TCP/IP, then you will have to use the VLM utility rather than the Windows 95 client. If you need to have the NCP packet signature for security reasons, you must use the VLM utility rather than the NetWare client. If you meet these requirements, you will have to install the NetWare shells in the Windows 95 client.

System Requirements

Windows 95 can be installed only on a DOS system (including MS-DOS, PC-DOS, and Novell DOS), OS/2 (if dual-boot DOS is installed), Windows NT (if dual-boot DOS is installed), Windows 3.x, and Windows for Workgroups 3.x.

You will need to have at least version 3.2 of MS-DOS or its equivalent. While this is the minimum, we recommend that you upgrade to version 6.x or its equivalent before installing Windows 95, as this will ensure that Windows works as smoothly as possible.

The computer on which you are installing Windows 95 must have at least 417 kbytes of conventional memory and at least 40 Mbytes of disk space for the system. If you are using a disk compression utility, you will need to set aside an uncompressed area on the drive for Windows 95 purposes.

As with Windows 3.1 and Windows for Workgroups 3.11, you need to have at least an Intel 80386 CPU (or equivalent). While the 386 may be the minimum required for Windows 95, performance is very slow on this computer and runs much better on a 486 or a Pentium chip computer.

RAM requirements are given by Microsoft as 4 Mbytes as a minimum, but for normal operation you will want at least 12 Mbytes with 16 Mbytes (or more) as an optimum. Because you will most likely be opening a number of Windows, the RAM amount is critical to the operation.

Installing Windows 95

Even though Windows 95 is considered to be a separate operating system, differentiated from the previous versions of Windows, you cannot install Windows 95 on a computer that does not have any other operating system on it. And, for reasons known only to Microsoft, the setup routines cannot install Windows on a computer that has only the HPFS or NTFS disk partitions installed on the hard disk.

Before starting the installation of Windows 95, there are several things you should do to make sure that the installation will go smoothly. You will need to defragment the hard disk to ensure that Windows 95 can perform the modifications to DOS as necessary. If you have Windows or applications and data on the computer, it is a good idea to do a verified backup in case something goes wrong during the installation. Since Windows 95 will use the network files during installation to configure itself, you need to have all network shells operational before starting the install routine.

While you can get Windows 95 on floppy disks, we highly recommend getting the CD-ROM version as the installation will be much smoother and faster. You will have to install the DOS CD-ROM drivers (e.g., manufacturer's disk driver and MSCDEX utility). The SETUP.EXE utility will be on the CD-ROM disk. Run that to start the installation.

There are a number of switches available for SETUP.EXE. The /? is the universal help switch that will give you information about the options available for this utility. The /D switch prevents Windows 95 from using the *dynamic link library* (DLL) files from previous versions of Windows during setup. If you are experiencing problems during setup, try this option to see if the problems go away.

Specifying /ID will disable the check of amount of disk space before Windows 95 is installed. The /NOSTART switch installs only the required Windows 3.x DLLs that are needed for the installation. There are some Windows 3.x DLLs required for installation, and these will be installed during the normal installation process.

You can also specify the setup ASCII file (normally MSBATCH.INF) that controls the setup options. When installing Windows 95 on a number of different computers, you can customize it as you can with SETUP.INF and SETUP.SHH when Windows for Workgroups is installed.

When the setup program starts, it will search the hard disks on the computer for any versions of Windows 3.1 or later. If the desired version of Windows is found, you will be asked if you want to start that copy. If you choose OK, that copy of Windows is started and the setup routines start for Windows 95. If you do not want to run that version of Windows, some of the DLL files from Windows will be installed that will enable the Windows 95 setup utility to run. By running the currently installed version of Windows, you will be able to upgrade the applications and groups into Windows 95.

The setup program also checks to see if there is an extended memory driver installed and loads an XMS driver if it cannot find one. It will also look for a disk caching utility, installing SMARTDrive if one is not loaded and operational.

As in standard versions of Windows, the setup routine will check for TSR files that may be present in memory. The TSR utilities that may cause problems are listed in the SETUP.INF file. If one of these problem TSRs are found, the Windows 95 setup utility will warn you about the problem.

The opening screen will describe the setup process and the steps required (including which steps have already occurred). Because you are just starting the installation, only the first option (gathering information) will be highlighted.

Type of installation

The next screen will ask what type of installation you wish.

Typical. This is the most common installation option for most desktop computers. It requires the fewest decisions and places a complete installation on the computer hard disk, requiring about 40 Mbytes of disk space. The next screen asks if you want to default the directory to C:\WINDOWS or another directory. If you click on the other directory option, the "change directory" screen appears and you can type in the drive and directory in the space provided.

After the disk drive (by specifying the drive letter) and directory are specified, the next step is for SETUP.EXE to check the disk (unless you specified the /ID switch) to ensure that there is enough space free to install Windows 95.

Note: The utility that checks the disk space may report the wrong values on a disk drive that is compressed. While there may be enough room to install

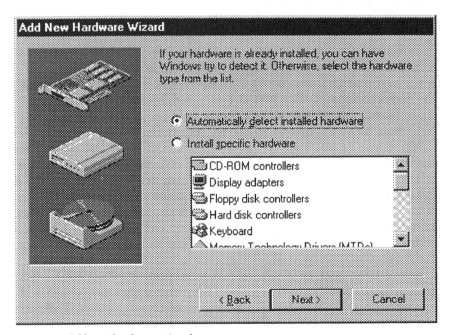

Figure 11.4   Add new hardware wizard.

Figure 11.5   Keyboard language dialog box.

Windows 95 because it is compressed space, you may still get warnings that there is not enough room.

After checking for disk space, you will be asked for user information by entering your name and your company's name. This completes the beginning steps for the installation.

The next step is for the installation routine to review and detect the computer hardware (see Figs. 11.4 to 11.6). SETUP.EXE will look at the CPU, disk drives, video display, mouse, and keyboard. During the analysis, the analysis progress bar will display the status of the analysis.

A complete scan is performed on the system, including all peripheral hardware devices and external devices connected to the computer. The Windows 95 setup utility also scans IRQs, I/O, and DMA addresses, and builds a list of

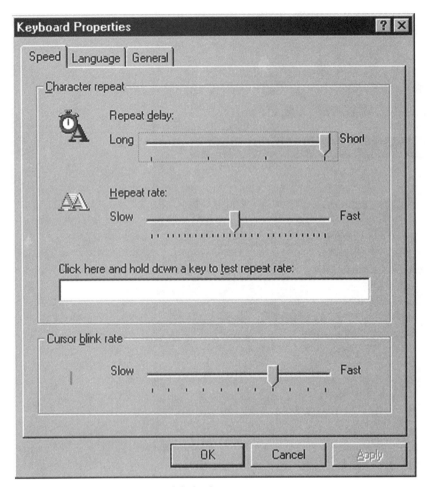

Figure 11.6 Keyboard setup speed dialog box.

hardware on how it is connected in the Windows 95 Registry (a system database in Windows 95).

If you have a new computer that adheres to the plug-and-play specification (Fig. 11.7), the setup utility will access the plug-and-play system to identify the peripheral devices. If you have a computer that does not support plug-and-play, Windows 95 will reference a database of known hardware devices and then will try to determine each hardware device in the computer.

There is a potential for access to certain hardware systems to cause SETUP.EXE to hang. You may be able to click on the Cancel button. If that doesn't work, try pressing the F3 key, which is the standard key for exiting the setup process. In the event that those options don't work, you will be forced to try <Ctrl+Alt+Del> or power the computer off and back on again.

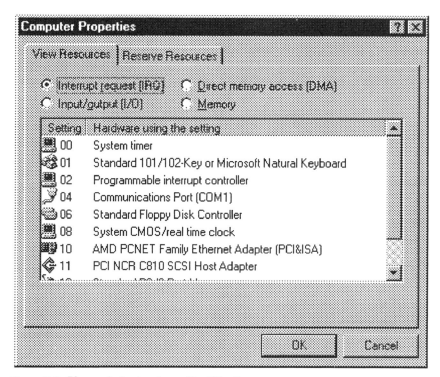

Figure 11.7 Plug-and-play hardware identification.

Next, you will be asked if you want to create an emergency startup disk like that used in Windows NT. This disk contains a series of files that will start Windows 95 in the event the startup files on the hard disk are corrupted. If you choose not to create the startup disk, it can be created at a later time.

After the creation of a startup disk, the next step is to describe how the computer will appear on a Microsoft network (this is not for Novell NetWare). It requires entering a computer name, the workgroup you will be a part of, and the description. The computer name is what appears on the computer's list on other systems, the workgroup is for segregating the computers on the network, and the description is a multiword logical description.

The computer name must be one word, different from any other computers on the network, with a maximum of 15 alphanumeric characters and/or these special characters: ! @ # $ % ^ & ( ) − _ { } ′ ~.

The workgroup should not be unique (unless you are starting a new group) but should indicate the name of the group in which you want this computer to appear. The workgroup name must be one word, with a maximum of 15 alphanumeric characters and/or these special characters: ! @ # $ % ^ & ( ) − _ { } ′ ~.

After all this setup is done, the actual creation of the startup disk is performed (depending on what you chose earlier). You can insert a high-density floppy disk regardless of whether it is formatted or empty. The setup program formats the disk and creates the startup files on that disk.

The purpose of the startup disk is to enable the system to start Windows 95 whenever there is a problem with the startup files on the computer hard disk. Because this is an emergency method of starting, you will not be able to access any network systems or any special hard-disk systems that require special drivers in CONFIG.SYS.

The setup utility will format the floppy disk, if required, and then install IO.SYS, MSDOS.SYS, and COMMAND.COM on the disk to ensure that it becomes bootable. After the disk is created as a system disk, the following files are copied to the disk.

File	Description
ATTRIB.EXE	DOS file attribute utility
CHKDSK.EXE	DOS disk checking utility
DEBUG.EXE	System debugger utility
EDIT.COM	DOS ASCII text editor
EDIT.HLP	DOS ASCII text editor help file
FC.EXE	DOS file compare utility
FDISK.EXE	DOS disk partition utility
FORMAT.COM	DOS disk format utility
MEM.EXE	Memory display utility
MORE.COM	System viewing utility
MSCDEX.EXE	CD-ROM disk driver utility
MSD.EXE	System diagnostics utility
SCANDISK.EXE	New disk status and repair utility (can be used instead of CHKDSK)
SCANDISK.INI	Configuration file for SCANDISK.EXE
SETVER.EXE	DOS version utility
SYS.COM	Disk system setup utility
XCOPY.EXE	File copy utility

If you wish, you can copy other utilities to the startup disk that may help you recover the system if there is a problem.

After the creation of the startup disk, the computer is restarted (you need to remove the floppy disk) and Windows 95 will start up again. This step will convert groups found in the current version of Windows (if you are upgrading Windows 3.x).

The final steps of installation is setting the time zone, date, and time (see Figs. 11.8 and 11.9), and installing a printer. The time-zone setting has a unique method of choosing the time zone as it shows a map of the world, and you can choose the time zone by clicking on the map location where you are or, if you wish to use the more traditional method, you can use the dropdown

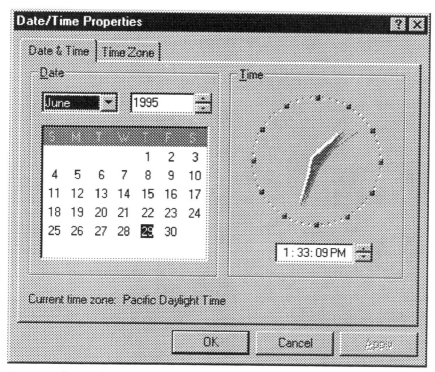

Figure 11.8 Date and time dialog box.

list above the map, which lists the text version of time zones, to choose the time zone. There is a check box below the map that you can use to adjust for Daylight Savings Time.

The same screen has a tab to allow you to change the date and time of the computer system. If the system time of the computer is correct, then there is no need to choose this option.

The installation of a printer is guided by the "add new hardware wizard" (see Fig. 11.4) to enable you to easily select a printer.

Custom

This option gives you the option of better control for the installation of Windows 95. It requires a number of decisions and places a complete installation on the computer hard disk, requiring about 40 Mbytes of disk space. The next screen asks if you want to default the directory to C:\WINDOWS or another directory. If you click on the other directory option, the "change directory" screen appears, and you can type in the drive and directory in the space provided.

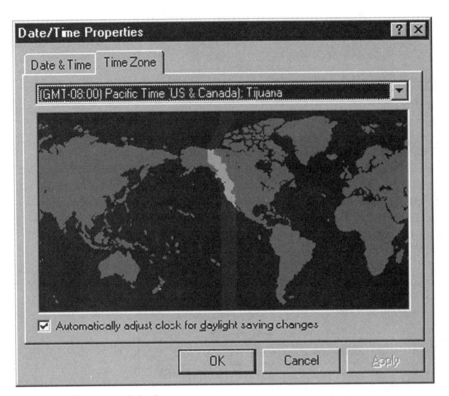

Figure 11.9 Time-zone dialog box.

After the disk drive (by specifying the drive letter) and directory are specified, the next step is for SETUP.EXE to check the disk (unless you specified the
/ID switch) to ensure that there is enough space free to install Windows 95.

The next option allows you to select the individual systems in Windows 95
that you want to install. These options give the name, an icon, a check box,
and the amount of disk needed for each option. Backup, bitmaps, disk compression, games, and other utilities can be deselected. All items are selected
by default, and you can unselect them as desired.

You will next be asked for user information by entering your name and
your company's name. This completes the beginning steps for the installation.

The next step in the installation routine is the review and detection of the
computer hardware. SETUP.EXE will look at the CPU, disk drives, video display, mouse, and keyboard. During the analysis, the analysis progress bar
will display the status of the analysis.

Access to certain hardware systems may cause SETUP.EXE to hang. You
may be able to avoid this by clicking on the Cancel button. IF that doesn't
work, try pressing the F3 key, which is the standard key for exiting the setup

process. If those options don't work, you will have to try <Ctrl+Alt+Del> or power the computer off and back on again.

You will then be asked whether you want to create an emergency startup disk similar to that used in Windows NT. This disk contains a series of files that will start Windows 95 if the startup files on the hard disk are corrupted. If you decide not to create the startup disk at this time, it can be created later.

After creating a startup disk, your next step is to describe how the computer will appear on a Microsoft network (this is not intended for Novell NetWare). You must enter a computer name, the workgroup you will be a part of, and the description. The computer name is what appears on the computer's list on other systems; the workgroup is used for segregating the computers on the network, and the description is a multiword logical description.

The computer name must be one word, distinct from any other computers on the network, and must contain no more than 15 alphanumeric characters and/or these special characters: ! @ # $ % ^ & ( ) − _ { } ' ~.

The workgroup should not be unique (unless you are starting a new group), but should carry the name of the group in which you want this computer to appear. The workgroup name must be one word, containing no more than 15 alphanumeric characters and/or these special characters: ! @ # $ % ^ & ( ) − _ { } ' ~.

Following all this setup, the startup disk is actually created (depending on what you chose earlier). You can insert a high-density floppy disk, regardless of whether it is formatted or empty. The setup program formats the disk and creates the startup files on that disk.

After you create the startup disk, the computer restarts (remember to remove the floppy disk), and Windows 95 will recommence. This step will convert groups found in the current version of Windows (if you are upgrading Windows 3.x).

The custom installation brings up the option of selecting network components. The network options allow you to install a variety of network connects. It is possible to connect to virtually every network system available through Windows 95. You can select the primary client even though you have added several different network systems.

To add another network component, click on the Add button (see Fig. 11.10), and you will be given choices for specifying the client, adapter, protocol, and service. The network clients can be Artisoft LANtastic, Banyan VINES, Beam and Whiteside NFS, DEC Pathworks, Novell NetWare, SunSelect PC-NFS, or TCS 10-Net.

The final steps of installation involve setting the time zone, date, and time, and installing a printer. The time-zone setting, as mentioned earlier, displays a map of the world, allowing you to choose the time zone by clicking on the map location where you are located or, if you wish to use the more traditional method, you can use the dropdown list above the map, which lists the text

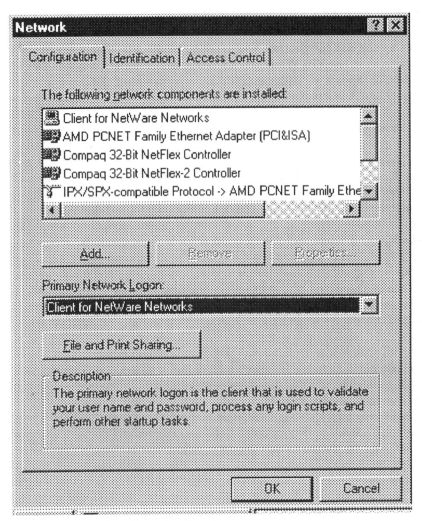

Figure 11.10   Network configuration dialog box.

version of time zones, to select the time zone. There is a check box below the map that you can use to adjust for Daylight Savings Time.

The same screen has a tab to allow you to change the date and time of the computer system. If the system time of the computer is correct, there is no need to choose this option.

Printer installation is guided by the "installation wizard" (mentioned earlier) to enable you to easily select a printer (Fig. 11.11).

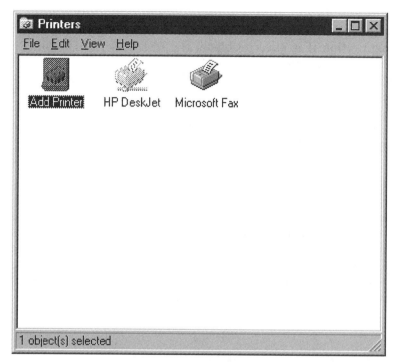

Figure 11.11   Printer folder.

System modification

After the installation process is complete, the setup routine will replace the existing system files for DOS with its own files to boot into Windows 95. If you are running MS-DOS, the IO.SYS file is renamed "IO.DOS" and MSDOS.SYS is renamed "MSDOS.DOS." For other versions of DOS, the system files are renamed differently. After placing the new files on the disk, the setup routine reboots the computer and the system restarts in Windows 95.

Log files

Several log files are created during the installation of Windows 95. If the installation goes fine, then there is little need to view them. However, in the event of a problem, they can become very useful in troubleshooting the problem location.

SETUPLOG.TXT

This file is similar to the BOOTLOG.TXT file found in Windows 3.x and Windows for Workgroups 3.x. It records each and every step of the process and its status (was it successful or not). While the information is useful for you to read, it is also used by the setup routine when the installation fails and you have to restart. In a small, but important, installation enhancement, Microsoft wrote code that would check this file and avoid a step, if it could, during the reinstallation if it gave problems the first time. This avoids a nasty habit of some installation programs of hanging on a minor step that will not greatly impair the operation of an application or utility, yet it hangs the installation routine. Usually, this means that a hardware device that gives problems during installation will not be installed.

You can find SETUPLOG.TXT in the root directory of the disk drive on which you are installing Windows 95.

DETLOG.TXT

This file contains information about what hardware devices have been detected during the scan of the hardware system. Hardware detection occurs not only during installation but also whenever the Add New Hardware icon is selected in the control panel (Fig. 11.12). Information about the hardware items is stored in MSDET.INF. A binary file named DETCRASH.LOG has been created to provide information to the Windows 95 setup utility about any problems encountered during the hardware scan.

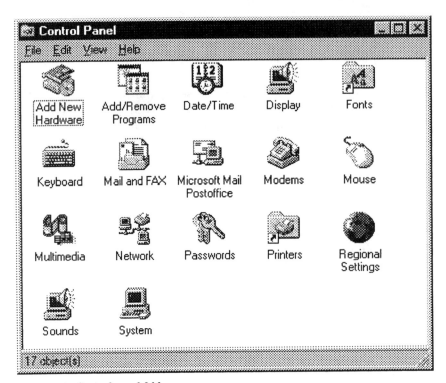

Figure 11.12 Control panel folder.

The information in DETLOG.TXT is ASCII text and can be read by any text-based editor. It lists the hardware item, whether the item was found, and current status of the system. Items detected include not only peripheral cards but also internal systems such as keyboard, all disk drives, and parallel port.

Setup utility files

A number of files are used in the setup of Windows 95. These files fall into two categories: binary programming files and text configuration files. SETUP.EXE is the primary utility that starts the installation routine. This file does some of the installation and then starts other routines as needed. It works in close conjunction with SUWIN.EXE, which does the actual starting of DLL files used during the installation.

SETUPC.INF is a text file that has information on how to install the base system and some computer configuration items such as those in CONFIG.SYS. SETUPX.DLL is the main code for installing Windows 95 as it contains utilities for copying files, disk access, and reading the .INF files.

Another utility used in the installation process is NETDI.DLL. It is dedicated to detecting and configuring networking systems in Windows 95.

When installing Windows 95, a directory called WININST0.400 is created. The number 0 at the end of the file name can change but usually will be 0. A number of files will be copied to this directory for installation purposes. After installation is complete, the files and this temporary directory will be deleted.

The files copied from the installation disks or CD-ROM are (listed alphabetically):

ADAPTER.INF	KEYBOARD.INF	MSPRINT.DLL
APM.INF	KOMMCTRL.DLL	MSPRINT.INF
APPLETPP.INF	LAYOUT.INF	MSPRINT2.
APPLETS.INF	LOCALE.INF	MULTILNG.INF
ATWORK.INF	LZEXPAND.DLL	NET.INF
AWFAX.INF	MACHINE.INF	NETAPI.DLL
CDROM.INF	MCA.INF	NETCLI.INF
COMCTL31.DLL	MF.INF	NETDI.DLL
COMMAND.COM	MIDI.INF	NETOS.DLL
COMMCTRL.DLL	MODEMS.INF	NETSERVR.INF
COMMDLG.DLL	MONITOR.INF	NETTRANS.INF
COMPLINC.DLL	MONITOR2.INF	NODRIVER.INF
DELTEMP.COM	MOS.INF	OLDSETUP.INF
DISKDRV.INF	MOTOWN.INF	OLE2.INF
DLLMSTCP.DLL	MSDET.INF	PCMCIA.INF
EISA.INF	MSDISP.INF	PENDRV.INF
ENABLE.INF	MSDOS.INF	PENWIN.INF
FONTS.INF	MSFDC.INF	PRECOPY.INF
FORCEIOS.INF	MSHDC.INF	PRTUPD.INF
FWINTEMP.400	MSMAIL.INF	RNA.INF
ICM.INF	MSMOUSE.INF	SCSI.INF
JOYSTICK.INF	MSPORTS.INF	SETUP.HLP

SETUP.INF	SUWARN.BAT	WARNING.EXE
SETUPC.INF	SUWIN.EXE	WAVE.INF
SETUPPP.INF	SYSDETMG.DLL	WINHELP.EXE
SETUPX.DLL	TAPI.INF	WINPAD.IN
SHELL.DLL	TIMEZONE.INF	WINVER.INF
SHELL.INF	UNKNOWN.INF	WORDPAD.INF
SUCHECK.BAT	VER.DLL	
SUEXPAND.DLL	VERX.DLL	

Directory structure

Although you can change the directory name for Windows 95, a number of subdirectories below that name are fixed and cannot be changed. Figure 11.13 shows the directory structure of Windows 95. For purposes of this illustration, we have kept the top directory name of WINDOWS even though you can make it anything you want.

These directories contain the following utilities (listed alphabetically):

C:\WINDOWS   Base Windows 95 files

COMMAND   MS-DOS

FONTS   Font files

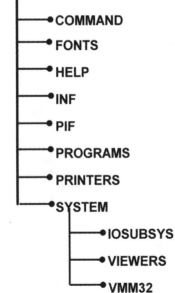

C:\WINDOWS
- **COMMAND**
- **FONTS**
- **HELP**
- **INF**
- **PIF**
- **PROGRAMS**
- **PRINTERS**
- **SYSTEM**
  - **IOSUBSYS**
  - **VIEWERS**
  - **VMM32**

Figure 11.13 Windows 95 directory structure.

HELP	Help system files
INF	Information files
IOSUBSYS	Input/output subsystem
PIF	DOS program information files
PRINTERS	Printer drivers
PROGRAMS	Applications
SYSTEM	Drivers and VxDs
VIEWERS	Viewers
VMM32	VxDs installed after initial setup

Starting Windows 95

There are some new files that are used in Windows 95 that will have an effect on the operation of Windows 95.

MSDOS.SYS

This file is flagged as "hidden" and "read only" and is placed on the root of the boot drive (usually C:). It has critical information about the computer system for Windows 95, which is required before Windows 95 can start. The parameters in MSDOS.SYS are tabulated as follows:

Parameter	Description
BootDelay	When starting Windows 95 you can choose from startup options and not start Windows 95. The value specified is in seconds. The default entry is BootDelay = 2. To disable the delay, set the parameter to BootDelay = 0.
BootFailSafe	This parameter is used by vendors to disable the Fail-Safe Startup. Not recommended for normal use unless directed by a hardware vendor.
BootGUI	By setting this to BootGUI = 0, the automatic graphical startup will be disabled and you will have to start Windows 95 manually.
BootKeys	This parameter can be used to secure a computer system. By setting this to BootKeys = 0, the user cannot press any of the startup function keys in Windows 95 (F5, F6, and F8) when starting the computer system.
BootMenu	This is the opposite of BootKeys. Setting BootMenu = 1 will display the Windows startup menu by default.
BootMenuDefault	This parameter will set the default menu item on the startup menu. The default is BootMenuDefault = 1.
BootMenuDelay	After you have selected the default startup menu in the previous parameter, this parameter will determine how many seconds the startup menu is displayed before the default item is run.
BootMulti	Set this parameter to BootMulti = 0 to disable the ability of the user to run DOS rather than Windows 95 on startup. It will also disable the <F4> key that can be used to start DOS.

Parameter	Description
BootWarn	The default is 1, and if it is changed to 0, the safe-mode boot warning will be disabled from the startup.
BootWin	If you set this value to 1 (the default), Windows 95 will boot by default. Setting it to a 0 will boot to MS-DOS. You can start Windows 95 after booting to DOS by moving into the C:\WIN95 directory (or any directory you have installed with Windows 95) and run the WIN.COM file. (*Note:* This option will not work if you don't have MS-DOS 5 or 6.)
DblSpace	This is similar to the DOS feature of loading double-space compression from CONFIG.SYS. Set this parameter to 1 (the default), and DBL-SPACE.BIN will load automatically. A value of 0 disables it.
DoubleBuffer	This parameter is similar to the SMARTDrive utility in DOS. By setting this to 1, double buffering for the disk drive controller will be used when needed, a 2 will make double buffering unconditional (this would be in case Windows 95 couldn't determine whether double buffering was needed), and the default of 0 disables double buffering.
LoadTop	On bootup, Windows 95 will load COMMAND.COM, and other drivers (e.g., DBLSPACE.BIN) between 640 kbytes and 1 Mbyte. If your system is incompatible with this option, set this value to 0, and these drivers will be loaded in conventional memory. A value of 1 enables you to load these files high.
Logo	If you want to bypass the starting logo (equivalent to running WIN : in previous Windows versions), then set this value to 0. It will also disable the annoying beeps upon startup.
Network	A value of 0 disables this feature, while a 1 adds a new menu choice to start up "Start Windows, bypassing startup files, with network support" as an option. This allows you to start Windows in a stand-alone mode without network support.

Editing MSDOS.SYS

MSDOS.SYS is a read-only hidden file in the root directory. You will need to change the attributes before opening the file for modification. The fastest method is to use the "find" command in the main ("start") menu and select the Files option. You can search for the file, turn on "read only" and "hidden" attributes, and click on the OK button. After you have modified those attributes, choose the "open with" option and choose a text editor (you can use the built-in WordPad utility). Make the changes you want and then save the file. Choose "properties" in the find menu and reenable the read-only and hidden attributes.

At the bottom of the file you will find a series of dummy statements that are not used by Windows 95. This is designed to keep the file larger than 1 kbyte. Some virus systems might flag a hidden file smaller than 1 kbyte as virus-infected and cause a false alarm. Some virus detectors in their cleanup mode will delete this file before continuing. You will be able to continue to run Windows 95 but will not be able to start it again without MSDOS.SYS.

Novell NetWare Client Utilities

Even though Windows 95 has utilities built in to handle connections to the network, it can also connect to a file server through Novell-supplied utilities.

You can use the VLM shell to connect to a NetWare file server from Windows 95. To use the Novell-supplied utilities, you need to load the TSR shells in the normal method from AUTOEXEC.BAT before Windows 95 is installed.

To use the Novell NetWare client software, boot the computer under DOS, install the NetWare client software from a floppy disk, load the network shells, and then run the Windows 95 setup. It is important that the NetWare shells be loaded and working properly before Windows 95 is installed because it reads the configuration of these shells to help set up its communication to the network. The setup utility will configure Windows 95 to work with the ODI shells.

Windows 95 will support the old IPX monolithic drive configuration, but we believe that no one should be still using that configuration now but rather should have migrated to the newer, more efficient ODI standard. The same goes for the NETX shell. You should not be using that utility because VLM is the preferred shell, and eventually Novell will drop support for NETX.

Using the VLM network shell with Windows 95 does not eliminate the use of Windows 95 "client" utility. In certain situations you want to connect to other network systems such as the Windows NT "advanced server" in addition to Novell NetWare servers.

Installing Virtual Loadable Modules in Windows 95

Once Windows 95 has started, choose "custom setup," "network," and add options, then press the Client button and then the Add button for the client option. You will be presented with a list of manufacturers, from which you can choose Novell NetWare (Workstation Shell 4.0 and above). After choosing the network shells, you may be asked to reinstall the VLM files and run the NetWare install program for the network shells.

NetWare Login Scripts

Windows 95 will process the login scripts of NetWare 3.x and 4.x (in bindery emulation mode) by creating a DOS session that will process the login script and then close down after the script is complete. A special processor in Windows 95 will take the MAP, SET, and CAPTURE commands in the login script and make them global in Windows 95. This will make them available to all graphical and DOS applications running under Windows.

If you have special utilities or applications that run in the login script, they will unload after the DOS session closes down after running the login script.

If you need to have these utilities, load the ODI and VLM drivers in DOS before starting Windows 95.

Printing in Windows 95

You can print to a NetWare print queue through the print manager, which allows you to choose the print queue on a temporary or permanent basis.

Windows 95 coordinates printing much better than previous editions of Windows did. In Windows and Windows for Workgroups, it followed the DOS method of printing, in which data was dumped to the printer until the printer buffer was filled and the printer signaled to stop sending data until the buffers were cleared and more data could be imported. The Windows 95 spooler checks with the printer first to see if data can be accepted and then sends data only if the printer is ready to accept the print job. You will probably find this method to be faster and to provide a smooth, even-paced document printing process.

New printing method

The purpose of spooling is to allow the user to return to the application as soon as possible. This is enhanced in Windows 95 by printing not a direct print file but an *enhanced metafile* (EMF). Under Windows for Workgroups, the printer driver processed the print job and created an output image file (see Fig. 11.14). Control was returned to the user only after the driver finished converting the file to an output file. This resulted in delays for the user and long waiting periods.

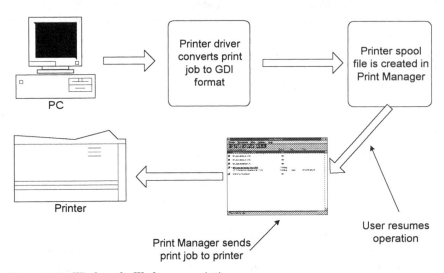

Figure 11.14 Windows for Workgroups printing.

What the programmers have done with Windows 95 is to shift the time when conversion to the printer language is performed. By returning control to the user before doing the conversion, the user perceives the printing as being faster. Although there is an increase in speed because the printing is done in a 32-bit environment, getting users back to the application sooner allows them to focus on their work and forget about the printing cycle.

Spooling DOS applications

In Windows for Workgroups, DOS applications printed directly to the hardware printer port and printing were actually slower than if the print job were done outside Windows. This is because DOS applications running in Windows run slower than otherwise and because the applications couldn't use the print manager.

Windows 95 provides the ability for DOS applications to run inside Windows 95 and spool their print jobs through the Windows 95 print spooler (see Fig. 11.15). The spooler diverts all print jobs destined for a hardware port and redirects them through the print spooler. Even though these DOS applications can't gain access to the EMF function of printing, you still get spooling and background printing.

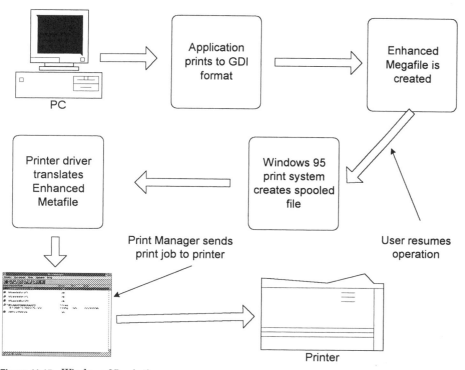

Figure 11.15 Windows 95 printing.

In addition to standard spooling, print jobs in Windows 95 can be held and printed later. This allows the user to continue operation even though they may not be able to connect to a printer right away or want to hold the print job until a time when the printer is not busy.

Printer control

Windows for Workgroups had a confusing setup for printers as it required two different locations to handle printing control. In the control panel, configuration of the printer takes place including connection to a network printer (see

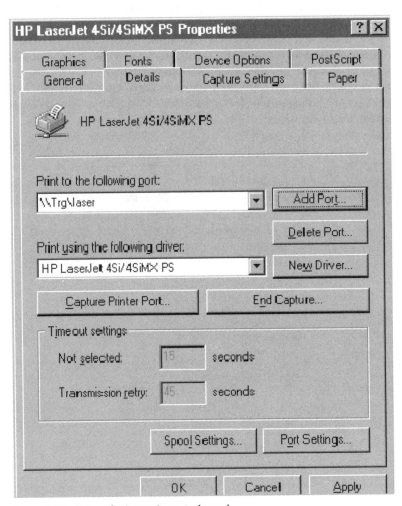

Figure 11.16 Setup of printers in control panel.

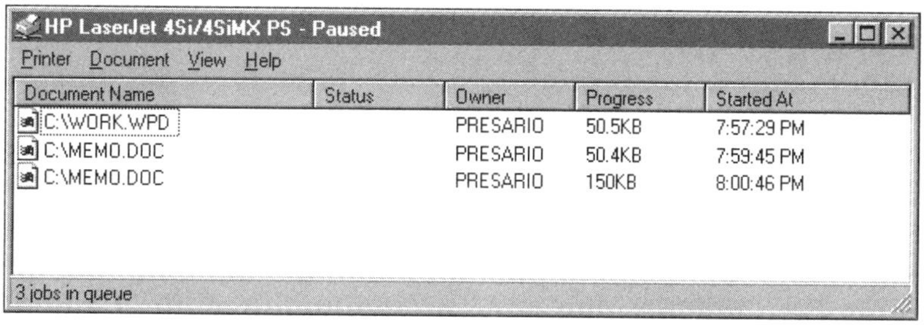

Figure 11.17 Print manager.

Fig. 11.16). But you need to go to the print manager (Fig. 11.17) to control the print jobs.

Printer folder

Rather than having the multiple locations for printer control, Windows 95 just has a printer folder that lists all of the printers and how you can control them there. If the printer you are installing conforms to the plug-and-play specifications, then Windows 95 can detect and install it automatically. When installing a printer from the printer folder, the "installation wizard" (a Microsoft standard help utility) gives you the parameters required to install the printer.

The plug-and-play utilities can detect and install a printer when Windows 95 is first installed, when Windows 95 starts, or when you invoke the detection module.

Note: The plug-and-play utilities require bidirectional ports to install the printers. Some manufacturers do not install bidirectional parallel ports in their computers. If that is the case, you will need to purchase and install a separate parallel port card that is bidirectional.

Once a new printer is found during the detection phase, you will have a choice of installing the internal driver (if available), installing the driver on a floppy disk provided by the printer manufacturer, or ignoring the printer and not installing it in Windows.

When connecting to a NetWare server, it is a good idea to preload all printer drivers on the file server(s) so that when a user wants to install a printer, the drivers will be automatically available on the file server. All the user has to do is to point to the directory location, and Windows 95 will complete the installation.

When a Windows 95 computer loses connection to the network, it will hold any print jobs on the local hard disk until the computer connection resumes and then will print to the network printer.

Windows 95 has the ability to act as a remote printer for a NetWare printing queue without the hassle of RPRINTER or NPRINTER and Windows for

Workgroups. This still allows you to control the print jobs centrally yet still have the printers directly attached to a local station.

Note: Although using a locally attached printer as a network printer is a viable option in Windows 95, we are still partial to using a printer network card (e.g., HP JetDirect) directly attached to the network. The increase in speed of transmitting a print job to the printer via network protocol rather than a parallel or serial port is significant. In an unscientific test, we have performed comparison tests between a serial connection and network printer card. The serial connection to a laser printer completed a full page of graphics in just under 5 min, while the network card connection saw a print time of under 1 min. Because the network printer connected to a computer running Windows 95 would most likely be connected through a parallel cable, the speeds would be definitely slower. This does not include problems with the printer being disabled if the user's computer was turned off.

All activities related to the printing can be done just by dragging or clicking on the printer icon shown in the printer folder.

Network Utilities

We believe that Windows 95 is the first graphical version of the Windows family that was designed to operate in virtually any networking environment. While other versions have network connectivity available, it usually is through great effort and frequently with third-party utilities. For example, to run Windows for Workgroups on TCP/IP, there is a large amount of work required to install third-party software and configure it for the network.

Windows 95 has focused on the TCP/IP, IPX/SPX, and NetBEUI protocols as they are the most commonly used in networking. However, even though the focus is on these protocols, Windows 95 can connect to a number of other network systems (see Fig. 11.18).

Network connectivity is a series of layers that communicate with each other, giving wide options as to the type of communication (see Fig. 11.19).

- Artisoft® LANtastic® version 5.0 and later
- Banyan® VINES® version 5.52 and later
- Beame and Whiteside BW-NFS version 3.0c and later
- DEC™ Pathworks™ version 5.0 and later
- IBM® OS/2® LAN Server
- SunSelect PC-NFS® version 5.0 and later
- TCS® 10-Net version 4.1 and later

Figure 11.18 Additional networks supported by Windows 95.

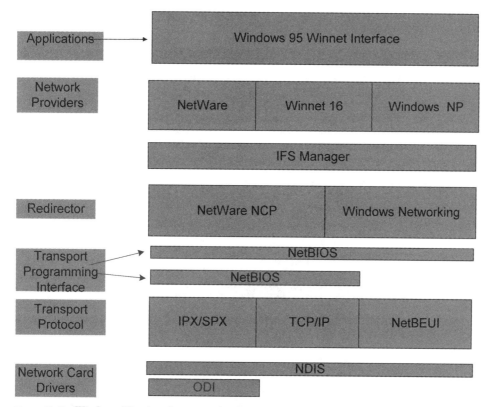

Figure 11.19 Windows 95 network communications.

The Microsoft developers have provided an open system to enable third-party vendors to integrate their networking environments into Windows 95. There is an application programming interface (API) available to network providers that enables customization of networking services and acts as a translator between the low-level network services and Windows 95. This API set is so rich, the network providers can create their own network login dialog box (see Fig. 11.20). This allows a consistent look to logins but yet attach to different network systems.

NetWare Connectivity

Microsoft has developed a client for NetWare that is fully integrated with Windows 95. If you desire, you can also use the NETX or VLM shells to run with Windows 95. Microsoft claims up to 200% increase in network operation speed over Windows for Workgroups. This number comes from Microsoft, and we have not been able to perform exhaustive tests to confirm or deny this claim.

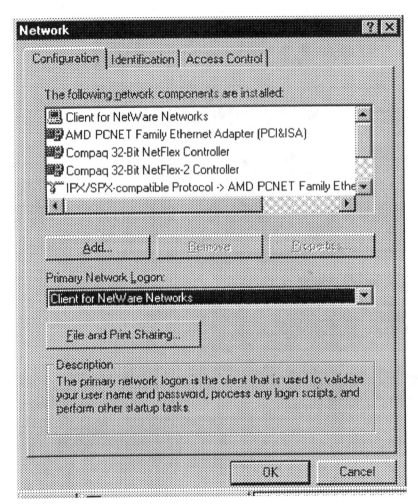

Figure 11.20 Network configuration dialog box.

This client utility does not take up any conventional memory and will reconnect automatically to the NetWare server if there is a disruption in communication. Microsoft has included support for the packet-burst feature of IPX/SPX to enhance network communication, plug-and-play for network cards, and ability to operate with any NetWare 3.x and 4.x file servers (remember that only the bindery mode is supported in NetWare 4).

If you are using a docking station for a laptop, the laptop can be hooked and unhooked from the docking station, and Windows 95 will sense the network communication automatically and ask for a user login. There is no need to shut down the laptop before connecting it to the docking station.

The NetWare client module has a setup screen that allows the user to specify a preferred server, and to determine what letter should be assigned to the first network drive, the level of search mode (SMODE), and whether the login script will be run on login.

Other Networks

As mentioned earlier, Windows 95 has a connectivity to a number of other networks. However, discussion of those details are beyond the scope of this book.

Communications

If you believe the broadcast and print media, there is no other type of computing except for remotely accessing information between computers. While this level of communications has been and will always be important, there is much more to computing than just that. Microsoft has created a number of levels of access in Windows 95 for "reaching out and touching" another computer.

Windows for Workgroups has never been able to handle high levels of communications traffic without special drivers. For years, many have used utilities such as King Comm to handle communications into Windows, especially with the high-performance UART 16650 chip.

Also, many who tried to run a communications session in the background of Windows for Workgroups while running another application in the foreground frequently noted that the communications session broke down and had errors. These problems virtually disappear in Windows 95, as it can handle the high communication rates.

The first communications feature to be implemented in Windows 95 was the increase in communication speed through the 32-bit communications subsystem. They included routines ensuring that time-sensitive communications sessions would not be starved for CPU access and cause the communications to fail.

The developers of Windows 95 extended the printer-driver concept to communications by providing a unified platform for communication routines and then translating those into specific modem access. Now, a software developer only has to write the communications program to this common set of programming calls, and by installing a driver for the specific modem, can have seamless communication while the software program is blind to the type of modem used. This will make setup for communication programs much easier.

Windows 95 also employs the Microsoft Telephony API system for controlling multiple communication programs that seek access to a single communications device such as a modem (see Fig. 11.21).

Windows 95 on the Internet

The growth of the Internet in the last couple of years has been nothing short of amazing. While those of us in the industry knew and used the Internet, the

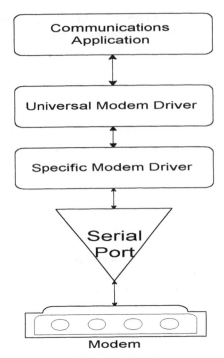

Figure 11.21 Windows 95 modem communication.

current number of users exceeds 20 million and grows by thousands each month. While we could debate how useful Internet access is, we do acknowledge that it is the latest fad in the industry and everyone is allowed in the pool. Windows 95 is configured to provide access to the Internet in a way that no other desktop system has.

Microsoft Network

The Microsoft Network (see Fig. 11.22) provides access to the Internet in the same way as do other online providers (e.g., CompuServe, America Online, Prodigy). This controversial new service from Microsoft is a latecomer to the online services market but has the potential to take a substantial portion of the market from the other providers. Microsoft has received criticism because they will be integrating Microsoft Network in many of their products. Windows 95 has Microsoft Network utilities built in.

Accessing the Microsoft Network from Windows 95 is just a matter of clicking on the install New Modem button to set up your modem, choose the

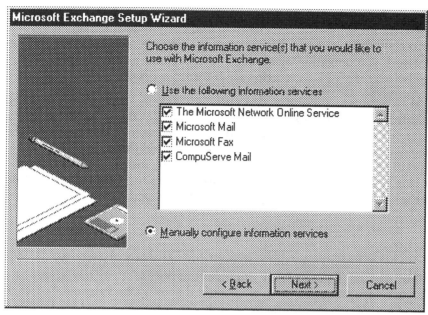

Figure 11.22 Microsoft exchange setup dialog.

"install Microsoft Network" option, and then choose the "sign up for the Microsoft Network" option in the "accessories" menu. You will need to provide your name, your company's name, and street address, city, state, ZIP code, country, area code, and phone number. The next dialog box will handle the billing information (usually a credit card), and then you can enter a password and user name.

The Microsoft Network uses terms similar to the Internet with a "home page," which lays out the basic information about the network. Like other online services, the Microsoft Network has daily updates on system information, electronic mail, member services, and folders that define different forums on a variety of topics.

Direct Internet access

You can take several steps to gain access from Windows 95 to the Internet. You need to get an account with an Internet provider and get a PPP or SLIP account. PPP is Point-to-Point Protocol, a standard for framing and authentication protocols, and it handles configuration setup for several layers of the OSI network model. From Windows 95, you can dial directly into a computer system that provides communications through the PPP standard. You do not need to purchase any additional software to provide those connections.

A SLIP (Serial Line Internet Protocol) is an original communication standard for UNIX (on which the Internet is based). It provides the same connection services available through PPP but doesn't provide automatic negotiation of the network configuration or security of encrypted authentication. If you have the choice, get a PPP connection for Internet access.

Note: SLIP support is not provided automatically in Windows 95, and you must install the modules from the CD-ROM installation disk. The code for SLIP is found in the ADMIN\APPTOOLS\SLIP directory. Just click on the "add/remove programs" icon in the control panel to add this support.

After getting an account with the online provider, install TCP/IP from the network icon in the control panel, install the "dial-up networking" connection and enter an IP (Internet protocol) address in the property sheets.

Internet addressing

There are several things to note about Internet connectivity. While this book is not designed to provide comprehensive information about the Internet, there are several things we should discuss. The Internet Network Information Center is the controlling body for Internet connectivity. They have divided the network into the groups listed in Fig. 11.23). These names appear at the end of the Internet address (e.g., *commercial_company*.com).

Name system

Before connecting to the Internet, you will need to set up an IP address, subnet mask, and gateway IP address. (This is done in the network option of the control panel.) This information is required for the "domain name" system used by the Internet to translate those addresses into IP addresses.

Name	Type of Organization
COM	Commercial Organization
EDU	Educational Institution
GOV	Governmental Organization
INT	International Organizations
MIL	Military
NET	Networking Organization
ORG	Noncommercial Organization

Figure 11.23 Internet standard addressing extensions.

TCP/IP addressing

When using TCP/IP addressing, you need some basic information on how the system works. Each address is 32 bits in length and must be unique for each computer and router on the network. An address will look like this: 111.222.333.444. This address contains the network ID, which is a logical network, and the host ID, which is your computer on the network.

Of course, a random assignment of address numbers would mean chaos on the network as each address must be unique. If you are using a TCP/IP system that is unique to your organization and will never communicate with another TCP/IP network, then you can create any addressing scheme you want. If you want to communicate with the rest of the world, you need to make sure that the address you use is unique. This is done by having a network address assigned by the Internet Network Information Center (InterNIC), which assigns all network IDs. They can be reached at (800) 444-4345 from within the United States and (619) 455-4600 from all other countries. You can also send requests on the Internet to hostmaster@internic.net. The number you receive will be a network address, and you can add your own unique number at the end to identify each computer in your network.

The Internet uses address classes to identify systems. There are different network classes, and the type of address you get depends on how many computers will be connected to the network through this number. There is a theoretical limitation of many millions of computers available on the network. This addressing scheme was never designed to handle the large number of computers joining the network as they are doing now. The classes are known as A, B, and C; class A has values 1 to 126 and occupies the first octet of the address (e.g., 100.xxx.xxx.xxx). This allows the computer address to occupy the x values shown above, allowing over 16 million addresses. Class B can contain values 128 to 191 and occupies the first two octets (e.g., 100.150.xxx.xxx). Class C is the most common and has values of 192 to 223 in the third octet (e.g., 100.150.200.xxx). This allows up to 254 computers to be attached to the network address. As a result, many organizations will have more than one class C address. The addresses you put in the dialog boxes in Windows 95 will be given to you by the Internet access providers according to the addresses assigned to them.

Windows Project Checklist

Planning the Project

Every project, unless it is very small, needs to have a work plan on how to achieve the intended goal(s). The checklist given here is designed to give you some ideas on how to structure your project. While it is impossible to plan the project for you, we hope this helps. This checklist lists items you should be aware of while planning your project.

I. Planning the project
   A. Setting project goals
      1. What do you want out of the Windows project?
      2. Will every desktop system have Windows?
      3. Will Windows be the primary desktop environment or intended only for part-time usage?
   B. Time frame
      1. When is the project deadline?
   C. What is the knowledge level of users?
      1. What level of training is required?
   D. User freedom
      1. Should users be able to change the Windows environment?
      2. Change hardware settings?
      3. Local station setups?
      4. Command-line access?
      5. Installation Windows versions?
   E. What level of uptime is required?
   F. Will users need to move from computer to computer?
   G. Will users need to access Windows remotely?
   H. Is host connectivity required?
   I. Creating the project plan

  J. Staff members required
  K. Working with users
  L. Training key users
  M. Working with management
  N. Budget calculations
    1. Conversion
    2. Implementation
    3. Maintenance
    4. Technical support
    5. Training
    6. New applications required
II. Reviewing current environment
  A. Number of users
  B. Number of desktops
  C. LAN setup—configuration information
  D. Protocols
    1. Is the speed high enough?
    2. Type and speed
  E. Current level of bandwidth utilization
    1. Making bandwidth utilization calculations
  F. DOS applications retained
    1. Do they require EMS or XMS memory allocation?
  G. Users who have remote access now?
  H. WAN links?
    1. WAN transmission speeds?
  I. Links to host systems
  J. Multiple users per machine?
  K. Current IS (information system) staff Windows knowledge
  L. What is the support capability of the IS staff?
  M. Network infrastructure
    1. Servers
      a. Number
      b. CPU
      c. Speed
      d. RAM
      e. Expandability
      f. Network interface cards
      g. Bus type
      h. SFTIII installed?
    2. Communications
      a. LAN or WAN?
      b. Cabling
      c. Routers
      d. Bridges

    e. Backbone
    f. Protocol
    g. Multiple protocols on wire?
    h. Hubs
    i. NICs
  3. Workstations
    a. CPU
    b. RAM
    c. Speed
    d. Monitor
    e. NICs
    f. Bus type
    g. PCI or VESA local bus?
    h. Mouse type
III. Workstation configuration
  A. Amount of RAM required for calculations
  B. Understanding memory
    1. Memory issues
      a. Memory sizes
      b. Core memory systems
      c. Memory extension schemes
      d. ROM shadowing
      e. Memory terminology
      f. ROM chips
      g. Buying memory
      h. Wait states
      i. Page-mode chips
      j. Interleaved memory access
      k. Memory cards
      l. Memory types
      m. Expanded memory
      n. LIM-EMS 4.0
      o. Upper memory
      p. TSR loading problems
      q. Hard-disk memory configurations
      r. CMOS ROMs
      s. Remapping EMS page frame
      t. Accessing the high-memory area
      u. Computer setup
      v. CONFIG.SYS
      w. DOS-HIGH
      x. DOS-UMB
      y. File handles
      z. File control blocks

2. Order of loading?
3. SMARTDrive
4. Buffers
L. Network drivers
   1. Monolithic drivers
   2. ODI
   3. NDIS
   4. NETX
   5. Virtual loadable modules
   6. NET.CFG
     a. Link driver statements
     b. Packet burst
     c. Large Internetwork Packets
     d. Loading VLM modules
     e. File handles required for Windows
     f. Cache buffers required for Windows
IV. Installing Windows
  A. Windows v3.0 currently installed?
  B. Windows v3.1 currently installed?
  C. Windows for Workgroups v3.11 currently installed?
  D. Windows 95 currently installed?
  E. Location of Windows
    1. Compressed files on server
      a. Local installs from compressed files
    2. Uncompressed files on server
      a. Setup commands
      b. Used for install
      c. Used for running Windows from server
      d. File attributes
    3. Split installation
      a. Run files from server and local station
      b. Decreased network traffic
      c. User mobility
  F. User setups
    1. User directories
    2. Files in user directories
    3. User rights required
  G. Automatic installation
    1. SETUP /A
    2. SETUP /H
    3. SETUP /O
    4. Modifying .INI files
      a. .INI file Structure
      b. WIN.INI
      c. Section names

        d. Variable standards

        e. String variables

        f. Integer variables

    5. Lines that can be removed

    6. Rewriting setup files automatically

    7. Setup scripts

    8. Setting colors automatically

    9. Setting desktop automatically

    10. Removing groups

    11. Removing applications

    12. Adding new groups

    13. Adding new applications

    14. Adding new video drivers

    15. Automatic detection of hardware

  H. SETUP.INF file

    1. Lines not needed

    2. Removing network choices

    3. Adding drivers from OEMSETUP.INF

    4. Removing v3.0 upgrade lines

    5. Adding changes for network setup

    6. Running modified version of SETUP.INF

    7. Personalizing display boxes

    8. NETSETUP-TRUE

    9. Default directories

  I. NETWORK.INF

  J. CONTROL.INF

  K. APPS.INF

    1. Modifying detection of applications

  L. Groups

    1. Adding and modifying

    2. Sharing groups on the network

    3. Restricting modifications

  M. User training

    1. Types of training needed

    2. Timing of training

    3. Refresh training

    4. Conversion from old applications

  N. User support

    1. During conversion

    2. Ongoing support

  O. Using project software for installation planning

  P. Installation problems

V. Windows and NetWare customization

  A. Swap files

        1. Temporary
        2. Permanent
        3. Size of swap file
        4. 32-bit file and disk access
    B. Setup files
        1. SETUP.INF
        2. SETUP.SHH (automated setup)
        3. NETWORK.INF
        4. APPS.INF
        5. CONTROL.INF
        6. OEMSETUP.INF
    C. Customization of initialization files
        1. SYSTEM.INI
        2. WIN.INI
        3. PROGMAN.INI
        4. CONTROL.INI
        5. PROTOCOL.INI
        6. WINFILE.INI
        7. MSMAIL.INI
        8. SCHDPLUS.INI
    D. Source files
        1. SYSTEM.SRC
        2. WIN.SRC
        3. CONTROL.SRC
VI. File servers
    A. Focal point of computing
    B. Server CPU configuration
    C. Hard-disk configuration
    D. Cache
    E. RAM requirements
    F. Open files with Windows applications
    G. Duplexed drives
    H. Mirrored servers
    I. Network cards
    J. Multiple network cards
    K. Server configuration
    L. Communication and receive buffers
VII. Windows printing on NetWare
    A. Printing objectives
    B. Installing printers
    C. Printer configuration
    D. Generic printer
    E. Updated drivers
    F. Multiple printers

G. Printer connections

H. Additional ports

I. Print job settings

J. Using print manager

K. Corrupted drivers

VIII. Network printing issues

A. NetWare printing

B. NetWare 3.x utilities

C. NetWare 4.x utilities

D. NetWare print systems

E. Configuring print services

F. Workstation printing utilities

G. Startup procedure

H. NetWare Windows utilities

IX. Network DOS applications

A. Application types

B. DOS environment

C. PIF setup

D. Automatic application setup

E. Program file name

F. Window title

G. Optional parameters

H. Startup directory

I. Memory parameters (standard mode)

J. Memory parameters (386 enhanced mode)

K. Advanced options

L. Application multitasking priorities

M. Program priority

N. Memory options

O. Lock program memory

P. Uses high memory

Q. Display options

R. Other options

S. Command-line access

T. Changing the DOS prompt

X. Windows and NetWare security

A. Removing run command

B. Modifying icon properties

C. Levels of security

D. File manager

E. Monitoring user activity from the file server

F. Monitoring user activity from other utilities

G. Tracking user activity through NetWare accounting utility

XI. Applications
    A. Sharing applications
    B. Installing application for multiple users
XII. Additional resources
    A. CompuServe
    B. Microsoft BBS
    C. Microsoft TechNet
    D. Novell Support Encyclopedia
XIII. Windows 95
    A. New desktop system
    B. Using Explorer
    C. Network connection
    D. Network login to Windows NT and NetWare
    E. Hardware requirements
    F. Software requirements
    G. Using DOS applications
    H. Diagnostic utilities

Getting Help

In most projects it is difficult to do everything by yourself. Integrating Windows and NetWare is also impossible to do yourself. That is why you bought this book—to make the job easier. There are many other sources of help you can turn to for a great amount of assistance while working on this project. Novell and Microsoft provide a wide range of services you can turn to for help.

Telephone Support

Novell

Novell has two main offices: in Provo, Utah and Austin, Texas. The addresses are

Novell, Inc.
122 East 1700 South
Provo, Utah 84606

Novell, Inc.
5918 W. Courtyard Drive
Austin, Texas 78730-5036

Here are some telephone numbers you can use to reach Novell for technical and sales support:

Technical support	(800) NETWARE; (512) 794-1775 (fax)
International technical support	(801) 429-5588 (outside USA)
Novell education	(800) 233-EDUC; (801) 429-3900 (fax)
International education	(801) 429-5508
Novell developer programs	(800) RED-WORD; (512) 345-7478 (fax); (512) 794-1796 (outside USA)

Microsoft FastTips

Toll-free, 7-days-a-week, 24-hours-a-day access to automated information about key Microsoft products is available, including access to common questions and answers, and technical articles, via fax and U.S. mail.

Desktop Applications FastTips (Word, Excel, Works, etc.)	(800) 936-4100
Home Products FastTips (Encarta, Golf, Kids, etc.)	(800) 936-4100
Personal Operating Systems FastTips (Windows, etc.)	(800) 936-4200
Development FastTips (VB, VC++, etc.)	(800) 936-4300
Advanced Systems FastTips (Windows NT, MS Mail, etc.)	(800) 936-4400
Microsoft Download Service	(206) 936-6735; (905) 507-3022

Standard support

No-charge support from Microsoft support engineers is available via a toll call. Support is available in the United States between 6:00 A.M. and 6:00 P.M. Pacific time, Monday through Friday, excluding holidays. In Canada, call between 8:00 A.M. and 8:00 P.M. Eastern time, excluding holidays.

Support for personal operating system products is available for 90 days from first call to a support engineer. Support for development tools products is available for 30 days from first call to a support engineer. The following phone numbers are in the United States and Canada:

Desktop applications	(905) 568-3503
Microsoft access	(206) 635-7050
Microsoft Automap	(206) 635-7146
Microsoft Bob	(206) 635-7044
Microsoft Excel for the Macintosh	(206) 635-7080
Microsoft Excel for Windows and OS/2	(206) 635-7070
Microsoft Magic School Bus and kids' products	(206) 635-7140
Microsoft Money	(206) 635-7131
Microsoft Bookshelf, Encarta, Cinemania, and other multimedia products	(206) 635-7172
Microsoft Office for the Macintosh	(206) 635-7055
Microsoft Office for Windows	(206) 635-7056
Microsoft Office—Switcher Line	(206) 635-7041
Microsoft PowerPoint	(206) 635-7145
Microsoft Profit	(800) 723-3333
Microsoft Project	(206) 635-7155
Microsoft Publisher	(206) 635-7140
Microsoft Schedule+	(206) 635-7049

Microsoft Scenes and Games	(206) 637-9308
Microsoft Video for Windows	(206) 635-7172
Microsoft Windows entertainment products	(206) 637-9308
Microsoft Word for the Macintosh	(206) 635-7200
Microsoft Word for MS-DOS	(206) 635-7210
Microsoft Word for Windows	206) 462-9673
Microsoft Works for the Macintosh	(206) 635-7160
Microsoft Works for MS-DOS	(206) 635-7150
Microsoft Works for Windows	(206) 635-7130
Personal operating systems (90 days from first call to support engineer)	(905) 568-3503
Microsoft Mouse, Microsoft Ballpoint, Windows Sound System, and other Microsoft hardware	(206) 635-7040
MS-DOS 6.0 and MS-DOS 6.2 upgrade	(206) 646-5104
Microsoft Windows and Windows for Workgroups	(206) 637-7098
Development Tools (30 days from first call to a support engineer)	(905) 568-3503
Microsoft Basic PDS	(206) 635-7053
Microsoft C/C++	(206) 635-7007
Microsoft Delta	(206) 635-7019
Microsoft Excel SDK	(206) 635-7192
Microsoft FORTRAN	(206) 646-5109
Microsoft Fox products for MS-DOS, Windows & UNIX	(206) 635-7015
Microsoft QuickBasic	(206) 646-5101
Microsoft QuickC	(206) 635-7010
Microsoft Source Safe	(206) 635-7014
Microsoft Test for Windows	(206) 635-7052
Microsoft Visual Basic	(206) 646-5105
Microsoft Visual Basic Professional Toolkit	(206) 646-5105
Microsoft Visual C/C++	(206) 635-7007

Related Microsoft services (U.S. phone numbers) are

Microsoft Support Network Sales Group	(800) 936-3500
TT/TDD (text telephone)	(206) 635-4948
Microsoft Wish Line	(206) 936-WISH
Microsoft Authorized Training Center Referral	(800) 636-7544
Microsoft Certified Professionals	(800) 636-7544
Microsoft Consulting Services (MCS)	(800) 426-9400
Microsoft Developer Network	(800) 759-5474

Microsoft Press	(800) 677-7377
Solution Provider Sales and Information	(800) 765-7768
Microsoft TechNet	(800) 344-2121

CompuServe

CompuServe was the first bulletin-board provider to recruit a wide variety of vendors to create forums on their system. Now, you can get support on virtually any product through an account with CompuServe. To open a CompuServe account, call one of the following numbers:

From within the United States or Canada, call (800) 524-3388.

From within the United Kingdom, call 0800-289-378.

From within Germany, call 0130-37-32.

From the rest of Europe, call 44-272-255-111.

From outside of the United States, Canada, and Europe, use the appropriate country code for the United States to call (614) 457-0802.

CompuServe Information Manager

The CompuServe system is divided into forums that contain message areas where everyone can exchange messages and libraries in which vendor and third-party files can be accessed. Navigating around the forums can be difficult at first, but using several communication programs designed for CompuServe can help. The most common communication program is CompuServe Information Manager (CIM) (see Fig. B.1). The Windows version is known as WINCIM.

The Windows-based version has icons associated with forums and services, and you can customize it to your needs. Figure B.2 shows the forum message box and a message being posted. By writing these messages offline, you can save connect charges by going online only to post messages or get new ones.

The latest version of WINCIM also includes a version of the SPRY Internet access software enabling access to the Internet through CompuServe (see Fig. B.3).

Novell NetWare CompuServe Forums

NetWare 2.X Forum (NETW2X)

1. Printing
2. NetWare Utilities
3. Disk Drives/Cntrls
4. LAN Cards/Drivers

Figure B.1   Windows version of CompuServe Information Manager.

    5. Install/Upgrade

  14. 2.1x & Below/OS

  15. Operating System

NetWare 3.X Forum (NETW3X)

    1. Printing

    2. NetWare Utilities

    3. Dsk Drvs/CDs/Cntrls

    4. LAN Cards/Drivers

    5. Install/Upgrade 13, SFT III

  14. NLM/OS/Console Util

NetWare 4.X Forum (NETW4X)

    1. Printing

    2. NetWare Utilities

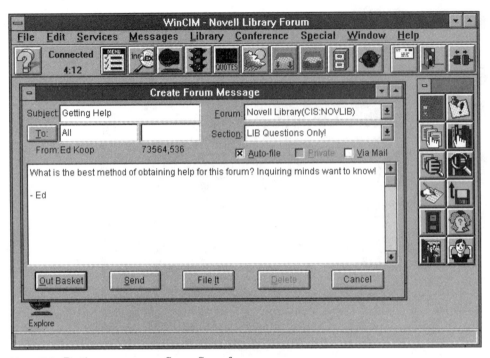

Figure B.2   Posting messages on CompuServe forums.

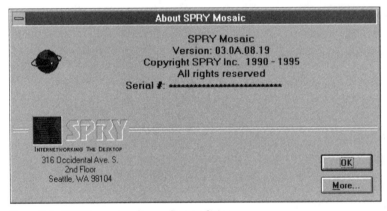

Figure B.3   SPRY mosaic—CompuServe edition.

3. Dsk Drvs/CDs/Cntrls

4. LAN Cards/Drivers

5. Install/Upgrade

6. ElectroText/Doc's

7. Directory Services

8. Closed See Sect 7

13. SFT III

14. NLM/OS/Console Util

UnixWare Forum (UNIXWARE)

1. Core OS

2. Mail System

3. Developer Support

4. DOS Merge

5. Installation

6. X Windows

7. Networking

8. Device Drivers

9. Printing

10. Applications

Novell Client Forum (NOVCLIENT)

1. IPX/ODI Issues

2. NETX Issues

3. VLM Issues

4. ODINSUP Issues

5. NetBIOS Issues

6. NetWare & Windows

Novell DSG Forum (NOVDESKTOP)

1. NWDOS/DRDOS Apps

2. NWDOS/DRDOS Disk

3. NWDOS/DRDOS Memory

4. NWDOS/DRDOS Utils

5. Customer Service

6. Programming ?'s

7. Dataclub

8. NetWare Lite

9. Personal NetWare

14. NetWare NT Client

NetWare OS/2 Forum (NOVOS2)

1. OS/2 Printing

2. Client/Server

3. OS/2 Requester

4. NSM [OS/2]

5. NW 4.x for OS/2

6. GUI Tools

7. WINOS2/DOS

Connectivity Forum (NCONNECT)

1. NACS

2. NW Connect

3. NW for SAA

4. AS/400 Connectivity

5. Host Printing

6. SNA Links

7. LAN/LAN Links-MPR

8. NetWare Macintosh

9. NW/DEC Connectivity

10. Portable NetWare

11. NW/IP NFS-TCP/IP

12. Email/MHS/FAX

13. LANwrkplce/Group

14. Other Conn Issues

NetWare Management Forum (NOVMAN)

1. Network Mngmnt

2. NetWare Mngmnt Sys

3. ManageWise

4. Lanalyzer for Win

5. NW for SAA Mngmnt

6. NW Navigator

Novell Hardware Forum (NOVHW)

1. Power Monitoring

2. Token Ring

3. Ethernet

4. ARCnet

5. Backups

6. Cabling

7. RPL / Remote Boot

17. Other Hardware

Novell GroupWise Forum (GRPWSE, GROUPWISE)

1. General Features

2. Windows Client

3. Remote Client

4. Other Client

5. Gateways

6. Administration

7. Connectivity

8. Message Servers

15. Enhancements

Novell SoftSolutions Forum (SOFTSOL)

1. General Features

2. Integrations

3. ODMA

4. SEM

5. DSS

6. Indexes

7. Conversions

8. Upgrades

9. Document Desktop

15. Enhancements

Novell InForms Forums (INFORMS)

1. General Features

2. Filler

3. Designer

4. Security

5. Calculations

6. Databases

15. Enhancements

Novell PerfOffice Forum (POFFICE)

1. Installation

2. OBEX

3. PerfectScript

4. DAD

5. QuickTasks

6. OLE/DDE

7. Oject PAL

8. Paradox Usability

9. GroupWise QuickLook

10. Borland Office

11. Misc

12. Enhancements

WordPerfect for Windows (WPWIN)

1. 6.x Gen Features

2. 6.x Installation

3. 6.x Networking

4. 6.x Print/Fax

5. 6.x Template/Style

6. 6.x Macros/Merge

7. 6.x Tables

8. 6.x Graphics

9. 6.x Spell/Grammar

10. 6.x Draw/Chart/OLE

11. 5.x Gen Features

12. 5.x Installation

13. 5.x Networking

14. 5.x Print/Fax

15. 5.x Styles/Outlines

16. 5.x Macros/Merge

17. 5.x Tables

18. 5.x Graphics

19. 5.x Spell/Grammar

20. Enhancements

WordPerfect for DOS (WPDOS)

1. 6.0 Gen Features

2. 6.0 Installation

3. 6.0 Networking

4. 6.0 Print/Fax

5. 6.0 Styles/Outlines

6. 6.0 Macros/Merge

7. 6.0 Tables

8. 6.0 Graphics

9. 6.0 Spell/Grammar

10. Shell 4.0

11. 5.1 Gen Features

12. 5.1 Installation

13. 5.1 Networking

14. 5.1 Print/Fax

15. 5.1 Styles/Outlines

16. 5.1 Macros/Merge

17. 5.1 Tables

18. 5.1 Graphics

19. 5.1 Spell/Hyph/Thes

20. Enhancements

WordPerfect for Macintosh (WPMAC)

1. General Features

2. Macros/Merge

3. Conversions

4. Graphics

15. Enhancements

WordPerfect for Unix (WPUNIX)

1. 6.x Gen Features

2. 6.x Installation

3. 6.x License Mgr

4. 6.x Printing

5. 6.x Macros/Merge

6. 6.x Tables

7. 6.x Spell/Write Tls

8. 6.x Grphic/Drw/Chrt

9. 5.x Gen Features

10. 5.x Installation

11. 5.x License Mgr

12. 5.x Printing

13. 5.x Macros/Merge

14. 5.x Tables

15. 5.x Spell/Write Tls

16. 5.x Grphic/Drw/Chrt

17. Enhancements

Quattro Pro Forum (QPRO)

1. News & Forum Help

2. QP/DOS-General

3. QP/DOS-Printing

4. QP/DOS-Macros

5. QP/DOS-Networks

7. QP/Win-General

8. QP/Win-Printing

9. QPW Macros/UI Build

10. QP/Win-Install

11. QP/Win-Graphs

12. QPW Data Exchange

13. QP/Win-Networks

14. QP/WIN Sug Box

15. QP/DOS Sug Box

16. Developer Toolkit

18. Non-Tech Cust Serv

Novell Presentations Forum (PRESENTATIONS)

1. 3.0 Gen Features

2. 3.0 Installation

3. 3.0 Drawing Tools

4. 3.0 Printing

5. 3.0 Slide Shows

6. 3.0 Bit-Map Editor

7. 3.0 Clip-Art

8. 3.0 Charts

9. 3.0 35MM Slides

10. PRWin 2.0

11. PRDos 2.0

15. Enhancements

Novell PerfectHome Forum (PERFHOME)

1. InfoCentral

2. PerfctWorks/WPWorks

3. Grammatik

4. ClipArt

5. TaxSaver

6. ExpressFax

7. Random House Dict

8. Home Education

9. Family Entertain

15. Enhancements

Electronic Publishing Tools (ENVOY, ELECPUB)

1. Envoy

2. Market Messenger

3. SGML/HTML/Int Publ

4. Language Modules

5. ConvertPerfect

6. Electronic Dict

Patches, Fixes, and Utility Files

1. Novell Technical Solutions Database (GO NTID)

2. Novell Files Library (GO NOVLIB)

3. Novell Files Area (GO NOVFILES)

4. Novell Applications Solutions Database (GO GWTID)

5. Novell Applications Library (GO GWFILES/WPFILES)

6. Novell Applications Solutions Database (GO APPTID)

7. Novell Applications Library (GO WPFILES)

Microsoft CompuServe Support Forums

MS Windows News Forum (WINNEWS)

Libraries available

1. Hot News

2. Microsoft Uploads

Microsoft DevCast Forum (DEVCAST)

Message sections

1. General Information

2. DevCast1 May 14, 93

3. DevCast2 Aug 31, 93

4. DevCast3 Dec 9, 93

5. DevCast4 Mar 30, 94

6. DevCast5

Libraries

1. General Information

2. DevCast1 May 14, 93

3. DevCast2 Aug 31, 93

4. DevCast3 Dec 9, 93

5. DevCast4 Mar 30, 94

6. DevCast5

11. Bus Soln Telecast

MS Dev Network Forum (MSDNLIB)

Message sections

1. Peer Help/Chat

2. Non-Tech Cust Serv

3. MSDN Suggestions

4. Dev. Library Help

5. Dev. Platform Help

Libraries

1. New Uploads

2. Technotes & Samples

15. Gen./Admin.

Developer Relations Forum (MSDR)

Message sections

1. Non-Tech Info

2. Strategic Issues

Libraries

1. General/Dev Service

2. Strategic Issues

Microsoft TechNet Forum (TNFORUM)

Message sections

1. WW Comments/Sugg
2. US
3. Benelux
4. Central Europe
8. TechEd
9. TechNet Lib Cmnts
15. Gen/Admin
16. TechNet CD Prob Rpt

Libraries

1. Index and Info
2. TechNet Files
3. TechEd
4. MS Press Releases
15. Gen/Admin
16. TechNet CD Prob Rpt
17. Member Uploads

MS Access Support Forum

Message sections

1. Getting Started
2. Tables/DB Design
3. Queries
4. Forms
5. Reports/Printing
6. Macros/Builders
7. Modules/DAO
8. Import/Export
9. Multi-User/Networks
10. Interop/OLE/DDE
11. ODBC Connectivity

12. Converting 1.x to 2

13. Setup

14. Mktg/Sales/Info

15. 3rd Party/User Grp

16. ADK/ADT/Security

17. Open Discussion

Libraries

1. Getting Started

2. Tables/DB Design

3. Queries

4. Forms

5. Reports/Printing

6. Macros/Builders

7. Modules/DAO

8. Import/Export

9. Multi-User/Networks

10. Interop/OLE/DDE

11. ODBC Connectivity

12. Converting 1.x to 2

13. Setup

14. Mktg/Sales/Info

15. 3rd Party/User Grp

16. ADK/ADT/Security

17. Open Discussion

MS Home Products Forum (MSHOME)

1. Forum Info-No Suprt

2. MS Games

3. Simulators

4. Encarta

5. Bookshelf

6. Cinemania

7. MM (oth-titles) Mac

8. MM (oth-titles) Win

9. MS Kids/Children

10. Scenes

11. Money

Libraries available

1. Index and Info

2. MS Games

3. Simulators

4. Encarta

5. Bookshelf

6. Cinemania

7. MM (oth-titles) Mac

8. MM (oth-titles) Win

9. MS Kids/Children

10. Scenes

11. Money

MS Desktop Forum (MSDESKTOP)

1. Forum Info-No Suprt

2. Publisher

3. Works-DOS

4. Works-Mac

5. Works-Win

6. PowerPoint-Mac

7. PowerPoint-Win

8. Project for Windows

9. Project for Mac

Libraries available

1. Index and Info

2. Publisher

3. Works-DOS

4. Works-Mac

5. Works-Win

6. PowerPoint-Mac

7. PowerPoint-Win

8. Project for Windows

9. Project for Mac

The Microsoft Excel Forum (MSEXCEL)

1. Forum Info/News

2. Excel Setup

3. MS Office Setup

4. VBA for Excel

5. Excel Macros

6. Gen Functionality

7. Windows Environment

8. Mac Environment

9. NT/OS/2 Environment

13. MS Query Tool

14. EIS Pak Mac/Win

Libraries available

1. Index and Info

2. Excel for the Mac

3. Excel for the PC

4. VBA for Excel

13. Desktop III Prods

14. EIS Pak Mac/Win

The Fox Software Forum (FOXFORUM)

1. Mktg/Sales/Info

2. Getting Started

3. DOS/WIN Config/Inst

4. MAC Config/Install

5. Screens/Menus

6. MAC/WIN Reports/Prt

7. DOS/UNIX Rpts/Print

8. Language

9. Queries/SQL/BROWSE

10. LCK/API/Externals

11. Project Manager

12. OLE/DDE/Interop

13. Networking/ODBC

14. Convert/X-Platform

15. FoxBASE+

16. DK/Application Dist

17. UNIX Config/Install

Libraries available

1. MS Info/Indexes

2. FP Cross-Platform

3. FP Win-Platform

4. FP Win-API/FLLs

5. FP DOS-Platform

6. FP DOS API/PLBs

7. FP MAC-Platform

8. Mac Externals/XCMDs

9. FoxBASE + DOS/MAC

10. FP UNIX-Platform

11. Private

12. Maintenance

13. Miscellaneous

14. International

15. FoxPro NEW Updates

16. FoxPro OLD Updates

MS Fox Users Forum (FOXUSER)

1. New Forum Users

2. FoxPro Publications

3. Consultants Corner

4. What's New

5. Developers Exchange

6. Fox User Groups

7. Conventions/Events

8. Chatter

9. 3rd Party Products

Libraries

1. MS Info and Index

2. FOXGANG

3. Want Ads

4. Archive

9. 3rd Party Products

MS Programming Apps Forum (PROGMSA)

Message sections

1. Forum News/Info

2. WordBasic

5. Excel SDK

Libraries

1. Index and Info

2. WordBasic

5. Excel SDK

Microsoft Word Forum (MSWORD)

1. Forum News/Prod Sug

2. Wrd Suprt-Win 2.0x

3. WrdAssist/TTMstrSet

4. Wrd Suprt-NT & OS/2

5. Word Support: Mac

6. Word Support: DOS

7. W4W6-Setup/Networks

8. W4W6-Printing/Fonts

9. W4W6-System/GPFs

10. W4W6-Conversions
11. W4W6-Templts/Wizrds
12. W4W6-Styls/MstrDocs
13. W4W6-Frmtng/Nmberng
14. W4W6-MailMrg/Dbases
15. W4W6-OLE/DDE
16. W4W6-Fields/Spell
17. W4W6-Other/Misc

Libraries

1. Index and Info
2. Files from MS PSS
4. Word for Windows
5. Word for the Mac
6. Word for DOS
7. Word for OS/2
10. TT Master Set (Mac)
11. Word Asst (Win/Mac)

MS Wrkgrps Apps Forum (MSWGA)

2. MS Mail for PC
3. Remote/Modems
4. MS Schedule Plus
5. MS Mail for Mac
6. PC/Mac Connection
7. MS Eforms
9. GTWY-MHS Fax
10. GW-SMTP X400 FAPI
11. GTWY-PROFS SNADS
12. GTWY 3COM MCI
15. Non-Tech Info
16. WRKGRP Templates
17. Forum News/Info

Libraries

1. MS Info and Index
2. MS Mail for PC
3. Remote/Modems
4. MS Schedule Plus
5. MS Mail for Mac
6. PC/Mac Connection
7. MS Eforms
9. GTWY-MHS Fax
10. GW-SMTP X400 FAPI
11. GTWY-PROFS SNADS
12. GTWY 3COM MCI
16. WRKGRP Templates

MS Sales & Info Forum (MSIC)

1. Pre-Sales Info
2. Registration
3. Training Info
4. Product Promotions
5. International

Libraries

1. Index and Info
2. Registration
3. Training Info
4. Product Promotions
5. International
7. MS PRESS RELEASES
17. MS Job Opps

MS DOS Forum (MSDOS)

1. Forum News/Info
2. Setup & Install

3. Hardware Issues

4. Compatibility

5. Networks

6. Commands/Utilities

7. DOS Shell

8. BASIC Conversions

9. Shareware (MS-DOS)

10. Developers Exchange

11. Doublespace

12. Mem Mgt/Optimize

13. Unmonitored Chat

14. Stacker Conversion

15. Scandisk

Libraries

1. Index and Info

2. Setup & Install

3. Hardware Issues

4. Compatibility

5. Networks

6. Commands/Utilities

7. DOS Shell

9. Shareware (MS-DOS)

10. Developers Exchange

11. Doublespace

12. Mem Mgt/Optimize

15. Scandisk

MS Win for Wrkgrps Forum (MSWFWG)

2. Mail/Sched Plus

3. Installation

4. File/Print Share

5. Novell

6. Other Networks

7. Accessories/Utils

8. 32-Bit Access

9. MSDOS Add-On

10. 3rd Party Apps

11. At-Work FAX/Comm

12. Remote Access

17. Forum News/Info

Libraries

1. MS Info & Index

2. Mail/Sched Plus

3. Installation

4. File/Print Share

5. Novell

6. Other Networks

7. Accessories/Utils

8. 32-Bit Access

9. MSDOS Add-On

10. 3rd Party Apps

11. At-Work FAX/Comm

12. Remote Access

MS Windows Forum (MSWIN)

1. Forum News/Info

2. Setup

3. Mouse

4. Video/Display

5. Enhanced/Std Modes

6. Swapfile/32 Bit Acc

7. Memory/Optimization

8. SMARTDrive

9. Prog Mgr/File Mgr

10. MS Accessories/OLE

11. MS-DOS Apps/PIFs

12. Printing/Fonts/WPS

13. Multimedia Ext/Serv

14. Terminal/Comm

15. Networks

16. Win Sound System

17. Video for Windows

18. Mouse/Paintbrush

19. MS Natural Keyboard

Libraries

1. Index and Info

2. Setup

3. Mouse

4. Display Drivers

5. Enhanced/Std Modes

6. Swapfile/32 Bit Acc

7. Memory Optimization

8. SMARTDrive

9. Prog Mgr/File Mgr

10. MS Accessories/OLE

11. MS-DOS Apps/PIFs

12. Printing/Fonts/WPS

13. Multimedia Ext/Serv

14. Terminal/Comm

15. Networks

16. Win Sound System

17. Video for Windows

18. Mouse/Paintbrush

19. MS Natural Keyboard

MS BASIC Forum (MSBASIC)

Message sections

1. Forum News/Info

2. Setup Wizard/Kit

   3. Data Access Objects

   4. The Data Control

   5. Programming Issues

   6. ODBC Connectivity

   7. SQL Queries

   8. ProEdition Controls

   9. Calling API's/DLL's

   10. Using OLE/DDE

   11. MSCOMM control

   12. MCI/MAPI controls

   13. DOS Visual Basic

   14. DOS and Mac Basic

   15. Non-Tech Info

   16. CDK

   17. 3rd Party Products

Libraries

   1. MS Info and Index

   2. Setup Wizard/Kit

   3. Data Access Objects

   4. The Data Control

   5. Programming Issues

   6. ODBC Connectivity

   7. SQL Queries

   8. ProEdition Controls

   9. Calling API's/DLL's

   10. VBWIN-ODBC/Database

   11. MSCOMM control

   12. MCI/MAPI controls

   13. DOS Visual Basic

   14. DOS and Mac Basic

   15. Non-Tech Info

   16. CDK

   17. 3rd Party Products

Foundation Classes Forum (MSMFC)

2. Beginners Section
3. Database Classes
4. OLE 2.0 Classes
5. OLE 2.0 Automation
6. VBX Usage
7. Printing & Graphics
8. Doc/View/UI
9. DLL & Memory
10. Wizards/DDV/DDX
14. Non-Tech Info
15. Unmonitored Chat

Libraries

1. MS Info and Index
2. Beginners Library
3. Database Classes
4. OLE 2.0 Classes
5. OLE 2.0 Automation
6. VBX Usage
7. Printing & Graphics
8. Doc/View/UI
9. DLL & Memory
10. Wizards/DDV/DDX
14. NonTech Cust Serv
15. Unmonitored Chat

MS C & Other Lang. Forum (MSLANG)

1. Visual C++ Setup
2. Microsoft C++
3. Microsoft C
4. Assembler
7. Workbench (PWB/VWB)

9. App Studio

11. QC/QCWin

12. CodeView/IDE Debug

13. FORTRAN

14. Non-Tech Info

15. Unmonitored Chat

17. Utils/Link/Nmake

Libraries

1. MS Info and Index

2. Microsoft C++

3. Microsoft C

4. Assembler

7. Workbench (PWB/VWB)

9. App Studio

11. QC/QCWin

12. CodeView/IDE Debug

13. FORTRAN

14. NonTech Cust Serv

15. Unmonitored Chat

17. Utils/Link/Nmake

Microsoft Win32 SDK Forum (MSWIN32)

Message sections

1. Non-Tech Info

3. Far East Win32-beta

4. API-User/GUI

5. API-Graphics/GDI

6. API-Base/Console

7. API-Security

8. Tools-Win32 SDK

9. Tools-SCT

10. Tools-MS Test/Setup

11. Porting-OS/2 & UNIX

12. API-WinNet/RPC

13. Windows NT DDK

14. API-Win32s

15. API-Unicode/NLS

17. Unmonitored Chat

Libraries

1. MS Info and Index

3. Far East Win32-beta

4. API-User/GUI

5. API-Graphics/GDI

6. API-Base/Console

7. API-Security

8. Tools-Win32 SDK

9. Tools-SCT

10. Tools-MS Test/Setup

11. Porting-OS/2 & UNIX

12. API-WinNet/RPC

13. Windows NT DDK

14. API-Win32s

15. API-Unicode/NLS

16. Tools-Third Party

17. FAQ Library

Windows Extensions Forum (WINEXT)

Message sections

1. Non-Tech Info

2. MS Test for Windows

3. TAPI SDK

4. WOSA/XRT

5. WOSA/XFS

6. MS Delta

7. Arabic/Hebrew SDK

8. Pen SDK

9. Far East SDK

10. ODBC

11. ODBC Dsktop Drivers

13. MAPI SDK

15. DSPRMI and SPEECH

Libraries

1. MS Info and Index

2. MS Test for Windows

3. TAPI SDK

4. WOSA/XRT

5. WOSA/XFS

6. MS Delta

7. Arabic/Hebrew SDK

8. Pen SDK

9. Far East SDK

10. ODBC

11. ODBC Dsktop Drivers

13. MAPI/Schedule+ Libs

15. DSPRMI and SPEECH

MS Win Multimedia Forum (WINMM)

2. MDK

3. MediaView

4. Video for Windows

6. Viewer 2.0

7. WinSndSys DDK

10. MM Strategy

11. Third Party S/W

12. Windows Game Dev.

Libraries

1. MS Index and Info

2. MDK

3. MediaView

4. Video for Windows

6. Viewer 2.0

7. WinSndSys DDK

10. MM Strategy

11. Third Party S/W

12. Windows Game Dev.

MS Windows Objects Forum (WINOBJ)

1. Non-Tech Info

2. Component Obj Model

3. Structured Storage

4. OLE:User Interface

5. OLE:Drag&Drop

6. OLE:Naming/Monikers

7. OLE:Interop issues

8. OLE:Automation

10. OLE Controls

12. OLE:Mac issues

13. OLE 1 issues

14. OLE:MFC

17. Strategic Issues

Libraries

1. MS Info and Index

2. Component Obj Model

3. Structured Storage

4. OLE:User Interface

5. OLE:Drag&Drop

6. OLE:Naming/Monikers

7. OLE:Interop issues

8. OLE:Automation

10. OLE Controls

12. OLE:Mac issues

13. OLE 1 issues

17. Strategic Issues

MS Windows SDK Forum (WINSDK)

1. Non-Tech Info
2. USER-Dlgs/Controls
3. USER-Msgs/Hooks/DDE
4. USER-Menus/MDI
5. USER-Misc. Topics
6. Common Dialogs
7. GDI-Printing/Fonts
8. GDI-BMPs/CURs/ICOs
9. GDI-Misc. Topics
10. KERNEL-Memory Mgmt.
11. KERNEL-DPMI/TSR
12. KERNEL-DLLs
13. KERNEL-Misc. Topics
14. COMM API/Networking
16. WinHelp/Tools
17. DDK/WIN386 Peer Hlp

Libraries

1. MS Info and Index
3. Public Utilities
4. Training
5. USER
6. Common Dialogs
7. Printing
9. GDI
10. KERNEL-Memory Mgmt.
11. DPMI/TSR
12. Libraries/DLLs
13. KERNEL
14. COMM API/Networking

16. WinHelp

17. DDK/VxD/Drivers

Microsoft Networks Forum (MSNET)

1. Non-Tech Info

2. Install and Config

3. LM on OS/2

4. LM on WinNT

5. LM/WFW Interop

6. LM/NetWare Interop

7. LM/Remote Access

8. LM/Macintosh Introp

9. NDIS (Net Cards)

10. NDIS (Transports)

11. LM Programming

12. Network Mgmt

15. MS TCP/IP

16. SMS

Libraries

1. MS Info and Index

2. Install and Config

3. LM on OS/2

4. LM on WinNT

5. LM/WFW Interop

6. LM/NetWare Interop

7. LM/Remote Access

8. LM/Macintosh Introp

9. NDIS (Net Cards)

10. NDIS (Transports)

11. LM Programming

12. Network Mgmt

15. MS TCP/IP

16. SMS

Microsoft SQL Server Forum (MSSQL)

    2. MS Server Topic

    3. MS SQL Connectivity

    4. MS SQL Prog Topic

    5. ODBC Drv for MS SQL

    6. MS SQL Server Tools

    7. Front Ends

    8. Host Connectivity

  16. Sales/Non-Tech Info

Libraries

    1. Index and Info

    2. MS Server Topic

    3. MS SQL Connectivity

    4. MS SQL Prog Topic

    5. ODBC Dvr for MS SQL

    6. MS SQL Server Tools

    7. Front Ends

    8. Host Connectivity

  16. Sales/Non-Tech Info

MS WinNT SNA Forum (MSSNA)

    1. Forum News/Info

    2. General Discussion

    3. Setup & Admin

    4. SNA Svr 3270/5250

    5. 3rd Party Products

    6. Diag Tools

    7. Hardware/Drivers

    8. NetView & Net Mgmt

    9. Application APIs

  10. EIS, SNADIS APIs

  11. Doc, Online Help

  12. SNA Server Beta

Libraries

1. MS Info and Index
2. Fixes and Updates
3. Problem Reports
4. 3rd Pty/Unsupported
5. MSSNA Archives
12. SNA Server Beta

WinNT Forum (WINNT)

1. Forum News/Info
2. Remote Program Load
3. Setup & Install
4. MS-DOS/Win3.x Apps
5. 32-bit Windows Apps
6. OS/2 & POSIX Apps
7. Utilities/Applets
8. H/W Compatibility
9. FT & File Systems
10. Device Drivers
11. Net Services/Conn.
12. Printing
13. Admin & Security
14. Srvcs for NetWare
15. TCPIP/DHCP/WINS
16. WinNT RAS
17. MS Mail (32-bit)

Libraries

1. Index and Info
2. Fixes & Updates
3. Problem Reports
4. Support Tools
5. WINNT Archives

6. Windows NT Surveys

7. Released Software

See also Fig. B.4.

NetWare Support Encyclopedia

One of the products available on CD-ROM is the *NetWare Support Encyclopedia* (see Figs. B.5 to B.8). To those subscribing to this service, updates are sent periodically. This CD-ROM provides all the manuals, documentation, support notes, engineering notes, and other miscellaneous information that can be easily found through an excellent search engine. You can search for any topic by entering any and all words relevant to the topic. As you type the words, each word is displayed and the number of "hits" are shown. After you have entered the complete phrase, the number of "cards" where all the words in the phrase are found is shown. After the search is complete, the titles from each "card" are shown, and you can choose from the desired items.

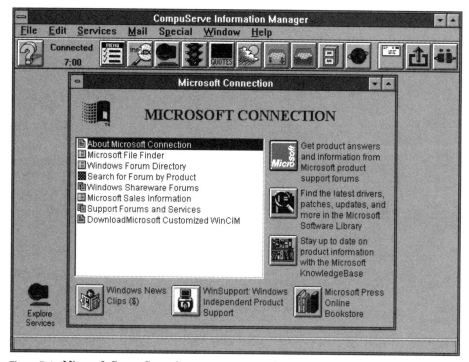

Figure B.4 Microsoft CompuServe forums.

Figure B.5 *NetWare Support Encyclopedia.*

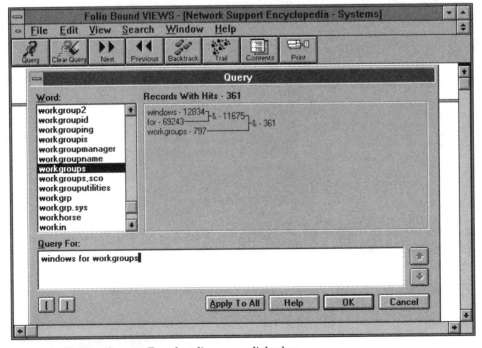

Figure B.6 *NetWare Support Encyclopedia*—query dialog box.

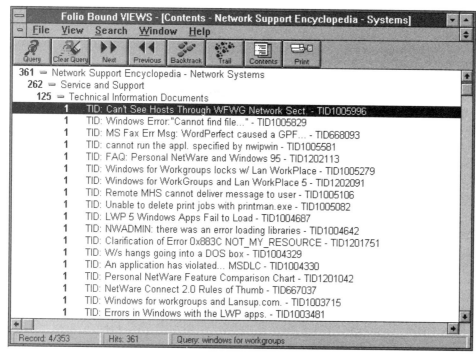

Figure B.7 *NetWare Support Encyclopedia*—result of search.

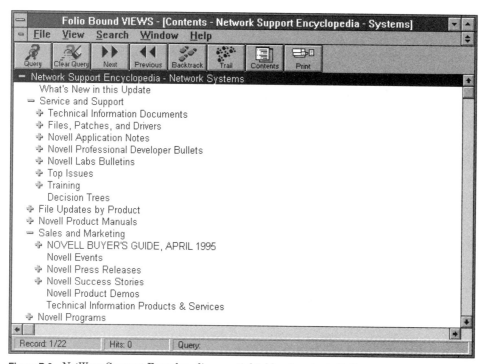

Figure B.8 *NetWare Support Encyclopedia*—partial table of contents listing.

We can testify that this reference CD-ROM has been extremely useful. We use it almost every day in our work as it is much easier to answer a question than looking the information up in the paper (hard-copy) manuals or calling technical support.

There are two types of NSE subscriptions: NSE standard and NSE professional. Both are the same, except the professional edition has patches, fixes, and utility files stored on the disk. The standard edition has only the manuals and textual information.

NetWare Application Notes and Research Reports

Novell publishes a monthly collection of notes and research items that are available by subscription. These notes and reports explore technical items, and we have found them to be great for tutorial purposes rather than technical reference. In North America, these documents can be ordered by calling the Novell Research Order Desk at (800) UPDATE1. From outside the United States or Canada, call (801) 429-5380.

Microsoft TechNet

This product (see Fig. B.9) is similar to Novell's NSE as it provides notes and manuals for Microsoft products on a CD-ROM issued monthly. Subscription is much less expensive than Novell's NSE, but we find the search engine to be less user-friendly and slower than the NSE (see Fig. B.10).

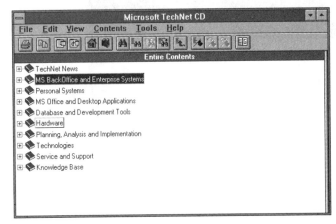

Figure B.9   Microsoft TechNet.

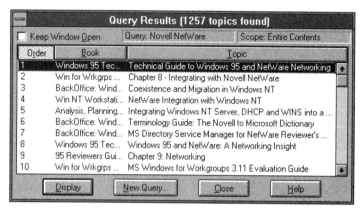

Figure B.10 Microsoft TechNet query search results.

Internet Access

Microsoft and Novell also have home pages on the worldwide web and can be reached through the Internet. Most of the patches, updates, and information available on online systems like CompuServe and America Online is also available on the Internet.

Microsoft can be reached at www.microsoft.com, and you will reach the home page shown in Fig. B.11.

Topics available on the Microsoft Internet access are shown in Fig. B.12.

Novell has a home page at www.novell.com, as shown in Fig. B.13.

Taking Advantage of Resources

These are just some of the sources you can use to obtain help for your network and Windows installation. We turn to these sources almost daily, saving ourselves many hours of fruitless labor.

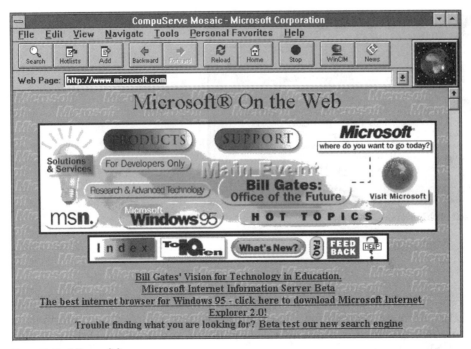

Figure B.11   Microsoft home page.

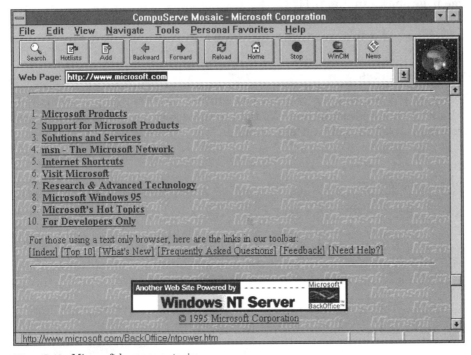

Figure B.12   Microsoft home page topics.

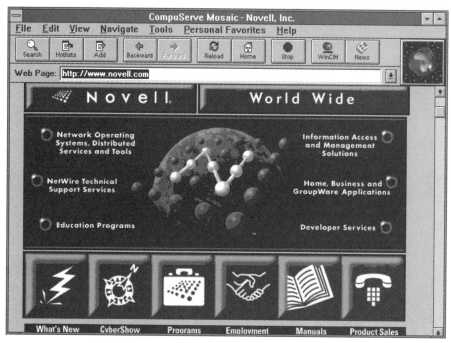

Figure B.13 Novell Internet home page.

Glossary

There are a number of terms used in this book that we haven't defined when discussing other topics. The following list may give you a good understanding of terms and clear up any confusion.

address A numerical identifier (usually in hexadecimal code) that uniquely identifies each node (either file server or workstation) so that data packets can be sent and received for each node.

advertising A method in which a computer or application will broadcast its availability on the network so that other computers or applications will know how to reach it.

algorithm A set of rules and/or computer code that determines how data will be processed.

American National Standards Institute (ANSI) A board that sets standards for a number of computer (and other) systems. Any hardware, software, or data item or device that adheres to the standard will be interchangeable with another.

American Standard Code for Information Interchange (ASCII) A standard code that enables computers to exchange data through this common set of information.

analog A method of transmitting data as a continuous variable voltage. This is different from the digital method where data is broken into physical blocks.

application A computer program or utility that accomplishes a certain activity.

application binary interface (ABI) A set of specifications that calls for development of applications that access hardware. Usually used to access hardware through direct commands to the operating system.

application programming interface (API) A method of communicating with system resources, usually in communication with another application. A programmer can create applications that access the data of another application through the use of APIs.

Arcnet A network communications standard that uses a token-bus architecture (similar to Token Ring) and was used widely by third-party vendors in the 1980s.

attribute A value associated with a device or system that will determine how it operates. In Novell NetWare, this is the file and directory properties (e.g., read, write, create, modify, delete).

authentication A method of identifying users that does not require the user to supply a login name and password in each attempt to access a service. In Novell NetWare, once you have logged into a NetWare 4.1 Directory Services tree, there is no need to resupply a login and password to access another server on the tree. The user information is supplied in the background.

backbone A term used to describe a high-capacity network communications system that carries a large portion of common data traffic. By connecting to the backbone, each computer has the ability to reach another computer.

bad-block table A list of hard-disk blocks that are damaged and cannot be used for data. When a bad block is encountered in NetWare, the physical address is entered in the bad-block table and then a spare hot-fix block is used for storage of the data.

base memory address The address location in RAM that is used by a peripheral card with which it can send information from the peripheral card to RAM.

binary A method of determining numbers using only 1s and 0s. The placement of these values determines what the value will be.

bindery A database on a NetWare server that contains information about users, groups, passwords, and other system information. On versions prior to 4.x, the server cannot run without the bindery file.

BIOS The basic input/output system in the computer ROM that standardizes the transfer of information back and forth between the individual hardware elements in the computer system.

broadcast A method of communicating with nodes on the network by sending the same information to all users. A very efficient method of sending the same information, as only one packet has to be sent and the address is generic, so that all nodes will receive the information.

buffers A memory location that is designed to hold data temporarily before it is moved to another location in memory. This helps speed up the access to information.

burst A method of transmitting data in groups for efficiency. There may be high-volume traffic at one time while at other times, the network may be quiet.

cache Dedicated high-speed areas of memory that the CPU has direct access to and is intended for temporary storage of data while it is being processed.

character Eight bits grouped together to create an alphanumeric character (also known as a *byte*).

client A workstation that connects with a file server and performs all computation itself.

client/server computing The execution of data processing by two different computers, usually over a local area network. One part of the application (server) runs on a file server or host machine and provides database services. The other segment (client) runs on the user workstation and communicates with the server system. This type of computing is very efficient and is best for applications that have large amounts of data.

CMOS (complementary metal-oxide semiconductor process) A very efficient memory chip that is used for handling hardware internal systems storing information about hardware settings.

collision The transmission of network data on the same network wiring system at the same time. The data collides and is not useful to any user. Both transmitting nodes must transmit again.

compression A method of reducing the number of bits of data in a file by using mathematical formulas that represent repeating elements (lossless compression). Graphical images can be compressed efficiently by throwing away selected bits that decrease the quality of the image but do not destroy it (lossy compression). This is very efficient compression, as 20:1 ratios can be achieved.

Connectionless Network Protocol (CLNP) A protocol standard in OSI that handles the delivery of data between two nodes that are not directly attached to each other. The data is sent out without knowledge of whether the other node is present on the network. If the receiving node doesn't respond that the data has been received within a prescribed time period, then the transmitting node determines that the communication failed. Prior schemes for data transmission required a connection to be established before data transmission took place.

console A monitor and keyboard on the file server that is used to communicate with and display information from the file server. Some operations can be performed only on the console.

conventional memory The memory in a PC that exists between 0 and 640 kbytes (hexadecimal 00000h and A0000h). It is the only location where DOS applications can run unless special utilities modify the memory mapping (e.g., the DOS virtual sessions in Windows).

data A series of electronic voltages that represent characters. This term is usually reserved for information input into an application rather than the actual application code itself.

database A set of information contained in one or more files that contain information about an entity. This information can be searched and retrieved easily (usually!).

datagram A set of data (packet) sent on a common wiring system shared by many other computers. It contains addressing information in addition to data. The sending computer does not know whether it has arrived at the destination until an acknowledgment packet is sent back.

data-link layer The second layer in the Open Systems Interconnect (OSI) mode of network data transmission. This layer defines how data will be grouped in packets and how those packets will be transmitted and received by each node.

decryption The reverse of data encryption. Unscrambling of data from an unreadable form to a human-readable form by applying various algorithms to the data and re-creating the original data.

demand paging Used to activate data from the swap files in Windows. When an application requests a page of memory (4 kbytes in size) from RAM and that data is not available, a page fault is generated. When the page fault occurs, the Windows virtual-memory manager is activated and brings in the desired data from the swap file.

device driver   A software utility that receives hardware access requests from the operating system and translates them into a format directly readable by the hardware device. This allows the operating system to transmit or receive hardware information in a standard format, and the device driver will translate for the hardware item.

direct memory access (DMA)   A method of transferring data from a peripheral on the computer to RAM without going through the processor. Commonly used in backups or other systems that require faster access to data.

directory caching   Used in Novell NetWare to increase speed of access by copying the directory entry table into server memory, thus increasing access speed.

directory rights   Specifications as to what type of activities can take place in a given directory. In NetWare, the rights are very similar to file rights (read, write, create, erase, modify, file scan, access rights, and supervisory).

Directory Services (the NetWare)   A new method of tracking user and system items in NetWare 4.x replacing the bindery in older systems. This new system tracks all items in a network on more than one server and allows administrators to efficiently handle a multiserver network.

directory structure duplication   A method of storing directory and file information about a file server in more than once place. In the event of failure in one or more disk blocks where the directory structure is stored, the system can reference the secondary copy to determine file and directory locations.

disk cache   An area of memory reserved for temporarily storing data from the hard disk for faster access from the hard disk. When running Windows, this area is managed by the SMARTDRV utility. Disk caching can be used to manage reading from and writing to the disk. Not using some type of disk caching will result in greatly impaired performance.

disk duplexing   A method of storing the same data on two separate physical disks so that the failure of one disk will not mean data loss. Since the second disk contains the same information as the first, NetWare can access the second disk without interruption. Disk duplexing uses two different disk-controller cards and data channels to read and write data. This is very efficient, as data can be read from either disk for a greater throughput.

disk mirroring   Same features as disk duplexing, except data is transmitted through one controller card and the second disk cannot be accessed at the same time as the first disk.

domain name system   A naming convention used on the Internet that specifies an address through one-word names separated by periods.

DOS-protected mode interface (DPMI)   A standard from Intel that enables MS-DOS to execute applications in the protected mode of 286, 386, and 486 chips even though it wasn't designed to work in that environment.

double buffering   A method of using more than one buffer to handle the transfer of data to and from an I/O device. It can increase performance because one buffer can be receiving data while the other buffer is transmitting data to another system.

dynamic data exchange (DDE)   The original method of communication between applications in Microsoft Windows. It allows applications to exchange information even if they were developed by different vendors.

dynamic link library (DLL) Application or utility code in Microsoft Windows that can be loaded by another application as needed, linked (dynamic linking) as needed, and then unloaded from memory when no longer needed.

elevator seeking A method of organizing reads and writes to a hard disk and completing them in one pass across the disk rather than in random order (as in a DOS system).

encryption Scrambling of data by applying an algorithm to it and creating a modified set of data that is not in human-readable form. The receiving system will apply the same algorithm to unencrypt the data.

error detection A method of checking incoming data and comparing results against a given value to determine whether any data bits have changed during transmission.

Ethernet A method of network wiring and data transmission but now used widely for network communications. It uses carrier-sense multiple-access/collision detection (CSMA/CD) to list for other transmissions and then, if none are heard, transmit data and determine whether there was a collision and then retransmit later. Also a local area network communication system used widely in current LAN systems. It is an IEEE standard (802.3) and runs at 10 Mbits/s.

extended industry-standard architecture (EISA) A microcomputer bus standard developed in response to the IBM Micro Channel Architecture (MCA) in 1988. It featured high-speed data transfer and backward compatibility with ISA peripheral cards and was an open system for vendors to use.

expanded memory Memory above 1 Mbyte that can be made available to DOS applications that normally would not be available. While DOS cannot access beyond 1 Mbyte, the expanded-memory drivers provide access through temporary locations in upper memory. An expanded-memory driver (EMM) is required to be loaded on computer bootup before expanded memory can be used. The DOS application also must have a special code added to access expanded memory. Expanded memory is controlled by the expanded memory specification (EMS) originally developed by Lotus, Intel, and Microsoft.

extended memory Memory in the computer that is beyond 1 Mbyte and can be accessed directly. While the expanded memory uses "gateways" in upper memory to move data to and from memory beyond 1 Mbyte, extended memory is designed to have direct access and handle memory like a UNIX system or other non-DOS operating system. Windows uses extended memory through the extended memory manager (HIMEM.SYS).

fault tolerance A method of duplicating hardware or software whereby the failure of one system signals the other system to take over automatically and continue to provide services. Mirrored and duplexed disk drivers in NetWare are examples of fault tolerance, as is SFTIII.

FCONSOLE A NetWare utility used to view information about a file server and to make changes to the system (see Fig. C.1).

file allocation table (FAT) The listing of files and their locations on the hard disk in a computer system. The FAT is the index for all files and is used by the operating system to retrieve information as requested by applications.

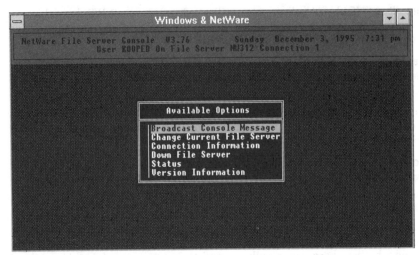

Figure C.1 FCONSOLE utility.

file server   In its basic mode, a computer on the local area network that provides file and print services to other systems also on the network. Some file-server operating systems provide other services than just file storage and printing. It is a common storage place for applications and data for multiple users to gain access.

gigabyte (Gbyte)   One billion characters of storage on a hard disk or in memory.

grabber   A utility running in Microsoft Windows that enables the exchange of data in video memory from DOS applications and Windows. It is found in the following files (specified in the SYSTEM.INI file):

```
[boot]
386grabber=CPQVGA.GR3
286grabber=cpqvga.gr2
```

graphical user interface   A screen style that uses graphical pictures and allowing the user to make choices with a keyboard or a pointing device.

group   A logical gathering of application icons in Windows. This enables better organization of the Windows desktop.

groupware   Software that permits more than one user to access simultaneously across a local area network.

high-memory area (HMA)   An area just beyond the first 1 Mbyte of RAM that can be used for utilities, DOS, or other TSRs. Even though it is beyond 1 Mbyte, it still can be accessed directly by DOS.

Host   A centralized computer that not only stores applications and data but also runs applications for users. Frequently used to refer to minicomputers.

hub   A hardware device which connects several local area network nodes. It connects the different nodes together into one common communication path so that they can exchange data. It is not uncommon to hook several hubs together to increase the capacity of the network.

IEEE The Institute of Electrical and Electronic Engineers organization, which is responsible for a number of standards of wiring and communication used in networking.

interface A computer term, now used in many different situations. A screen design where there is a format for keyboard and pointing device commands. It is also a standard for peripheral hardware communications and communication standards between those devices and the computer.

Internet packet exchange (IPX) A method of communication between server and workstation in Novell NetWare networks.

internetwork packet exchange (IPX) A method of transmitting data between computer systems. Used by Novell NetWare file servers.

interrupts A method allowing hardware devices to gain access to the CPU. An efficient method of giving each piece of hardware time with the CPU, as the interrupt will signal the CPU time required for processing input from the hardware device.

ISA The designation of the type of bus in original personal computers. It stands for industry-standard architecture and is rarely used on computers now.

ISO/OSI A model on which most networks are based. It is published by the International Standards Organization (ISO) and is called the open-systems interconnect (OSI). It defines how data will be formulated in each node and transmitted to another node. The steps are divided into seven sections: application, data link, network, physical, presentation, session, and transport.

kernel A core file for operating systems and Windows. It allocates memory into sections and sets the environment for operation. The kernel also acts as a controller of the system during operation.

local area network A common term used to describe a number of methods of connecting two or more computers so that they can communicate together. Through a common wiring system, these computers can share data. Several users can share common data and computers (file server).

login script An ASCII text file that contains instructions to be performed whenever a user logs into a file server. In NetWare, there can be a system login script and user login script. For NetWare 4.1, login scripts can also be in organization unit and company containers.

media access control (MAC) A level of communication (the data-link layer in the ISO/OSI model) that communicates with the network card and ensures that there are no errors when transmitting information.

memory protection Intel 386 and higher CPUs can run in protected mode, enabling more than one application to run simultaneously without interfering with each other.

millions of instructions per second (MIPS) A method of measurement that determines how many machine-language instructions can be performed by a CPU in one second. Early mainframes ran about 10 MIPS, while early microcomputers were 1 or 2 MIPS. Current Pentium computers are currently rated as high as 66 MIPS.

monolithic protocol stack A term given to the IPX and NETX network shells that can handle only one network communication protocol at a time. Even though the

Novell NetWare shells are most commonly called monolithic, this term can apply to any network drivers.

movable-code segment A portion of application code in Windows that can be moved to different locations in RAM as needed.

MSIPX A driver provided by Microsoft that has an NDIS-compliant IPX protocol stack and is used in Windows for Workgroups.

Multicast A broadcast of data to more than one node on the network but not necessarily all nodes. It usually means that a specified group of stations on a predetermined list received these broadcast packets.

multitasking The ability to perform two or more tasks at one time in a computer. It requires the CPU to perform activities for each application a few milliseconds at a time before switching to another application. It appears that all programs are running simultaneously, but this impression is due to the fast switching of the CPU between the applications.

NDIS A network communication standard developed by Microsoft and 3Com. The term stands for *network device interface specification* and covers the MAC layer and transport protocol drivers (in the OSI model).

NetBEUI An extension to NetBIOS (NetBIOS extended user interface) designed by IBM in 1985 that provides network communication with additional functionality to NetBIOS.

NetBIOS A method of communicating on a local area network between workstation and file server.

NetWare Access Server A Novell computer application that runs on a dedicated computer to provide remote access services to users running on other network systems.

NetWare shell A series of small utility programs loaded into memory that provide communication services to the network. NetWare shell takes all requests that are not directed to the local computer and reroutes them across the network to the file server.

network adapter A term used to describe the peripheral card that goes inside a file server or workstation that provides an electronic communication path to the network. A network cable connection will be attached to the card to transmit the data signals to the remainder of the network.

network layer This is the third section or layer of the OSI model which defines how data is routed through the network.

Node A computing device on the network that can communicate with other devices. Usually it is a file server or workstation that is considered a node.

object The basis of all graphical systems. Any item, value, icon, data element, window, or application can be regarded as an object. If these items are divided into individual elements, they can be accessed separately by more than one application or utility.

object handler This is a component of the OLE system in Windows. It is between the client and server applications and updates the object in the client application if the server application has been modified.

object linking and embedding   The utility in Windows that enables applications to link data between two applications. The data from one application can be imported from another application with a link created between the two applications. For example, a drawing created in a computer "draw" program can be imported into another program. Because this link exists between the two applications, if the graphical drawing is changed in the drawing program, the changes will be seen in the second program. The drawing is not actually stored in the second application; only a copy of the image is stored there.

open-systems interconnect   See **ISO/OSI model.**

operating system   A special class of computer program that acts as the intermediary between the hardware and applications. It creates a common method of accessing hardware devices much more easily than writing code directly to the hardware.

packet   The division of data into small logical groups. These groups of data will have information about the transmitting and receiving stations, how the packet is constructed, as well as the actual data itself.

page fault   An interrupt that is created when data in a memory location is accessed but is not available. The page fault will cause the memory manager to access other memory storage locations (e.g., swap file).

page frame   The sectioning of data in memory into a fixed size so it can be passed through the expanded memory manager to memory storage locations above 1 Mbyte.

paging   A method of passing data from RAM to swap files by dividing the data into logical pages so it can be placed in the swap file and retrieved easily.

peer-to-peer communication   The ability for two or more workstations to communicate together directly without going through an intermediate system (e.g., file server).

physical layer   A section or layer in the OSI model that handles physical factors of communication such as signal voltage, transmission timing, and other similar factors.

pipe   This term comes from UNIX systems where the output of one utility or application can be routed as the input into another application or utility. The pipe symbol (|) is used to signal that the output of one system is to be transferred to another.

platform   The hardware and operating systems of a computer that make up its unique environment. Only applications created for that environment can be used.

plenum   The space between the ceiling of one floor and the rigid structure of the floor above. This space is an excellent location for laying computer communications cable. Only a special type of cable (called *plenum cable*) can be used that adheres to fire and safety codes.

plenum cable   Cable that is wrapped in special material that is fire-resistant and will not give off large amounts of chemical fumes or smoke in case of fire.

presentation layer   A layer or section in the OSI model that deals with the protocols for file transfers, format, and network security.

print server   This can be a computer that handles all printing chores for a printer or group of printers; it can also be an NLM on the file server, or a separate box connected to the network and printers. The print server feeds data to the printer as needed, handles communication, and performs other printer functions.

protected mode A method of CPU design found in 286 and higher Intel chips which can run more than one application at a time—each in its own protected space.

protocol Communication rules on data communications as set forth by a standards committee (e.g., OSI, IEEE, ANSI).

queue A method of lining up electronic communication for access to hardware or software systems. The objective of the queue is to process the data as quickly as possible so that the data will be unaffected by the transmission speed.

read-after-write verification A method of checking data written to a hard disk before the original data in memory is discarded. After writing the data to the disk, the information is read the next time the disk spins around. The data read from the disk is compared to the original data in memory, and if the two are identical, the original is thrown away. If they are not identical, then the area on the disk is marked "bad" and another block is used.

registration database A database system inside Windows that provides pathing information to other applications. This enables OLE to find a path between the different applications. Whenever a new application is installed that supports OLE, the pathing information to the application is built into the database. The database file is called REG.DAT.

relational database A highly efficient database that breaks data into several different tables to prevent storage of redundant data. Data from one table can be used to "relate" to other data.

rights A method of assigning security to files and directories on the file server. This sets the limits as to what the user is allowed to do.

ring A communications system for a local area network in which there is one continuous path without a beginning or an end to the wire. Data packets flow continuously through the ring.

scalability The ability for computer hardware or software to increase capacity without major interruption to the user. An application that is scalable is one that can be installed on a larger computer and still have the same functionality without loss of data.

sequenced packet exchange (SPX) A method of communication between two or more workstations on the network. SPX works together with IPX to ensure that the messages are delivered and in the right order.

software development kit (SDK) A series of software routines available from Microsoft to enable development of applications and utilities in the Windows environment.

server While there are many names for this term, the most common is a computer that contains common programs and data to be accessed by users. It runs on the network and can be accessed by anyone granted permission through rights assignment.

service advertising protocol (SAP) A method of advertising the availability and resources of an applications server. The message of availability is broadcast to all stations, and those that need the services respond to the messages.

session layer A section or layer of the OSI model that handles network management through passwords, monitoring, and reporting.

shadow ROM   Used by some computer manufacturers to speed up operation by temporarily copying system ROM BIOS routines into RAM memory where it will run faster. This will speed up operation of the computer but will take away scarce space in upper memory.

spanning   Hard-disk reading and writing performance can be increased through placing data across more than one disk. This enables the operating system to retrieve data from more than one disk simultaneously.

spooler   A utility that "receives" print jobs from an application and writes it to disk in a temporary file for later printing. This enables users to return to work on the application sooner than if they had to wait until the printer was finished.

Structured Query Language (SQL)   A language designed to retrieve data from a relational database. These are standard elements that can be used on many different database systems. SQL attempts to make searches for data in more common everyday language rather than arcane computer code queries.

timeslicing   A method of multitasking that can run on only one CPU. The processor spends only a small fraction of time on each application running in a "round robin" system. To the user it appears that all applications are running simultaneously, but in reality, the CPU can run only one application at a time.

Token Ring   A communications system that uses a local area network wired in a ring and passes packets back and forth between nodes on the network. A token is used to determine which station has the ability to communicate. It is a standard of the IEEE (802.5).

topology   The physical elements of a local area network, including all wiring, nodes, routers, hubs, and similar hardware communication items.

Transport Control Protocol/Internet Protocol (TCP/IP)   A communication system widely used in UNIX computers that is also a standard for communications on the Internet. This protocol defines all segments of the communication system, including file transfer, messaging, and management of the network.

transport layer   A layer of the OSI model that handles the flow of information on the network and any transmission errors that occur.

TSR   Acronym for *terminate and stay resident,* which is the ability to write a program or utility that will load memory into and stay in the background of a DOS system until activated by a keyboard sequence or other activity.

twisted-pair cable   Two single-strand metal wires twisted around each other to cancel out general interference and electromagnetic interference. This cable is widely used in network wiring because it is stable and inexpensive.

upper memory   An area of RAM ranging between 640 and 1024 kbytes (1 Mbyte) that is used for hardware access to the computer but can also be used to run utilities such as network shells, thereby freeing conventional memory.

upper-memory blocks (UMB)   An area of memory between 640 and 1024 kbytes not in use for hardware systems (e.g., used by video drivers). This can be used for loading utilities and saving conventional memory.

user   A person who accesses a file server or host through a computer or terminal.

user account   Information in the bindery- or directory-based service that is used for identifying a user. It also keeps password information and any other notes about their environment on the network.

value-added reseller (VAR)   Also known as a *value-added remarketer.* A computer reseller who specializes in a limited number of products but provides installation and customization services in addition to selling hardware and software.

virtual control program interface (VCPI)   A memory management system developed by Phar Lap Software. It provides 386 and 486 CPU memory management to applications using MS-DOS extenders and those applications using an expanded memory manager.

virtual device   This is a computer "device" that doesn't physically exist but can be emulated in software.

virtual machine   A software utility or routine that emulates a hardware device. In Windows, each DOS session resembles a single DOS session on a computer. Even though there may be more than one DOS session running, each session seems to be the only one running.

virtual memory   A method of extending memory beyond the physical limits of the installed RAM. By creating a space on a hard disk that can be used to store applications and data, one can extend RAM without additional hardware purchases. The drawback to this method of memory extension is that it runs much slower than regular memory.

virtual-memory manager (VMM)   A software routine in Windows that handles the swapping of applications and data from physical memory to the swap file (virtual memory).

volume   A directory and disk structure in Novell NetWare. The volume is a logical group of files and directories which is separate from any other volumes on the server or network. When mapping a drive letter, you can assign a new letter for each volume.

wide area network (WAN)   A network that provides services to users spread over a large geographic area.

workgroup   A new user classification used in NetWare that allows partial supervisory rights to be given to a user for the control of users and creation of new users.

workstation   A computer that is connected to a network or large computer host system that shares resources with other users.

D

Automated Installation Utility

Install Utility

We have included with this book a customized Windows installation program that will assist network administrators in configuring and installing Windows and Windows for Workgroups on local PCs. By using SETUP /H, you can automate the entire setup process. Along with the automation, we have developed a utility that also allows you to set a number of setup parameters such as machine type, monitor resolution, and mouse type. To help alleviate unauthorized access to data and applications, WINNW will increase security and remove unneeded groups.

To install WINNW on the network (where we suggest), simply insert the installation diskette in your A: or B: drive, change to that drive, and type "INSTALL." The install routine will expand the WINNW.BCF file to create WINNW.EXE and a shareware subdirectory.

WINNW basically does two things: it performs a SETUP /A of your Windows or Windows for Workgroups (WFW) files to your network and a SETUP /H automated install using the setup parameters you specify. By editing the SETUP.SHH file, which is included on setup disk 1, you can tell Windows how to configure your system ahead of time, allowing the setup process to be automated.

Other files that can be edited are the SETUP.INF, PROGMAN.INI, and CONTROL.INI files. Each one of these configuration files dictates which features and functionality the user will have once Windows starts up.

The WINNW program is most useful when installed on a local area network and used to install multiple copies of Windows or WFW to PCs attached to the network. Using the automated setup can easily save hours of work. It also gives the person installing Windows or WFW much more control than they might otherwise have.

To copy the necessary Windows files to the network, you simply choose "copy windows files to network" and tell the program which disk drive you will be installing from. At this point, WINNW performs an administrative setup (SETUP /A), copying and expanding all Windows files to the selected directory. Once this is complete, the system is in place for the automated install.

In performing an automated install, you will be asked to specify a number of parameters with reference to the machine on which you will be installing Windows. If you choose not to make any changes to the defaults, your computer will be set up using the following values:

Machine type	MS-DOS system
Monitor resolution	Super VGA 800 × 600 16 colors
Mouse type	Microsoft, IBM PS/2
Windows directory	C:\WINDOWS
User name	<Name>
Company name	<Company>

For group restrictions, you have the option of not installing the games, start-up, and accessories groups. If you place a check next to these entries, they will not be installed. To effect these changes, either the SETUP.SHH file or SETUP.INF file is modified, depending on the group chosen.

For security, the options are "no run," "no close," "no editing," and "no file menu." "No run" means the user cannot go to the file menu and select "run." "No close" means the user cannot close the program manager. "No editing" takes away the right for a user to edit any program information or properties for a file. The "no file menu" option takes the file menu away completely. If this is done, the only way to exit is to do an <Alt><F4>. These restrictions are all handled by adding a [Restrictions] entry to the PROGMAN.INI file and adding the appropriate lines.

Once these options are set, you are shown the current setup parameters and their values. If everything looks okay, you simply hit <Enter> and the setup process begins. At this point, a SETUP /H is performed using the information you supplied inside WINNW. Control of the machine is given to Windows until the install is complete, at which time you are exited to the DOS prompt. It is important to note that after the Windows install is complete, you *must* run the Novell NetWare client install to fully integrate Windows and NetWare.

As an added bonus, we've included some of the best Windows/NetWare shareware programs we could find. You can find these programs under the SHARWARE subdirectory where you installed WINNW. For a brief description of these programs, please see the SHARWARE.TXT file located in the same subdirectory.

Please note that WINNW is itself shareware. Please pass it along to others who might benefit from its use. If you would like the source code for WINNW

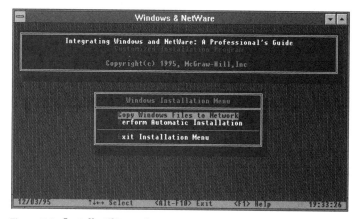

Figure D.1 Install utility main menu.

or want to purchase the enhanced version, please see the ORDER.FRM and README.HLP files included on the supplemental diskette. (See also Fig. D.1.)

Other Utilities—Shareware Program Descriptions

Use PKUNZIP to unzip these files. Syntax: PKUNZIP <filename>.zip

AMPS20.ZIP*

This program will print the contents of the entire Windows screen when the Print Scrn key is pressed. Print Screen for Windows will print the currently active window when the user presses the Alt-Print Scrn keys. Output from this program can be saved to a .BMP file.

File listing

BWCC.DLL	PACKING.LST
FILE_ID.DIZ	PRNTSCRN.HLP
INSTALL.EXE	PSEVAL.EXE
INSTALL.INI	README.TXT
ORDERFRM.TXT	VENDOR.DOC

---

*Requires an additional 644 kbytes of free disk space to unzip.

WMWHOHAS.ZIP*

This Novell NetWare utility will identify which users are using specific file or files on the network. It will also list all files in use by a user or users. Program features include a user defined refresh period for "real-time" monitoring, the ability to send broadcast messages or clear connections of all or specified users, and an option to set the sort order of user information by connection or name.

File listing

CMDIALOG.VBX	REGISTER.TXT
CSCOMBO.VBX	SPIN.VBX
CSFORM.VBX	THREED.VBX
MSAFINX.DLL	TRUEGRID.VBX
NWCALLS.DLL	WMWHOHAS.EXE
README.WRI	

NWMENU.ZIP†

NWMenu shows different users different applications depending on their NetWare group assignments. It can also automatically attach to a server, map a volume, start an application and detach from the server when the application closes. NWMenu fully supports both bindery users and NDS.

File listing

CTL3DV2.DLL	NWMENU.WRI
DISCONN.EXE	PASSENCR.EXE
DISCONN.INI	README.TXT
NETCDROM.INI	WHATS.NEW
NWMENU.EXE	

INRNET.ZIP‡

Inner-Net is a network communication program for Windows that enables group discussions from each user's desktop. It allows instant conversation without the complexities of an inter-office telephone conference call. Users can create their own "channel" and converse in separate groups if they wish.

---

*Requires an additional 732 kbytes of free disk space to unzip.

†Requires an additional 180 kbytes of free disk space to unzip.

‡Requires an additional 146 kbytes of free disk space to unzip.

File listing

FILE_ID.DIZ	INNERNET.HLP
INNERNET.DOC	INNERNET.INI
INNERNET.EXE	PICCLIP.VBX

UNGAME11.ZIP*

UNGAME searches, detects, and optionally deletes games for your network file server's disk. It can also eliminate games on individual PC disks (i.e., on the local C:\ drives of PCs on your network). UNGAME searches through the files in the specified directories for a special unique signature. These signatures are not based on the file name so renaming a file won't help.

File listing

FILES0.OVL	README.TXT
FILES1.OVL	UNGAME.CFG
FILES2.OVL	UNGAME.DOC
FILE_ID.DIZ	UNGAME.EXE
LICENSE.DOC	UNGAME.LOG
MAIN.OVL	VERIFY.OVL
ORDER.ME	

WMENUN.ZIP†

Winmenu is a state-of-the-art menu program for Windows users designed to facilitate access to all applications and provide authorized access for the users. Winmenu provides easy and intuitive access without the complications of Program Manager.

File listing

ADMIN.EXE	MAIL16B.ICO
ADMIN.HLP	NETCOM.DLL
DOS.ICO	NEWS.TXT
FILE_ID.DIZ	NWCALLS.DLL
GENERIC.ICO	ORDER.TXT
IPXERROR.TXT	PHONE08.ICO

---

*Requires an additional 153 kbytes of free disk space to unzip.

†Requires an additional 643 kbytes of free disk space to unzip.

UPGRADE.TXT	WINMENU.INI
VENDINFO.DIZ	WINMENU.TXT
WCONVERT.EXE	WINMNEWS.EXE
WINMENU.EXE	WMENU.DLL
WINMENU.HLP	

OB30.EXE*

Observer is a LAN analyzer (packet viewer and decoder), network load monitor, Novell network statistics gatherer, and more. Observer was designed to be useful to the average LAN administrator and the computer professional. Observer allows you to keep track of your network conditions, warns you about network overload, and captures packets from a single computer (or multiple computers) on the network.

File listing

COLORS.NIC	NIVIEW.DLL
DEMOETH.LST	OBSERVD.DLL
DEMOTOK.LST	OBSERVER.ADR
DISCOVER.EXE	OBSERVER.EXE
DISCOVER.HLP	OBSERVER.FLT
DISCOVER.NIC	OBSERVER.HLP
INSTALL.DAT	OBSL.DLL
INSTALL.EXE	ORDER.WRI
NIBAR.DLL	README.WRI
NICHART.DLL	VPACKD.386
NIMODES.DLL	VPACKODI.COM

---

*Requires an additional 848 kbytes of free disk space to expand.

Index

SOFTWARE AND INFORMATION LICENSE

The software and information on this diskette (collectively referred to as the "Product") are the property of The McGraw-Hill Companies, Inc. ("McGraw-Hill") and are protected by both United States copyright law and international copyright treaty provision. You must treat this Product just like a book, except that you may copy it into a computer to be used and you may make archival copies of the Products for the sole purpose of backing up our software and protecting your investment from loss.

By saying "just like a book," McGraw-Hill means, for example, that the Product may be used by any number of people and may be freely moved from one computer location to another, so long as there is no possibility of the Product (or any part of the Product) being used at one location or on one computer while it is being used at another. Just as a book cannot be read by two different people in two different places at the same time, neither can the Product be used by two different people in two different places at the same time (unless, of course, McGraw-Hill's rights are being violated).

McGraw-Hill reserves the right to alter or modify the contents of the Product at any time.

This agreement is effective until terminated. The Agreement will terminate automatically without notice if you fail to comply with any provisions of this Agreement. In the event of termination by reason of your breach, you will destroy or erase all copies of the Product installed on any computer system or made for backup purposes and shall expunge the Product from your data storage facilities.

LIMITED WARRANTY

McGraw-Hill warrants the physical diskette(s) enclosed herein to be free of defects in materials and workmanship for a period of sixty days from the purchase date. If McGraw-Hill receives written notification within the warranty period of defects in materials or workmanship, and such notification is determined by McGraw-Hill to be correct, McGraw-Hill will replace the defective diskette(s). Send request to:

Customer Service
McGraw-Hill
Gahanna Industrial Park
860 Taylor Station Road
Blacklick, OH 43004-9615

The entire and exclusive liability and remedy for breach of this Limited Warranty shall be limited to replacement of defective diskette(s) and shall not include or extend to any claim for or right to cover any other damages, including but not limited to, loss of profit, data, or use of the software, or special, incidental, or consequential damages or other similar claims, even if McGraw-Hill has been specifically advised as to the possibility of such damages. In no event will McGraw-Hill's liability for any damages to you or any other person ever exceed the lower of suggested list price or actual price paid for the license to use the Product, regardless of any form of the claim.

THE McGRAW-HILL COMPANIES, INC. SPECIFICALLY DISCLAIMS ALL OTHER WARRANTIES, EXPRESS OR IMPLIED, INCLUDING BUT NOT LIMITED TO, ANY IMPLIED WARRANTY OF MERCHANTABILITY OR FITNESS FOR A PARTICULAR PURPOSE. Specifically, McGraw-Hill makes no representation or warranty that the Product is fit for any particular purpose and any implied warranty of merchantability is limited to the sixty day duration of the Limited Warranty covering the physical diskette(s) only (and not the software or in-formation) and is otherwise expressly and specifically disclaimed.

This Limited Warranty gives you specific legal rights; you may have others which may vary from state to state. Some states do not allow the exclusion of incidental or consequential damages, or the limitation on how long an implied warranty lasts, so some of the above may not apply to you.

This Agreement constitutes the entire agreement between the parties relating to use of the Product. The terms of any purchase order shall have no effect on the terms of this Agreement. Failure of McGraw-Hill to insist at any time on strict compliance with this Agreement shall not constitute a waiver of any rights under this Agreement. This Agreement shall be construed and governed in accordance with the laws of New York. If any provision of this Agreement is held to be contrary to law, that provision will be enforced to the maximum extent permissible and the remaining provisions will remain in force and effect.